TO

BARRETTS;

Titans you ?

For your Hospital....

Tom

210315

COMING UP FOR AIR

A true novel, about you.

TONY MARTURANO

a Different Angle

Published in the United Kingdom and the rest of the world by
a Different Angle 2015

Cambridge, UK

ISBN - 978-0-9540137-2-1

Printed and bound in Great Britain by Clays Ltd, St Ives plc

Author's Note

All of the stories in this book, including my own, are true, to the best of my knowledge. All of the recreated scenes and associated dialogue are as recounted to me by the protagonists, and supported by any evidence and or corroboration I could lay my hands on.

However, the names and some locations have been changed to protect the identity of the characters, unless otherwise stated.

Any and all of the official research contained herein was correct at the time of discovery, and remains the copyright and property of its author/s regardless of whether or not I managed to correctly attribute credit where credit was due!

My special and heartfelt gratitude goes to the United States military for allowing personnel to take time out of their very important mission of protecting and safeguarding freedom to contribute to this book, in the hope that it may help others.

I should also make clear that while the United States Air Force and the United States Marine Corps fully supported and facilitated my research for this book, neither has reviewed, nor edited, nor endorsed the final manuscript.

You'll find more detailed and gracious acknowledgements on the last page, but for now, take a comfy seat, strap yourself in safely, and secure all loose items as your roller coaster ride is about to begin.

Although it may feel like it sometimes, you are not alone. Your best friend is reading this text right now. You just need an introduction.

Allow me.

For M, without whom…

TONY MARTURANO

EPISODES

EPISODES (continued)

FOREWORD

What is this moment worth to you?

These seconds that are ticking by as you read these pages, were they snatched from other activities—your job, your chores, your family, your friends?

Or is this special time, quality time, saved up and set aside by you for the purpose of doing something that pleases you?

So?

Are we alone?

Are you ignoring everything and everyone to be here with me?

Have you set your phone to silent?

If so, thank you; I appreciate it.

I really appreciate that you've chosen to spend your time with me because I know these minutes, these seconds that you are spending here are not being spent elsewhere with anyone else, especially since these minutes, these seconds that are trickling by as you read this very text can never be taken back by you.

You will never be able to reclaim a refund on these seconds. Never.

What a sobering thought that is, right?

When I first stopped to consider that, especially as I was approaching midlife and I was ripe for the whole crisis thing, I thought I was going to have a panic attack. I was getting old, and so I, like many, started going through that whole re-evaluation thing: What have I done with my life? Have I done enough? Have I lived it well? What should I really be doing right now? Have I spent my time wisely?

Most importantly, have I squandered too much from my trust fund?

What—you didn't know I had a trust fund?

Sure you do. You have one too.

As does every other living and breathing creature on this earth.

Each and every one of us was endowed, at birth, with a finite trust fund of time on this earth, a bank account of a somewhat predetermined number of years, months, days, hours and seconds that are spent with every breath we take. No matter if we're conscious or unconscious, happy or sad, we're all spending from our fund, whether we like it or not.

You're spending right now.

So take a few seconds to ask yourself, given the choice, what exactly would you spend your time doing? And, in years to come, would you consider that a wise expenditure/investment?

It's so easy to 'write off' (there's that financial expression again) bad experiences as a waste of time—but are they really?

For example, is time spent on a bad relationship really a waste of time?

Is it?

Have a think about that.

Did you have fun for at least some of the time you were together? Was the sex good and pleasurable? Did you travel? Did you get to experience different things? Different foods? Different ways to pass your time? Different perspectives?

What did you learn from it?

Anything?

Nothing?

Really?

Are you not at least stronger for it?

Wiser?

Of course you are.

Each experience on this earth, good or bad, teaches us something; the good becomes the valuable, the bad becomes perspective.

Time spent on a good and/or (as a bare minimum) pleasurable relationship is time spent wisely. Time spent on a great friendship is a wise investment as it will yield dividends when you need them the most.

For richer, for poorer, in sickness and in health.

Your time is priceless; guard it. As is that of others; respect it.

I respect the time you're spending here with me, right now. You should too.

So, why are you here?

Is it because something about this book felt oddly familiar to you?

It should.

Because this book is about you.

Well, maybe not specifically you, but it's about us, all of us humans: about how our biological intricacies compel us to crave specific interaction with others.

This is the true story of love, passion, obsession, lust, friendship, marriage, narcissism, sex, betrayal, and all of the other things we feel, do and are done unto us throughout our very short time on this planet.

It's the story of each and every one of us who has, at some stage or another of their life, loved, been loved, cared about, hated, envied, lusted after, lost, mourned, and interacted in any way with one of the billions of other souls in our world.

And it's all one hundred per cent true.

I made a point of that.

I made a point that if I was going to bring you these stories, then they would have to be delivered to you as they occurred/were recounted to me, free from any creative preservatives and one hundred per cent natural.

That said, they have been somewhat 'packaged'.

By that I mean that I've used my experience as a novelist to set each and every scene for you as if it were a chapter from one of my novels or a scene from a movie, but the source of the information is based on my first-hand experience, the testimony of the interviewee and any evidence I could lay my hands on.

This book isn't a medical journal, nor is it the findings of a specific scientific study—although it does, from time to time, draw on the published work of the scientific community—but it is the culmination of my life's obsession with human beings and how they interact with each other.

Don't expect a lazy read.

I will be putting you right in the thick of the action, by writing the scenes as they unfolded, but, from time to time, I'm going to ask you to stop reading, and I'm going to challenge you.

I'm going to ask you to pause for thought and consider what you would have done or would do in that specific situation. I will also, on occasion, in the true spirit of audience participation, ask you, the reader, based on what you've gleaned from a particular story, to challenge yourself into predicting what happened next. I'll even give you a multiple choice option before going on to reveal exactly what happened.

I'll also be adding my own assessment for most chapters, based on the extensive research that I've conducted over my lifetime.

Yes, I'm in my, uh-hum, forties, and I've been studying human behaviour ever since I was a teenager. Interestingly, it's only through writing this book that I found out why exactly I developed such a fascination with us humans and how we tick.

You will find out too.

The people you'll be reading about are average folk from all walks of life, be that straight or gay, and of all professions, including that of the American Military, such as the Marine Corps and the Air Force, both here in England and in the United States where this book is dually set.

So expect some Americanisms and Briticisms!

I chose to feature some relationship stories from military personnel because these are the people who spend a lot of time away from their loved ones and I was interested in learning just how well they cope—and you won't be surprised to read that many didn't cope very well at all, with devastating consequences.

But then they are human; they breathe, they feel—just like the rest of us.

Just like you.

Most of the names of all of the voluntary and involuntary contributors to this book have been changed, since many of the protagonists became involved in this project over a decade ago and have since moved on with their lives. Others would rather this book never see the light of day because they'd prefer their secrets remain, well, um, secret.

So what about you?

What secrets are *you* hiding right now?

What kinds of stories are you giving refuge to deep in the recesses of *your* mind?

You know they're there. Some shared, others buried, many forgotten but most on display; in your personality, your temperament, your compassion, and your love.

Who you are today may not necessarily reflect who you will

be tomorrow. That's what it means to be a biological, continuously evolving entity.

The trick is knowing how to deal with each and every element of life: to appreciate the good, cherish the joyful, relish the love and accept the bad for what it is—a stage, a process, a curse, and maybe even a way of life.

Most importantly, no matter what challenges life sends you, just make sure that sometimes, occasionally, perhaps even reluctantly, you keep Coming Up for Air.

1 THE AWAKENING

Of all the stories I'm going to share with you, there is one that has undoubtedly had its fair share of angst, drama, betrayal, revenge and downright weirdness.

My own.

To be perfectly honest, despite the fact that the inspiration for this book came from my own experience, I wasn't in any particular rush to share it. This isn't just because I'd be revealing, well, my own personal business, but also because I couldn't help but feel that it was somewhat egocentric to presume that my story is anywhere near as interesting as everybody else's.

But then I asked myself one simple question: *"How can you interview all of those people and ask them to share some of their most intimate experiences if you aren't willing to do the same?"*

And I had a point.

So, here I am.

I was born in England to Italian parents who decided to repatriate to Italy when I was ten.

Forenza is a very small town in Southern Italy, in the province of Potenza. The type of small town where everybody knows everybody else, as well as their business.

I was an English boy and I may not have known one word of Italian, but I was nonetheless sent to *scuola media* (middle school) with my cousin of similar age.

It turns out that the fact that I was the only person in that classroom who spoke English was actually good for me since it evolved some kind of survival skill—which in this case was to learn fast!

I did.

By the time I finished *scuola media,* I knew how to read, write and speak fluent Italian.

The year was around 1986. I was sixteen years of age.

Like many teenagers, I wasn't particularly sure about what to do with my life. Not that I was really spoilt for choice; career choices in a provincial Italian town like Forenza are fairly limited: agriculture, local government office (or town council), agriculture, a small shop, or agriculture.

I chose agriculture.

Well, when I say *chose*, I use the term loosely.

My mother, ever the pragmatist, wasted no time in finding me a job on a local estate that, believe it or not, owned lots of arable land as well as dairy cows and horses. My mother sold me the idea of working on the estate by first explaining that I'd be earning my own salary (which I remember being quite impressive, especially to sixteen-year-old me), then by adding that it was a 'live-in' position (which meant I'd be getting away from home), and then that I'd be sharing the role with another young lad of similar age which meant I'd be in good company.

So I met with the estate owner, *Signorina Natale* (Miss Christmas).

We hit it off immediately as she was a fifty-five-year-old English teacher who could not only speak my mother tongue but also welcomed the opportunity to converse in English as frequently as possible. She was also a modern thinker and talked about how she wanted to automate the farm, including the milking process, and how she'd like me to be very much involved in that process.

I signed that day.

I met Franco, the farmhand, the next.

To say that his response to my arrival was cool would be an understatement. He'd been working on his own for a couple of months now (ever since an older colleague of his decided to move on) and whilst he may well have been eager to have another pair of hands around the place, I don't think he very much liked the idea of having another *spy*.

After all, Franco and his brothers, who just happened to live with their all-seeing, all-knowing grandma on a farm on the opposite hill, had had the run of the place.

Until now.

My arrival meant that he would no longer need nor could he justify the presence of his siblings on the farm, and thus they'd perhaps no longer need to visit as often (the Signorina's words).

I would soon learn that the reason for the Signorina's comment was the fact that she had good reason to believe that

'The Clan', as she called them, were pilfering from her estate to take to their grandma's farm.

I had, albeit involuntarily, indeed become her reluctant spy.

Just short of six feet with a toned body, piercing blue eyes and wavy black hair, Franco was from a well-connected and somewhat feared Italian family of traditional Italian customs, and while the following may well sound somewhat dramatic, I can tell you that there were many similarities between them and the notorious Corleones of *The Godfather* fame.

It took me a while to learn the ways of the estate: the early morning (04:30) starts, moving expertly between penned cows so as to avoid a drenching (or worse), disinfecting cow udders, administering medicines and injections, and getting to grips, literally, with the milking apparatus, and so on and so forth.

It was all alien to me.

As was grooming, feeding and bareback riding, from one location to another, the five or so horses who shared the estate with some twenty calves (at any one time), numerous chickens, several swans, some ducks, a few turkeys, a couple of peacocks, and I lost count of the dogs.

Of course my struggle with farm life was something that delighted Franco, who would often refer to me not by my actual name, Antonio, but by the nickname *l'inglese—the Englishman.*

However, his smugness soon came to an abrupt end when one day, about a month into my role, true to her word, Signorina chose to invest in an automated cow-feeding system.

It was the first of its kind that controlled actual portions of feed and dispensed these into troughs at specified time intervals. It was believed that this method, coupled with the additional staple of hay, actually increased the cow's milk production.

The best part was that the system was controlled by a computer, another first—and guess who was chosen and trained to operate the new machine?

That's right, yours truly.

And whilst it didn't help the already strained relations between my colleague and I, it did offer the perfect opportunity to improve them.

Franco was a country boy; he'd left school early and the whole concept of a computer was as foreign to him as Italy was to me. I, on the other hand, instantly fell in love with the thing, and working with the machine became second nature which, of course, put me in the enviable position of being able to give Franco lessons.

Naturally, he rejected my offer of help at first, but he eventually came to the realisation that my knowledge inevitably put me at an advantage and, some would say, in a more powerful position.

He was taking lessons from me within a week.

At least they started that way until they turned into an opportunity to play video games. No, it was no Xbox or PlayStation. In fact, I think it was actually a Commodore 64, which, back then, was the equivalent.

Most importantly, the activity served its purpose and earned me some major respect credits which were eventually cashed in for something else that Franco, the country boy, wasn't at all familiar with: friendship.

Work days soon turned into fun, for the most part, and we'd all too often hurry our chores to maximise our free time together when we'd disappear on horseback into the surrounding forest and countryside. An activity that was reliably communicated to Signorina via her trusty estate manager, a middle-aged man who spoke little, but said very much (at least out of our earshot).

Before long, I was summoned into Signorina's office and warned off Franco. I was told, in no uncertain terms, that whatever friendship I may think I was developing with him was not and should not be trusted; 'The Family' were expert manipulators.

Of course, I may have been young but I was also very much aware of the possibility that Signorina's concern wasn't just for my welfare but also for the fact that my friendship with Franco often saw us challenge her estate manager (whose instructions and/or advice we'd often ignore), and eroded the usefulness of her having recruited me as her reluctant spy.

Our rebellion against the estate manager saw Franco and I united in a common cause which served to solidify our friendship.

Our forays into the forest for picnics became a common practice. By *picnic* I'm naturally not talking about bonnets and straw baskets, but more fresh Italian bread and homemade cheese, wine, and water (for me as I wasn't much of a drinker).

It was in the secluded woods and to the gurgling sounds of a nearby brook that Franco and I would share deep and meaningful conversations about life. It was there, away from his family, friends and his duty to be one of the hard-core males of 'The Family' that he would reveal a softer, more sensitive side.

He'd talk to me about the world and ask about life in England. He'd share all of his hopes and dreams, many of which did not necessarily include his family, and, of course, we talked about love. He'd tell me about all of the girls he'd been with and who wanted to be with him.

Of course, had I known then what I know now, I would have recognised that he was actually grandstanding as he was finding himself in a strange, unusual and somewhat uncomfortable situation; he was allowing himself to be open and vulnerable with another human being whilst attempting to suppress a truth about himself so abhorrent he despised the very notion of it.

Yet, one day, I remember we were having an argument about something meaningless, and suddenly he leapt up from his position on the grass, grabbed me by the scruff of the neck and shoved me violently up against a tree, all in one motion.

He held me there for a few seconds as he bored his way deep into my soul with a pair of the most menacing icy-blue eyes I've ever seen. I was very much expecting him to punch me in the face, but instead he grabbed it with his other hand, scrutinised me further, as if I were an alien being, and then kissed me, roughly.

It took me a few seconds to actually understand what the hell was going on. I didn't know whether to just stand there as he pinned me against that tree, and let him work whatever it was out of his system, or to do something about it.

Interestingly, I didn't reject the action but instead found myself accepting it. It was one of those moments that I'd seen many times on television: actors grabbing their female counterparts and clamping their mouths on them for interminable seconds—but I'd never actually experienced anything like it, not until that moment, and I liked it.

I reciprocated.

Now, of course, I could have described that moment as him grabbing me 'passionately', but I actually don't think that would have accurately described the act. To me, it felt as if Franco kissed me with the same vigour one adopts when swallowing bitter cough medicine.

There was an urgency, a need as well as a somewhat palpable resentment.

Almost like it was something he *needed* rather than *wanted* to do.

That moment had awakened something in him. But it was a momentous realisation for me. Sure, I had become very fond of the rogue, especially his broodiness and his reluctant smiles around me, but I had no idea that he might actually 'feel' something for me—and vice versa.

Today, I read this action as you probably already have: the handsome young man was well and truly conflicted. He wanted me, but at the same time he hated wanting me. It, us, went against everything he knew and that was acceptable.

Yet, our passionate and somewhat turbulent affair started that day and I can tell you that it pretty much followed the same vein: his conflicted 'need' becoming my aphrodisiac. From then on, we sought out every opportunity to be together, away from the prying eyes of everybody else.

Our love, our passion was always urgent, illicit, angry and deeply satisfying. A bit like make-up sex, only every time.

Yet, no matter how careful we were, 'The Family', in particular Grandma, noticed that Franco was visiting them less and spending more time 'at work'. Oddly, we both suspected that she might be watching us from inside the dark ocular windows of that farm perched on the opposite hill. Indeed, it had become a rule that nothing about who we were in private would ever be displayed in public—not a slap on the back, the touch of a hand or even a 'wrong' smile.

Anything that could rouse suspicion was banned.

And I was fine with that arrangement.

However, 'The Family' started to question him and, despite his attempts to disperse idol talk, they began to suspect since it followed that if Franco was spending more time on the estate, then he was spending more time with me, and thus I became 'The Accused' since, in their own words, Franco had changed ever since he started working with me. Not only had he become 'weak', but rumours had started to spread about us.

"What kind of rumours?" he asked.

"The kind that can ruin your credibility," his grandma told him in one of those sentences that encapsulates a whole speech (his words).

"Do you feel weaker?" I asked.

He just looked at me with those troubled blue eyes and then, after a very long pause, left the room.

But I knew the answer and I knew he was struggling with it.

I also knew that Franco could be as dangerous as he was passionate. He came from a family that was notorious for violence. One of those families that seem to attract trouble whilst always managing to evade and/or reapportion responsibility for it.

He was eighteen and of the age where he was expected to take more of a direct involvement in family affairs, and he was called on by his family—but nowhere near as much as he'd soon be called upon by the Italian Government; National Service beckoned and, unbeknown to me, it was the prelude to our end.

I walked into the horse's stable one morning to find him there, grooming one of the horses with a hand brush.

"*Buongiorno*," I said with a big smile. "You're earlier than usual."

"Morning," he responded without looking up.

I paused. "Hello?"

"I said good morning," he mumbled, still not looking at me. The only sound being that of the brush on the horse's mane.

"Everything okay?" I asked.

"I've received my National Service notice this morning," he said flatly, as he busied himself.

"Oh," was all I could say; the words had dropped lead into

my stomach.

"When for?" I asked.

"A few months."

"A few months," I echoed. "That isn't much notice."

Silence.

"Franco?"

"It's the government. What do you want me to say?"

I walked up to him so he was in profile.

"Well don't you at least want to talk about it?"

"What's to talk about? I'm leaving in a few months—what else is there to say?"

I put my hand on his in an attempt to stop him from brushing.

He snatched it away and looked up with watering, cold blue eyes.

"What's wrong?" I asked.

Something had changed.

He held my gaze but not in his usual brooding kind of way. I noticed something else in there: anger, yes, but there was something else. At first I thought it was the usual internal conflict, the one that I could usually coax him out of, but today, well, there was something else: pain, turmoil of some kind, and it worried me.

Eventually he said, "Nothing's wrong. I'm just busy."

Of course, that was my cue to let the man work through whatever he was struggling with in his head, but I couldn't. I cared about him and he was hurting. I needed to get to the bottom of it. I needed to 'fix' it, now.

"*Franco, dimmi, che cosa c'é?*" "Tell me, what's the matter?"

"*Lascialo,*" "Leave it," he said, moving to the other side of the horse and pushing a bundle of hay in front of the animal that immediately began to chomp on it.

I followed him. "I can't leave it alone. You're upset. Tell me what's wrong."

"I said leave it…" He moved away from me again. This time to the opposite side of the room.

I followed him. "But…"

…The rest of the words were snatched from my mouth as, suddenly and powerfully, something hard hit my face and I was propelled off my feet, back through the air for what felt like minutes, until I landed heavily on the concrete, the impact shooting pain up my spine that metamorphosed into a wave of nauseousness.

As I lay there, reeling from the impact, I tasted blood in my mouth. In fact, I was bleeding from the nose and lip; Franco had punched me so hard, the force of the impact had literally sent me flying through the air.

It took me a few seconds to get up on my haunches and gawp, somewhat stupefied, into those steely blue eyes that were now crying.

Seconds went by during which neither of us spoke. The room was silent but for Franco's deep rasping breaths and the rustling, munching sounds of the horse as it devoured hay.

Eventually he said, "I'm quitting this job. I'm quitting because…" He faltered, his tears falling. "Because of you…" He pointed at me. "Us…" He shook his head as he struggled with something deep inside. Something that I could not see. Something that had possessed him and was consuming him from within like a cancer.

He swallowed as his right hand turned into a fist, and he gritted his teeth. "I'll be leaving for National Service in a few months and I never want to see you again. If I do, I'll kill you."

With that he left the building—and that's pretty much the last time I saw him up close and that personal.

Franco did quit his job that very day, and he went to live with his grandma.

Me, well, I spent the next few days nursing my jaw and going through a series of phases, the primary ones being confusion, sadness and anger, but I definitely preferred those to the one that came next: loneliness.

I missed my work colleague and companion. I missed our talks and ached for the intimacy. I'm not necessarily talking about sex; I'm talking about the fact that we both shared a secret that nobody else knew, and I loved that. It was something that was exclusive to us and I'd become addicted to it.

I had become addicted to *him*.

I longed for answers and struggled to understand exactly what had changed that day.

Of course, looking back on it now, it's obvious that whatever Franco felt for me terrified him and was incompatible with who he was as a man and, most crucially, who he was *expected* to be. Our relationship could not continue, and National Service was the perfect opportunity to start anew.

And while this analysis may well seem plausible now, teenage me had no clue. All teenage me knew is that the man who had made me feel special enough to affect him as I did had suddenly disconnected all ties. He had rejected me and, in the infamous words of Alanis Morissette, 'washed his hands clean' of me—and that was very hard for me to handle.

Now, I could bore you with what came next but I believe all of the elements appertaining to affairs of the heart are covered extensively in different forms and stories throughout this book, so all I will say here is that I spent the next few months mourning what I believed to be my first love.

I ached for that man, and I did everything I could to be with him; I'd even developed an affiliation with Grandma in the hope that she may assist me with getting in touch with him.

But it wasn't long before it became clear to me that Grandma's sympathetic ear to the loss of my 'friendship' with her grandson was simply her way of recruiting me to replace him in the practice of feeding her farm by stealing property from the Signorina's estate.

Then one day, a few months later, I actually bumped into his brother.

Forenza is a small village built on a hill. Its ancient origins date back to 317 when it was occupied by Rome but was subsequently destroyed in the Greek war of 535. It was rebuilt shortly after—and if you were to visit you'd be forgiven for thinking that nothing has changed since then.

The stone buildings, the stone steps, the endless *vias* (roads) of steps that lead up to and down from the main piazza, many of which are adorned by buntings of pulley-system washing lines.

I was coming down one of these *vias* as Giuseppe was walking up. He was a few years Franco's junior and the only one of his brothers I actually liked. He was similar to Franco in character albeit lacking that element of danger. Even back then,

I remember thinking that it was only a matter of time before Grandma's training would take hold.

Given the current state of play, I half expected him to walk on by and ignore me but he didn't; he stopped.

"Come stai?" "How are you?" he asked.

"I'm okay," I replied. "How are you?"

We shared some small talk about the estate and his grandma for a few minutes and then, mercifully, he surprised me by introducing the only subject on my mind.

"You know Franco is very sorry about how it ended between you."

It? I remember being interested in his choice of word, a sort of 'make of that what you will' kind of word.

"What do you know about that?" I asked as casually as my feelings would allow and feigning interest in the distant view of rolling fields and forests that this particular perch on top of these particular steps afforded.

"I know that he punched you."

"Do you know why?" was my quick reply.

He sighed, *"Perche nella vita ci sono cose complesse e difficili,"* "Because in life there are things that are complex and difficult."

I just nodded as if I understood him, but it was actually an instinctive reaction as I processed the fact that such existential wisdom had just left the lips of this teenager.

Then, almost as if he had read confusion on my face, he clarified, "The family…" he said.

"Oh, the family…" I nodded.

"…It's difficult for him…"

"It's difficult for me!" I snapped, much more angrily than I had intended. I was sick and tired of hearing about the family.

"He has responsibilities, and you…"

"And me… And me what?" I asked.

"You were a bad influence."

I let out a short laugh, *"I* was the bad influence?"

"He changed when he met you."

"So I keep hearing. I was the evil English friend who led him astray."

"You were the English who made him want to be a different

23

person," he said calmly.

Yes, I look at this now and I don't know if I could have written such a great line. Of course I didn't notice it at the time, but I do remember being surprised by his candid comment.

"Yet being a better person," he continued, "does not necessarily make you a better man."

More wisdom. Seriously?

"What does that mean?" I asked.

He just gave me a knowing smile and then put his hand on my shoulder, *"Stai bene, Inglese, e fatti un favore, dimenticatevi di lui."* "Stay well, English, and do yourself a favour; forget about him."

With that, he turned and continued his ascent up the steps.

"What if I can't?" I called after him. (I actually wanted to yell).

But he didn't answer.

Some things were simply easier said than done. Didn't he think I'd tried? Didn't he think I did everything I could to consign the whole dysfunctional relationship, including its somewhat dramatic climax, to history?

I tried.

And I couldn't.

It was all I could think about.

I couldn't eat.

I couldn't sleep.

There was something about that boy. Something about his brooding personality, his publicly dangerous demeanour and his private vulnerability that made me want to be near him, his rejection always my aphrodisiac.

I'd become the moth to his flame.

A few more months went by during which I slowly but surely managed to come to terms with the fact that this thing was over. And, of course, my loss of appetite, the pining and the seismic shift in my mood swings was not lost on my superstitious mother who didn't hesitate to share with me her belief that Franco's rather eccentric grandma had placed a hex on me!

Yes, somebody had placed a hex on me all right—but it wasn't Grandma; it was what I believed at the time to be love.

On the other hand, I didn't completely dismiss the idea of

Grandma actually being a witch. She definitely fitted the stereotypical profile; she wore black, walked with a stoop and had a somewhat hooked nose and even the obligatory hairy mole. I had visions of her poring over a cauldron on the open fire spitting into a bubbling brew whilst mumbling a spell. Yes, a ludicrous theory in hindsight but, in the absence of an actual explanation, I was prepared to cling to any rationalisation that made me feel better.

To this day, I'm sure my mother still thinks that it was thanks to her own intervention to remove the so-called granny 'hex' that I was saved from eternal pining damnation.

It was in fact my encounter with Giuseppe and his odd pubescent wisdom that proved to be the turning point for me. I concluded that I needed to understand not just why *Franco* had behaved the way he had, but more so why *anybody* would.

So I enrolled on a psychology course at the local college. I say 'local', but I use that term loosely, since the college was at least an hour's drive away. But I was taking driving lessons, would soon have my driving licence and was ready to start anew.

With college came a new circle of friends, some of them from my hometown, one of whom introduced me to the manager of the one and only radio station in town. The station manager of Radio Forenza asked me if I'd be interested in hosting a dance-music radio show (Italians love dance music almost as much as they love the English language). I asked what I could possibly bring to a show that the other DJs couldn't.

His somewhat bemused reply was, *"Ma sei Inglese, no?"* "But you're English, no?"

I nodded reluctantly. But it wasn't a trick question; it turns out that he wanted me to host a two-hour show every other day—with the obvious twist being that I introduce all of the tracks in English, not Italian. Of course, I jumped at the opportunity and, before long, my notoriety changed from *L'Inglese* to *Tony DJ*.

I remember thinking, *if only it were that easy to change other things about myself.*

I still ached for Franco, but I buried that pain deep in the pit of my stomach and I rationalised my affair with him by telling myself it had been conducted not by me, but by some alter ego of mine. The evil twin who enjoyed a dalliance into the sinful, the forbidden, and the perverse.

At least that's how I believed that small town of devout Catholics would have viewed me.

Who the hell had I become?

I had no idea.

What I did know is that this new trait had led me, for the first time in my life, to experience deep emotional pain and it was an experience that I was in no hurry to repeat.

So I threw myself into my new role at the station, which in itself brought a most welcome and unexpected change. Hosting a show in a small town actually turned me into a local celebrity which, by association, meant that people viewed me differently, and for all the right reasons.

I'd managed to change the course of my life, but there was trouble ahead, the kind of trouble that threatened to destroy everything.

2 THE ONE

So, did you, like many, often find yourself fantasising about it? Perhaps it was the first thing on your mind from the moment you opened your eyes in the morning.

I know I did.

Many have.

Including the next girl I'm going to introduce to you.

Her name is Sarah.

Sarah thought about it most of the time.

Ever since her mother first read her the story of Cinderella, she would dream that one day, a man (her prince) would walk into her life, sweep her off her feet and introduce her to the rest of the world, beyond London.

Yet, at the age of eighteen, Sarah had barely dated.

In fact, it seemed that she'd managed to get through school by circumnavigating any meaningful relationships. Not unless you counted Peter Taylor with whom she'd experimented with 'French kissing' behind the proverbial school bike shed.

The truth was that, with tied back mousy blonde hair, scrawny body, brown eyes and freckles, Sarah didn't exactly consider herself a stunner like some of the other girls in her class—and it seemed most of the boys agreed.

And she was okay with that since she was rarely attracted to boys of the same age, because she believed they lacked the maturity and sophistication of older men. She wasn't into middle-aged men, but someone several years her senior would suit her just fine.

It was this thought that was crossing her mind as she gawped at the middle-aged man behind the bar. He wasn't exactly drop-dead gorgeous, but he was handsome in that mature middle-age kind of way, with short red hair and a beard to match.

She sighed as that man's wedding band glinted under the overhead lights.

She looked at her watch. It had gone eight in the evening.

She was sitting in one of the pubs on the Old Kent Road in London; her best friend was late and she was alone and feeling a bit nervous. She hadn't frequented many pubs; in fact she rarely left the house since she spent most of her free time caring for her bedridden mother.

Suddenly and mercifully the sound of the traffic rushed in and she looked over for what must have been the twentieth time that evening. Finally, it was Zoe.

"Where have you been?" she asked as her friend rushed in and unwrapped herself from her coat.

"I'm sorry, I got caught up."

"Blimey, if I'd known I wouldn't have rushed Mum's dinner," Sarah said, rolling her eyes.

"I thought you said Mel would take care of that tonight," Zoe said, taking a seat next to her friend.

"She did, but you know my sister—something came up with the kids and she couldn't come over after all."

Zoe sighed. "You know, I think they really put on you. They can't expect you to single-handedly take care of your mum."

"They don't."

Zoe threw her friend a look.

"They don't," Sarah reiterated. "It's just that Mel has a husband, kids and a household to run too."

"Oh, and just because you haven't, you don't have a life, right?"

Sarah was about to respond, but changed her mind. "Do you want a drink?" she asked, searching in her purse for some money.

"No, I'm okay, let me get this round… what do you fancy?" Zoe asked, standing up.

"I'll have an orange juice."

Zoe shot her a look.

"What?"

"Seriously? One of your rare nights out and you're going to drink orange juice? For God's sake, try and live a bit dangerously, will you?"

Sarah forced a fake smile at her friend who returned the grin and added, "Okay, I'll have a vodka and coke then."

Zoe grinned, happy that her friend may well be letting her proverbial hair down—literally, she thought as she noticed that Sarah's normally mottled hair had been washed and brushed and was sitting nicely at her shoulders.

"You're hair looks lovely," she said.

"Oh, thanks," Sarah smiled and instinctively touched it.

"I won't be long. Try not to get abducted by some hunky fella whilst I'm at the bar, will ya?"

"I'll try," Sarah grinned, still feeling somewhat self-conscious after her friend's compliment until her thoughts turned to her father and whether or not he had looked in on her mother.

She glanced up at Zoe and contemplated calling home, but promptly pushed the thought from her mind; Zoe would never let her hear the end of it, and it was this thought that reminded her of her friend's comment.

Okay, maybe she did assume a lot of the burden of taking care of her mother, but somebody had to, and it made sense that it be her since she was unmarried and, unlike her sister, didn't have children and a husband to take care of. At least this is how she explained it to herself, and it was good enough for her.

And it was as Sarah was considered these thoughts that she noticed him for the first time. He had just walked in from the street and immediately made for the bar, where he slapped the back of a lanky fella while shaking the hand of another. He was wearing a broad grin on a very handsome face.

Sarah felt her stomach roll and her face prickle hot and cold. It was a new experience for her. She hadn't felt this way about anybody for a long time, not since her maths teacher—but then nobody knew about that.

She sneaked another peak.

Yes, he was definitely good-looking; about twenty six, standing nearly six feet tall, with wavy black hair, shaved at the sides, and a goatee beard.

Sarah couldn't stop staring at him until they inevitably ended up locking eyes with each other.

"Oh, shit!" She put her hand to her face, covering her eyes whilst finding unusual interest in the scuffed bar table before her, although that wasn't cover enough so she decided to rummage in her handbag for her mirror so that she could look in it and adjust her non-existent fringe.

Her heart was pounding. He had seen her gawping at him. She felt foolish, and as much as she felt compelled to look up again, she resisted the urge.

Mercifully, Zoe finally returned with the drinks.

"Oh, God, Zoe!" Sarah said urgently in a hushed tone, grabbing her friend's arm and nearly causing her to spill the drinks she was carrying.

"What? What?" Zoe asked as she was being tugged down to her seat with urgency.

"Quick! Quick! Sit down!"

She fell into her chair.

"What is wrong with you?" she exclaimed, shaking the spilt drink off her fingers.

"Across the room, at the bar," Sarah said in a loud whisper—though she needn't have bothered since the pub was a cacophony of loud voices over the already loud music.

Zoe was about to turn around.

"Don't look! Don't look!"

"Sarah, will you get a grip? I don't even know what I'm looking at."

"Behind you, the bloke with the goatee... don't look though!"

"If I don't look, how will I be able to see what you're going on about?"

Zoe turned around and saw goatee guy talking to his friends and pause from time to time to look over at their table.

He smiled at Zoe.

Zoe smiled back.

"Ooh, he's a bit of all right," she said appreciatively.

"I saw him first!" Sarah pointed out, as if they were schoolchildren, as she persisted with her charade of fixing her hair in the mirror of her compact case, and surreptitiously glancing up from time to time.

"Oh, God!" Zoe exclaimed.

"What? What?"

"He's coming over."

"Oh, no! Let's go! Quick!"

"We can't just get up and leave. Besides, it's too late."

"All right, girls? How's it going?" Goatee man spoke in a deep cockney accent.

"We're good, thanks," Zoe replied with a big smile, while Sarah still seemed to be struggling with a deformity that inhibited her from lifting her head.

"I'm Steve. I haven't seen you girls in here before," he said.

"No, this is the first time in ages that I've managed to drag my friend out for a drink," Zoe said, nodding at Sarah.

"Lucky me," he said with a sexy smile, holding out his hand.

"I'm Zoe and this girl behind the non-existent fringe is my mate, Sarah."

Sarah glared at Zoe and then looked up slowly to see a pair of jeans-clad legs, a well-defined torso wrapped in a white T-shirt, a strong jawline smothered with stubble graffiti, a roman nose and a smiling mouth with thick kissable lips, creased into a broad grin, and then two adorable hazel eyes.

"Hi," she squeaked.

"Hello," he said, grin still intact. "You okay? You seem to have a bit of a sore throat?"

"I'm fine," she squeaked once more and then urgently took a sip of her drink, cleared her throat, shrugged her shoulders, flicked her hair, smiled and then added again, "I'm fine."

And that is how it began. A chance encounter in an old London pub; Sarah met the man of her dreams.

Steve walked her home that night and the two made plans to meet again.

And they did.

True to her fantasy, Steve was every bit the gentleman: he sent flowers nearly every other day with various notes about why she was special to him; he'd randomly buy her gifts and take her out for meals in places she had only read about.

One day he had a posh dress delivered to her home, asked her to dress in it and be ready by seven in the evening, when he showed up in a chauffeur-driven limousine to take her to the ballet. It was a unique experience for Sarah who had often dreamed of going, but was never able to afford it.

She cried that night as she listened to the rousing music of the orchestra with the occasional interlude of scuffling slippers on stage.

She was so happy.

But it wasn't all plain sailing.

There were occasions when Steve would make plans with Sarah, only to let her down at the last minute because of work commitments, without so much as an apology.

Other nights, after they had made plans to go out, Sarah would be dressed and ready, but when Steve turned up he'd say that he'd much prefer staying in and spending the evening with her, in front of the television.

She didn't particularly mind, especially as he would often recount amusing stories to her mother, who would explode into fits of laughter.

He was so good with her.

And it was in these moments that Sarah's love for Steve was at its strongest. He appeared to possess a unique sensitivity that she had never seen before, especially in a man. And whilst she had no idea which direction their relationship would take, she did know that she loved him, and she really could not imagine ever being without him.

So, a few months drifted by, and the two of them would often find themselves lying on the bed talking about life. Sarah shared stories of her childhood, of growing up in Billericay, East of London, and of how her ambitions to go to college were dashed when she came home from school one day to discover that her mother was very sick with a disease that was attacking the muscles in her body and would eventually paralyse her.

Knowing that her father could never afford to give up his job to take care of his wife, Sarah offered to do so until they could get live-in help. In the meantime, her sister, Melanie, agreed to do all she could to share the burden, but then got pregnant, married her boyfriend and moved into a small terraced house, where she subsequently gave birth to two more children.

Consequently, the responsibility of taking care of her mother, her father and the house fell to Sarah.

Three years later, things were still pretty much the same.

Steve, on the other hand, didn't have much to say about himself or his family. Other than, he was born and bred in the East End of London and grew up in a household with a father who was a drunk and who'd often return home in the small hours of the morning and pick violent fights with his wife that would often culminate in her receiving a beating.

Little boy Steve grew accustomed to falling asleep to the sound of his mother's sobs and to the dream that one day he would grow up and give his father a taste of his own medicine—although that dream was never realised because the man walked out on his family before his son reached puberty.

Sarah melted every time she witnessed this sensitive and vulnerable side of this man who was an otherwise very confident, cocky, streetwise male.

And it was this very diversity that she loved about him. She loved that she was the only person in the world to whom he would truly open up and allow himself to be vulnerable. It was something special and exclusive between them.

Sarah had never felt this kind of connection with any other man, except for her father who, whilst good to his wife and daughters, was often somewhat insensitive.

She wanted to know everything about Steve because she knew that he was the one: the man she wanted to marry and spend the rest of her life with. She wanted to have his babies and make a home for all of them, together.

The fact that, beyond his relationship with his father, she didn't really know much about her man—what he actually did for a living, where exactly he lived—was something she chose to ignore. He had obviously told her what he felt comfortable sharing right now. She was under no doubt that he'd share more about himself when the time was right, and that was fine with her.

And so another couple of months went by and their relationship went from strength to strength. Until one day, when Steve told her that he needed to go overseas on business. Her immediate assumption was that he would be gone a few days, but this changed when he told her it would be for over a month.

Although unhappy with the arrangement, Sarah knew better than to question him. If there was one thing she had learned during their time together, it was that this man was his own person. She doubted there were many people, if anybody, who'd dare question or indeed try to tell him what to do.

That included her.

As much as it made her sad to think so, Sarah felt that she did not figure as strongly in Steve's life as he did in hers, and she was afraid of ever doing or saying anything that might confirm this.

Steve left.

And it had been nearly one whole month to the night. Melanie was paying Sarah a rare visit without the children. They were both sat at the kitchen table, drinking coffee.

"So, how is the part-time job going?"

"It's good," Sarah said cheerfully. "Thanks for helping out with Mum."

"It's no problem. You know, as soon as we get the kids sorted with school and stuff, I should be able to help out more."

There was silence as they both drank from their cups. This was broken by Melanie. "So, have you heard from Steve?"

Sarah forced a cheerful smile. "Yeah, he called a few days ago and said he would be back soon."

Melanie nodded. "Right."

Sarah noticed that her sister had more to say. "Right?"

"What?"

"Come on, Mel. I'm your sister. Think I don't know when you've got something to say?"

"Oh, I don't think now's the right time," Melanie said, fiddling with the handle on her mug.

Sarah gave her a look. "Now, is the perfect time…there isn't anybody else here. Come on, spit it out. I assume it's about Steve, right?"

"I'm just wondering what it is the two of you have between you."

Sarah laughed, "Eh? I don't even know how to answer that."

"Well, it's been nearly a month now and this bloke is never here."

"He's working overseas, Mel. Plenty of men work abroad."

"Yes. But do you know exactly what it is he's doing over there?"

"If you mean do I know what exactly he is doing over there and who he is doing it with, then the answer is," Sarah paused and then shrugged, "I *don't* know."

And this was something that played on her mind a lot. But she wasn't going to share that information with her sister. Just like she wasn't going to share the fact that she'd actually overheard Steve speaking to someone, who could only have been a female, on the phone one night. She'd actually heard the words *underwear* and *teeth*.

When she questioned him, he told her he was messing about with his best friend, John.

"Well, you have no idea what he's doing when he's over there, but that actually isn't what I mean."

"Then what do you mean, Mel?"

Melanie hesitated.

"I mean... I mean…" she was obviously struggling to say something.

"Go on, Mel, just spit it out—it's bound to be a load of rubbish anyway," Sarah urged with a stony face.

34

Melanie met her sister's gaze, gripping onto her mug as if her life depended on it. "Steve steals for a living, Sarah. He breaks into other people's homes, lifts their stuff and sells it on."

Sarah laughed. Whether it was a genuine or a nervous laugh, her sister couldn't tell. "Yeah, right... Steve deals in second-hand stuff, Mel..."

"And where did you think he gets that stuff from?"

"I don't know, and I don't care," came Sarah's petulant reply. Much more petulant than she'd intended, but she'd just heard news, horrible news, about her boyfriend that she didn't particularly want to hear. News that probably wasn't a complete surprise to her, but nonetheless the kind she didn't want to hear from her judgemental sister who had her perfect marriage and her perfect children.

"Sarah, I am telling you that..."

"Why are you doing this?"

"Doing what?"

"Why are you telling me this stuff? Why are you being so cruel?"

"I'm not being cruel, Sarah. I just thought you needed to know that ..."

"...No, Mel. I don't want to hear it," Sarah interrupted, even as her stomach suddenly felt hollow and her drumming heart was resonating around it. "So what if Steve steals? We've all done it. Remember you with that bar of chocolate?" she said, almost desperately.

Melanie looked at her sister, incredulously. "Don't be so bloody ridiculous, Sarah. We aren't talking about bars of chocolates here; we're talking about old grannies with nothing else but the bare furniture in their home."

"I don't care," Sarah repeated obstinately, drinking from her cup.

"Did you just hear what I said to you?"

"I heard and I don't care." Sarah's words were delivered decisively, even if she actually felt like throwing up. "It's none of my business where Steve gets his money from."

"Really?" Melanie asked, and then continued in a hushed, almost conspiratorial tone, "What do you think Mum and Dad would say if they knew you were going out with a….." the word eluded her, "...a villain?"

Sarah laughed once again, only this time it was clearly nervous laughter. "You make him sound like he's part of some mafia or something."

"Maybe he is."

"For God's sake, Mel. Don't you think you're getting carried away just a tad here? Anyway, where the hell are you getting all of this information?"

"Pete got talking to one of Steve's mates who apparently has worked with him on one of his so-called *jobs*."

Sarah shook her head and smiled broadly despite the fact that smiling was the last thing she felt like doing right now. "So, some piss artist starts giving your husband some story about my Steve and you just believe it?"

"Why wouldn't I?"

"Well, you could have at least given my boyfriend the benefit of the doubt. After all, your husband isn't exactly perfect."

"I'm going to pretend I didn't hear that."

"Pretend all you like, Mel. You know Pete has dabbled in the odd thing off the back of a lorry himself. I know my Steve wouldn't…"

"*My* Steve?! *My* Steve!" Melanie exploded. "Jesus Christ, you hardly know this bloke, Sarah. You have no idea where he's been and what he has done."

Sarah gawked at her sister for a few seconds and then spoke. "You're right, Mel; I don't really know where he has been or what he has done. But what I do know is that I love him. I know that might be hard for you to understand. *I* don't even understand it! I just know that I want to be with him and when he isn't here, my…" the words dried in her throat, "…my heart aches, and the only thing that keeps me going is the thought that one day he'll come back to me."

There were tears welling up in Sarah's eyes and it was clear that the subject was causing her a great deal of pain. Melanie wasn't immune to this.

"I'm sorry, Sarah." She placed a hand on her sister's arm. "I didn't mean to…"

"I know you're worried about me," Sarah said. "I'm worried about myself. You see, Mel… well, I wasn't really going to say anything about this but Zoe knows and you're my sister. It's just that Steve…well, he was my first. And you know me, I'm not the kind of girl to fall for any bloke, but with him, well, there is something about him, a certain connection… I just feel like he's the one. I *know* he's the one for me."

Melanie squeezed her sister's arm reassuringly, as they both exchanged a smile, the kind where words aren't necessary; they were sisters and they would always be there for each other, no matter what.

On cue, the doorbell rang.

"I'll get it," Melanie said, and she left the table.

From her seat, Sarah could hear muffled voices, but couldn't quite work out who was speaking until she saw him walk into the lounge, with that unique confident swagger of his, followed closely by her sister who was sporting a somewhat grim look on her face.

"Steve!" Sarah squealed before launching herself out of the chair and into his arms.

"All right, darlin'?" he said with his trademark grin and his masculine tone before he clutched her thin body to his chest.

"Miss me?" he asked in between kisses.

"Oh, God, tons," was all she could say.

Eventually, she emerged and asked, "So, was it a good trip? I want to hear all about it."

"Yeah, not bad," he said, peeling her off him and looking deep into her eyes. "I can't stay long, but I had to talk to you. I think you'll need to sit down," he said.

He led her to a chair and sat down opposite her. "I've been doing a lot of thinking while I was away."

Sarah's heart skipped a beat.

"And, well, I realised that some things are just too important to risk losing…"

She swallowed hard.

"I realise that I haven't treated you right, Sarah. We've been seeing each other for a while now and I haven't really shown you any kind of serious commitment. Then I bugger off for a whole month and you hardly hear from me. It's rubbish, Sarah. See, I don't think this is going to work…"

Her eyes widened and her pounding heart tried to pick-axe its way out her chest.

"…not unless I start treating you as you deserve to be treated. You see, I think about you all the time, babe. From the moment I wake up to the second I fall asleep, and even if we're not talking, I'm still thinking about you. And that's because, well, that's because I love you, Sarah. I love you more than life…"

He paused as Melanie held her breath, dreading what may well be coming next.

"…I need you to be with me. I need you to spend the rest of your life with me, Sarah. Please say yes. Please say you'll marry me."

His big hazel eyes were brimming with tears as her suffocating sense of dread shifted to giddy, overwhelming happiness whilst Melanie's stomach turned to lead and a dramatic silence enveloped the room.

"Oh my God, Steve… I don't know what to say…"

Her eyes leaked tears and she wrestled with the lump in her throat.

"Just say yes."

"Oh my… Yes! Yes!" she squeaked.

They hugged tightly and he kissed her long and hard, and she felt safe in his arms once more.

Then, when they finally emerged from the embrace, he joked, "You really should get your throat seen to."

He flashed her another of his grins as he reached into his pocket, pulled out a small satin violet-coloured box and opened it; the diamond-encrusted gold ring sparkled even in the dim of the house lights.

Sarah took in a sharp breath whilst Melanie momentarily stopped breathing.

He slipped the ring onto her finger and they kissed once more.

"Are you okay?" he asked, his dark eyes shining with love.

"Am I okay?" Sarah asked, incredulously. "I'm more than okay… I'm so excited… I can't believe this is happening to me!"

I can't believe this is happening to me.

It's interesting how one phrase can have different meanings in different contexts. In this case, it was sheer delight. Sarah loved Steve like she had never loved anybody else before in her life. The fact that this gorgeous man had asked her to be his wife was, at that moment, the best thing that had ever happened to her.

Melanie, on the other hand, did not share the same rose-tinted view of the situation. What she saw was a man who appeared incapable of holding down a job and someone who, at least until that moment, hadn't treated her sister particularly well.

Melanie knew that her husband was hardly a paragon of romance, but he was a decent man who cared deeply for her and his children, and provided for them—priorities that she believed Steve did not possess.

Furthermore, the discovery that he might be affiliated with some of London's most *unsavoury* characters disturbed her. She had heard stories, rumours about these villains. If Steve was indeed part of that mob then her sister had no business getting involved with him.

But what could she do?

Not much, since she knew all too well that there wasn't a great deal she could say to her sister that would make her reconsider her relationship with Steve.

Most of us have been confronted with a similar situation: we see someone we care deeply about getting themselves into a situation we know or believe will ultimately cause them pain, and our instinct is to react, to do or say something that will protect them. However, we don't often stop to think about how exactly our intervention will be perceived.

In this instance, Sarah took her sister's comments pretty well considering the fact that her emotions were already running very high; as far she was concerned, she had found the man of her dreams.

The conversation could quite easily have taken a completely different direction; Sarah could have felt affronted by her sister's comments and launched into a fierce defence of her boyfriend. Just as Melanie felt compelled to protect her sibling, Sarah would have felt compelled to protect the man she loved.

That whole thicker family blood can soon thin when confronted with affairs of the heart. Indeed, families have and still do fall out over less emotive topics.

Melanie was right, as well as brave, to discuss what she did with her sister, even if she could have perhaps approached it in a different way.

The aim is to get the loved one to consider, if not act on, our advice—not to alienate them, but to relay information without judgement. In this case, Melanie could have shared what she had learned with her sister rather than applying the filter of her own feelings on the subject.

For example, she could have posed questions rather than statement, and added less weight to her words:

"Did you know that Steve was involved in something like this?"

"How do you think you would feel if this turned out to be true?"

"You know there's no love lost between Steve and I, but this? You obviously know him much better than I do."

Et cetera.

And, of course, there's a good chance that Sarah would have seen right through this. But the point here is that the approach should not set out to be confrontational. Mel would have been sharing her feelings with her sister, but not purporting to know better than her (considering she is the one now engaged to the man), nor is she *projecting* her own emotions; consequently, isn't perceived as being on the offensive, which inevitably forced her sister to go on the defensive.

Most importantly, the seed would have been planted. Maybe Sarah would not consider her sister's words instantly; indeed, she may choose to ignore them. However, you can bet that as soon as something relevant happens, that conversation will return to her and suddenly things will start to fit into place. And at that time, if Sarah needs to talk with somebody, there is a distinct possibility that she will visit her sister because of her familiarity with the situation.

Don't get me wrong. I'm not for one second suggesting that it's practical, or within the mindset of many, to tiptoe around this type of situation. I'm from an Italian family. Trust me, all they ever try to do is interfere. Moreover, we, my sister and I, are renowned for tackling sensitive situations head-on.

And no, it's not that we enjoy confrontation—we both despise it, but what we also despise is time-wasting, skirting around an issue when we can just get straight to the heart of the matter, deal with it, talk it through and then move on with the rest of our lives.

What we perceive as 'delicate' subjects have a way of inserting themselves into all our lives. The trick is knowing how to manage the potential flashpoints as well as the fallout.

If you're a person who confronts things head-on, that's great—but you must stop to consider the weight of your words and the appropriateness of your interference. If you believe yourself to be the proverbial bull in that china shop when it comes to speaking your mind, then pause to consider, "Is what I'm about to say really helpful right now?" and/or, "If I were in this situation and somebody told me what I'm about to say, how would I feel?"

Ultimately, the best technique is to ask questions rather than make statements. This works all the time for me and is highly effective. You'll come across as interested and not judgmental, which in turn will inspire trust and not invoke defence shields or indeed tit-for-tat retaliation. As was the case with Sarah and Mel. *You say something 'mean' about my husband and I'll just start on yours.*

You'll appreciate as well as me that this is not a constructive way to get your point across. In fact, I've often found that, by asking questions, I help the other person actually reach the same conclusion as me for themselves, rather than me having to impose my opinion on them—and you will know how effective it can be sometimes to let the respondent think that the idea was theirs in the first place.

So, does this all mean that we should stand idly by and watch those we care about get hurt?

Absolutely not.

What it does mean, though, is that you must not only choose your battles, but when to fight them.

Telling somebody you care about that their partner is a waste of space when they're deeply submerged in the glow of love and happiness is clearly a bad call because not only are you seen to be ruining the moment, but you're also making yourself out to be the villain in what may well be their own personal fairy tale.

I've already said this before, but I'll say it again because I know you want to hear it: sometimes, it doesn't matter how much life knowledge you may have nor how much you can relate to a specific situation, your word will mean nothing in the face of the human will to learn, understand, and experience a particular situation first-hand.

Many of us, more often than not, choose to make our own mistakes and will not be told—be that because we live in eternal optimism that our situation will turn out much better than the woe tellers predicted, or simply because we're too pig-headed to be told what to do.

Sarah wanted to pursue happiness, as she had never known it before. Could or should she abandon that possibility based on the word of somebody else or even on her own unfounded suspicions?

All will be revealed.

3 THE PERFECT MAN

When I wrote my first novel, Nimbus, I introduced my leading male character, Blake Hudson, as a handsome man, the kind most girls would kill for: tall, handsome, and strong, with a good sense of humour and style.

Yet, when I handed the manuscript over to the first focus group, Blake received a very tepid response from all involved.

The reason?

They said that they liked Blake as a character, but that he was 'too unbelievable'. I found this curious since I had written Blake with attributes desired by most women—yet when they got to know him, they resolved that he was just too good to be true.

And it's for that reason that I had to actually go back to the drawing board (or manuscript) and rewrite Blake with some 'flaws', to make him more 'believable'—because such a good man doesn't exist, right?

Well, I'll let you make up your own mind.

I met Al (his actual name) during a series of research interviews I was conducting for this book.

At the time, he was a Tech Sergeant stationed at an American Air Force base in Suffolk, England; RAF Lakenheath.

When he first walked into the room, my initial impression was of a quiet man, the kind of guy who isn't easily rattled, someone who prefers to keep himself to himself—and, of course, I managed to notice that he looked very good in the uniform that complemented his blue eyes, close cropped dark hair and disciplined posture.

Al sure was handsome, but in an understated, underrated kind of way, and when he spoke, his words were delivered in smooth measured servings laced with a subtle southern flavour.

Born in Florida and raised in North Carolina, Al was forced to come to terms with the divorce of his parents at the tender age of five, which resulted in him spending most of his weekends with father—well, at least the time it took his father to drop Al off at his grandparents who pretty much became surrogate parents to him during his teenage years.

In fact, Al told me that some of his most treasured memories are of the times he spent with his grandparents, including some particularly heart-warming stories of loading cars with water melons, driving down to the beach at Topsail Island, North Carolina, and selling them to the tourists.

Whilst a stark improvement on that with his father, Al's relationship with his mother wasn't the warmest either. She believed in tough love, one that equips children for the harsh realities of the world and not something idealised in Disney movies.

And it was as teenage Al was finishing high school and working his way through his first semester at college that he found himself discussing his tuition with his mother. He candidly explained that, whilst he felt that he was doing well, he couldn't particularly see himself finishing on a high.

His mother was very understanding but, with equal candour, told him that nineteen was old enough for him to consider getting a place of his own.

Al was shocked by his mother's comments, especially when she went as far as suggesting that, since he didn't believe he could go much further with college, he may as well go ahead and enlist in the military.

Al conceded.

His first choice was the army, but he wasn't particularly impressed with the recruiter. In fact, he couldn't get out of that small stuffy office, resembling a goldfish bowl, fast enough.

Coincidentally (or not), it was as he was exiting the building that he was approached by an altogether different kind of recruiter who, in comparison, managed to sell him the idea that the United States Air Force promised far greater career opportunities with even better rewards.

Al enlisted. Mum was pleased.

One rainy night, a few weeks before he was due to leave for basic training, Al found himself walking home from the mall. Many cars passed him, but only one stopped. Why can only be attributed to Al's handsome looks, his rain-soaked hair and the big smile he flashed the blonde driver.

Her name was Missy.

The two started dating.

And even when Al left for tech school, they continued to correspond with each other because the young airman was in love.

Missy felt the same.

Or at least it seemed to be that way until she met somebody else.

Al was heartbroken.

Many months later, whilst he was home on leave, the two bumped into each other at a gas station. Missy had split from her boyfriend and was now single once more. They started seeing each other again. Only this time it became more serious and Al found himself travelling from South Carolina to North Carolina on a regular basis just to be with her, and on an airman's salary, that was a pretty expensive trip.

So they moved in together.

It was a small apartment but good enough for the two of them.

Missy found a job as a receptionist at one of the local hotels, even if more of what little money she earned went towards her relatively extravagant lifestyle than the bills.

One day she told Al that a colleague had called in sick and that she would have to cover for her which meant a gruelling eight-hour night shift.

Feeling sorry that his girlfriend would have to work through the night, Al set his alarm for early morning, cooked breakfast and drove it over to her. However, when he got there, he was surprised to find the girl, who was supposed to be on sick leave, behind the front desk.

When she saw Al arrive, the girl got flustered and, when questioned, had no other option but to reveal that Missy had indeed spent the night at the hotel, but that she wasn't working; she had checked herself into one of the rooms with one of 'the regulars'.

When confronted, Missy was mortified and suitably remorseful, washing the whole scene down with a waterfall of tears. She explained that she did not know why she'd ended up spending the night with a complete stranger, but vowed that it would never happen again.

Young puppy-loved-up Al believed her, but things were understandably strained for a few weeks after. So much so that Missy announced that it would probably be best for both of them if she left to spend some time with her friend in Florida. Al agreed.

When Missy arrived in Florida, she called to let him know that she had arrived safely. He wished her a good time and hung up only to remember that he hadn't told her he would be going home to visit his grandparents for the weekend.

He called back.

"Hello."

"Hi, Beth, it's Al. Could I talk to Missy?"

"Al?"

"Yeah."

There was silence on the line.

"Beth?"

A pause and then, "Al, Missy isn't here."

He forced a laugh. "What do you mean she isn't there? I just spoke to her."

In that moment, he heard a distinct bleeping on the line; call waiting.

And that is when it occurred to him.

"That's her, isn't it?"

"What?"

"Come on, Beth, that's Missy isn't it? She's calling you to agree her alibi."

Silence.

"Beth, I need to know what is going on," he appealed, his heart beginning to pound, for he was afraid of what the truth might be. "Please, Beth," he continued.

There was a long pause and then, "I haven't spoken to Missy in a long time, Al. She certainly had no plans to stay here with me."

"Then where is she?"

"I have no idea."

He believed her as much as he had no doubts that Missy was the caller on the other line.

"Beth, is there anything you could tell me that might help me understand? Please, Beth, I am going out of my frigging mind here."

He explained everything that had happened. After which there was yet another pregnant pause, then, albeit reluctantly, she told him everything.

Missy was hooked on drugs and had been for a long time but, worse still, she prostituted herself to pay for the habit.

The news hit Al like a truck. In all the time he'd thought he had known this girl, in reality he had not known her at all. And, whilst Al represented stability, a loving home, both of the things that Missy had always craved, he was incapable of funding that to which she had become enslaved.

It was a gut-wrenching moment, but one that would define a turning point in his life.

When Missy returned home the following week, he confronted her with the findings. Naturally, she denied everything and cursed her friend for betraying her, but the truth—and, most importantly, the damning facts—were irrefutable.

He gave her two weeks to move out, and, because Missy didn't have anybody else, even offered to move her furniture for her. He borrowed a trailer and called upon his best friend for help. Although it turned out that his 'best friend' had better things to do that day, like go to the beach, and so a complete stranger, somebody Al had never met before from the Air Force base at which he was stationed, offered to help. And thus a landmark was reached in his life.

This handsome young man, whom you'd expect to love and leave all of the girls, had devoted himself to one and had been seriously hurt.

And it was then, but only after several weeks of pining for Missy, that he moved to become every bit the stereotype by dating many girls and committing to none.

Until one day.

There's a popular saying, normally used in a negative context: *A leopard never changes its spots*. In this case, Al may have tried to play the part of the player, but his heart longed for more since, albeit subconsciously, he sought to create that which had been denied him as a child: a stable home in which to raise children to parents who loved each other and them.

And one unexpected day, his dream came true.

Al was home, sick; he had a cold and was feeling particularly lousy and sorry for himself. One of the girls he had dated a couple of times offered to visit him with some hot soup, a friend and lots of sympathy.

Al welcomed the visit.

That was the day he met Kayla, a sweet-looking twenty-something brunette with a slender body and a killer smile. She was holding her thirteen-month-old daughter, Emily, in her arms. Together, they were a dream—and the perfect ready-made family.

Al was smitten, totally oblivious to the fact that it would be this relationship that would reintroduce him to renewed heartache beyond anything he and maybe even you could possibly imagine.

4 YOU MEAN NOTHING TO ME

Of all the stories I'm going to tell you, the one that will most likely stick out in your mind the most will be Katy's.

Her father spent many years in the British Army before leaving to marry his wife and live the much easier life of a farmhand—or, more specifically, a herdsman on a farm in Hampshire, England.

Katy loved growing up on the farm, and although she sometimes felt isolated from the other schoolgirls, who lived in town, she didn't really miss being with them because farm life, the cows, the pigs, the ducks, the chickens, racing on motorbikes, and dirt-riding old cars meant much more to her than primping hair and painting nails.

Yes, Katy was a bit of a 'tomboy' as a teenager—and proud!

Or at least she was until she hit fifteen and her parents decided to move the family to Portsmouth, England where she started her first full-time job with her mother on the perfume production line at Estee Lauder.

She loved that job, she loved working with her mum, but probably loved receiving that brown wage packet even more.

At seventeen, Katy was introduced to her own femininity; she started to take more pride in her appearance and used these new and improved features to attract some of the many British sailors who often dock in Portsmouth.

But it wasn't just the sailors Katy was attracted to; it was their uniforms and what these represented.

Before long, she had enrolled in the Navy.

And although military rules forbid applicants from applying to two military branches at the same time, it didn't deter this wild child; she signed up for the Royal Air Force on the same day and, as fate would have it, it was the Air Force that accepted Katy first, and that's how, two months later, she found herself, along with a group of other girls, stepping off the train at Hereford Station and into basic training.

The six weeks she spent there, sharing barracks (among other things) with twenty other girls were a far cry from her purple bedroom and posters of The Bay City Rollers, David Essex, and Donny Osmond.

This was the world of adults, and Katy was ready to devour it whole.

A few months later, she successfully graduated from training as a Telephonist at RAF Cosford in Shropshire, England, and that's where she met him.

The sun was signalling the start of another warm summer's day, she was being marched to one side of the camp whilst a group of Airmen were being marched to the other when, suddenly, one of them shouted, "Hey, blondie!"

Her immediate thought was, *who's the idiot who's looking to get written up first thing in the morning?*

It was only when she made eye contact with him and he winked at her that she realised he was actually referring to her!

She quickly turned the other way, irked that the brash, six-foot-something northerner, with massive dimples and a round face, even had the audacity to address her, let alone do so during a march.

Had he lost his mind?

She would later learn that he hadn't, but that this was just part of Tom's personality: forever causing mischief, defying convention, and generally getting himself into trouble—and that's most likely why everybody loved him.

Tom could be your best friend, as loyal as he was funny, but he could also be your worst enemy, with a quick temper to prove it.

And it was that element of danger, that cheeky, happy-go-lucky, laddish attitude that had girls flocking to him. But Tom wasn't interested in them for he only had eyes for one girl, and her name was Katy.

But he meant nothing to her. He was an arrogant so-and-so

who may well have revelled in the attention of many of her colleagues, but she wasn't one of them. He was brash and all out trouble, if you like that kind of thing. But she did not, and she told him so.

"Why won't you go out with me, blondie?"

"Well, the fact that you keep calling me that is just one of the reasons."

"But you are blonde, blondie, Come on. You know you want to."

"Um, actually I don't," she retorted.

"You will. You'll see," he said with a cheeky grin.

Not long after that, Katy was posted to her permanent station at RAF Stanbridge in Bedfordshire, England, and it's there that one day she once again heard that now haunting line, "Hello, blondie!"

Sure enough, when she turned around, there he was, all six foot of him with that trademark grin she just wanted to slap off his face.

"Well, well, well. Now who would have thought we'd both be posted here together? It must be fate."

Katy rolled her eyes. What were the chances of that? Whatever, she didn't hang around to consider them; she simply walked away.

But there was no escaping that guy. He was persistent as much as he was charismatic. And that's how she found herself talking to him one night at one of the discos on base. He showed an avid interest in her, her history and, before long, the ice thawed.

Her fate was sealed the moment he kissed her.

They were married the next year at their relatively tender age of eighteen at a small church in Hampshire, although his family did not attend, since, as Roman Catholics, they did not approve of the fact that Katy was not christened. Not that the bride and groom were particularly perturbed by this, since, in their minds, the wedding was about them and nobody else.

And so they moved in together.

Tom, now a telegraphist, continued to go out and get drunk on a regular basis, and Katy continued to be his favourite drinking pal. But that all changed when he was posted to

Cyprus.

They were about a year into their marriage and his departure affected Katy for she missed him dearly.

That was, of course, until she was posted to the same base, where they both spent another three adventurous years together. They absolutely loved their jobs—almost as much as they loved the lifestyle that being in the military in a Mediterranean country offered.

However, there was more change on the horizon.

After approximately four years, three of which were spent in a foreign land, Katy started to get restless. While she enjoyed being posted to Cyprus which, in her own words, was an extended holiday, she missed England, and when she received orders to return home, she welcomed and even pre-empted them by one month.

Tom, on the other hand, wasn't eager to go back. He was having a good time exactly where he was.

However, several months later, they were reunited in England, once more having both been posted to the same base—which then led them to buying a house together.

They were now six years into their marriage and something had changed.

Katy was tiring of the drinking routine that Tom was still enamoured with—more, it seemed, than he was with her. She felt it was time to grow up, lay down some roots and start being a family. Tom didn't feel the same and, after several months of arguing about pretty much the same thing, he decided to leave.

Katy, whilst saddened by the loss of her best friend, realised during that time that that is exactly what Tom had become to her: a friend, a drinking pal. And she hadn't even realised until that time that her yearning for Tom was more about his companionship and their partnership than it was about love.

It was over.

Tom started dating other girls and Katy spent most of the next few months agonising over this; whilst she didn't desire Tom anymore, she didn't want any other girl to have him either.

Eventually, she had no choice but to accept that which was inevitable and the two divorced.

From there, Katy found herself on the rebound with a string of relationships that were more about fun than they were about anything substantial—until she met a married man called Andy. This, however, was not meant to be since he spent the majority of their illicit affair together promising to leave his wife, but never living up to this, until one day he just stopped calling.

Katy was devastated.

After this, she decided to sell her house along with its memories and move into a new three-bedroom home of her own.

She was now twenty seven years of age and what she hadn't considered was that her new house was actually a few miles from the base she was stationed at, and that she did not drive.

Luckily, one of her colleagues knew of a mechanic who lived in Katy's village and who worked at the aircraft hangers near her base.

His name was Mark.

Mark was a lanky, twenty-something-year-old recently divorced man with a mop of mousy blonde hair and a laid-back demeanour.

He agreed to be Katy's ride until she passed her driving test.

Through their journeys to and from work, the two learned a lot about each other, including the fact that he came from a family of three brothers and that the reason he had divorced his wife was because he had come home to find her in bed with his best friend.

Katy and Mark started dating somewhat casually for approximately four months without much more than a kiss, and this worked really well for her since she wasn't particularly attracted to him as a sexual partner but more for his personality. He was every bit the gentleman—until one night when a kiss led to him staying over.

Unlike Katy's previous relationships, she was in no hurry to move in with him nor have him move in with her, and it was during this time that she went away on a six-week course, where she became involved with another man—although the longevity of this was dictated by the duration of the course.

When she returned home, she found herself being questioned

by Mark who suspected all may not be well since she appeared to have grown distant of late.

Katy reassured him that everything was fine, and he accepted this despite the fact that during the year that they had known each other, she had refused to marry him no less than three times.

However, fate intervened when she received orders to report to RAF Valley in Wales, a base which, in her words, was in the middle of nowhere.

Katy didn't want to go but there was only one way to avoid a career progression in the Air Force and that was to marry Mark and abandon it.

What do you think she did?

Have a think about that.

We'll catch up again with Katy later.

5 AN HONOURABLE MAN?

Do decent, honourable men really exist?

I guess that depends on how such a man is defined. Your definition of a 'decent' man may not necessarily match mine or anybody else's.

That's why I'm curious as to what you'll make of the following quick story.

It's about a young man called Luke. He was raised in a very small town in Georgia, the kind where if you catch a cold in the morning, it's public knowledge by the afternoon.

Luke was a single child so he never had to compete for the affections of his mother, who single-handedly raised him from his eighth birthday, after his father walked out on them both.

All they had was each other and, consequently, shopping outings became family excursions, decisions became family meetings and, of course, they both regularly attended and volunteered at their local Baptist church.

Religion meant everything to both mother and son since it was but for the grace of God that the two managed to survive without a man in the house.

They were indeed an effective team.

But that was about to change.

Luke had just turned eighteen when he met Haley at the local cinema where they both worked. She thought he was cute and he thought she was sweet. They both came from broken homes and had something in common.

They hit it off and, away from the prying eyes of their colleagues, they began to date—secretly because it was not company policy to encourage or condone fraternisation between employees.

So, a few months went by and, like most relationships of its kind, it wasn't without the usual angst; they'd fall out, make up, fall out and make up again.

So what?

The match may not have been perfect, but there was always one thing that would bring the pair back together again, and that was their strong religious beliefs.

Yet, despite the strict teachings of the church and the vow that they had both taken before their peers and God to 'wait until marriage', the two were nonetheless teenagers; a young man and a young woman with hormones and desires that often replaced quiet introspection with wild abandonment.

Consequently, one night, in the backseat of his car, the kissing that they had both practised somewhat regularly during their time together progressed to something much more exerting, the consequences of which, if not provided for, can be life-changing.

It was a late Saturday evening and the cinema's foyer was buzzing with activity; there were lines at the popcorn stand and lines at screen entrances as the general public queued to see the latest blockbuster.

Luke, a shift supervisor at the time, was helping out by taking tickets when he was joined by one of his friends.

"Hey, Luke, Luke! Are you and Haley dating?"

Luke finished ripping a ticket and looked up, glaring at his colleague and then glancing at the line of customers. "What are you talking about?" he asked with a forced smile.

"Are you and Haley dating each other?" the boy repeated eagerly.

It was a direct question that required a direct answer but Luke had to consider this before opening his mouth; he knew full well that if his relationship with Haley became public knowledge, it could jeopardise his promotion to management.

"Why do you ask?" Luke replied as he ripped more tickets and allowed more people through.

"Well," the boy began in a conspiratorial hush, "I just heard her talking to one of the girls about the other night."

Luke's heart skipped a beat. He looked through the throng and caught a glimpse of Haley by the ice cream stand.

"Take over for me," Luke said, pushing his colleague into his place.

"Hey, I've got my own..."

But Luke wasn't listening. He was already making his way through the crowd and over to Haley who was laughing at a comment made by one of her colleagues when she felt a hand on her arm and was tugged to one side.

"Hey!" she complained.

"What do you think you're doing?" Luke demanded through clenched teeth.

"What are you talking about?"

"Why have you been telling everybody that we're dating?"

"I haven't," she replied, struggling to release his grip on her.

"Yes, you have. You've been telling people about the other night."

Haley paused and then replied, "So what if I have?"

"What do you mean, *so what*? You know that if he finds out, I can kiss goodbye to my promotion."

Haley let out a short laugh. "You're worried about not making manager in a shithole like this?"

Her apathy irked him but he reeled in his anger with a sigh and said, "You know how I feel about people knowing about us." His words were quiet and deliberate and her reply was equally so.

"I only told one of my friends. She won't say anything, and even if she does then you are just going to have to deal with it," she said, finally shrugging him off and rubbing the ache from her arm. Then she added, "I don't have a problem with this relationship; if you do, then that's your problem."

With that, she left and strutted across the foyer that was slowly emptying of its visitors as they disappeared into various screenings throughout the complex.

Luke watched her go but he wasn't done yet. He could not and would not let Haley trivialise his career progression. He needed this promotion and, most importantly, he needed the pay rise that it offered. He hurried to catch up with her, and when he did, he spun her around to face him once more.

"Are you insane? Get off me!" her tone was loud and caused some of the people from Luke's recently abandoned line to turn in their direction.

"I've worked hard for this promotion and I don't like the idea of you pissing it away for me."

"Get off me!"

"Why are you being such a bitch about this?"

"Get off!" she struggled.

"What on God's green earth is going on here?"

Luke turned to find his manager standing, cheeks flushed and eyes wide with irritation, behind him.

He searched his brain for a reply but Haley spoke for him. "Not much, except for the fact that he's all bent out of shape because I've been telling people that we've been dating."

Luke closed his eyes.

The manager smiled at the two members of the public who were showing an unhealthy interest in the scene. He then turned back to his subordinates. "Is this true?"

The question was directed at Luke, who didn't reply for he was too busy wrestling with the blanket of anger that was smothering him, making him want to lash out, scream at Haley and at himself for ever getting involved with her.

"Luke?"

He opened his eyes and glared at the girl who contemptuously grinned at him whilst rubbing her aching arms.

"You bitch," he muttered under his breath.

"Okay, that does it," the manager said. "Go wait for me in the front office."

Luke heard the words, but was unable to disengage from the icy glare in which he and Haley were locked.

"Luke," the manager repeated.

"It's over," he told her through gritted teeth and with a piercing stare.

"Yeah, whatever," Haley dismissed once more.

"It's fucking over!" Luke yelled, swiping his hand in a chopping motion.

His outburst caught the attention of a group of people at the concession stand, making one of them, the teenager in the party, giggle—that was until she received a smack upside the arm from her parent, warning her to mind her own business.

With that, he walked off, leaving Haley smirking and his boss to smile apologetically at the nearby duo of cinemagoers.

Five minutes later was enough time for Luke to consider his outburst and the fact that he had almost certainly ruined any chances he had of being promoted, and the thought gutted him. He had worked hard for the position of assistant manager, and now he was looking at the prospect of kissing that goodbye.

The office door opened and his boss walked in.

Before the man even had a chance to speak, Luke began to apologise. "I know what you are going to say and I know what I did out there was totally unprofessional and I understand that I may have thrown away any chances I may have had of a promotion, but I was mad and…."

"Luke…"

"…I can only say that it will never happen again…"

"Luke…"

Luke stopped and met his boss's gaze.

"You're fired."

And that was it.

Luke's appeals for clemency went unheard. His boss wanted both him and Haley out and there was nothing that he could say to change his mind.

It was over.

And so a few months drifted by, during which Luke carefully considered his future. He needed a job, but his small hometown didn't offer many professional opportunities. There was only one organisation that was recruiting, and they were also offering him a chance to see the world: the United States Air Force.

He signed up.

It was a big decision, but one he knew offered new opportunities with the chance to leave the past behind—or did it?

He hadn't spoken to Haley in a few months, yet it took just one phone call to reawaken the bitterness between them.

"What do you want?"

"We need to talk," she said bluntly.

"We don't have anything to say to each other," he said.

"I'm telling you, we need to talk. I wouldn't ask if it wasn't important."

The gravity of Haley's tone made him hesitate. Then, "Fine, whatever, but it won't change anything."

They agreed to meet at a local park.

It was late evening and the crimson glow of dusk had long given way to darkness.

They were both sitting at a picnic table. Around them, street lamps sprang to life as if ordered by a director before calling action on the movie scene that was about to unfold.

"So, what's so important that you needed to see me?"

Haley looked Luke in the eyes as if she was about to say something, but then turned away.

"Well?" he prompted.

"I'm pregnant" she said flatly.

His laugh was spontaneous, "Yeah, right."

She turned to look at him. "It's the truth."

"No way can you be pregnant."

"I am."

"Then who's is it?"

"I'm pregnant and it's yours."

She pulled out a large ziplock bag full of pregnancy kits and thrust it at him. "I'm three months pregnant and it's yours," she reaffirmed.

Luke paused as if to digest the information; he then forced a smile and added, "So, who knocked you up then?"

Haley held his gaze and her eyes narrowed with determination. "You did," she repeated.

An owl hooted somewhere in the distance as Haley's words buried their way deep into his brain then scuttled down his back, and he could suddenly feel the blood pulsing in his neck.

I'm going to be a father?

It took a few more seconds for the reality to sink in, and suddenly he was having trouble breathing, the streetlamps were dimming and the darkness threatened to swallow him whole.

Seconds seemed like hours.

"Say something," Haley said anxiously, snapping him out of the moment.

But Luke was unable to speak, unable to articulate as a myriad of thoughts rushed through his mind like rapids down a rocky canyon: his age, his mother, the congregation. What would everybody say? What would everybody think? What were they going to do?

"I'll take care of it," he blurted out, without even thinking.

"I'm scared, Luke."

"So am I. But it's going to be okay. We'll figure something out."

He was speaking the words, but they sounded as if they were coming from somebody else's mouth, some other person, not the now nineteen-year-old him.

With that, he stood, told Haley he would be in touch, climbed behind the wheel of his car, and drove off at great speed.

He drove most of the night, south, until he reached Florida where he parked up at one of the many piers and simply stared into space until the sun rose over the Atlantic Ocean.

He was going to be a father.

He was going to be a father and no matter how many times he repeated that statement in his head, he still could not negotiate the full weight of what it entailed. Life, as he knew it, had changed.

He glanced at his phone on the passenger seat as it angrily bleeped indicating that he had now missed ten calls and had five voicemail messages.

He switched it off and began to cry. He felt ashamed. He'd let everybody down—the congregation, his mother and himself.

An hour later, with a tearstained face, he started up the engine of the car and drove north once more, towards a new reality.

By the time he finally arrived home, his mother was beside herself with worry and consequently assaulted him with a barrage of questions as soon as he walked through the door; he had stayed out all night and had never done that before, and her anxious interrogation continued until he finally managed to silence her long enough to listen to him.

Although she wished he hadn't.

The news made her knees go weak and she had to grab onto the dining table for support as she eased herself into a nearby chair. She didn't even know her son was dating, so the fact that he was going to be a father was somewhat of a shock to her.

Luke had failed to tell his mother about Haley because he didn't feel that he had been dating her long enough to make the customary family introductions. Of course, the irony of his thought process was not lost on her; he had known Haley long enough to make a baby, but not long enough to take her home.

Nonetheless, her son was going to be a father. Or at least, this girl, whomever she was, claimed this to be so.

"Are you sure it's yours?" she asked. "Do you know if she has been with other boys? Maybe she is trying to trap you. Some girls do that; they realise the relationship is over, they get pregnant and then…"

And the questions just kept on coming.

But Luke was incapable of answering any of them, for he was busy dealing with his own psychological struggle. And the more he didn't answer, the more the questions kept on coming: Did he realise what he was being committed to? Didn't he learn anything from church? How did he think everybody was going to react when they found out? How could he do this to her? How could he embarrass her in this way after everything they had been through, everything they had discussed?

Not that any of her son's answers would have mattered, since, as far as she was concerned, that girl had trapped her son. This could be the only explanation for what had happened.

And so the rumours began, spreading around town like wildfire; Haley was a girl with loose morals who spent hours in the backseats of cars where one night she had got careless, and now that everything had gone wrong, she was trying to take advantage of Luke's good southern values, telling everybody that the child was his when it obviously wasn't.

At least this was the truth according to some of his loyal friends from church who believed that if he had been dating Haley then they would have known about it, and they hadn't been told anything, until now.

Luke's dilemma: defend Haley's honour and risk alienating the rest of the community or allow the tongue-wagging to continue and save himself?

What do you think Luke did next?

A)   The honourable thing; he focussed on the fact that, no matter their differences, Haley was carrying his child. He accepted the consequence and told everybody the truth.

B)   The dishonourable thing; he stayed quiet and allowed the rumours about his ex-girlfriend to flourish.

The decision was pretty much made for him when his orders came through; he was to leave for a United States Air Force base in England within weeks.

Haley was ostracised by the community and her local Baptist church who, quite clearly, frowned on such reckless and sinful behaviour.

Luke allowed the rumours to grow rather than quell them, and he took the only way he believed was right, a way out of the gossip, the guilt, a way that would leave his and his mother's standing in the community untarnished.

He left.

Three years later, he found himself wondering if he did the right thing. Was he right to leave or should he have stayed?

Again, the answer is subjective.

In this case, the simple fact was that he didn't have a choice; our new recruit had signed up to the Air Force, he was under contract; therefore, like it or not, he had to leave. The question is more about whether or not he could have done more for Haley's reputation.

Eventually, regardless of her treatment by Luke, Haley allowed his mother to visit with her granddaughter who would share photos of this time with her son. And it was through these that the now senior airman had a change of heart.

His baby girl was growing up, without him and it broke his heart.

He regretted leaving and felt that he had abandoned his daughter and her mother when they needed him the most.

Consequently, having had the counsel of time, he concluded that there was only one thing that this good old-fashioned southern boy could do to see his child and spare her the heartache of a broken home—and that was ask the girl he barely knew to marry him.

In a somewhat peculiar similarity to another story you'll read later on this book (in that both protagonists come from the same state, Georgia), Luke chose to do what he believed was right for his baby.

But is marrying somebody you do not love or have anything in common with really the best thing for a child?

I asked Luke why he felt this was the best way forward, and his response was pretty empathic, "It's the right thing to do. I want to give my daughter a stable home. One I didn't have, with a mother and father who love her. That is why I am hoping to convince Haley to come over here [to England], to be with me."

But it was too late; Haley had already moved on.

After all the gossip died down, she started to date other men and slowly began to rebuild her life the best way she could.

For me, whilst admirable (albeit belated), Luke's intentions are somewhat misguided.

There is no disputing that he abandoned Haley and his daughter when they needed him the most, yet soon after arriving in England, Luke made contact and stayed in touch as often as Haley and his job permitted. In addition to this, he provides for his daughter. Unlike many, the senior airman did not run out on his little girl, at least not financially.

Does this absolve him?

Maybe not, but for me, the real disservice here would have been if, in a moment of madness, Haley had agreed to marry Luke and move to England, since it was clear, from what little time they spent together, that the two were not exactly madly in love. In fact, we know they spent the majority of their time together arguing.

Most would conclude that, regardless of the peer pressure, Luke should have stayed and stepped up to his responsibility regardless of how young and/or how terrified he was, and they'd be right.

Yet we all make mistakes.

Let he who is without sin, etc.

Luke and Haley's story ends here.

Last time I spoke to him, the two were still 'negotiating' a possible reconciliation.

So I'll leave you with this question: are the interests of a child best served when he or she is growing up with two loving parents who happen to live in separate homes or with two strangers who live in the same home but are too busy battling with each other's traits to be concerned about the needs of their offspring?

You decide.

6 THE STEREOTYPE

Meet Ethan.

He's twenty five years of age, five foot eight, short dark blonde hair, blue eyes and designer stubble. He's handsome, a Calvin Klein photo model in the making, and a smooth talker with a mid-western accent that charms girls as successfully as it makes friends of boys.

I met him on a warm Monday night in downtown Oklahoma.

I was standing near the canal as a gentle breeze swayed the trees almost in rhythm with the pulsating dance music from the nearby nightclub.

Ethan was at the front door, dressed in black, and with a frown that could strike fear into even the most hardened of club goers.

He certainly fit the profile of the stereotypical blue-eyed boy with the charisma of James Bond and the scowls of Mr Darcy, and I got the initial impression that he was a player, a man who loved every woman but committed to none.

As it turned out, during his teens, Ethan played the girls with the same vigour as he did football. To him, dating was just another game: how many girls he could bed in one week. Consequently, he shattered hearts as casually as he captured them.

So, can you see him?

What's your first impression? Have you formed an opinion of this young man?

Sure you have.

But what if I told you that Ethan isn't anything like the picture I just painted?

Okay, let me rephrase that. What if I gave you a typical psychological assessment of Ethan and told you that he is but the mere by-product of a broken home and that he actually desperately wants a relationship with a 'special' girl but simply hasn't managed to find the right one yet?

Would you believe me?

You may. Many wouldn't.

I'll elaborate.

Ethan does appear to have a head start on most; he's young, handsome, has a great personality—you know, one of those unassuming characters: non-threatening, very witty, warm smile and eyes that, when he chooses, make you feel like there is nobody in the world but you.

You know the type, right?

Now, if I were to compare him to the stereotype, I'd conclude that he's somewhat exceptional since a common theory would have us believe that, given the fact that Ethan is good-looking and everybody flocks to him naturally, he should, by consequence, have an undeveloped personality.

Yes, if you're eating or drinking right now, try not to choke. I did just say that good-looking people are less socially engaging than ugly (okay, not *ugly* because that's such a, well, *ugly* word—let's say *facially challenged*) people.

As beauty being in the eye of the beholder is a given, we don't need a study to know that someone with typical good looks need not try as hard as somebody else of typical average or limited beauty. By *try* I mean to attract friends, potential partners or even business partners. Nor do they have to work hard to stand out in a crowd full of other people, evade a speeding ticket, and so on.

This is a fact and, as much as your moral sense may be telling you otherwise, if you took a second to consider this basic rule of nature you would conclude that, as horrible as it sounds, if you had a comparative choice to make between two people, forgetting personality or anything else, then you would most likely opt for the most aesthetically appealing.

And this is not a reflection on you but it's basic human programming; we're biologically programmed to perpetuate the species. It's the very reason flowers, otherwise known as females, work on being as well scented and as colourful as possible, to attract bees, otherwise known as males.

For some of us, finding the right mate—or for those of a discerning nature, a *lifelong partner*—goes beyond physical appearance and digs deeper, into personality, morals and values. It's the very reason some of the best-looking people in the world need only open their mouths to turn some of us right off, and vice versa: average Joe instantly becomes an Adonis if he gets the opportunity to show off all of his best attributes (Timothy, who you'll meet later, is a great example of that).

If things come to us easily, then why would we try hard to achieve or indeed retain them? And how can we really appreciate their true worth?

A handsome person (who is aware of their aesthetic appeal) will always have the pick of the crop, so why bother developing a personality and consequently a mind that will appeal to others?

Ethan is from a broken home. His wealthy father left when

he was still at junior school and, without a job, his mother found it very difficult to make ends meet. She was forced to rely on welfare to feed Ethan and his brother. And, like many single-parent families, it was a very difficult time for the trio, aggravated further each and every time Ethan would travel to Colorado to visit his father who enjoyed nothing more than to shower his son with gifts in a somewhat cynical and sadistic attempt to make his ex-wife feel inadequate.

And it did.

Ethan wasn't impervious to the power struggle taking place between his parents, but he enjoyed the attention it yielded. This trend continued throughout his puberty and it wasn't lost on him that the more his manly characteristics matured, so did the attention he started to receive from females.

And thus, the cycle continued.

Ethan actually became addicted to the attention and dated many girls, until his education demanded that he take on a part-time job in a local restaurant, where he met Megan, a girl quite his opposite, one who would change his world.

Born in Oklahoma to abusive parents, Megan was a cynical twenty-something-year-old with a waiflike body, black hair and piercing green eyes, who believed that true happiness could only be found in romantic Hollywood movies, Jane Austen novels and the drugs she indulged in on a regular basis.

Her fatalistic approach to life meant that she had no ambitions, especially since she believed that her destiny was already predetermined the moment she was born, by the alignment of the planets, thus there was nothing she could do to improve the quality of her life.

The only reason Megan had taken up a job in one of Oklahoma's dreariest of eateries was because the capitalist world she lived in enslaved her in exchange for hard cash necessary to survive and, of course, to score.

She hated her work and the people that frequented it, including her colleagues who bored her with their dull talk of family and vacuous love.

In fact, Megan had concluded that she was never going to date since there was no man who could ever live up to her heroes from the silver screen, and real life would always fall short of the style and sophistication recreated in movies like *Sabrina*—but not the remake, the original black-and-white version starring her idol, Audrey Hepburn. These films truly captured the nostalgic innocence of romance and marriage, the way it should be, not the chaotic mosaic of arguments her parents exemplified.

"Can I help you with that?"

Megan looked up from the debris on the table she was trying to clear away.

It seemed that the parents of the family she had been waiting on had failed to instruct their kids that the food was there to be eaten and not to decorate the table and floor; they'd even managed to get tomato ketchup all over the booth seat and wall.

The young man with stunning blue eyes and short blonde hair had not failed to notice the devastation before them.

"No, thanks. I've got it," Megan said as she hurriedly proceeded to mop up the red slick on the floor.

Much to her surprise, she could feel her face flushing. This guy was cute. But then, they were all cute at first—but ultimately all after one thing, and most of them couldn't even do that properly. She had lost count of the awkward fumbling of anxious and inexperienced teenagers in various bedrooms in several houses, where the fact remained that the only good thing they had to offer was weed, and even that sometimes left a lot to be desired.

When she stood up, he was still there, leaning against the doorframe, and still smiling. "I'm Ethan," he said, holding out his hand.

She looked at his blue eyes and then his outstretched hand. "And I'm busy," she said, grabbing dishes and dirty napkins and hurrying towards the kitchen.

He followed her. "Yeah, I noticed that; it's why I asked if you needed a hand."

"No, thanks. I'm not allowed to accept help from customers."

"Great," Ethan said with a grin, "because I'm not a customer."

And that was it

What Ethan saw in Megan that day is unknown, but my money would be on that age-old cliché of *opposites attract*—

she was everything he did not want in a girl: she suffered from acute low self-esteem, appeared to take little pride in her appearance, didn't fawn all over him, lacked any ambition and was very unpopular.

Everything he didn't find attractive in a girl.

Yet, for some reason, he enjoyed being around her.

There's an argument for the theory that the initial attraction was in the challenge of being with someone like her. She was completely different to any other girl he had dated. For the first time in many years, Ethan had to work harder and, perversely, there was something sexy in working for the attention of a female, and empowering in the knowledge that he, above all other men, could date, hold, kiss and love her like no other.

And the feeling was mutual; Megan had never felt this way about another human being. He, unlike every other man, made her want to be a better person. A compulsion she'd never experienced before.

She started to look at herself differently and she didn't even know why. She styled her hair and actually considered what to wear in the morning rather than dragging on the first thing her bedroom floor presented.

He made her feel good inside, made her miss him, and flush hot and cold every time he moved near. It was a feeling she had never experienced before, along with another alien feeling: pride. It was something she felt every time he held her hand in public and each and every time she'd catch other girls looking at him.

She loved him and it seemed that he loved her too.

But Megan came from a very unhappy place and, sometimes, when you've been living under a negative shroud for so long, it becomes all you know and all you believe you deserve. In this case, she had developed traits that, no matter how happy she might be, proved hard to shrug.

When Ethan first saw Megan take drugs, he wasn't so much shocked as he was surprised, for he had heard a few things about her past, but she had failed to mention or allow him to become aware of the fact that she enjoyed inhaling every now and then, and this was one of her negative traits that he was not prepared to accept.

They argued.

Megan swore that her dalliance was precisely that and not an addiction. And that she would never touch the stuff again.

At least not until the next party.

Thus a battle of wits ensued—his to ensure Megan kept her word, and hers to ensure he never found out.

At least that's how she thought things would go. As it happened, she actually found herself being able to keep her promise, albeit by picking up another vice, one she truly became addicted to and without which she wouldn't be able to survive.

It was Ethan.

Low self-esteem, loneliness, hunger for affection and the dreaded feeling of being unloved were all gone, replaced by just one thing: love.

In turn, Ethan's philandering ways waned as his devotion to his new girl grew. Not that he wasn't presented with ample opportunity during his trips out of state to visit his father, at college or through his work as a doorman, but he wasn't interested.

But could this be?

Could it be that Ethan had finally changed his ways? Was this girl truly giving him enough of the fix he needed, to the point where he no longer sought attention from others?

You'll find out.

7 LOVE, SEX & A CRISIS

Timothy and Aubrey were college sweethearts.

She was a beauty with a voluptuous body, long flowing blonde hair and dreamy blue eyes that beckoned boys like rats to the Pied Piper.

Timothy, on the other hand, was just your average-looking college boy, slim with curly mousy hair, a somewhat nondescript young man that most girls wouldn't even look at twice.

Yet Tim managed to get Aubrey to fall for him.

Now, how do you think he managed that?

Simple: he talked to her.

What Tim didn't have in looks he made up for with personality.

From an early age, his talent for salesmanship surpassed that of many of his peers. So, what better talent could any man wish for but that of being able to sell himself to the ladies? And sell he did, not in the literal sense of course, but Tim wooed, loved and left many girls broken-hearted.

That was until he met Aubrey.

Of all the girls, she captured his heart with her fiery personality and her voracious joy for life. It wasn't long before the college jock was smitten, lost his philandering ways and devoted himself to her, fully.

They both graduated from college, she moved into a job in the hospitality business and he, naturally, moved into sales where he flourished.

Tim never stayed in any one job more than three years, and before long he was commanding a managerial role in one of America's largest pharmaceutical companies. However, this new position often took him away from home and this was something that Aubrey started to have a problem with. After all, what's the point of 'being' with someone if they are never there, right?

I think that depends on your point of view. There is an argument for the fact that Tim was negotiating his way into these good jobs in order to provide them both with a good standard of living. There is also the argument that Aubrey may have been happier with a humbler existence rather than be parted from her man for so long.

Was Aubrey right to feel aggrieved or was she being selfish?

What do you think?

Take a few seconds to consider: what would *you* do in a situation like this? Then take a look at the options below and ask yourself, what do you think they actually did?

A)   Realising that their relationship was suffering,

COMING UP FOR AIR

Aubrey and Timothy booked a table at a nice restaurant, discussed the situation and decided to move into a smaller house, thus reduce their cost of living. Tim then accepted a job with lower pay but was able to spend more time with Aubrey.

B)   They married, wrongly believing it would bring them closer, but divorced soon after.

C)   They talked about it but were unable to reach a mutually satisfactory conclusion and split up.

So? What was your assessment?

Well, there's no doubt that, if you're a romanticist, then you'll probably go for option A because it is the most sensible and, of course, it saves the day. But is it really the most realistic of the three? Would the two really sit down and talk about things before they got worse, or would they just leave it until the eleventh hour? You don't have to be a pessimist to think that sometimes you can be so close to something that you're unable to take a step back and 'see the wood for the trees'.

Those everyday sayings, peppered throughout this book, must have originated somewhere.

In Timothy and Aubrey's case, they were unable to reach the most sensible and practical solution for both of them because, rather than putting time aside, sitting down and discussing the issue in a mutually neutral environment (i.e., away from home and everyday life), the subject was instead discussed (argued over) as a supporting role to a separate argument.

It was never resolved.

Instead they chose to get married, wrongly believing that the 'official' commitment to each other would resolve the long-distance issue. But what they both failed to see was that the discontent wasn't just about trust, but a genuine need to be with each other and, for want of a better expression, service their relationship.

Thus, Timothy filed for divorce and moved to Colorado, leaving a devastated Aubrey behind. Which means that if you chose option B, you will not burn for being cynical, but should be praised for being *real* and appreciating that sometimes we can be so close to and affected by something that we're unable to look at it, objectively, until it is too late—hence why therapists can often help in situations like these as they are an independent, unaffected party who is able to look at the 'evidence' objectively.

That doesn't necessarily mean that they can fix whatever the problem is, but they can make a realistic assessment and work with clients, to find the most suitable solution.

So is this the end of this story?

No, actually, it isn't.

This is the part where I tell you that, in the original draft of this book, I was going to leave this story here and move on to a different one—but I'm not going to do that to you

Timothy and Aubrey had a beautiful home with a gigantic (at least by British standards) garden, and a manicured lawn at the foot of which was a large lake overlooked by a lush green forest.

Aubrey ended up owning that home as part of her divorce settlement, although this was little consolation for the woman who had lost the man she loved dearly. In fact, the split had such a profound impact on her that she turned to her nearest and dearest friend for solace: alcohol.

Meanwhile, forty-nine-year-old Timothy, in his quest to stay forever young, became obsessed with his body and visited the gym on a daily basis. And it was through this that he met a young lady, twenty years his junior, who just happened to be emerging from her own divorce.

Tim, the orally gifted king, knew exactly what to say to make her feel better. She found comfort in the older, wiser man. He found youth in the younger woman. They started dating just months after their respective divorces.

Well, Tim always did like a challenge. In this case he was dealing with a variety of things all at once, which is not an uncommon situation for a middle-aged man.

Firstly, he was dealing with a divorce that may have well been based on a bed of disputes, acrimony and pain, but he was still very fond of Aubrey who was the only woman who managed to truly capture his heart.

Secondly, the aftermath of the breakdown of his marriage brought into focus the fact that he was getting older. Youth was no longer on his side and he was terrified of being left on the shelf, for his 'gift of the gab' would only get him so far, and that was only after he was given a chance by the opposite sex to actually speak with them.

Yes, Timothy found himself grappling with the reality of getting old and began to suffer from something common in most middle-aged men: a midlife crisis.

Which brings me nicely onto my next question. Have you seen a 1990s film called *Falling Down*?

It stars Michael Douglas. It's the story of a man who one day simply, for want of a better expression, 'loses it'.

In the film, Douglas reacts, somewhat impulsively, to the things that are wrong in his life, acting out scenarios that most of us have probably thought about but seldom realised. Such as abandoning his car and walking off when the traffic jam on a hot day goes on for way too long (yep, I can relate to that), exacting revenge on staff at a fast-food outlet when they refuse to serve him breakfast minutes after they've switched over to the lunch menu (oh, and that one), after which he also takes issue with the fact that the marketing poster depicting the burger he purchased does not in any way resemble reality (um, well). From there, the character goes on to 'right wrongs' with a bunch of racists as well as with his ex-wife.

In my opinion, the film literally 'lost the plot' halfway through, yet it was met with relative success, and I think that success was due to the fact that many were able to relate to the character because they too, at one stage or another in their lives, had fantasised about acting out the events portrayed in the film.

When I say 'one stage or another', I'm actually talking about the thirty-something-slash-fifty-something age, considered to be the 'midlife'. It's the time when we, as human beings, find ourselves, often inadvertently, considering our own mortality; the fact that we're halfway through our existence on this earth. For many, this realisation can prove a somewhat distressing time, with symptoms of depression, anxiety, sense of failure and loss, to name just a few!

Does this sound like somebody you know? If it's you, don't

worry about it. Most of us are said to experience this 'phase' at one stage or another in our life so you're not alone.

Research suggests that men in midlife become members of a buffer generation, unsure whether to emulate their elder, more traditional and perhaps somewhat austere father, or become more like their younger, progressive, individualistic sons.

So, what's your definition of someone going through a midlife crisis?

Go on, take a few seconds to consider that.

Done?

Okay. Now read on...

The stereotype for somebody going through a midlife crisis is generally a bloke (as we say here in England) in his forties or fifties desperately trying to recapture his youth. Generally, it's a character we pity because he tends to be blind to the fact that he may have taken on board a few pounds and is thus perhaps not as sprightly as he used to be, nor does he look as cool in the clothes that perhaps suited him better several years ago. He also tries to lead a lifestyle that is perhaps more compatible and socially acceptable to a twenty-year-old, yet this still doesn't stop him making a fool of himself as he desperately tries to recapture his youth by seeking to realise adolescent fantasies of taking up adventurous activities and possessing the 'dream' sports car. This is often accompanied by a re-evaluation of his libido as well as his stamina, so he seeks to partner with or get the attention of a member of the opposite sex (if you're into that kind of thing), many years his junior. This is both to score a psychological boost as well as the opportunity to project his ongoing virility onto his peers with the metaphorical tag of, "I still have it". This self-delusion feeds the fantasy that, by being able to 'pull' and (in theory) 'keep up' with his younger model, his physical appearance is in no way an accurate representation of his actual maturity.

Other aspects of his life on the slab for re-evaluation include career (humiliation and angst as comparisons are made against more 'successful' colleagues or peers), children (or lack thereof) and maturity, which in turn reflects his age, spousal relationship (was it the right choice?), life choices made, and many regrets.

Is that how you envisaged him?

Of course it was.

It is, in various forms, the stereotype.

Yet there is actually a lot more going on with this character who is actually going through another stage of his evolution.

It's a time when key 'life anchors' are receiving the once-over. It's a dangerously 'hormonal' time for most men, who seldom discuss these feelings with anybody—rarely their life partners and certainly not their buddies (as this is often way too touchy-feely a subject). This in turn makes for a very lonely and thoroughly depressing time during which the search for 'fulfilment' goes on.

In fact, it's believed that this transition can last for three to ten years in men and two to five years in women (yep, the fairer sex are clearly much more resilient against this physiological onslaught).

And whilst I'm on the subject, what about women? Well, as depicted above, generally, when we picture a midlife crisis, the image is normally of a mature man—but the reality is that an increasing number of women are suffering the same fate as their male counterparts and, worse still, this so-called 'afternoon of life' is no longer exclusively reserved for those forty-something-year-olds; cases have been reported as early as thirty to thirty-five.

This traumatic time is marked by the onset of angst, boredom, self-doubt, a loss of identity (the struggle to identify with physical evidence of maturity) as well as a terrifying sense that 'time is running out'.

For women, it's the reawakening of the proverbial biological clock, but often for different reasons that include 'empty nest' and the menopause, and it's terrifying.

It's believed that this new physiological phenomenon is yet another symptom of women's quest for equality.

In the noughties, there was a lot of pressure on women to seek success not only in the office, but at home, in the bedroom, in front of the school-gate crowd, and within their social circles, which in turn led some childless women to wake up to the possibility that they may never experience a 'family life' of their own, a distressing concept when you consider a woman's biological urge to give life.

Add to this a smorgasbord of images of scantily clad twenty-something-year-olds with their metaphorical world in their hands, and it's suddenly really easy to feel passed your prime and deeply unfulfilled.

Cue *Eat, Pray Love*, a biographical novel of how an unsatisfied woman quits her marriage and her job then embarks on a world adventure—or if you're looking for a much less glossy rendition, you could opt for *Shirley Valentine,* who quits her home for a Greek adventure only to end up right back where she started.

The reality is, whether you're a man or a woman, there'll come a time in your existence when the fragility of life will be brought to you with all of the delicacy of a charging rhinoceros. You'll just wake up one day and think, "How the hell did I end up here and looking like this?" And then you'll try to work out who or what exactly put you in a coma twenty years ago and left you to wake up somewhere in your forties feeling that you'd accomplished sod all, and done absolutely nothing with your life whilst meanwhile discovering that those things you had an endless tolerance for have now turned out to be the things that grate you the most, and that the one thing you thought was on your side, your body, has equally turned traitor as well as its back on you and has embarked on its own journey south, leaving you feeling psychologically saggy and all too keenly aware that feeling sexy is no longer a state of mind but a daily battle; you and your daily ablutions versus the mirror and the cold, cold light of day!

You didn't sleepwalk your way here. You simply allowed the years to slide by, thinking you'd never get here. Forty seems as far away when you're twenty as does sixty when you're forty, but we all get there nonetheless.

We all suffer a crisis of confidence from time to time, and those who don't are either lying or in denial.

On the other hand, not every crisis can be attributed to midlife.

There's research that suggests that many people mistake everyday stressors for a midlife crisis: that is, the converging of a series of stressful events, such as the death of a loved one, career failure, relationship troubles and so on. These amalgamated stresses eventually manifest themselves in the form of mood swings, angry outbursts, emotional and mental breakdowns and, in some acute cases, the not-so-uncommon practice of 'going postal', and even suicide. This turmoil can often take place at midlife but it isn't necessarily a midlife crisis.

Some research even goes as far as stating that the whole midlife event may well be cultural—it is not as prevalent in Japan and India—and that the 'culture of youth' in Western countries is to blame for later angst.

A flower has many petals. And life has many roads. Which path you choose is up to you.

Timothy chose to leave the marital home, move away and choose a new partner much younger than his former wife, and himself for that matter—about twenty years younger.

So what do you think of that?

'Good on him?' 'He's old enough to be her father'?

The practice of disparate ages when it comes to relationships is something that is generally frowned upon because we find it socially unpalatable. The socially acceptable rule is that we partner with mates of a similar age to us.

But why? Why should Timothy, you or I care about age differences when we're in 'love', and does age really matter? How old is too old?

Well, stereotypically (once again), 'The man old enough to be her father/grandfather' scenario tends take place between a twenty-something-year-old lady and, uh-hum, a much older gentleman who happens to have a few pennies in the bank. She, generally, has assets of a different kind.

A good example of such an 'alliance' would be Hugh Hefner, notorious publisher of that sophisticated mag known as *Playboy*. Hefner was in his eighties when he ditched his wife to be with the new love of his life who was just twenty-seven.

And who said romance was dead?

Yes, in this fast, frenetic world we're all living in, time is precious and nobody wants to waste several months and maybe even a few years of their life in a relationship that may 'come to nothing'. That's why more and more people are turning to the law to ensure that their marriage vows stay as fresh as the day they were mumbled.

Some of the most scandalous pre-vow wows include the wife who demanded that her husband retain his washboard torso or be kicked to the curb; the husband who demanded compensation if his wife exceeded a weight threshold; the husband who demanded four cooked meals a week or the wife lost her shopping allowance; the husband who in a divorce would get the pool boy; and the wife who'd get the gardener (well, good help is hard to find). Then there was one football game a week with friends for one husband; one visit by the mother-in-law per quarter for a wife; fines for positive drug-testing for a husband; sex once a month for an elderly lady and no more; sex a minimum of once a week for one young couple and no straying. Then there's the relatively famous 'No Nappy' clause for those couples who agree before marriage not to have children and want to avoid any change (or lack of) contraception later.

I could go on but I'm sure you're already thoroughly nauseated by such public displays of love.

No?

What do you mean that isn't love?

Sure it is. It's just *organised* love.

What do you mean you haven't heard of that either?

Organised love is where two people can go about their daily existence relatively free from the danger of everyday relationship breakers—you know, like money pressures, straying terrors, neglect, and so on. If you both stipulate your likes and dislikes before you tie the knot and then enshrine it in a legal document with severe penalties, then you've sanitised your marriage, sterilised it to make sure no pesky bugs come along and make you both physically sick at the sight of each other further down the line.

Still not convinced that's love?

What is love, anyway? Do you even know?

If you took thirty seconds to consider that before moving on to the next paragraph, do you think you'd come up with a definition for me?

Go on; think for a few seconds—in your opinion, what is real love?

Whatever your conclusion, one thing is for sure: the conclusion you reach is yours and yours alone, because the true meaning of love is yet to be defined.

Many throughout the centuries have tried to define love through music, paintings, photography, food and a whole medley of artistic expression, but each and every one has always been unique to the protagonists involved, because the truth is that love is one of those things that is truly subjective. My definition of love may well differ from yours; some things that you interpret as romantic would probably do nothing for me, and vice versa.

But it's the difference in our interpretations that make us unique and it's this uniqueness that stands us apart from others of our kind and what makes us attractive to our partners.

Age differences in relationships may no longer be that unusual, although gargantuan differences, such as the ones highlighted above, will most likely continue to set our tongues wagging, as will those we deem just a tad too close to the cradle.

And it's this very thing that legislators have been wrestling with for years. Underage sex both in heterosexual and homosexual relationships; when is young too young?

Well, some doctors have asserted time and time again that the brain of a young female is two years more developed than that of her male counterpart—which technically means that girls should be old enough to consent to sex at the age of 14 here in England!

Yes, there's that old uncomfortable feeling again.

When you see it in black and white, it just doesn't sit well. The truth being, of course, that if you tried to use this defence in a court of law, they'd laugh at you.

Whatever your opinion, the harsh reality is that girls do tend to prefer older boys and, by association, men—despite the fact that this goes against years of evolution (there's a clear reduction in sperm count in older men compared to their younger counterparts).

A study conducted in the early eighties concluded that a young female's preference for an 'older' man is due to the belief that older males will have accumulated more 'attractive' (or life) resources, otherwise known as 'resource acquisition'. This, scientists argue, also makes evolutionary sense because, by allying herself with a man 'of experience' the female feels secure in terms of 'safety' and 'protection' and thus more likely to 'survive' (although I'm sure there are a few women out there who would beg to differ).

There is no denying the fact that love—and I'm talking about 'real love', not the one fabricated inside the laboratory of a contract, or the one you hope will germinate and grow from persistent exposure, I'm talking about the love that makes you smile, your stomach giddy, sets your pulse racing and your heart pounding just at the mere thought of the object of your affection; does exist and is indeed blind. It compels us to perform acts way out of our own character and often to our own detriment, and yet it is the embodiment of bliss. It knows nothing of age, gender, beauty or creed, nor does it know what may or may not be socially acceptable.

Love, in its true form, simply *is*.

In Timothy's case, he hadn't found new love, but somebody to fill the empty chair. A younger person who made him feel better about himself whilst at the same time drawing an underscore beneath the 'age' issue. However, she was eager to go out and celebrate her newfound freedom; he, on the other hand, after the novelty had worn off, soon tired and was much happier kicking his shoes off, putting his feet up and snuggling on the couch at the end of a hard day—not that he'd share that information with his new partner. Not that he needed to either, because she was already coming to her own conclusion.

She enjoyed being around Timothy, he was great company, and he had been a great comfort to her when she needed him after her divorce, and, yes, that comfort even extended to the bedroom. But when their honeymoon of lust was over and their bodies reclothed, how much did they really have in common?

Not much.

This realisation came on the eve of a major event in Timothy's life: he needed to undergo surgery on his eye. Doctor's orders were to rest as much as he could and this included omitting strenuous exercise from his daily routine.

This meant no gym visits; a severe blow for a man for whom the prospect of not working out, running or cycling was terrifying; they were the very things he believed were keeping him anchored to his youth.

She, on the other hand, wasn't particularly excited about the prospect of redefining her role of lover/girlfriend to that of nurse, either.

They split. She left.

In all, their relationship lasted no longer than three months.

Timothy was devastated.

Not only had he lost his companion, but he had also lost one of the things that made him feel young, and now, with the imminent surgery, he had few places to turn to for support.

He considered his family but he knew that arrangement would never work out.

No, there was only one place, one person he could rely on, because he knew that door was always open no matter what he did. Wasn't it?

You'll find out.

8 MONSTER IN THE CLOSET

It had been over a year since Franco and, given my new commitments, I too handed in my notice at the estate and moved into town, which made it easier to get both to college and to the radio station on time.

I was eighteen, I'd passed my driving test and life was good.

Whilst my local celebrity continued (it was a small town after all) I found that knowledge of the fact I was studying psychology started to spread and I'd often find myself 'profiling' friends and their partners by conducting my course-learned profiling techniques on them with the aim of achieving an overall score (picture) of their personalities. They loved this and I needed the experience.

It was through one of these so-called 'readings' that I met

Peppe. I had seen him around, but we'd never actually met until that night.

Peppe had always appeared to be a fairly laid-back kind of guy, with generous eyes yet economic with his words, at least that was until he witnessed me 'profile' one of his relatives, then he erupted into fits of incredulous laughter and asked me to 'do him next'. We hit it off instantly and became good friends.

Before long, I was introduced to the rest of his so-called 'posse' and we became, in today's vernacular, 'tight'. There was rarely a day when we didn't hang out together, be that for car drives, trips to the movies, or just generally wiling away the evening in the town square.

Yes, if you are not accustomed to Italian life in a small town, performing a continuous turn (walk) around The Square, chatting about everything and anything with the occasional stop at one of the many bars, is considered a national pastime and one still practised to this day.

Peppe, Gaetano and Raffaelle (Raff) were my age and we had a lot in common, although I developed a certain affinity with Peppe that I did not have with the other two, especially Raff; there was something about how he behaved around me that made me think he trusted me almost as far as he could throw me, but I just put this down to the fact that I was the newcomer to the clan and that he perhaps just saw me as some kind of threat. Something I hoped I'd be able to change.

There was another member of the group; his name was Nick.

Nick, or so I had dubbed him, after the eighties heartthrob Nick Kamen (you know, the guy who famously took off his jeans in a popular 1985 Levi's laundrette advertisement and then subsequently released, in collaboration with Madonna, the rather ironically titled hit *Each Time You Break My Heart*? Remember? No? Well—him. Nick—his real name Angelo (Angel)—had all the looks of Nick Kamen but with the curly black locks of a cherub, and I liked him. I liked him very much.

Some would call this 'love at first sight', but those who know me would know that I do not believe in such a thing since it's impossible to love someone just by seeing them (not unless you're just in love with their likeness).

To truly love and be in love with someone is to love that which makes them whole: their personality, their traits, their good and bad, and, ideally, how they love you. Flaws and all.

And to those romanticists who disagree with that notion, I say this: picture the most attractive being you have ever clapped your eyes on; someone you have never spoken to nor heard speak; someone for whom you have done nothing nor witnessed them do anything.

Ask yourself: do you love them or just the image of them?

Now, in your mind, picture that person speaking, about themselves, about how good-looking they know they are, about how everybody keeps fawning over them and about how irritating and inconvenient it is for them to keep repelling such advances.

How do you love them now?

Now picture them looking you up and down, as if you were something they'd just scraped off their shoe, as if you were something that shouldn't even have the audacity to look at them let alone love them.

Still in love?

Beauty lives on the skin, but real loves lives in the mind (or if you prefer, in the heart). Romantic love at first sight is a myth.

I could feel myself falling in love with Nick. I knew this because it had been a while since Franco and, until the day I first clapped eyes on Nick, I had managed to do a pretty good job at repressing and/or ignoring my feelings for any other man, at least romantically speaking. But that day, when I first saw Nick, I thought, *wow*. Then, as I got to know him, his personality, his kindness, his unassuming demeanour, the way he laughed at my jokes, cared for his sick nan, and how affectionate he became when he'd had a few too many drinks, I knew that I felt more for him than friendship.

But I also knew nothing could ever come of it. I told myself this from day one.

Nick's sexuality was no mystery to me—not that I'd asked, but because I knew he and the other guys were very much into girls, a pursuit they, and to a certain degree even I, believed we shared.

Months went by and I became really close with the lads (well, most of them), including Nick, but it was most definitely a case of unrequited love. We fooled around, sure, as friends, but that was about it, and I have to confess that this wasn't as easy as it sounds. There's nothing easy about being around the object of your desire yet never being able to truly express it beyond a hug and maybe even a kiss on the cheek (not so unusual in Italy when you think that it was Mediterraneans who pretty much invented the dual-cheek-kiss greeting so popular today). However, I kept telling myself that at least I was lucky enough to be around him every day and that, until I figured it out, had to be enough.

And it was—until one evening.

Now, I've never been much of a drinker, especially back then, I don't think I drank more than fizzy orangeade or cola.

Yes, you already have an idea of what's coming next. Well, you'd be right.

That particular night, we were out celebrating something very important: little old me, the local DJ from a small town, had just won a monthly slot on a radio station in the nearby city of Potenza. This was a much bigger station with a much wider audience, and the lads were insistent that fizzy pop was good enough only to take a bath in (their expression), but certainly was not the nectar of men, and that I should join them for beers.

Much to my repulsion, and in the need to fit in, I did.

Towards the end of the evening, I'd well and truly had a few too many (not that it would have taken much for such a lightweight), and who should I find myself deep in conversation with? No, not Nick but Raff.

The dynamics of our relationship hadn't changed; I think we just learned to tolerate each other, and I have no clue as to why we, of all people, ended up having a heart to heart at the bar. I guess seeing me with a bottle of beer in my hand as opposed to a can of fizz made me seem more like one of 'them' and thus more acceptable to him.

Whatever the reason, the red-haired guy with freckles, a thin body and a very pale complexion (for a southern Italian) took me into his confidence. He shared with me the fact that his life was a tough one, and that he lived with his abusive father, but that he could not leave the family home, for his mother's sake. He then went on to tell me about the group: this band of brothers meant everything to him, for we were the brothers he'd never had. I wasn't sure if that included me, but I didn't question it. Instead I commiserated with him, and I remember being somewhat grateful that he had deemed me worthy of such intimacy, and that the ice wall between us was finally starting to thaw.

I told him that I shared his affection for the group, all of whom I considered true friends (I stopped short of calling them brothers since I already had three real ones of my own), and that I loved them all.

Fair enough.

But then I added, "…Especially Nick. He's so handsome…"

Duh!

The words just slurred out of my mouth before I even registered what the hell I was saying. And I can still remember Raff's reaction: he was just about to take another swig from his bottle of Peroni, but paused to look at me.

My stomach lurched. He'd obviously registered what I had just said but I, like the proverbial rabbit in the headlights, was unable to recover. My normally sober mind just didn't appear to be functioning as fast as I was used to. Eventually, I forced a laugh and chinked his bottle, foolishly hoping that I could just steamroller over those words that were still hanging way too heavily in the air between us.

No such luck.

"You fancy Nick?" he asked with an incredulous velociraptor smile.

I forced another laugh. "I didn't say I fancied him, you fool. I just said he was handsome. What's wrong with that?" I tried, using all of my acting skills to appear unfazed by my bold statement.

Remember, this is 1988. Today, after a few drinks (or even before), you can kiss your best friend and nobody will even bat an eyelid—but back then, especially in that small town, well, it was unheard of. It was like another world

Raff started laughing at me. *"Tu lo vuo mettere a Nick?"* "You want to put it into Nick?" He laughed some more.

I remember looking around for the others—who, mercifully, were out of earshot—and then back at Raff who was still laughing. I guess this was one of my movie scenes; you know, the moment where the protagonist just wants to stop the other character from laughing and smacks him or her in the mouth or over the head with the nearest heaviest object.

No such drama here.

Just me shrinking in horror to the back of my bar stool, desperately seeking some words, a line that would dilute or even erase Raff's thought process.

But he wasn't having any of it, and this terrified me.

And it was just as I was considering my fate that the others broke up the moment by joining us at the bar. Nick wasn't with them and I breathed a sigh of relief. Until I felt an arm over my shoulder.

"Eh, Tony DJ!" Nick said, kissing me on the cheek.

He was very drunk.

If only he knew.

I looked at Raff, who returned my gaze, smiled his predator smile, took a swig from his bottle and then started a conversation with Peppe.

It's strange because it wasn't until that moment, until I came face-to-face with the risk of losing these friends and the bonds that I had managed to forge with them, that I realised just how much they meant to me—and that included Raff. For all of his blustering, although I knew we would never go down as best friends, I'd believed that we'd managed to find an accord, some kind of mutual respect. And tonight, with his taking me into his confidence, I had thought we'd turned a corner.

Obviously not.

Worse still, I started to panic about what any potential revelation would mean to my fledgling career. An idea which sounds so ludicrous to me now, but back then, well, I was young, albeit very much aware of the fact that a high demographic of my audience was female. I was content with my life. I didn't want anything to jeopardise that.

However, my fears were misplaced. Raff said nothing to the others. Instead, we had a few more drinks and then staggered home, arm in arm. I was safe.

Or so I thought.

The next evening, there was no car honk outside my house at the usual time. The lads didn't call for me as they had pretty much done for the whole time we'd known each other. I waited as long as I could, but then had to leave as I was already late for my show during which it occurred to me that something may well have happened. They may have had a car accident or something. This was pretty much all I could think about the entire evening, and those two hours seemed like two days. I resolved that I was going to spend the rest of the night tracking them down.

But I didn't need to, for it was as I was walking back from the radio station, through the Town Square, that I spotted them sitting outside one of the bars, joking and laughing as if nothing had happened.

But it had.

It was a warm evening, one of those oppressively stifling ones that threatens to storm but never does. The storm, as it turns out, was deep inside of me.

I walked up to them as they lounged on plastic white patio chairs. They were all there: Raff, Peppe, Gaetano and Nick.

"What happened to you lot today?" I asked without any preamble.

I didn't need to draw on anything I'd learned at college about body language to know that all was not well; Peppe's bowed head, the sudden seriousness in their faces, the exchanged looks all made it pretty obvious.

I sat next to Nick who promptly stood up and said, "I need to get home. I have work in the morning." He looked me straight in the eyes, big brown eyes full of a sentiment even I couldn't quite place: sadness, loss, anger? Whatever it was, it spoke loudly, but said nothing.

He turned to leave.

"Wait up," said Raff enthusiastically. He paused next to me and looked me in the eyes as if sizing me up, smiled and said, "Goodbye, Tony DJ," in forced English before jogging off to join Nick and put an arm around his shoulder.

"Wait for me!" It was Gaetano. He smiled at me and then hurried after the other two.

At least Peppe had not forsaken me.

Not yet.

"What's going on, Peppe?" I asked.

"Ma e vero?" "Is it true?"

"Is what true?" I asked impulsively, although I knew exactly what he was talking about.

"Dimmelo... ma e vero? Tu sei un finocchio?" "Tell me...is it true? Are you a fag?" he asked with a sideways glance.

(I so hated that expression) "Peppe..."

"...Just answer the question," he said without looking me in the eye.

"Peppe... You know me."

"Do I?"

That hurt. "Where is this all coming from?" I asked.

"Answer the question..."

"I don't know what you're talking about," I said.

I wanted him to tell me what he knew. I needed to know exactly how Raff had relayed the information, although I was sanguine enough to know that if he had shared what I'd said with the rest of the group, there wouldn't be much I could do from here on in terms of damage limitation.

"You told Raff that you fancy Nick. Is that true?"

"I didn't say that..."

"What did you say?"

"I said that I thought he was handsome—but then everybody says that."

"I don't say that."

"Peppe..."

He stood up. "I don't think we should see each other anymore."

"Peppe, you're not even giving me a chance to explain. You're just accepting what Raff told you as the truth..."

"...You should never have lied to me."

"About what? I haven't lied to you." I was getting angry now.

"All the times we've been together. All of the times you've embraced me and my cousin."

"What about them...?"

He said nothing.

"What about them, Peppe?"

"Tell me. Is it true?" he persisted.

"There's nothing to tell, Peppe! What exactly do you want me to say?"

He turned to me and seethed, *"Dimmi che not ti piace il cazzo! Dimmelo!"* "Tell me that you don't like cock! Tell me!"

I stared at him in disbelief. Don't get me wrong—I was a teenager; it wasn't the language that was alien to me. It was the context in which it had been spoken.

I considered this as I contemplated the way in which this whole thing was playing out. I was being judged for one stupid remark and I was being treated like some kind of social criminal, interrogated, and bullied into answering one single question rather than having a rational conversation about what had really transpired that evening; a conversation that was actually in context as opposed to just an excerpt.

And I could feel myself getting angry. I could feel myself getting *very* angry. I resented being spoken to in that way for something I hadn't even done. I don't know if my rage was to do with Peppe playing judge and jury or the fact that, once again, my sexuality was causing me pain. What I do know is that I actually felt the birth and the growth of my anger that night; it was like a tidal wave, washing up my legs through the pit of my stomach, prickling my chest and burning my cheeks before I spat out, "Who the hell do you think you are?" I seethed, "Do you know what? Go fuck yourself!"

"You'd like that, wouldn't you," he retorted with a sneer.

I was speechless. I couldn't believe it had come to this.

"Don't contact me or any of my family again," Peppe said, and walked away.

I don't know how long I sat in that chair, smiling absentmindedly at passers-by as they greeted me. I just could not believe it. History was repeating itself all over again. Franco, the lads; I kept losing these people—and for what?

At least I now had an understanding of what Franco must have struggled with: his sexuality, our illicit affair and the consequences of his family or anybody else ever finding out. I understood that. But I couldn't understand this. I was being judged and condemned for something I had not done.

Or had I? Should I have said something sooner, at least to

Peppe? But what would I have said exactly? That question rattled around in my head all night and into the next day. But there were no answers. A situation I was somewhat familiar with.

And I didn't like it.

It seemed that *not acting* on my so-called impulses got me into as much heartache as *acting* on them. And so I came to one inevitable conclusion: there was something fundamentally wrong with me. I was a defect and this thing, my attraction to other men, was indeed an abomination. It was something that may well have started out as something beautiful, but it soon became as rotten as it was terrifying, ugly as it was hurtful, and I didn't want to feel that way anymore.

I had had enough.

I didn't try to reconnect with Peppe. I concluded that even if, by some miracle, they took me back into the fold, they'd never trust me again. They'd always be 'wondering' about me, and I hated that thought; I hated the idea of being some kind of outsider.

I hated *me*.

And I was disgusted with the notion that the person I had come to love from afar most likely saw me as some kind of deviant, a creature that had infiltrated itself into the group disguised as a friend, that was biding its time before making its move.

It seemed that no matter how much I resisted, how much I suppressed or protested, there was no escaping the truth: I was gay, a homosexual, a faggot, an abomination! Just some of the adjectives used to describe someone like me, depending on the point of view.

Did I really use those words in the same sentence? Yes, I did—and they may even have tickled your revulsion trigger, even today. Sadly, some of these words, or the very notion of their meaning, do indeed invoke that reaction, and more, in some.

The generally acceptable adjective for a homosexual is 'gay'. We adopted this word into the English language in the twelfth century from the French word, *'gai'*. Its primary meaning is 'joyful', 'carefree', which implies 'uninhibited by moral

COMING UP FOR AIR

constraint'—hence the reason seventeenth-century prostitutes were sometimes referred to as 'gay', as were womanising men, whilst brothels came to be known as 'gay houses'.

The use of gay to mean homosexual is believed to have happened around the 1920s through its definition of 'uninhibited and carefree', and thus 'unrestricted by convention or acceptable social comportment'.

By the mid-twentieth century, the word had become well established in reference to 'hedonistic and uninhibited lifestyles', as had its antonym, 'straight', which has connotations of seriousness, respectability and conventionality.

In the UK, practising gays were deemed criminals by law and, as such, punished by death until 1861 when punishment was reduced to imprisonment. In the 1950s, the police moved to clamp down on gay practices by actively seeking out homosexuals in 'sting' operations (of the type used for fraud and drug trafficking today) via a series of high-profile arrests and trials.

One of the most notorious was that of eminent mathematician, scientist and wartime code breaker, Alan Turing, who was charged with 'gross indecency' and who eventually committed suicide.

Since 1967, the act that specifically targeted homosexual practices (lesbian practices were never acknowledged or deemed illegal) has undergone various reforms, including the lowering of the age of consent from twenty-one to sixteen.

In the 1980s, campaigning by right-wing groups led to the passing of a law that prohibited the 'intentional promotion of homosexuality by any local authority', and 'the teaching in any maintained school of the acceptability of homosexuality as a pretended family relationship'. The provision was known as 'Section 28' which, apart from sounding like a secret American Air Force base, was eventually repealed and led to a public apology by British Prime Minister Cameron, who stated that it [Section 28] was a "mistake" and "offensive to gay people".

Today, in England, same-sex couples are able to marry and enjoy the same rights as other married couples, although where they can actually marry, as in who will perform the ceremony, is still being debated, with some churches fully endorsing this diversity whilst others remain staunchly in favour of 'traditional' values.

It's no secret that God, according to the Bible, never intended for love, marriage or any kind of bedroom naughtiness to exist between those of the same sex. Correction: the Bible doesn't worry about two people of the same sex; it just has a problem with two men.

"If a man lies with a male as he lies with a woman, both of them have committed an abomination, they shall surely be put to death; their blood shall be upon them" (Leviticus 20:13)

And...

"Do you not know that the unrighteous will not inherit the kingdom of God? Do not be deceived, neither fornicators, nor idolaters, nor adulterers, nor homosexuals, nor sodomites, nor thieves, nor covetous, nor drunkards, nor revellers, nor extortioners will inherit the kingdom of God."(1 Corinthians 6:9-11)

Oh dear.

One of my American (practising Christian) friends made that clear to me a few years ago. I was in the passenger seat of her car as we drove home after a weekend away when, out of the darkness, I heard her say, "I'm really worried about you, Tony."

I thought, "Blimey, what does she know that I don't?" So I asked, "Why?"

She said, "That you won't be joining me in heaven."

The comment was so sudden and unprompted that I was temporarily speechless (yes, unusual for me) but I eventually uttered, "Oh, well. We're just going to have to make the most of this life, I guess," and I laughed.

It was only upon reflection that I realised how sad her statement made me feel—not necessarily for me, but for her. The thought must have seriously been troubling her.

Most rational human beings will understand that loving somebody isn't like ordering pizza; there's no menu to choose from (at least not in the conventional sense)—it just happens. Some would say that it's destiny, and sometimes, maybe, careful scheming but, ultimately, we're all just pawns for the mischievous machinations of Eros and Cupid who one day, as we're going about our business, see fit to ethereally bind us to another human being.

Sometimes, we'll notice it immediately, as soon as we lay eyes on them, and at other times it takes a while, but those who are bitten by the proverbial love bug succumb and become, in the immortal words of Brian Ferry, 'slaves to love'.

(What? You don't know that song either? I give up.)

So why does a gay person choose to be, well, gay?

Many will know that they don't. It's not like choosing to be vegetarian, where you just wake up one morning and decide that you're done handling meat (yes, I know—bad choice of words, but you get my meaning).

Gays are born gay.

So what sets them apart from their heterosexual counterparts? Razor-sharp sarcasm, wit, good sense of humour, excellent fashion sense, or is it their capacity for oodles of fabulously creative ideas, darling?

Um, I'd say that pretty much does it, but, physiologically, what makes them different is still unknown. Whilst there have been numerous studies, there's still no quantifiable proof or data that can actually explain why gay people 'lean' towards partners of the same gender. What is undisputed is that they yearn, love, feel and hurt in the same way as other human beings (some would say a tad more dramatically) because, believe it or not, they too are human.

Shakespeare once said, "Prick us, do we not bleed?" Gay men and women are no different from every other heterosexual soul on this earth and, as such, are entitled to the same basic human rights as the rest of the civilised world.

But then, I'm biased.

Sadly, there are still many in the world, generally zealots, who see gay love as unnatural, a scourge that must be eradicated by any means possible.

So what to do with the gays?

Enter conversion therapy, the origins of which are believed to go back to Christian fundamentalist groups (shocker) who believe that it is often possible to 'pray the gay away'. In these tragic cases, parents believe and their children are often brainwashed (via personal tuition, peer pressure and subjection to hell-house performances) into believing that sexual orientation can be 'cured'.

Conversion therapy often involves psychiatric, pharmacological and even electroshock treatment. Yet, homosexuality is not recognised as a mental disorder and thus, as such, cannot be treated with psychotherapy.

Even the famous Freud reluctantly attempted to cure a lesbian of her 'illness', only to conclude that it was not possible. He later wrote (in a letter to a mother who wanted to have her son treated for homosexuality) "…Is nothing to be ashamed of, no vice, no degradation; it cannot be classified as an illness."

Punishment-based therapy became prevalent in the 1940s and 1950s, with misguided doctors believing they could 'cure gayness' by subjecting male 'patients' to erotic images of females and then those of males whilst administering an electroshock. The therapy was then repeated and the wattage increased each time the patient failed to declare themselves cured. The same therapy involved intravenous delivery of a pharmaceutical compound that would induce vomiting in the 'patient' whilst he (or she) viewed erotic images of those of the same sex.

Needless to say, the 'therapy' proved ineffective, although some declared it a great success since there were a few sessions that did, albeit temporarily, reduce attraction to the same sex. The report's authors just missed out the part where it did not increase attraction in members of the opposite sex either.

Conversion therapy for homosexuality remains controversial today, with numerous cases still doing the rounds before the courts the world over, with campaigners calling for the practice to be declared illegal.

So, if not that, then what?

There's only one solution. It's the final solution, first identified by Hitler and now enshrined in Uganda's Anti Homosexuality bill of 2009. The bill originally sought the death penalty for 'Aggravated Homosexuality' and life imprisonment for 'The offence of homosexuality'. It was later downgraded to just life imprisonment. *Just* life? Wow—one century later, and Uganda has managed to go full circle. Now that's what I call progress.

Of course, I didn't know all of this back in the Eighties. What I *did* know is that I was living in a small town at a time when gays didn't have co-starring roles in mainstream movies and sitcoms. Instead, AIDS, the disease some believed was sent by God to clear the Earth of the scourge of gays, was beginning to rear its ugly head. A time when being gay literally turned you into some kind of pariah. And the teenage me couldn't face that. I'd been hurt enough.

So, like many in a time of crisis, I ignored the ugly truth and instead threw myself into trying to understand what makes humans tick, and my work at the radio station.

These became my salvation. Studying psychology helped me understand, whilst hosting the radio show made me feel like part of the community. Something I so desperately needed.

But the knocks kept coming.

My new job offer at the larger radio station fell through. Of course, in my paranoid state, I did consider the notion that this may well have happened because the station managers may have heard rumours about me, but I luckily had the presence of mind to dismiss this as ludicrous. Why would these people even care?

Would they?

And this is how it went. Constantly second-guessing myself—and at the time there wasn't really anybody I could really confide in, either. All of my siblings were in the UK or the USA, and I couldn't tell my mother, a devote Catholic and pained sufferer of the well-known small-town neurosis of 'what will the neighbours think?'

I focussed instead on the radio show I did have, and my new friend: writing. Not books but a diary.

I first adopted the practice when I was ten and I left to live with my Italian-speaking aunt, uncle and cousins for nearly three months while my parents organised our emigration from England to Italy.

I was English and I couldn't speak any Italian, which meant that there really wasn't anybody I could literally *talk to* during that time, so I took to writing my thoughts down on bits of paper.

I remember that I'd sometimes do this while attending *scuola media*. I've lost count of the amount of times my teacher would castigate me for not paying attention. Hey, I was English; I could hardly understand a word the woman was saying. What did she expect?

Interestingly, the more I developed the ability to articulate, the less I found the need to write, and so I eventually abandoned the practice.

Until the fateful night that I watched Peppe walk off and away from me.

Writing therapy is something counsellors often recommend to their clients (patients). It's a cathartic process that provides relief for those who are unable to share their feelings openly, be that because they're unable to trust someone else with such thoughts or because they are incapable of articulating them.

In my case, I started keeping a diary; I committed every single controversial thought to paper and, in doing so, erased it from my mind whilst banishing me to the proverbial 'closet' for what would turn out to be a whole decade.

My beloved mother, never one to miss a beat, noticed my newfound love for journal writing and bought me my very first mechanical typewriter, which I adored and still have to this day, along with boxes full of those typed (what can I say? I never did like my handwriting) diaries. The typewriter was also put to very good use on papers for class as well as some short stories. Not that I ever dreamed of having these published, for my mind was elsewhere; I was with Sister Sledge, *Lost in Music* (metaphorically speaking).

The idea of cutting my own record had occurred to me before, but I had never seriously considered it. Where on earth did one start? Why, Yellow Pages of course. At least that's where Patty, my new girlfriend, started on one of her visits to the radio station. She told me I should look up recording studios and cut a demo. I told her she was crazy and that if it were that easy then everybody would do it.

"You're not everybody," she said, thumbing through the pages of the book and highlighting potential candidates.

And so a whole new chapter in my life began.

I travelled to a studio in Bari, Southern Italy, for an audition and I apparently impressed the songwriter so much that he 'gave me' (I didn't know then that he'd still enjoy royalties) one of his songs. It was called *Nothing Can Be the Same*. It became the B side to my first single, *Into Emotion*, which I went on to perform on several stages throughout Italy, including San Remo, which is an Italian pop music show televised on RAI (the Italian equivalent of the BBC).

The rest is history.

Tony DJ became Tony the pop star, who now had a toned body and a modern haircut that complemented those dreamy brown eyes.

I garnered a whole new legion of female fans, and that suited me just fine.

Once again, my life had changed. But I was nineteen and in Italy, and that meant, despite my place of birth and my British nationality, only one thing: National Service.

I had a choice: return to England, as my mother had done before me, join the rest of the family, or put my life on pause for a year and try to pick up the pieces when I got out.

I chose the former and cashed out. I came back to England where I focussed on the true love of my life—writing.

I wrote my first full-length manuscript, *Dark Crossing*, which I later turned into a play and, rather ambitiously, produced, directed and starred in! This was followed by another five plays and a semi-professional career in photography as well as some business investments.

My first novel, *Nimbus*, was published in 2001 (there are rumours of a sequel but I have no idea who started those). I've finished the manuscript of a supernatural thriller, *Unspeakable*, the publication of which has been bumped back by a few months in favour of these very words I'm writing to you now.

Needless to say, the days of Franco and the gang are firmly in the past—but don't get too comfortable here in the present, as I'll be taking you back to a night in 1998 where a young corporal in the United States Marine Corps would set in motion a series of powerful and dramatic events that would put an end to my ten years of self-imposed exile deep inside the closet, and would out me, somewhat unceremoniously, to everybody who cared to know.

9 WHO DO YOU THINK YOU ARE?

Coming to terms with how I felt about Franco, another male, wasn't something I managed very well. In fact, I often found myself pausing to wonder how exactly to define my relationship with him since, in my teenage opinion, I wasn't showing any obvious 'signs' of being gay.

After all, to everybody else, I was Tony: a slim young man with a very masculine Roman nose, a mop of black hair, big brown eyes and a sexy English accent—a package that proved very popular with those of the opposite sex.

Conveniently, I had read a few magazine articles on the natural 'experimentation' of teens, and I was more than happy to consciously attribute my dalliance to that.

Subconsciously, it was a different story.

So what about you?

What kind of person are *you*? And no, I'm not specifically talking about your sexuality, but more about who you are.

Take a few seconds to think about that.

When somebody meets you for the first time, what kind of person do you think they see? What kind of impression do you think you make? Do you think they see the real you or do they see a 'projected' part of you?

Maybe your best trait/s.

Are you confident? Shy? Aloof? Warm? Welcoming? Or downright disinterested?

They say you should never judge a book by its cover. They (whoever they may be) also say that you should never 'judge' somebody just by their appearance. By *judge* I mean know what *type* of person they might be, the things they like, the kind of life they lead, and what type of personality they may sport.

There's an Italian proverb (yes, you're going to find quite a few of these dotted throughout this book) that says, "You don't really know somebody until you've eaten a tonne of salt together".

Wow, a *tonne*?

But the point remains the same; you don't really know someone until you've spent a considerable amount of time with them, truly understanding who they are, their goals, values, intricacies and nuances.

And even then, humans are quite adept at hiding that which they do not wish to be revealed. And one doesn't need to train as a special agents to acquire these skills—no, just one skill in particular; seduce other humans into caring so deeply they'll choose (albeit subconsciously) to become blinded to the things they do not wish to see.

This has been evidenced time and time again in a multitude of long-term relationships where partners learn, sometimes after decades, that their partner was having an affair with somebody else, often of the same sex, or that their partner is actually leading multiple lives with multiple family members.

Scary thought, huh?

Think about that.

Imagine being married to someone for multiple years and then learning that they have an identical family life somewhere else with someone else, sometimes just a few miles away.

It appears inconceivable.

Yet, I've regularly come across stories of husbands with two sets of wives and associated children.

Some of these stories lead to tragedy when the protagonist is in danger of being exposed. Some are so shocking they'd make Jerry Springer's hair stand on end.

Like the story of the man who had two different homes with a wife and a girlfriend just ten miles apart in Hertfordshire, England. The fifty-year-old carried on the charade for twenty-one years and had ten children. He eventually committed suicide when the women found out about each other.

Another story is that of Stephen King (no, not the writer) who was known to his American neighbours, in a small town in America, as a family man who worked as a cable engineer—yet Eddie Maher was actually a wanted criminal back in good ole' sunny England for a notorious van heist that had netted him a cool £1.2m. Maher lived his double life in America for twenty years.

There are many similar stories.

The truth hidden behind closed doors is often inconceivable to the outside world.

"How could she not know he was like that?" "How could she have not seen what was happening?" "How could he have not realised sooner?"

Like a picture hidden inside of a picture, the chameleon of truth reveals itself to those who look upon it with a fresh perspective, yet often remains hidden to those up close and personal. That's because most humans will strive to see what they *want* to see—and nothing else.

Indeed, most people would prefer to see their relationship as something that is blissful, brimming with love and mutual respect, rather than something that is frayed around the edges and patched with complacency and deception.

The truth is often on display—we just need to want to see it.

So, tell me, how often have you heard somebody say that they like to people watch?

You might even be one of those who, like me, enjoys this simplest of pastimes. Nothing better than enjoying a latte or a meal and 'watching the world go by'. By *world*, I mean a group of strangers who, like ants, go about their lives unaware of the curious eyes following their every move until they disappear out of sight.

Yes sinister, yet it remains a favourite pastime of many.

I've always enjoyed people watching. I like to try and work out what 'type' of person they might be just by what they wear, the way they comport themselves and, if they're speaking, the accent and intonation of their voice.

I developed this fascination when I was a teenager and, if I may say so myself, I've become fairly adept at 'reading' people because of it. Give me an hour with somebody and I'll give you their secrets.

Ever since Franco, I developed an obsession with understanding humans, and my 'talent' was often called upon by friends who'd ask me to 'check out' prospective partners with the view to forming a 'profile' of their personality and thus their compatibility.

I sharpened these skills by studying psychology, and have been honing them in life ever since, including the time I spent interviewing literally hundreds of people whilst researching this book—and, indeed, I have become an unofficial couples' therapist for some, who have often told me that I have a talent for such things.

The thing is, I believe everybody has this talent; they just need to want to use it.

It is ultimately about being observant, picking up on subtle mannerisms and social cues, and comparing these for similarities with other individuals—and after a while, this reveals a 'type'.

So, can you really judge a book (or a person) by its cover?

Some would argue that you cannot.

I would have to disagree.

I believe you can 'profile' people just by looking at their demeanour and backing this up with a few minutes of conversation. In fact, you'll already know that government agencies around the world use specially trained forensic psychologists, known as profilers, for this sole purpose: to 'build a picture' of character traits of people they've never met before simply from case notes, by visiting crime scenes and, sometimes, interviewing witnesses involved in the case.

Yes, you can read a person by their cover.

It's the very reason profilers exist in blue-chip organisations where personality traits, capability and compatibility are crucial to the success of the candidate within their new environment.

You may well have heard of, and indeed participated in, one or more of the many personality tests on various websites or social media. These are, after all, just a series of questions thrown into a formula to reveal a 'type'.

All of this tells us that, whilst it isn't possible to 'know' somebody just by asking a battery of questions, it's most certainly possible to build a 'profile' or ascertain a 'type' of person. You just need to know where to look and what questions to ask.

After all, the nineties did spawn one of the most popular

partner-selection practices based on this very premise. Originally conceived to help Jewish singles meet and marry, it then rapidly became a popular and somewhat commonplace exercise around the world. I'm talking of course about speed dating.

In speed-dating sessions, participants have just seconds to form an opinion about any one person before moving on to the next. In that short period of time, they have to make the most of their social observations and glean as much as they can from their instincts whilst all the time trying to avoid the first and most obvious cue: aesthetics.

The whole process of speed dating is the source of an endless stream of information: Grooming and wardrobe tells us whether or not that person takes pride in themselves and their appearance. Slouching or sitting up straight in their chair indicates their level of confidence and self-esteem. Whether or not they pose questions or wait for the questions to be asked tells us if they're an introvert or extrovert, which in turn tells us about their confidence, and so on.

So who do you think *you* are? Did you take a few seconds to consider that?

If somebody met you on a speed date, what kind of impression do you think you'd make in the first five minutes?

Who would the other person see?

Would they be the one making the small talk, or would you offer that up willingly with a barrage of nervous (or perhaps not-so-nervous) chatter?

What would you talk about—the weather? Would you want to sound easy-going? Or would you want to sound a tad more intelligent, perhaps touching on current events somewhere in the world?

Perhaps you wouldn't want to stick out at all and you'd go more mainstream, play it safe by talking of things you know, 'project' that you are a 'normal' person by sticking close to subjects like family and or your job.

Or maybe you'd be incapable of talking about *anything*; you'd wait for the other person to say something and try and ride out the uncomfortable silences?

Either way, know that whoever or whatever you're

projecting may not necessarily reconcile with how you are perceived by others. That's because we think we know ourselves but, more often than not, the person we believe we know is just a projection of ourselves, often polarised by our life experiences and, of course, our current state of mind.

If you're an egotist, you'll undoubtedly believe that others see you as an attractive, confident person, somebody with whom they'd undoubtedly want to share a lot of time. (Ironically, many rarely perceive these traits as endearing.)

Conversely, if you're suffering from low self-esteem, you'll think that everybody is seeing that 'ugliness', which most likely doesn't even exist, but you are projecting on yourself.

However you play it, remember there's a distinct possibility that the stranger's receptors are up and scanning every possible thing about you too. That's assuming of course that they are actually interested in getting to know you.

They may well just be filling time; they may have already made up their mind as soon as they clapped eyes on you (or the projected you). Thing is, you won't necessarily know that about them, nor will they about you—and that's when kinesics may come in handy.

Kinesics, otherwise known as 'body language', is primeval in its origin and you'd be forgiven for thinking that it's just about how we hold and move our bodies—but it's actually about much more. Kinesics is about the space between us and other human beings, and how we allow this to grow or shrink depending on how we're feeling, also known as proxemics.

It was the anthropologist Edward T. Hall who first coined the term, back in the sixties. Hall's study looked at people's use of space as a crucial element of social interaction. It's believed that this was the origin of the term 'personal space'.

"Respect my personal space."

Personal space is carried with each and every one of us, wherever we go, and body spacing and posture are unintentional reactions to sensory fluctuations, such as the situation we're in, the person or persons we are reacting to, as well as the pitch of their voices.

Hall went as far as publishing a guide to the various distances between human beings:

Intimate distance for embracing, touching or whispering
Close phase—less than 6 inches (15 cm)
Far phase—6 to 18 inches (15 to 46 cm)
Personal distance for interactions among
good friends or family members
Close phase—1.5 to 2.5 feet (46 to 76 cm)
Far phase—2.5 to 4 feet (76 to 122 cm)
Social distance for interactions among acquaintances
Close phase—4 to 7 feet (1.2 to 2.1 m)
Far phase—7 to 12 feet (2.1 to 3.7 m)
Public distance used for public speaking
Close phase—12 to 25 feet (3.7 to 7.6 m)
Far phase—25 feet (7.6 m) or more.

These aren't meant to be an exact science but are more an indication of how, as humans, we are able to communicate with each other without even saying a word.

Now, it has to be said that body language is not an exact science. It actually takes a whole series of body cues to enable a capable 'reader' to understand what the other person is actually saying, but not verbalising or, more cynically, trying to suppress or disguise. Yet, there's one part of the human anatomy that never lies: our eyes.

They (*them* again!) say that *the eyes are the window to the soul*—but there is more to that saying than literally 'meets the eye'.

For example, a well-known eye cue is whether a person is looking to the left or right. Eyes tend to look to the right when the brain is imagining or creating, and to the left when the brain is recalling or remembering.

This is based on the NLP (Neuro-Linguist Programming) theory which was developed by scientists in the 1960s.

From this, you could conclude that subtle glances to the right would mean that somebody is 'fabricating', thus lying. This is a technique well deployed when you ask somebody to recount how a particular event took place.

Based on NLP, that person should be looking left, trying to 'recall' information; yet if they're glancing to the right, there's a distinct possibility that they're actually fabricating the memory!

Before you strap your partner into a chair and start pulling at his or her fingernails with a pair of pliers, however, a word of caution: just because your partner is looking right, it doesn't necessarily mean they're lying — it could well mean that they can't recollect the events as they happened and thus are talking hypothetically, speculating or guessing. This is the very reason many of these techniques work best as collective layers of analysis rather than an isolated assumption.

Ultimately, we are who we are. The trick is being comfortable in our own skin and loving ourselves enough to project who we are and not who we believe others wish to see.

The late Kurt Cobain (of grunge band Nirvana) famously said, *"I'd rather be hated for who I am, rather than loved for who I am not."*

Sadly, these pearls of wisdom weren't even a twinkle in Cobain's eye back in the 1980s when I was an English teenager in a foreign land and when I most likely would have put those words to good use.

10 M, FOR MARINE

So now that you've met most of the main characters, I guess it's time for me to introduce you to the main protagonist, the person who inspired this book and who is ultimately responsible for me sitting here writing to you today.

As you know, it wasn't long after the disastrous collapse of my friendship with Peppe & Co. that my music career as a DJ metamorphosed into that of a recording artist, and I owe this career progression to my eighteen-year-old (at the time) girlfriend, Patrizia (Patty).

Patty has got to be one of the most beautiful people to ever come into my life—and when I say *beautiful,* I'm not necessarily talking about aesthetic beauty; I'm talking about an inherent beauty, deep within.

Patty wasn't like the other girls who, whist keeping up with current trends, appeared to have no aspirations beyond the small-town mentality of growing up, marrying and raising a family. She was completely different: young, modern and forward-thinking.

Sure, she'd keep up with fashion and music icons, but she had ambitions beyond the town—not for herself but for me, her boyfriend. In fact, she'd often look beyond herself to my own well-being.

She was the perfect bride for any man.

Sadly, that man wasn't to be me, for obvious reasons.

Of course I didn't really appreciate that at the time I was dating her. Back then, she was perfect just the way she was, and it was I who was flawed. And I'm not actually referring to my sexuality here; I'm talking more about the fact that, in retrospect, I probably could have been a better boyfriend to her.

I'm not sure.

That's something only Patty can answer.

What I do know is that my inability to commit to her was because of that which I had vowed to suppress for the rest of my life. Again, had I known then what I know now: Patty and I probably would have been even better friends than we already were. We certainly did laugh a lot together; she had a wonderful personality.

However, I chose to return to England, where I didn't date for a very long time. In fact, I continued to correspond with Patty for several months after my return until I eventually started to 'fool around' with other girls, but never really connected with anybody for a few years, not like Patty, not until I met Sindy.

Sindy was a lovely girl with a cracking sense of humour, but I realise now that she lacked the altruistic goodness that was so inherent in Patty.

We started with casual dating that became more frequent and then, three years later, we were talking about marriage, and even selecting names for children. A concept that feels as alien to me now as it felt normal then.

So, you're probably thinking that I must have somehow used these girls, that I led them on in a somewhat cynical, premeditated way as proverbial 'beards' as I met my twenties and started my transition through them. But I can, in all honesty, say that I did not.

At least not consciously.

Sure, I knew that there was something different about me. I knew that I appreciated other men. But I don't think I truly accepted that I was actually sexually attracted to them.

It simply wasn't an option. For me, those days of 'experimentation' were over.

I was in a committed relationship and I loved Sindy.

Or at least I believed I did—for Sindy was nothing like Patty. She was English, for a start, and therefore had her own ideas on what dating meant and, if I were to look upon our relationship now, it would be the paragon of everything I don't believe a relationship should be.

Sindy was as possessive as she was domineering and, at the time, I believed that was part and parcel of being in a relationship. We spent nearly every spare waking moment with each other in a relationship that became as comfortable as it was familiar.

As a consequence, we approached every social occasion as a couple. In fact, I don't think I can remember, while we were dating, that I actually did anything without her.

But all of this was about to come to a screeching halt.

I was invited to a friend's birthday party. She was a mutual friend of ours, so naturally we attended together.

It's the 1990s; the video camera was the big thing, although, as a luxury electrical item, it was still rather expensive and therefore the ability to 'make home movies' wasn't as universal as it is today.

I was so fascinated with the technology that I filmed nearly everything I did—okay, maybe not *everything*.

That night I was asked, by the birthday girl, to film everyone and everything as a keepsake, and I was more than happy to oblige. My subjects included us, the guests, a bunch of strangers and, of course, the lads who were busy spinning the decks of the mobile disco.

They welcomed the opportunity to be filmed and it seemed they recognised me as a former 'pop star', which I thought was somewhat strange since my career had taken place sometime ago and in another country.

Then I learned that the birthday girl had been spreading the news about me being at the party.

I started chatting to my newfound fans.

Matt, a handsome teenage preppy with blue eyes and the looks of Jason Priestley (of the original *Beverly Hills 90210* fame) was the leader of the gang and showed a peculiar interest in me—and I welcomed the attention. It had been sometime since I'd actually engaged in deep conversation with a bunch of lads that wasn't monitored and/or edited by Sindy who, before long, interrupted the conversation in her usual inimitable style.

"Where the hell have you been?" she interrupted, angrily.

I looked at her and then back at the boys who were trying to suppress a snigger.

"You know where I've been. I went to get the spare camera battery from the car," I said with a smile, in an attempt to play down the awkwardness of the moment.

"That was ages ago," she retorted.

"I know, but I met these guys… This is Matt…"

"Can we go now?"

I smiled apologetically at the lads. I didn't particularly fancy making things worse by performing one of our explosive arguments in front of these strangers.

"It was nice meeting you," I said with a smile and turned to leave.

Interestingly, clearly undaunted by Sindy's attitude, as if it were something he was accustomed to, Matt called after me and asked if I wanted to 'hang out' with them the next evening.

I clearly remember shrinking inside, being thrilled to be asked, but at the same time wishing he hadn't done so in front of my girlfriend.

I have to say, just recalling this scene as I write it, I'm incensed that I enabled that kind of behaviour. I was her boyfriend, not her slave, and the fact that she disrespected me in such a way and I allowed it to happen is unforgivable.

Luckily, even then I had the presence of mind to accept Matt's offer and we exchanged contact information. (I could feel the hot breath of Sindy's temper over my shoulder, but I told myself I'd deal with that later.)

We walked home that night and, although we argued quite regularly, that must have been one of the worst confrontations we'd ever had.

It started with Sindy accusing me of abandoning and leaving her at the mercy of some strange bloke who could have quite easily molested her. She then went on to talk (or yell) about my new acquaintances and how I could have at least consulted with her before agreeing to go out with them the following evening.

We argued the whole thirty minutes it took to walk home and for another hour or so after that, her biggest complaint being that I had agreed to go out the following evening without her.

Crazy.

Now, it would have been much easier for me to say that I wouldn't go, because that's how we'd resolve such conflicts early on in our relationship; I would concede until, eventually, I simply stopped doing things without her.

It wasn't worth the hassle. (There's more about this later on in the appropriately entitled chapter.)

But that night, I didn't. That night something had changed. I told her that I was going and that she would have to deal with it.

And I did.

Matt, I and the whole gang of about ten became friends.

After nearly ten years my life had gone full circle; I was back in another group of lads, only these guys happened to be English.

Many of them were also single. Technically, so was Matt as he was on the verge of leaving his possessive girlfriend (I realised then why he was unfazed by Sindy's attitude at the birthday party; he'd personally experienced it all before).

Thus the rebellion began.

The arguments between Sindy and I continued, and when they weren't arguments they were throwaway remarks about me and 'my new pals'.

Now, I could bore you with the details of what came next but, quite frankly, I doubt it's anything you haven't heard before either in your own life, elsewhere, or indeed inside this book. Suffice to say that the relationship became toxic, to both of us.

The problem was, we'd become one of those monstrous insular relationships where we depended on each other for absolutely everything and, in the process, alienated all of our other friends to the point where there was nobody else, and if we ever did venture out socially with others it would only be if those others were couples that were known to both of us.

It was an oppressive, unhealthy state of affairs—and one I have seen time and time again since, and it simply makes me sad.

The worst thing is that when you're in one of these cancerous and claustrophobic relationships, it's so difficult to see the signs.

You just simply fall into the syndrome.

Your free time is no longer your own, it is always shared, and you don't often feel the need to question or revaluate this—not until something comes along that makes you wonder, *why don't I have any other friends beyond the other couples that we know? Why don't I ever spend any free time alone, doing other things, taking up a hobby?*

I realise now why I feel so strongly when I see this type of relationship in others. For me, this is everything that is unhealthy about a union between two people who are supposed to care about each other.

Yet I swallowed that poison for years, until that night.

In hindsight, I can only conclude that I had been unhappy for some time, but had never been aware of this until the incentive to 'defect' presented itself.

Interestingly, my decision to go out with the lads the next day wasn't something I needed time to think about, consider or even consult. I knew it was something I wanted to do and I also knew that, regardless of the marathon conflict, I was going to do it.

The time had come to break free, and I did.

My friendship with Matt and the gang continued.

And no, my interest in Matt didn't venture anywhere beyond friendship (we're still friends to this day). Sure, Matt was handsome and everybody literally flocked to him. He was the guy with the flashy car, the charisma, the looks and the sense of fun that attracted boys as it did girls, but I didn't see Matt in that way; that side of me had been well and truly suppressed— as had my inclination to jump into another serious relationship, until many years later.

Instead, I threw myself into my writing.

At the time, I was writing scripts for theatre. I love writing dialogue, and stage plays were the natural vehicle of choice— and, given my background in psychology and my fascination with relationships, I had plenty of material to draw on.

I even wrote a semi-autobiographical stage play about friendships called *A Stranger By My Side* which was never staged, but the script does accurately record all of the dialogue from some of my most meaningful relationships, including the very scene you've just been reading about.

What I didn't know is that I hadn't yet experienced my most meaningful relationship. The one that I would class as my first love, but you won't be surprised to hear that the first cut is well and truly the deepest.

Oddly, mine didn't happen until I reached the ripe old age of twenty-eight.

But first, as you know, everything you've read and will read in this book is one hundred per cent true. While I may well have changed names and some locations, everything you read is based on testimony, where possible, research, or, as in this case, first-hand experience.

In this particular story, the protagonist was directly involved with me. I am able to directly corroborate and substantiate, via my own testimony and photographic evidence that this relationship did exist in the format I am about to recount.

That said, it's been over a decade since these events, and I understand that this person, my ex, has since gone on to have a child or two, and get married (yes, in that order). He also works in public office and there's no doubt that the fallout from these revelations, whilst they shouldn't, may well have an impact on his career, not to mention his marriage.

Regardless of his status, I don't believe there's anything to be gained by naming and so-called shaming; I have therefore chosen not to reveal his true identity.

I'm going to refer to him as 'M'—no, not after the famous weapon maker, but after the marine that he was at the time.

The year is 1997. I can't remember which month, but what I do remember is that computers and technology were one of the fastest-growing industries at the time, since the 1990s really was the decade that connected us.

The whole concept of being 'online' and 'connected' to the rest of the world was as exciting as it was addictive.

I met M in a chat room.

Try not to raise your eyebrows so quickly.

Remember, this is the nineties; broadband as we know it today didn't exist. Back then, you still had to click that wondrous icon featuring two computer terminals, wait for the dial tone, listen to the screechy, scratchy dissonant sounds of two machines talking to each other and then cross your fingers that a flashing network icon would appear in your system tray to confirm that you were 'online'.

This was all before chat rooms inherited their stigma for lasciviousness, child (and adult) grooming and other unsavoury activities.

Back then, chat rooms were just online forums where people of like minds from all over the world could actually meet to discuss topics of mutual interest—although, to be perfectly honest, I have no recollection of exactly where or how a nineteen-year-old corporal in the United States Marine Corps and a twenty-something-year-old English writer slash photographer managed to meet online. All I know is that we did and that this young man would end up changing life, as I knew it, forever.

Marine Corps Base, Camp Lejeune, is situated in Jacksonville, North Carolina. It covers two hundred and forty-six square miles and is home to approximately a hundred and fifty thousand marines, dependents and civilian workers. It also features fourteen miles of private beaches used by the American Marine Corps for amphibious assault training.

Needless to say, I was instantly impressed with M's

profession. Well, he was a marine in the mighty United States Marine Corps. Up until that time, I'd only ever seen marines in movies—tough guys portrayed as invincible beings—and now here I was, chatting to a real-life one.

Now, before you start smiling at that somewhat naïve infatuation, I should tell you that a few years later, in 2000, M joined my family and me on a trip back to Forenza, and news that there was an *actual US marine in town* spread like wildfire.

We could barely walk down the street without him being accosted by people, generally young men, who went out of their way to chat with M (regardless of language barrier) and actually shake his hand!

It was surreal.

I guess the fact that he worked out a lot, was buff and therefore often bulging out of his T-shirts added to the whole image.

Anyway, I digress.

M and I became friends (or at least online pals) and started corresponding, often arranging to meet online on a daily basis.

Back then, video chat was just coming into its own. Our favourites were called ICUII and ICQ, and they had the ability to send instant messages, real-time video (albeit one that moved frame by frame rather than in one smooth motion) and chat.

It was awesome!

Again, remember, this was years before Skype was even a glint in Janus and Niklas's eye (that's Denmark's Janus Friis and Sweden's Niklas Zennström who, in August 2003, along with some collaborators, introduced Skype to the world).

We'd talk about films, Country (his preference) and Dance (mine) music, politics and a medley of other things. We'd also share links to websites, games and even photos of each other. He in uniform; me in, well, jeans.

One day, during a conversation, I directed him to the photography page on my website, which he found interesting albeit nowhere near as interesting as one of the female models featured there.

Her name was Cathy.

Cathy was—or should I say *is*—a very attractive blonde with gorgeous girly looks, a lovely body and a wonderful personality (or should I have written that the other way round?).

Cathy and I had worked on many photo shoots together. She was a natural, and M clearly enjoyed her pictures.

He was smitten.

So months went by and our online correspondence turned from casual talk about each of us visiting the other's country to actual planning.

It started with M's visit to England in March of 1998, during which he expressed a firm interest in actually meeting the new girl of his dreams, Cathy, and I was naturally happy to oblige.

As I drove to London's Gatwick Airport in the early hours of Saturday morning, I found myself really excited, but also inexplicably nervous. I was thrilled to be finally meeting my e-pal, whilst at the same time wondering what the hell I might be getting myself into. After all, I may have been corresponding with this guy for some time, but he was, ultimately, a stranger to me, and there's a huge leap from chatting to a bunch of pixels on a computer screen and listening to a disembodied voice on the phone to actually meeting somebody in the flesh.

Moreover, I'd signed up to spending two weeks with this person and to showing him the sights and sounds of my beautiful England—what if we didn't particularly like each other? Or, once the initial meet was over, we didn't have anything in common? What if we'd discussed everything there was to discuss online?

And so my thoughts raced just like the road before me. I really didn't know what to expect and, for a control freak like me, it was something that strayed way out of my comfort zone although I did draw some reassurance from the fact that we were actually meeting on my turf.

Yet, as I rode the escalator down to the arrivals lounge, my heart started pounding and I think I was moments away from breaking out in a cold sweat. I had to have a serious word with myself.

I reasoned that if I was feeling this way, on my homeland, then how on earth must M be feeling? He had just made the five-thousand-mile trip to see me. He was probably feeling just the same, if not worse.

And anyway, it was too late; a stream of people were emerging through the arrivals door like a bunch of animals evading a predator.

And so, like a game of spot the difference, I tried to identify him amongst the throng of fluorescent jackets, luggage trolleys, baggage and humanity.

And then, after what felt like an eternity, and what appeared to be the contents of two jumbo jets, he appeared, somewhat nondescript but for his military crew cut, among his fellow travellers, dressed in jeans and a simple khaki T-shirt.

My first impression was that he looked different to his online presence. Not different as in he had changed his appearance— that was all there: the large Roman nose, the big eyes, his buff frame, the ubiquitous haircut—but more his features looked harsher in the cold florescent light of English day.

To hug or not to hug?

I thought about that the whole time he was making his way inexorably towards me.

The actual meet was slightly awkward considering we knew each other fairly well and that, at least online, we were good friends, but that was to be expected.

His American accent helped here. One of the features I really liked about him. He didn't have a traditional southern accent; in fact, oddly, he sounded English but with an American lilt. I know that probably makes absolutely no sense, but all I can tell you is that there was something comforting about the way he'd annunciate his vowels, like sweet cherry pie.

The drive north from London Gatwick Airport started in silence, beyond typical small talk about the flight and first impressions of England—not that he was able to make much of an assessment, since he'd landed in darkness and we were currently travelling at high speed on a concrete jungle of motorway intersections.

At least that was until I had the brainwave of making him navigator designate. Well, that seemed to be the logical conclusion given the fact that, before that day, I hadn't really had much reason to drive to London Gatwick Airport. Let's not forget that this was before the advent of satellite navigation so prevalent today.

Interestingly, this became one of the topics of conversation. I remember discussing satellite navigation with M, and he explained how there were plans to release such useful military satellite technology to the civilian market. I joked that until such time that the travel revolution reached average folk, then we'd just have to make do with him and a road atlas (yes, that actual oversized printed book, the cause of many heated debates in cars all over the globe), and that with his military background and his regular field manoeuvres, it should be second nature for him. He laughed and said that may well have been the case, but for fact that he was confused and somewhat perturbed that all of the English roads he had seen so far resembled names of serious weaponry, such as the M1, A1 and M25.

We laughed, and it was in that moment that I knew we were going to be okay.

It took us a couple of hours to get back to the lake cabin I had rented in Cambridgeshire, but not long to settle in.

I had made sure the place was fully stocked with all sorts of groceries. In fact, I actually cooked that evening. Well, when I say *cooked*, I use that term loosely, I opened a few packets of frozen foods and slung them in an oven. Ironic really, because for M, a healthy eater who trained regularly as if his body were a temple, that kind of food should have triggered some kind of a nervous breakdown.

It didn't.

Over dinner, we reviewed the itinerary I had designed for his stay in the UK, which included obvious sightseeing in London and trips to theme parks, as well as time with my family. The trip was packed and, in hindsight, I probably designed it that way just in case we didn't get on; at least we'd be busy.

We also talked about Cathy and how, at some stage, we'd call her and arrange for the two of them to meet.

Thus, contrary to my earlier misgivings, once we got into the swing of things, there was nothing about M that I particularly disliked, and it seemed as if he felt the same. In fact, we talked about our nervousness and how silly it was considering how well we knew each other.

We actually laughed a lot for most of the first evening, primarily about how ridiculous our reservations were and how in awe we both were of the fact that, after so much online time, we were actually both in the same room together.

I have to confess to being somewhat mesmerised by that unassuming young man who, with that southern upbringing, was almost British in his politeness, and I encouraged him to regale me with stories of his time in the marines featuring details about his time at Camp Lejeune, the tough endurance training, the endless marching and 'yomping' across fields, along with how exactly he ended up there.

He explained, rather candidly, that he had been a bit of a wild child in high school (something I was finding hard to reconcile in the person before me) and that how, like many young men, he'd reached a juncture in his life where he had the opportunity to actually go to prison for typical juvenile misdemeanours, or knuckle under in the Marine Corps.

He chose the latter.

I remember loving this about him because it made him a more rounded person to me. He may have come across as unaffected, unassuming and, in a somewhat naive kind of way, like butter wouldn't melt, but there was a rebel beneath that cool exterior, as well as a dedicated, ambitious young man who was making a good name for himself in his platoon and was on course to making sergeant within a few years.

He also happened to be a fully qualified swimming instructor with the Corps (which I remember thinking was useful because I would have just sunk to the bottom of the swimming pool if placed in one), as well as a wrestler.

That last bit did make me laugh, as it seemed so disconnected from everything else, but then I learned that it's actually a popular American sport, particularly at high school and college.

And that's when he decided to show me some moves.

Of course, I wasn't in a hurry to go toe to toe (or should that be arms, legs and toes?) with this hunk of an American marine. Luckily, he made a point of not slamming lumbering old me to the ground too hard—but, boy, did we laugh as he put moves on me that had me surrendering before he'd even started.

117

And yes, I did at least try to hold my own but, hey, this guy was a professional; I was just an Englishman without so much as a game of Twister to my belt.

And it was then, as I was wheezing from the struggle, crying from the laughter, that he kissed me full on the lips.

It took a few seconds for me to realise what was happening; at first, I actually thought it was part of the game. I know how ridiculous that might sound right now, but that was my brain's first reaction to the event.

The second was surreal bliss, for his kiss was soft and delicate, unlike anything I had experienced before, and I remember closing my eyes and sinking into it, as one would into a bed made of fluffy cotton wool, as his warm hand gently cupped my cheek and I gradually became aware of the proximity of his body.

The moment must have lasted seconds, yet it felt like minutes and my heart seemed to switch gear, from practical pumping in response to the exertion of our play fight, through to rhythmic pounding that, somewhat bizarrely, seemed to increase when the kiss slowly ended and I dared to open my eyes.

He was looking down at me with glistening hazel eyes and a sleepy smile.

"Are you okay?" he asked, almost in a whisper.

I tried to speak, but I was inexplicably struck dumb. I just nodded and returned an incredulous smile.

If I were a teenager, this would most likely be the part where I type OMG! OMG! All over again, but I won't. I'm British and, uh-hum, much more mature now.

There is something incredibly unique about a first kiss. It's so special that it stays with you for the rest of your life, like a brand or a badge that is forever pinned on your heart.

So now you may well be wondering how on earth I can possibly say that with everything that came before.

You see, for me, all of the relationships that came before M may well have been my first loves, but none felt as true as that one kiss.

Needless to say, memories of Franco and everything after, all of the things that scared me into the proverbial closet and had me seek asylum there for nearly a decade, came flooding back.

Would this new love leave me heartbroken, as had those before it?

You'll find out.

11 BEAUTY & THE BEAST

So now you've met all of the main protagonists.

No doubt you will have formed an opinion about each and every one of them, and perhaps even drawn some conclusions—but, trust me, there's much more to all of these stories than originally meets your eyes.

Out of the many relationships I could have written about, I selected these because of the emotional impact I believe they will have on you.

Of course, I had no idea of their actual impact until I met with the first manuscript focus group.

If their reaction is anything to go by, then you'll need to ensure you remain seated with your seatbelt fastened because there's going to be some turbulence up ahead and, if you're receptive, perhaps even an awakening.

But first, I'm going to take you back to Al.

Remember him?

Al was busy recovering from his breakup with Missy after he discovered that she was sleeping with other men to fund her addiction, as well as a cold, that's when he received a visit from Kayla and Emily.

The sight of that woman and her beautiful baby girl was more than enough to lift his spirits and, after talking to them, he knew they were the girls for him.

He knew he had to be with them.

When I asked Al what exactly it was about Kayla that had such a profound effect on him, he rather sheepishly answered, "Her smile, her looks, I guess."

And that's exactly how it happens. One minute we're minding our own business—and the next, we're captivated by a complete stranger.

Yes, like it or not, rightly or wrongly, the first thing we all notice when we meet somebody for the first time is their looks and, consciously or subconsciously, we're rating them on our own internal beauty scale.

Yes, even you.

Of course, you may well believe that there's more to a person than 'meets the eye', but nonetheless it is indeed your eyes that meet a person before you do.

So, tell me, what are you? Are you a 'babe' or a swamp donkey? A fox or fugly?

Over the years, we've developed a fair share of adjectives that describe the beautiful, the bad and the ugly, of ourselves and others.

So what are you?

Go on; take a few seconds to really consider that. Remember, it's just you and me here so nobody else is listening or watching.

You can be honest.

If you have the opportunity, take a long, good look in the mirror or, if it's more convenient, switch off your mobile device and look at your reflection.

Now, realistically, if I were to ask you to rate your looks on a scale of one to ten, with ten being drop-dead gorgeous and one being, well, a swamp donkey (whatever that may be), how would you rate yourself?

Done it?

So what's your answer?

Chances are you're going to fall in with the majority of people and consider yourself of 'average looks'. That's somewhere around a five to a seven. Most people actually feel they rate, for one reason or another, a four to a six.

That's right, low self-esteem has never been so prevalent, and that includes whether or not you outwardly acknowledge it or keep it restricted to the privacy of your own bedroom.

Surveys continuously suggest that there aren't many women out there who wouldn't change one thing or another about themselves, now followed closely by the new generation of insipid and somewhat androgynous men who, in the aftermath of women's lib, appear to be somewhat confused about their evolutionary roles, with droves of them abandoning their alpha male machismo in favour of a good moisturiser and a pair of slippers.

Meanwhile, there does appear to be some truth in the claims that beauty/celebrity magazines make most readers feel ugly, be it because they crave the projected lifestyle, beauty or body of those who grace the magazine pages, or because the very products pedalled in these promise the illusion of perhaps not eternal but temporary youth. This is all complemented nicely with features about the prolific and successful use of lunchtime Botox or, if you fancy your chances, 'full on' surgery with interest-free payment plans 'to suit your budget'.

At my last look, the UK cosmetics industry was worth £15 billion (approximately $25 billion) a year. But this is dwarfed when compared to that of the United States, currently estimated to be worth a staggering $60 billion, and with the popularity of cosmetic surgery rising exponentially, what does that tell you? Beauty may be skin deep but it's that very skin that just happens to be the most valuable asset you'll ever own and, most likely, the one most deserving of your biggest investment.

So what's it all about? What's it for?

Well, we've all heard the saying, 'beauty is in the eye of the beholder'. Yes, that's precisely why many work hard to make the beholder like what they see, be that by applying a bit of 'lippy' and eyeliner, to a quick nip and tuck.

Much research has been conducted into what exactly we find beautiful in another person, and the answers tends to be the same: symmetry. This appears to be the case both in the human and animal kingdoms.

Faces with a high ratio of symmetry are typically considered much more agreeable to us than that of lesser ratios which, inevitably, feature overt deviations from the visually appealing, such as a lopsided mouth, a crooked nose, or one eye too small. All of these low ratios disrupt the perception of beauty and are often perceived as defective or signs of 'ill health'.

This is all part of nature's 'natural selection'. Our response to symmetry is down to that good old human compulsion to propagate; our evolutionary programming to ensure the survival of the best, the fittest. We believe (consciously or subconsciously) that it is to our advantage to seek a mate with the best possible genes to give our offspring the best possible chance of good health, survival and the ultimate perpetuation of our bloodline.

Studies on humans conducted by researchers at MIT (Massachusetts Institute of Technology) have shown that men in particular go for women with symmetrical faces and 'hyper-feminine' facial characteristics, such as a small pointed chin.

Men are also drawn to things that signal youth, such as full lips, clear and smooth skin, clear eyes, lustrous hair, and good muscle tone, which makes sense when viewing a woman for her reproductive potential (as clinical as that may sound).

The preference in women for symmetry is not quite as pronounced; however, for the judgment that is passed by women, men are apparently judged on the angle between their eyes and mouth and are considered more attractive based on cheekbone prominence and facial length. Those who have higher levels of testosterone are typically ranked as having more masculine faces, associated with the above characteristics.

It is thought that women may use facial attractiveness as a proxy measure for a male's physical strength.

So what do you look for in a mate? (How many times have you heard that question?)

Have a think about it.

What do you really like? Is it the eyes, the mouth, the pectoral region, the rear or some other fetishlike delectable attribute? And please don't be thinking about vomit-inducing stereotypical line that you're most interested in somebody for their 'personality' and 'their heart'.

It's just you and me here, remember?

Granted that most of us are interested in that, but not when we first notice somebody across the room. In those situations, we lack the ability to read their thoughts (not unless you're some kind of superhero) or the opportunity to hear them talk on all the subjects that are relevant to us—thus, inevitably, aesthetics is the only thing to be measured on the attraction barometer.

In fact, some of us are taking our intolerance of imperfection one step further by weeding out the 'fuglies' before they even get a chance to offend our eyes.

This is evidenced in a new breed of dating club reserved exclusively for 'beautiful' people, and it just so happens that, during my research for this book, I stumbled upon a website with that very name.

Websites like beautifulpeople.com have developed a whole new and somewhat radical business model; if you're 'facially challenged', you may as well not bother subscribing.

Hang on—before you condemn the website owners as arrogant megalomaniacs, allow me to explain exactly how your application is processed.

Oh, hell, I may as well just paste an excerpt from their website for you (just in case you're thinking of joining)…

"BeautifulPeople is the first dating community of its kind. To become a member, applicants are required to be voted in by existing members of the opposite sex. Members rate new applicants over a 48-hour period based on whether or not they find the applicant 'beautiful'. Should applicants secure enough positive votes from members, they will be granted membership to the BeautifulPeople dating community. The vote is fair and democratic. BeautifulPeople does not define beauty; it simply gives an accurate representation of what society's ideal of beauty is, as decided by the members."

Yes, that's a direct lift from their website. So here comes the disclaimer: details correct at time of printing.

Bottom line is, the owners do not process your application— existing 'beautiful' members do, and if "Yo ass is fugly" (I'm not sure what kind of accent that's supposed to be), basically your 'arse', as we say here in England, doesn't get in.

It's as simple as that.

The scary side (if you didn't find that scary enough) is that thousands of people are clamouring to join the site. Yes, there's that compulsion again, like dolphins on their hunt for schools of fish, many congregate to the one place that promises an abundance of beauty. Ironically, it's beauty (or at least the public perception of it) that will define whether or not they'll actually be in with a chance.

And before you start wondering how I happened across this website, allow me to explain: BeautifulPeople hit the headlines when a technical error (otherwise known as a computer virus, aptly named SHREK) allowed thousands of proverbial 'swamp donkeys' to join the site. You can imagine how the owners reacted to this disaster—well, it wasn't with humility. They promptly moved to evict the unsightly marauders, all 30,000 of them, at an estimated cost of £60,000 ($102,000).

"We have to stick to our founding principles of only accepting beautiful people—that's what our members have paid for," Greg Hodge, the company's managing director was quoted as saying. "We can't just sweep 30,000 ugly people under the carpet."

I dare say you can't, Greg. It'd have to be one awfully big carpet to cover up such hideousness.

Apparently, Greg and his sidekicks wised up to the virus, allegedly planted by a former employee, when "thousands of new members were accepted over a six-week period, many of whom were no oil painting." And if you're thinking Greg's company policies as well as his opinions somewhat non-politically correct, then you may be interested to know that 5000 members were allegedly evicted the previous year because they had 'put on weight'.

The UK's *The Guardian* newspaper quoted one of the site's subscribers, Rachel Godfrey, a 31-year-old Australian nanny living in LA, as saying that she received an email telling her she was rejected two weeks after being accepted.

"I was getting on really well with this American guy and we were going to go on a date and then they said I'd been chucked off and they locked me out of the site," she said. "Now I can't get in touch with him."

Godfrey said she is planning to have a makeover and professional photo shoot before reapplying to the website.

"What if he's the one? This is the only way I'll be able to get in touch with him," she was reported as saying. "If that doesn't work, I'll see what I can do with Photoshop."

Really? Rachel, love, are you for real?

It's sad to say that she is.

And whilst you're gawping at those very words, allow me to explain; there are multiple drivers here that poor Rachel is competing with.

Firstly, that whole inconvenient human compulsion thing we explored above. But then there's the rejection; they say it's the greatest aphrodisiac. Then it's hope; she may have met somebody who could have been the man of her dreams—she'd be foolish to let the opportunity pass her by, wouldn't she? Nobody wants to be lonely (I'm sure there's a song in there somewhere).

Now, I know what you're thinking: what kind of shallow, arrogant so-and-so would set up such a site and say those nasty, spiteful things about people?

Yet, if you think about it, none of this is really Greg's fault.

This situation is no different to that of those heart bleeders who condemn tabloids for stalking their favourite celebrities yet are generally the first people to buy those very publications.

The real villains here are the thousands who, like lemmings (or Rachel Godfrey), subscribed to the website in the first place. It's these vanity-fuelled egomaniacs who have given Greg both the resources and the arrogance to discriminate at will. But for the fact that these people are paying his salary, good ole' Greg would have no foundation upon which to preach what, quite frankly, many of us probably think.

Yes, you read me correctly.

As much as you may act all incensed, you, like the rest of the animal world, are programmed to seek and conquer the best genes to secure the survival of your species, which means that, unless you're dead in some areas, you aren't so dissimilar to Greg and his site's ethos.

Like it or not, there's a bit of that man in all of us (and I mean that in a non-sexual way of course since I don't even know what he looks like. No, wait—oh, whatever).

We're all guilty of judging that proverbial book by its cover. Be it personally or professionally, each time we meet a new person, the first thing we do, before we've even exchanged a word, is evaluate them: their looks, their demeanour, the way they're dressed, the way they look at us, the way they hold themselves, the way they greet us, shake our hand and then, last but not least (and I *mean* last), the way they talk, the intonation in their voice, the words they speak. We hang on these cues, these signals because most of us are incapable of mind-reading and we rely on our instincts and our ability to decipher human behaviour to secure our very existence on this earth. It's how we establish friend from foe, empathiser from antagonist.

Also true is something I already touched on earlier; our initial perception of someone is often shifted as our interaction with them continues. A not-so-attractive person may become more attractive if they have a good sense of humour, they're thoughtful, and they show a keen interest in us and our well-being, and so on. Conversely, somebody who may have initially stunned us with their beauty may rapidly become unattractive to us if they show more interest in themselves than they do in the conversation they're actually having with us, or if they lack the social graces necessary to engage our interest.

So, if we're all only interested in beautiful people, then how the hell do the uglies or the averages out there get a look in?

Well, they say there's somebody for everybody and this is absolutely true. Remember, as a species we're all about evolution; it's the civilian's response to the military's 'adapt and overcome'. There's much to be said about the theory that the harder it is for us to 'attract' somebody of the opposite sex, the more we'll develop alternate skills to attract them.

We've already heard about Timothy and his ability to attract girls regardless of his mediocre looks.

And here's another quick tester.

How many comedians do you know who possess stunning good looks? Think about it for a few seconds: of all of the comedians you know, how many of these are model-type, drop-dead gorgeous?

Chances are you don't know many.

Yet, how many average-looking and not-so-attractive comedians do you know?

Our natural evolution dictates that if we're unable to attract people just by our looks, then we need to develop other skills to attract them. Similarly, if we're well endowed with beauty and people are naturally attracted to us, why bother developing a personality? It doesn't matter if we repel a few; there'll be many more out there more than willing to take their place.

I learned this many years ago when I worked as a freelance photographer (didn't I mention that?).

I've had the fortune (or misfortune) of working with some beautiful people but, sadly, what they possessed in aesthetics they sorely lacked in personality, charisma or charm. The best fun I had wasn't with the models, but with those who worked behind the scenes.

And of course, as always, there are some exceptions to this rule—but, generally speaking, you'll find this theory quite solid.

On the other hand, if you found yourself disagreeing with what I said because you actually know some people who are either models or model material with cracking personalities, then ask yourself, how many of these people are aware of and believe in their own beauty?

You'll find that most of them don't believe they're all that.

There are plenty of people out there who are, for want of a better expression, gorgeous but they simply don't see it. And, conversely, there are some swamp donkeys who think they are God's gift when, quite clearly, at least to us, they're not.

That favourite line of 'there's somebody out there for everybody' remains true but only as far as our expectations permit.

Throughout this book, you're going to read a lot about the pains of seeking and finding a new partner.

Many, especially when still reeling from a breakup, believe they'll never find somebody as good as their ex, and it doesn't matter how bad things used to be sometimes, when he or she isn't there anymore (and if the breakup wasn't mutual or by choice), they will start to romanticise how perfect they were and how nobody will ever look at them in that way again, know them that well, make them feel that good, and so on.

If you or somebody you know is one of these people then know that the general rule of thumb is, if you're serious about a new partner, get real about your expectations. You may not be able to find somebody exactly like your ex—but isn't the point to simply find a companion who is good for you? Who loves you the way that you deserve to be loved?

Get real.

Make a list of your top ten 'must haves', be that looks, personality, wealth, physical attributes, and so on. You'll find, interestingly, that you'd actually be prepared to forfeit that list's favourite, 'good looks' in favour of a 'good personality' and/or 'somebody who is good to me'.

Now, narrow down those prerequisites to three absolute essentials.

If you're lucky, you'll find all three of these in a new partner. If you're luckier still, you may find more of your top ten. But, ultimately, get used to the fact that it's highly unlikely you'll find a perfect match who ticks all boxes.

Al was confident that he had found that with Kayla.

The then twenty-something-year-old airman's career in the Air Force was progressing very well and he'd been on several successful dates with Kayla. There was just one other technicality that hadn't yet taken place: meeting her parents.

But that was something they planned to change when they decided to take a vacation by the ocean and, a day before their departure, chose to invite Kayla's sister to go with them.

The teenage girl was thrilled and immediately asked her mother for permission to go. This was granted provided that the girl scrub every inch of her bedroom, including the walls, before she left.

It was a major job, and the disgruntled teenager shared the news with Al and Kayla knowing that it would take some time to get the chore done but Al cheerfully told her that, if they all worked together, they'd get the job done in no time.

They did.

They moved furniture, scrubbed walls, scrubbed floors, polished wood and windows before putting everything back in its place. They even left a note for Kayla's mother to that effect.

However, when Al dropped the young girl off, one week later, they learned that their efforts were not good enough for Kayla's mum, who flew into a blind rage. She not only accused her daughter of disobeying her but she also accused her of 'stealing' towels from the house to take to the beach without permission.

The whole scene was somewhat surreal to Al who had never witnessed such a display of rage. Sure, he'd witnessed and been involved in many disagreements with his parents, but he'd never witnessed such a violent outburst over what he believed to be something so trivial.

He tried to intervene.

"…Miss Ellis, I am sorry you feel Wendy didn't do a good job with the bedroom, but we did help her move…"

"…You shut the hell up! Who the hell asked you to speak? Who do you think you are coming into my home and sticking your nose in my business?"

To explain the scene as bizarre would have been an understatement and, for Al, the worse thing was that it unfolded in front of toddler, Emily, who was instinctively cowering in his arms.

What Al didn't know is this scene would be one of many, including a time when he'd been out shopping with Kayla and had called ahead to let her mother know that they would be late home. The woman accused Al and her daughter of lying to her, despite the recorded message evidence, which was flung out of the window in a fit of rage along with Kayla's belongings; her mother wanted her out of the house for there was no room at the inn for liars.

And this is how their relationship began.

But Al was committed.

They found a place to stay, but hadn't lived there more than a few months before he received orders to Germany.

Al was under no doubt that he loved Kayla and adored little Emily. He wanted both of them to be with him in Germany and he concluded that there was only one way he could do that.

He visited Kayla's father and heard exactly what he wanted to hear; in the old man's opinion, Al was a good man and would make a good husband to his daughter and father to his granddaughter. In fact, he actively encouraged Al to marry Kayla and adopt Emily.

And that is exactly what he did.

The next night, he left work early, fell on one knee and proposed to Kayla who, with tear-filled eyes, said yes.

They got married in the same church as her parents, in front of a gathering of friends and relatives, and spent that weekend relatively inexpensively at Myrtle Beach, North Carolina.

The following week they visited Florida and, due to their shoestring budget, picnicked in the back of his truck and thus were able to afford the entrance fees to all of the attractions.

It was a modest but very happy time for Al—but, sadly, one that would spell the beginning of eight of the most heart-wrenching years of his life.

12 SEX, LOVE & VIDEOTAPE

Al wasn't the only person embarking on a relationship that would change his life; I too had embarked on something as beautiful as it was surreal.

M and I didn't discuss the kiss. There was no need.

Anybody who is or has been in love will know that when you're lucky enough to make a connection with another human being, there's more than often no need for words. I think the proverbial *actions speak louder than words* truly applied.

That moment was probably one of the most surreal I have ever experienced—yet it also felt so right. Ironic when you consider that this guy was as straight and as masculine as they came and, in my perverse kind of way, I think this is one of the things that has drawn me to him and men like him my whole life.

You see, I may well be gay, but I've never felt the need to parade that fact. By that I mean I just consider myself to be a man who happens to be attracted to other *men*. I'm totally disinterested in men who believe that a prerequisite of being gay is to emulate a female (often a musical icon) to the best of their abilities.

It just isn't what floats my boat.

It was M who made me discover that.

Of course, if I were to assess myself I'd probably come to the conclusion that I may well have developed this propensity for men who behave like, well, men because they're more compatible with my need to keep my sexuality secret. However, as you already know, and as you'll discover later in this book, there'll come a time when the need to keep who I am secret will become null and void.

But that's later.

Right now, with just one kiss, M had awakened a creature in me, something that I had considered so ugly, I'd locked it deep inside the catacombs of my mind for over ten years, during which I played a farce, a pretence that I was somebody I was not…

…Until that kiss almost a decade later.

It seemed that the American marine from North Carolina had travelled the technology of the Internet, time and five thousand miles to meet with me and change my life.

That cabin by the lake became what I can only describe as our love nest for the next two weeks. Sure, we travelled to London and to theme parks all over the country as good friends, but at night we'd return to our sanctuary, draw the curtains and become lovers. In fact, much of that holiday was pretty much spent getting to know each other, if you know what I mean.

Now, the text that follows could have been written with a completely different tone, but for the fact that I was still into my videography.

Well, I had been a photographer for quite a few years and the videography was a natural field to include in my portfolio.

This meant that I documented most, if not all, of our time in that cabin. It's thanks to the six discs and hours of footage that I was able to go back in time and watch these two strangers tell a whole story of their own without the filter of time.

Given everything you will read before this book concludes, you'll most likely understand why this part of my relationship with M had become blurred, if not completely erased, which I have to tell you, in hindsight, is very sad, but an inevitable side effect of an acrimonious breakup.

But that would come much later.

Now, when I view the footage from back then, I see two people who are comfortable around each other, in and out of their clothes (yes, if you're eating, I apologise; please try not to heave).

We played, we laughed and we had a lot of fun in that cabin. Yet much of this was forgotten to me until, over a decade later when I viewed one of the discs.

Needless to say, much of this footage is very personal but, given that it's just you and me here, I'm going to share one of those video scenes with you now because I feel it will aid me in making a very important point, not least the one that it was all of these various elements that led me to my eventual conclusion: for the first time in my life, I was in love, and I think somebody else may well have been in love with me too. And they weren't in love with the person projected by me, but the real me, and that felt so damn good.

The scene opens with a fairly wobbly camera to reveal a young twenty-year-old dressed in a United States marine uniform. His surname is emblazoned on the left chest of his jacket. He looks up at the camera, smiles and asks in the most beautiful American accent, "Shall we go?"

I had no idea what was coming next, but the image pans out to reveal M standing in full camouflage uniform and cover (hat) on his head.

Then the music starts, it's Massive Attack's *Angel* which, for those of you who may not be familiar with the track, starts out slow and rhythmic with smooth vocals then gradually builds into a crescendo of raw and hungry guitar.

Now the Marine is smiling at the camera and his hand slowly moves to unbuckle the belt of his trousers (or pants for the Americans reading this), and slowly but surely, whilst smiling at the lens (me) from time to time, this man strips down to his well-filled briefs, revealing muscular thighs, before moving his attention to his T-shirt that, after flashing his midriff several times at the lens, he somewhat expertly yanks over his head and throws to the side of the room, revealing gym-trained pectorals and a beautifully sculpted body, before, somewhat bizarrely, deliciously replacing the cover on his head once more.

He then strides over off camera where, after a few seconds of wobbly frame, it's revealed that he's kissing me. The last sequence is captured from a low, off angle as I grapple to embrace the handsome young man whilst holding the camera in my other hand.

Yeah, OMG!

I won't lie; I was blown away by this footage. It was the sexiest thing, made sexier by the fact that this guy actually did that for me!

Now, take a few seconds and ask yourself: how many times has your lover dressed in anything and stripped for you?

I'm not crowing, I promise.

I do have a point.

Once?

Twice?

More? Or never?

I remember that M would often bring what were his work clothes on holiday just to dress in them for me, because he knew I loved seeing him in uniform.

Do you think that was a beautiful thing for him to do for me?

I think it was awesome—but do you know what? I'd forgotten that whole scene until I watched the video footage.

I had completely forgotten that person!

To be honest, I'd actually forgotten those two people. The two that sat for literally minutes just smiling at each other through the lens. The two people who from time to time would just touch each other on the cheek, smile and spontaneously kiss, or the weirdo (that would be me) who filmed this man as he went about his every ablution, like brushing his teeth and shaving, while all the time patiently smiling at me (the camera lens).

There were so many spontaneous acts of affection in that cabin of the kind that I had only ever seen in movies. I only appreciated them whilst watching my own home movie since my memory had done me a complete disservice. In fact, there was much about our time in that cabin that I had forgotten until this day, including his patiently posing for endless pictures, making me breakfast and serving it to me in bed, often with a flower, that I can only assume he'd plucked from the wilderness outside, as well as us playing challenge push-ups with him 'beasting' me, marine style!

But it wasn't all one way you know.

I asked the Rock, Country and Western music lover if he knew how to dance. When he said no, I seized the opportunity for perfect revenge.

Not that I can imagine myself as 'Madame Quickstep' with a cane in one hand and foppish stance in the other, but I took my role of dancing instructor seriously (oh, okay, quite seriously) as I showed him how to listen to the music and move left and right feet in tandem with the rhythm.

Oh, how we laughed.

And I laughed even more when I pictured at one stage what we would have looked like beyond the curtains to the outside world: two grown men; me in my pyjamas and he in nothing but his briefs (no, of course I didn't take advantage of that), shuffling around the room, arm in arm, to Vic Damone's rendition of *On the Streets Where You Live.*

Don't ask.

I think I somehow had a 'classics' compilation that was popular at the time—which would explain why the next class was on how to strut your stuff (and attitude) to Nancy Sinatra's rendition of *These Boots Were Made for Walking.*

We laughed a lot.

And kissed.

And hugged.

And it was so damn beautiful.

In fact, the last week of our first two weeks together continued pretty much in the same vein with both of us happy to be visiting my family and exploring England whilst equally eager to get back to the cabin and our own private sanctuary.

I was in love.

But I didn't know it then.

It only occurred to me the night before I was due to drive him back to the airport. I remember developing this terrible sense of foreboding like something bad was going to happen, and I realised then the feeling wasn't about something that *might* happen and more about something that was *going* to happen.

I didn't want M to leave.

And the feeling got worse as we drove to London Gatwick Airport the next day.

The Marine, on the other hand, was every bit that demeanour for the entire journey, but for the occasional stroke of my arm from time to time and the caress of my soul with those big hazel eyes of his.

Those expressive eyes that belied how he was really feeling inside.

I remember drawing comfort from this. It felt as if I wasn't going through this feeling alone, that it wasn't some kind of romantic fantasy artificially created by me, but that it was genuine.

Although it wasn't until we were standing in front of the departure gate and M reemphasising the fact that we needed to start planning the next trip, my first visit to the United States, as soon as we got home, that I realised just how much he too was hurting.

His eyes welled up in that moment and he spontaneously pulled me to him in one of the strongest hugs I have ever felt.

I remember being somewhat surprised by the action since, in the two weeks we had been together, he had never partaken in public displays of affection. I hadn't really internalised this fact because neither had I. It wasn't something that we had spoken about, but we'd just naturally kept a 'healthy' distance when in public or in the company of others.

But that day, whilst that embrace could have been construed as any brotherly farewell, the intimate way in which he whispered into my ear could not.

"I love you," he said.

With that, he broke away and hurried through security, stopping only to show his passport and boarding card to one of the officers.

Then, as if to add to the drama of the moment, I had a clear view through security and into the departure lounge. I watched the back of his shaved head and the nape of his neck that I had caressed so many times in that past two weeks as they ushered him forward, wondering if he would look back and wave but he didn't.

At least it seemed that way until he reached the far end of the corridor, just before he'd disappear out of sight. He then slowly turned sideways onto me, smiled and held up his hand.

I waved back, forced a smile and promptly blubbered like a little girl.

Then he turned and was gone, taking a proverbial part of me with him.

Blimey, that day was tough.

I didn't even know what was wrong with me since I had never felt that strongly about any other human being before, beyond family, but it was that day that I remember telling myself, "You're in love."

And I was as happy as I was terrified about how vulnerable I had become once more.

So, why is this so-called 'tie' with another human being so important?

I mean, do we really need another warm-blooded creature to 'complete' the puzzle that is us, or should we be equally content, alone?

Well, any therapist worth his or her hourly fee will tell you that you can't truly love someone else until you truly love yourself. And yes, I know that sounds very much like psychobabble. (If you think that's bad, wait until you read the next paragraph).

But the truth is, none of us can grow and lead a healthy mental existence unless we're allowed our own space, our own private thoughts in which to reconcile who we are as well as process everyday life events.

This processing is something that cannot be done comprehensively if it is interrupted by the influence, and sometimes the presence, of others.

I've often written about this common-sense theory; different friends bring different things into our lives. Some enjoy the same movies; others may enjoy the same music tastes; some are good listeners and some are not. Each and every one of our friends enriches our life in different ways. Why would anybody think that this should all change once we've committed ourselves to an intimate relationship with another human being?

The need to be able to share and vent thoughts (often about our partner) is an important process that enables us to deal with daily events.

How many times have you just talked something through with somebody and felt better for it? A problem shared and all that. You can't always do this with your partner, especially since your partner may well be the cause of your aggravation.

Don't get me wrong—I'd be the first person to tell you that the first step in any discord is to talk it through with the person who may be displeasing you. But the fact that your partner keeps leaving the toilet seat up (or down), regardless of how many times you've told them it bothers you, doesn't necessarily need a sit down and a therapy session, that's simply a good old- fashioned moan with somebody else who may be able to relate. This is how, as humans, we process some of the negative things that happen to us. The point being, demanding to spend every waking hour with your partner (beyond the time you're at work) is unhealthy for both of you.

Everybody needs 'me time', and if you don't, then ask yourself why you aren't content being alone with yourself.

So, what's the big deal with this whole relationship thing anyway? Why is it that many of us simply can't be alone? Is it because we're all absolutely terrified of facing big bad 14th February (Valentine's Day) or is there some other sinister force at work?

Well, believe it or not, researchers have actually established a scientific reason as to why we humans are compelled to seek out a partner or, more specifically, a connection and subsequent affection.

Apparently, it's all to do with the neurohormones.

Neurohormones are responsible for our 'love compulsions'. So much so that one of them, oxytocin, is actually called the 'love hormone'.

You may have heard of it.

Oxytocin is not just a hormone; it's also a neurotransmitter—hence the name.

It's oxytocin that is responsible for the bonds we forge with other human beings: family, friends and, of course, lovers. It's one of the reasons why, for many around the globe, hugs feel so damn good.

Often, just interacting with, talking to the object of our affection releases that good ole' hormone, making us feel all good, more than often, less stressed and, you've guessed it, loved.

Interestingly, studies have also revealed that those who did not have a positive relationship with their parents (or a parent) find it much more difficult to fully exploit the benefits of oxytocin.

The research focussed on a group of women—how many it doesn't say—who were subjected to the wailing sounds of a crying baby as they were given 'puffs' of oxytocin, whilst being asked to intermittently squeeze or relax their grip on a measuring device. Their response to the oxytocin differed between those women who had a tactile, loving relationship with their parents versus those who were disciplined more severely and deprived of affection. Women who had not been disciplined severely by their parents relaxed their grip, whilst those who had been disciplined did not.

In a separate study, women were given oxytocin or a placebo, and a questionnaire about how loving (or not) their parents were.

When the study was over, the women were paid for their time and then given the chance to donate to charity. It was found that the women of loving parents who were given oxytocin gave much more generously than their counterparts who received less maternal/paternal love.

The conclusion is that our relationship with our parents during our most impressionable years actually serves to build our oxytocin system. More specifically, the study suggests that if you've come from loving parents, then you're more likely to get a reward from oxytocin than if you did not.

This would also explain why often 'the first cut is the deepest' since in an 'unhurt heart' the oxytocin is more likely to be in free flow versus one that has been damaged by multiple romantic disappointments. This also explains why most of us become 'hardened' after each failed relationship, as well as why many of those not raised on tactile, affectionate relationships seldom go on to require this in adulthood: we're able to function quite happily without the receipt of constant or regular affection.

This study also puts some light on why men, often stereotypically, tend be less demonstrative of affection (as this is perceived as a sign of weakness) than the fairer sex. Although, generally speaking, this is a myth since I've often found that you can take the manliest of men away from his peers, into a safe space where he doesn't feel the pressure (or social obligation) to 'perform' at being a male, and find that he is more than capable of great emotive expression to rival even the 'fluffiest' of girlies.

That said, whilst it would be easy to surmise that only those who have been showered with affection as children are capable of giving and/or receiving it as adults, it wouldn't necessarily be true. Some people who were raised in a family landscape baron of affection actually go into adulthood overcompensating for that which was denied them as children and/or teenagers, more so when the proverbial 'first cut' happens later in life. This often results in a much needier and/or clingy individual.

Similarly, just because you had a bad childhood, it doesn't necessarily mean that you're doomed!

Far from it.

Conditioning, be it by therapy or own self-motivation, can quite easily influence the makeup of your Oxytocin system.

For example, I tend to 'condition' all of my male friends (my female friends give these freely) to give me a hug both when they meet and leave me (I'm talking strictly man hugs you know), and if I were to analyse the results of my own study, I'd be able to safely report that one hundred per cent of these straight men are conditioned into this act now. In fact, there's no doubt in my mind that if I were to shun them upon their departure, they'd actually feel as if something fundamental were missing from our friendship.

This is one of the simplest examples of self-conditioning.

Now, this may all sound somewhat tongue-in-cheek but there is a lot of seriousness in our ability to express affection in a relationship, and whilst there may be some sceptics out there (especially the men reading this), make no mistake: you too, not unlike your wife and/or girlfriend and/or family members, need to express and have reciprocated your acts of affection. Be that a kiss, acts of kindness or the ubiquitous act of sex.

This is the very reason many feel somewhat 'lost' when there is no one with whom to make that proverbial 'connection', be that lover or family member.

There's a need in all of us to 'connect' with another human being. It's one of the reasons females are much better at being single than men. Women are able to easily express and/or receive affection from friends and family members, thus satisfying that 'need' to make a connection.

Men, on the other hand, have that whole bravado to project; they aren't easily able to express affection. For them, the generally logical and socially acceptable relationship in which to act somewhat 'gooey' is with their girlfriends, wives, children and their mums!

Note the common denominator here.

Take away the female element and what are you left with?

Children.

Generally speaking, if our particular male lacks offspring, then he's left with nothing but an affection grey area, since, unlike his female counterpart, he's unable to glean and/or express affection elsewhere, such as with friends.

I should point out that there appears to have been a social shift in this theory over the past decade. If I were to go out on a limb and pin it to something specific, I'd say that the expression of affection between modern men is becoming almost as acceptable as confessing to a moisturising routine! It has indeed peaked in the brave—generally those confident about their sexuality.

However, regardless of the boom in the male cosmetic industry (yes, that means there are plenty of men out there, and not just the metrosexuals, who enjoy a good preen), not everybody is quite ready to confess the inner ablutions of the man cave.

So, what do we know?

Well, we know that matters of the heart are as blissful as they are complex—this book is testament to that—but how exactly did the heart come to symbolise 'lurve'?

Well, wise men such as Aristotle, believed that the heart was responsible for everything that takes place in the human body, including emotions.

Many centuries ago, the human brain wasn't believed to be anywhere as important as we all know it to be now. Back then, the heart was responsible for everything. That was because the heart is one of those organs that transmits a physical shift each time a situation arouses one of our senses—be it fear, nervousness, or simply that old thing called love. The memory, sight or smell of the object of our affection (or desire) is enough to send the organ into a whole pitter-patter.

In fact, one of the earliest depictions of the heart in the context of love is a French painting dating back to the 13th century. In it, a lover hands what looks like his heart to his mistress.

There's no doubt that, in its basic form, love is one of the most powerful of human conditions; it gives us the strength to overcome the impossible and the weakness to give our own life for that of another human being.

Powerful and dangerous stuff indeed. And, like most dangerous things, it should be used with caution.

If you're lucky enough to love or be loved by another human being, then you have the responsibility to treat it with care. Don't smother; nurture. Don't paw at it, nor take it for granted, but treat it with respect, and never assume it will be there forever.

Some of the most disintegrated human beings I know have made that mistake and have suffered for it.

I was one of them.

13 MISGUIDED

So, if giving and receiving love is a truly beautiful and wondrous thing, when is it not?

To explain that, let's revisit Aubrey and Timothy.

Having recovered from the immediate aftermath of the divorce, Aubrey set herself on the path of recovery, which meant 'drying out' and quitting smoking.

She did this, very effectively.

Now, several months later, a new rejuvenated Aubrey had rediscovered some of her former beauty as did someone else.

As you know, Timothy split from his younger girlfriend after a few months and was now contemplating the daunting prospect of having to undergo an eye operation and the subsequent convalescing that this would entail.

He contacted Aubrey and shared with her his delight at learning that she had turned her life around and was now feeling much more content about herself and the future.

He also happened to mention his imminent operation as well as the fact that during his convalescence he would need somebody to take care of him, but that, somewhat disappointingly, there really wasn't anybody he could trust to take on the role.

Timothy moved back into his beloved home, the very one he had forfeited to his ex-wife in his divorce settlement within weeks.

Aubrey could think of nothing better than to have the man she had loved so deeply for so many years return home, and to be able to nurture him.

Neither of them stopped to consider the long-term implications of this arrangement.

The definition of the word 'break' is to separate into pieces as a result of a blow, shock, or strain.

When something breaks, our first instinct is to see if we can fix it. The same thing applies to relationships, only they carry the added emotional need to be with that person, to have things back 'the way they were'.

But things cannot be the way they were.

Unlike a broken cup, you can't just glue a relationship back together and refill it. It takes time and, unlike an inanimate object, you are dealing with the complex fluidity of the human mind. That is pretty much the equivalent of shattering that cup into a thousand pieces and then hoping to put the whole thing back together again.

If you've ever tried this, you'll know it's pretty much impossible to restore the item to its former glory.

As humans, we change, we evolve, we adapt to everyday life. And, of course, part of that adapting process also relates to life after the breakup of a relationship. We realise that we're no longer accountable; we can come and go as we please, watch whatever TV show tickles our fancy, eat whatever, clean whenever, wear whatever, whenever and see whoever.

We restructure life as we know it to complement the new, single version of us.

Getting back together would mean conforming to the person our ex once knew—but maybe, just maybe, we don't want to do that. Maybe, now that we have tasted 'freedom', we don't want to go back to compromise, but prefer to continue to live a life of unrestrained hedonistic abandon.

My point being that we're constantly evolving, sometimes painfully, to our new surroundings, to our new life and often this happens without us even noticing. It is only when we revisit the way we were that we realise that somehow things have changed, that we have changed, that we are no longer the person we used to be.

Timothy was in the house less than a week when he started to realise exactly what he had committed himself to once more.

By returning to Aubrey, he had returned to the bad memories and he realised that he no longer wanted a part of that.

The consequence of which meant that he had decided that his return to the marital home was just temporary and that he'd be leaving for his own place as soon as he was fit and able to do so.

Asked how he thought Aubrey would react to his departure, Timothy said that she appreciated that the arrangement wasn't permanent. Perhaps this was true, but there's no doubt that, like others before her in such a situation, there was a good chance that she was hoping for something more. Hoping that their time together would somehow rekindle what they had. Something she hoped would be bolstered by the fact that he had now become, albeit temporarily, dependent on her.

Timothy left a few months later.

When it happened, Aubrey was devastated all over again. For her, it was a repeat of the divorce, but on a different scale.

She felt used.

I guess *hope springs eternal in the human breast* after all.

The truth was, they'd both grown apart during the separation, and as much as they liked the idea of reanimating their marriage, they were both unable to do so and instead only succeeded in reopening healing wounds.

So, at this stage you will have formed an opinion about Timothy

What exactly is that?

I'm guessing that it probably isn't a good one. I mean, this guy left his wife, shacked up with the younger model and then, when there was nobody else to take care of him, he went back to his wife once more, used her and then left her for the second time!

That's pretty rough.

But is Timothy really the only person to blame here?

Yes, you've guessed it; I'm going to play Devil's Advocate.

There is an argument that Aubrey used Timothy here, that she exploited his vulnerability to keep him close to her.

Don't you think?

And, by doing so, was enabling him to use her, once again.

Don't get me wrong. There's no doubting that he took advantage of her feelings for him. But that's what he does and has done his whole life. It's one of the very reasons the man excelled in his profession. Timothy knew how to exploit an opportunity and maximise its potential. You can't really fault the man for that. After all, he's just using the tools at his disposal.

Aubrey chose to allow herself to be used by Timothy. When I say *chose*, it may well have been a result of free will, but I think it's fair to say that it was executed whilst she was suffering from 'diminished capacity'.

She still loved her ex-husband and because of this she enabled him to use her.

Here's another definition for you—this one is from *The Oxford English Dictionary*: to 'enable' is to give (someone) the authority or means to do something; also, 'to give strength', 'to make firm and strong'.

Notice how all of these are positive interpretations, yet the word also has a very negative, if not corrosive, meaning.

As humans, we love. We really don't have any choice in the matter—be it a family member, a life partner, a friend or even our favourite football team, before we know it and without warning, we're bitten by the love bug and we love.

From that moment forward, we're generally putty in the hands of the object of our affection. There isn't much we won't do to be with them, please them, preserve their health and safeguard their happiness.

'A friend will help you move but a good friend will help you move a body.'

I think there may be more truth to that than initially meets the eye (or in this case, the text).

Ask yourself, if somebody you really loved took the life of somebody else, would you have the strength to see them brought to justice?

No, really, think about it for a second. Whilst you agonise over what may be morally correct, I can tell you, the reality is that the majority of people would be unable to forsake the ones they love.

Now, why do you think that is?

What exactly is it about the cruel and unusual scenario above that would stop a human being from doing what they are morally obliged to do?

It's love.

However irrational it may be, however wrong, the love of somebody else compels us to act in what we believe is the best interest of our loved one.

But are we?

In this particular circumstance, there's a very good argument in favour of the fact that, by lying to cover up the crime of our loved one, we're actually encouraging them to commit the same crime again.

Now hold up, just before you start arguing that.

Of course there are mitigating circumstances, as we don't know all of the details of this example: how and why the crime took place, whether it was premeditated, and so on. These things will all have a bearing (and certainly would in a court of law) on how we view the case. But the reality (or morality) remains the same: if our loved one does not assume the responsibility for their crime/actions then how on earth are they going to truly appreciate the severity of the deed and refrain from repeating it?

Here's a familiar, simple yet effective analogy.

Grandfather goes into the store with his five-year-old grandson who states he'd like some sweeties (candy). Grandparent refuses the child, stating that it's nearly time for dinner. Child throws itself onto the floor and proceeds to scream at the top of its lungs until the mortified man, with eyes of judgemental shoppers boring holes into him, concedes and buys the child some sweets.

Next time round, the process is repeated.

Who's at fault here—the grandparent or the child?

Why, the child of course... No, I'm kidding, it's the grandparent!

But for the fact that he indulged the brat previously, he wouldn't find himself in the same embarrassing situation once more. By yielding to and thereby condoning the child's behaviour, the grandparent set a precedent and sent just one message: 'If you scream loud enough, you'll get your way'.

It is this very reason governments do not negotiate with terrorists, because if they give into one, all of the freaks would come crawling out of the woodwork demanding the same treatment.

And am I comparing a spoilt brat to a terrorist? In this situation, hell, yeah! Is it not an act of terrorism to completely humiliate your grandparent and/or parents in public to get what you want?

Don't answer that.

This is a basic life lesson. Something we all become aware of pretty early in adult life: everybody knows that helping a child with their homework is good; doing it for them is bad.

Right?

Right?

Making excuses for a disrespectful loved one, consistently loaning them money and never asking for it back, solving their problems, doing things for them that they could and should do themselves are just a few of the crimes committed by an 'enabler'.

Now, there's a distinct possibility that you're going to see the above as just 'caring' for somebody—and you'd be absolutely right—but there's a fine line between being supportive and enabling.

"Give a man a fish, and you'll feed him for a day. Teach a man to fish, and you've fed him for a lifetime."

Why do you think somebody came up with this?

By not making excuses for someone, and by having them confront their own scenarios, you're teaching them that what they are doing is either wrong or unacceptable. Loaning somebody money and asking for this money back teaches them not only to respect the fact that you value your hard-earned cash and that it doesn't just get handed about, but that they too should take on the responsibility of keeping a job to support themselves and their potential future family. Supporting somebody in solving a problem rather than solving it for them, teaches them that life isn't always easy and there will come times when you're going to be confronted with challenges but, because you've been dealing with these throughout your life, you're not going to fall apart when you need your strength the most.

And so on, including some of the most famous enabling scenarios: parents who consistently clean up after their teenagers. This is not good parenting; this is bad parenting. You're enabling your teenage child to be a) a lazy slob, and b) stunting their psychological growth in becoming a responsible adult who respects themselves, others and their environment (as this kind of behaviour often translates into life; i.e., work, living with a partner).

Other basics things, like cooking for your teenager all the time without allowing them to ever step a foot in the kitchen, is hardly teaching them life skills.

There's a reason why they teach home economics in school. What do you think?

These are just some of the most obvious enabler traits and chances are you already knew this, didn't you?

So, ask yourself, are you guilty of any of the above?

I am. I've been known to loan money to people and not ask for it back.

Many times.

The only difference is it's not always the same person.

I love my family and my friends and so, of course, it comes natural to me to want to help them in their hour of need. But I don't think I know anybody with whom this has become a syndrome, because if it did, there's no doubt that I'd be re-evaluating the arrangement.

There's a fine line between love and becoming a 'feeder'.

What? You've never heard of that expression?

Sure you have.

And I'm not talking about someone who cooks you breakfast and dinner, like your mum; I'm talking about a person who actually gains sexual satisfaction from the act of gorging their partner.

'Feeders' are quite common and generally tend to be men who seek out overweight partners and encourage them to gorge themselves.

Yes, this is somewhat ironic, given the stereotypical practices of most heterosexual men today to seek out females, often much younger, 'fit' and as 'supple' as possible.

Not the feeder; he or she actually derives pleasure from the process of 'feeding' (gorging) their partner with the objective of making them gain more weight and thus become 'sexier' and, most importantly, more dependent on them, propagating the 'feeding' cycle.

Yes, it truly does take all sorts.

But that isn't the disturbing part of this story. What's disturbing is the fact that these days, unless you've been living under a rock, it will be difficult for you not to appreciate the fact that being overweight, obese or morbidly obese (which most of the feeder partners are) is in no way good for your health, since it elicits a whole battery of illnesses. Yet the practice continues.

Most importantly, the whole point of me sharing this story with you was to say that there's another term for 'feeder', and I bet you can't guess what that is.

Sure you can, it's 'enabler'.

This was the case for Arizona couple, Mark and Gina.

Mark actually left his wife when she decided to go on a diet to lose weight, but he was naturally delighted when he met Gina. Gina became Mark's project: to create the world's fattest woman.

And he succeeded; Gina reached a total weight of 380 kg, that's 837 lbs or 59 stone, 11 lbs.

Mark almost killed his partner in the process. In fact, things became so critical that Gina had to undergo surgery, much to Mark's dismay. Even now, he doesn't understand what the fuss was all about.

The grim reality is that Mark imprisoned Gina in herself. By 'feeding' her and by growing her weight, it became more and more difficult for Gina to do things on her own, so Mark would literally feed her, bathe her, and generally 'think' for her, which meant Gina's own personality disappeared and she became not just a surrendered person but a surrendered mind.

Her partner was killing her and she didn't even notice it.

So, okay, this is an extreme case and a distant relative to the everyday occurrences of enablement that take place in our homes, workplaces, and that many of us have, are or will be guilty of at some stage.

We've all done it, or do it—made excuses for and on behalf of somebody else because they were not fit or inclined to make the excuses themselves, be that pulling a 'sicky' so as to avoid a day at work or visiting relatives.

The issue here is not the act itself, but more the psychological impact that this has on the offending party.

Some psychologists believe that one of the most difficult aspects of battling an addiction, or other pathological behaviours, is not necessarily the psychological weakness of one person; i.e., it's not just the person with the behavioural problem, but he or she may have an unhealthy synergy with somebody who is an enabler or even, in the case of alcoholism or drugs, a co-dependent.

I've read a few cases where the partners of an alcoholic regularly lie or 'rationalise' on behalf of their partner to their partner's employer, making up excuses for why they are unable to report for work, inventing all sorts of creative stories about muggings, accidents and family traumas rather than the truth, which is that their partner is in a drunken stupor and in no fit state to be leaving the house.

I, like many before and after me, know this the most, as I lost a friend to alcoholism. She was enabled all the time by her rich family and those around her who, rather than seeking help for her, enabled her to slowly kill herself because she was such a 'lovely person'. Those very close to her just wanted to see her happy.

Oh, the irony.

There are stories of women who have stated categorically that they had no idea of their partner's criminal activity and yet had no rational explanation for how they were living a life of luxury. There are also stories of friends of dead heroin addicts who'd 'loaned' them money through the years right up to their eventual demise, who couldn't fathom, in retrospect, why they did that, knowing full well what their money was being spent on.

Enablers are not bad people, they're simply misguided; they believe that they are acting in the best interest of the person they care about.

Others have darker motives.

For example, there is the not-so-uncommon case where husbands or wives indulge their partner's addictions in order to gain a more meaningful relationship with their children (as the only reliable parent in the household).

There are those who seek out weaker business partners with the sole intention of undermining them to project a far more impressive picture of their own success.

And then there are the voyeurs, the sinister, psychological hitchhikers who actually get a kick out of watching the emotional train wreck of others; e.g., they'll watch and even encourage a gambler to lose a fortune, encourage an alcoholic to drink themselves into a state and goad them into performing dangerous and/or violent acts whilst they look on with amusement at no risk to themselves.

Excluding the sociopath/psychopath, we all have one or many people in our lives whom we care about. And it's this caring that compels us to look out for what we believe to be their best interests. We'll generally want these people to be happy, to live long and literally prosper, and it's in our makeup to do everything we can to support this—be that providing nourishment, support or a helping hand when they need it the most.

It simply gives us pleasure to make the people we love happy.

However, there are boundaries between expressing affection for the ones we care about and enabling them to avoid core psychological growth and moral responsibility.

A wife of a rude husband may feel inclined (some believe it's their duty) to justify his manners with those he may come into contact with.

Rationalising is something that women, primarily, do very well on behalf of their partners, but the reality is that, by supporting this unacceptable behaviour, the wife is actually perpetuating it rather than working with her husband to correct it. She isn't being supportive; she's enabling him to be a... well, one of those words... I'll let you fill in the blank.

Similarly, indulging a child every time they throw a fit so as to avoid 'distressing' that child is not in the child's interest, instead, boundaries should be set, defining what is and what is not acceptable behaviour.

In Aubrey's case, she was so desperate to have her husband back with her that she was more than happy to enable him into thinking that it was acceptable to leave her, be with another woman, return to convalesce, give her hope that things may well go back to the way they were, and then ditch her again once his convalescing was complete.

It is not acceptable, but this is a cycle that Timothy's next partner will either deal with or allow him to repeat once more.

And whilst the closing of this chapter may well spell the end of Tim and Aubrey's relationship contribution to this book, it doesn't necessarily mean we won't be seeing them again in later pages.

All will be revealed.

14 DEBT & RAGE

Germany was literally a whole new world for Al and Kayla, since neither of them had ever travelled out of the United States, and there was something very sobering about being in a foreign land and not being able to understand a word said by anybody other than United States Air Force personnel.

And things got worse for Kayla when Al was given orders to T.D.Y. (Temporary Duty).

One of these took him from home for nearly four months and, although he was technically but a few hours away by car, it was difficult for him to travel home often.

Home was a rented house off base. The American Air Force offers its married couples an allowance for accommodation. In this case, after looking for a short while, our couple found the perfect home. The only problem was that the rent was $350 above what they could afford.

However, when Al suggested that they keep looking, Kayla exploded into a fit of rage; not only did he expect her to move away from her family and everything she knew, but now he wanted her to live in some "shithole" too?

He felt guilty.

They took the house.

Yet because of his temporary duty, Al was unable to enjoy much time there. Furthermore, because of the house, Al could not afford to travel home. Consequently, in one month, Kayla managed to rack up a $1,200 telephone bill.

When Al confronted her with the debt, her answer was that she was lonely, and it was him and his job that had ripped her from her family and everything she knew and taken her to a foreign land.

And he couldn't argue with that.

He was the closest person to her. It was only natural that she'd want to talk with him. Only, Al wasn't the only person that Kayla would talk to on the phone; most of the charges came from long-distance calls back to the U.S. This, coupled with the unaffordable rent, and Kayla's compulsion to use her credit card meant that it wasn't long before they found themselves deep in a quagmire of debt.

So Kayla took a job on base, in an engraving shop, where, as a member of staff, she received a ten per cent discount on all products, including a series of mythical figurines.

The dragons, made of delicate crystal, were a fine example of German craftsmanship and the ideal birthday present for Al, who was indeed pleasantly surprised to receive such a glittering birthday treat—even more so when Kayla informed him she had spent more on him than she had on herself that day: an eye-popping $4,000 more.

It had to stop.

Kayla had just finished performing an impromptu fashion show of her latest purchases and left the crystal collection on the table to wink under the lights, reminding him of their value, as she left the room to pack her new possessions away in the bedroom.

He followed her, trying to stave off an overwhelming sense of dread that was pressing on his stomach; he had already experienced several instances of Kayla's somewhat violent and unpredictable bouts of rage and Al, a calm man by nature, was almost afraid of what demons this inevitable conversation may conjure.

He joined his wife in the bedroom where she was busy admiring herself in the wardrobe mirror and squeezing her recently purchased garments into the already bulging wardrobe.

He leaned heavily on the doorframe.

She noticed him in the mirror. "Hey," she said cheerfully.

"Hey." He forced a weary smile.

She was humming to herself and was too busy to notice his expression until she looked up from uniting a box of new shoes with the rest of the collection under the wardrobe.

"You okay?" she said brightly.

He nodded.

"You hungry? Want me to fix us something to eat?"

There was no other way to say it. "Kayla, I really appreciate the gifts, but I'm worried they're more than we can afford. Can we just keep the two I really wanted and take the others back?"

She stopped humming, frowned and turned to face him.

"What?"

"I know you really meant well and it's a beautiful set, really it is, but I really don't think we can afford them right now is all."

She paused for a few seconds and then said cheerfully, "Yes, we can. I'm working, and I can afford it."

She resumed unpacking.

"No, you can't."

"Yes, I can."

"You can't, Kayla." His voice was calm, but firm. "What you make at the shop barely covers the utility bills and now, with a baby on the way, things are only going to get worse."

Silence reigned for a few minutes; the only sound was the scraping of opening and closing drawers. This wasn't an uncommon occurrence; it was almost like the quiet before the storm.

"Kayla…" he began.

"What?" she snapped as she turned to look at him. "What do you want, Al? Want to tell me how much you hate the present I bought you, how much my birthday present means absolutely nothing to you?"

Al recognised the change in her demeanour: the flushed cheeks, her blazing eyes; she was staring right through him.

He proceeded with caution.

"Kayla, of course they mean a lot to me. I just think they're way more expensive than I expected and we just don't have the money right now. We don't even have anywhere to put them."

"We will when we move into a bigger home."

Al paused for a second as he took in the comment, and then added with very measured words, "And how are we going to afford *that*? The rate you've been spending, we're going to be in debt for the rest of our lives."

"So, that's it, is it? What's yours is yours and what's mine is yours too."

"You know that isn't..."

"Really?" she snapped, moving in closer to him. "Is that really how it is, Al? Because to me it seems that ever since we got to this shitty place, you've done nothing but bitch about me and how much I spend."

"That's because we can't..."

"That's because you don't love me! You don't give a shit about me!" Her voice was a progressive growl. "No matter what I do, it's never good enough for you. Even now that I've got my own job and I spent all that money on you, you still aren't satisfied with me. What is it about me, huh? What is it about me that makes you never want to be home with me?"

"What are you talking about?" he uttered, incredulously.

"You're never here! I'm alone in this place and you couldn't give a rat's ass about my feelings! You've no idea what it's like to be abandoned here *on my own*."

"Of course I do..."

"No you don't! No you don't! You don't know what it's like! You have no clue—because if you did, you wouldn't begrudge me those few things!"

Her voice was a loud shrill, bordering on the hysterical. Al held out his hands in a calming gesture, but it only fuelled the fire.

She swiped him away aggressively.

"Kayla, honey, just calm down."

"Don't tell me to calm down, dammit! I wouldn't be feeling like this if you weren't so damn selfish! It's all about you, isn't it? It's all about Al and how he's feeling—but what about *me*? What about Kayla?" What about me?"

"Kayla, please calm down."

"Why? Whatcha' gonna' do if I don't?" she teased.

"I'm going to start yelling too."

"Oh, really? Ooh, I'm so scared," she mocked. "You're going to yell too. So what?" She spat. "Think I give a shit? I hate you! I hate you, you selfish asshole!"

"Kayla... can we just talk about this without yelling..."

"We are talking about it, Al. We are talking about what a bastard you are, and how much you hate me!"

"Kayla…"

"Trample over my feelings in this way?"

"Honey…"

"You're no different to my first husband. He may have beat me, but what you do is worse; what you do is mental torture. You're no different than him. I hate you!"

"Kayla..."

"I hate you!"

"Kayla…"

"I *hate* you!"

"*SHUT THE HELL UP!*"

Al's voice resonated around the room like an explosion.

Kayla just blinked at him.

It was the first time she had ever heard him shout like that. She didn't even know how to react.

For the next minute, neither of them moved or uttered a word as they processed what had just taken place.

Finally, Kayla found her tongue and said contemptuously, with a flick of her hair, "Like I said, you're no different to that other asshole of a husband."

He took a few seconds to compose himself, such was his rage; it was as if the adrenaline that was coursing through his veins were some kind of anaesthetic on his tongue; it felt thick and heavy.

The comparison to Kayla's deadbeat husband who, according to her, cared nothing for his wife or their daughter, was one of the worst insults she could ever hurl at him, and one that she knew full well would affect him.

However, eventually, as his heart pounded, he uttered, "You're never making me yell like that again."

And, with that, he left the room and her standing, aghast, in the middle of it.

Since that day, the subject of returning the figurines was often discussed, but Kayla's promises to take ownership of the task proved empty. And then when their first son, arrived and she stopped working, the possibility of a refund proved even more unlikely.

It wouldn't be until a whole year later, as they packed to return to the United States, that the subject of the figurines would rear its ugly head once more.

Kayla had suddenly noticed that they were missing; Al had taken them back and was lucky to get somewhere near their original price in return. When his wife heard this, she launched a tirade of abuse at him. She accused him of being a selfish man who cared nothing for anyone but himself. How else could he take a birthday gift and sell it. He cared nothing for her or their family and was an ingrate and—nothing new—she added that she hated him.

And it was during one of these episodes that Al found himself mentioning the word divorce. He told Kayla that something had to give and that he could no longer live the way they were.

They had been married but a few years, yet unless something changed, as much as it would break his heart, it was over.

But who was he kidding?

They agreed to see a marriage counsellor.

These are often provided by the military free of charge.

And everything seemed to go okay, at least until the counsellor began to deal with Kayla's behaviour. In her mind, his unhealthy interest in her fits of rage were his way of blaming her for everything that was going wrong in her marriage and she wasn't to blame; it was her husband's fault. He made her the way she was.

She wasn't normally like that.

And when the counsellor, albeit tactfully, refused to accept Kayla's transference of blame, she gave him a sample of her volatility.

But then, of course, after the event, when she returned home and had a chance to calm down and realise what a fool she had made of herself, she would feel too embarrassed to go back again.

And so the cycle continued, and things were about to get worse, much worse.

15 THE GAMES WE PLAY

Ethan and Megan decided to move into a small apartment and a monogamous relationship.

Meanwhile, he continued to work as a club doorman during the evenings while studying for a business degree during the day.

Megan continued to work as a waitress.

Nearly two years went during which they even discussed marriage.

But trouble was looming.

Although their relationship thrived on their diversities, there was one thing that threatened to tear them apart: their ambitions—Ethan's to travel and see the world, and Megan's to marry, settle down and have children.

Ethan wanted Megan to travel with him, but she was a hometown girl, one who hadn't enjoyed a particularly harmonious relationship with her family. But that had changed now. More specifically, it had changed in the past year or so, under Ethan's influence. He had imprinted the importance of family on her and urged Megan to forge a more meaningful relationship with her parents. Now, she had no intention of abandoning them to pursue some whimsical quest with him.

What was so special about the rest of the world anyway? She had said. They both had everything they needed, right there in Oklahoma City.

But Australia was just one of the things that *was* so special about the rest of the world.

Ever since he could remember, Ethan had dreamt of journeying around the globe to discover new places, new cultures, and new people. He argued that they both had plenty of time, after their travels, to come home, get married and settle down.

But Megan wouldn't have any of it. She didn't want to go and she didn't want Ethan to go either.

So, talk turned to him going alone.

Six months isn't that long, right?

What do you think?

Take a few seconds to consider.

COMING UP FOR AIR

I think it'd take a strong, secure woman to trust her good-looking boyfriend alone for so long, thousands of miles away.

And we know that Megan wasn't strong. We know that she suffered from extreme bouts of low self-esteem and that it wasn't until now, until she'd been with Ethan that she actually started to feel much better about herself.

So she continued to apply pressure; she told Ethan that she didn't like the idea of him travelling and told him, in no uncertain terms, to abandon the idea and stay with her instead.

"If you love me, you'll forget this stupid idea; you'll stay and we'll get married."

Ethan refused.

He reiterated that he did want to marry, but not until after he had fulfilled his dream—and nobody, not even her, was going to hold him back.

It was a stalemate.

For Megan, all of her fears had come true.

"I don't really love you enough to give up on this and nor am I going to change my mind." At least that's what she heard.

And so a cold war started between them where, regardless of the fact that they were inexorably drifting towards Ethan's departure date, both chose to ignore the subject completely and carry on with life as if everything were fine.

I asked Ethan, "How could you let that happen? I mean, just not discuss the subject as you inch closer and closer to your departure date?"

He didn't really have a reply for me. It was just much easier to go on with everyday life and skirt around the elephant in the room, than it was to further debate an argument over which neither was prepared to budge.

Meanwhile, Ethan took on another job to support his studies and his travel fund while Megan would spend whatever free money and time she had on partying.

Things took a turn for the worse one night when, in one of her drunken stupors, Megan ended up in a strip bar that just happened to be frequented by one of Ethan's friends. There, she decided to perform a somewhat intimate and inappropriate lap dance for him.

The news got back to Ethan the very next day.

However, when confronted, Megan denied ever being at the bar.

She challenged Ethan: "Do you believe your best friend's word over mine?"

An argument, one of the worst they had ever had since moving in together, ensued.

So let's pause here and take a look at this for a second.

What on earth would motivate Megan to behave in such a way and why did Ethan ultimately choose to believe his friend's word over that of his girlfriend's?

To establish that, we're going to need to rewind to a few weeks earlier, when both Ethan and Megan found themselves at that very same strip bar.

Why they were both there is unknown.

What we do know is that, after a few drinks, Megan did exactly the same thing: she pulled up her top and exposed her breasts.

Ethan was incandescent with rage.

They fought until the early hours of the morning, and during this angry exchange, Ethan made it quite clear that he would not have her behaving like that, making a mockery of him and, most importantly, herself, and that if she ever did anything like that again, it was over.

So, fast forward a few weeks.

Can you see where I'm going with this?

They'd reached a stalemate.

And there's no doubt that they both cared very much about each other, but neither knew how to get past this particular hurdle in their relationship. Worse still, communication had broken down because the mere mention of the subject caused more arguments—hers because he wouldn't give up his dream, his because she would deny him it.

Megan found it particularly difficult, as she was unable to reconcile her man's behaviour. Ever since she had met the guy, she'd known exactly where she stood with him, and generally that resulted in her getting her way. But this time (not unlike Sindy and I) something was different and she couldn't understand exactly what.

Had he fallen out of love with her? Is that why he was leaving her? Is that why he refused to talk about it?

Sting once sang, "If you love somebody, set them free."

Instead, Megan took Ethan's actions as the perfect validation; just as she had always believed, real love, portrayed in some of her favourite black-and-white movies, did not exist. The man she had allowed herself to believe truly loved her for the past two or so years did not in fact care about her.

Certainly not enough to surrender his nomadic urge.

But Megan needed to know. She needed to know if Ethan even had any feelings left for her.

That's why she returned to that strip bar, that's why she sought out Ethan's friend, and that's why, buoyed by a few drinks and some sultry tunes, she pulled off her top and seductively gave the man his own private lap dance.

Megan was under no illusion that the news would get back to Ethan the next day if not that same night.

It did.

He was beyond angry.

But Megan was happy.

She'd managed to solicit a jealous reaction from her boyfriend. This meant he still cared, right?

"Oh, what a tangled web we weave."

Games are the staple of most relationships.

We play them when all other forms of communication have failed. We're afraid of expressing, admitting to our feelings, which often entails making ourselves vulnerable, so we'll find other ways of expressing or soliciting these, be that casually forgetting an item in the hope that a special person will return it, or giving ourselves the opportunity to go and retrieve it, or letting that phone ring way longer than it needs to so as to not appear too eager.

Other more complex games include creating an emotional scenario, a trap, and waiting for the other person to fall into it. When they do, a reaction will ensue and when it does, it can bring with it a wealth of information—but that information can be just as devastating as it is rewarding.

First and foremost, what should be considered is that the necessity to play a game in a relationship means that all is not well between the two protagonists. It means that they are unable to communicate effectively, that the lifelong skills they should have developed to deal with this precise situation are failing them, and that they need to address this first and foremost, as it's symptomatic of a dysfunctional, unhealthy, fragmented relationship.

When you play games of emotion, you're also running the risk that the very information you're seeking about someone else may be revealed about you: character traits that your partner may well have been blind to are potentially exposed, presenting yourself to your companion in a completely different light.

Most therapists will tell you that the number one ingredient for a tasty relationship is communication, the absence of which will result in a bland and unseasoned partnership; more food for sustenance than for the soul.

And before you stereotypically write this off as stuff of teenagers, know that it goes on all the time in different ways with different people for different reasons.

When information isn't forthcoming, then there's often only one way to get the so-called truth, and that's by orchestrating a 'game' and most of us, at one point or another in our lives, have been guilty of it (yes, including me).

Of course, we could just ask for information, but that's way too easy.

Life would also be so much easier if we all dealt with its challenges with the logic of Mr Spock. However, the majority of us humans are saddled with emotional complexities as infinite as a far-flung galaxy, and these inhibit our ability to see a planet for the stars.

Megan already had her answer.

Ethan told her he had every intention of returning, marrying and raising a family with her because he loved her.

But she didn't believe him.

He was 'just saying that' because it couldn't possibly be true, so she instead resorted to an unnecessary 'game' because what Megan didn't stop to consider is that the reason for her mistrust wasn't based on anything that Ethan had actually done and/or potentially was planning to do, but more on her own low self-esteem due to the emotional life scars she had sustained before meeting him.

But what do you think?

Do you think Ethan should give up his dream to please Megan?

Most importantly, should she have asked him to?

Have a think about that, we'll be revisiting them both one more time later in the book, to find out what actually happened.

Meanwhile, let's take a closer look at this.

For me, the issue about Ethan and Megan is not whether he loved her, but more about whether she truly loved him.

Megan's own insecurities meant that she was incapable of trusting her handsome boyfriend abroad for such a long (or in this case no) period of time, despite the fact that he had never given her cause for doubt.

Quite the opposite, he may have been passionate about his lifelong ambition, but he was equally as passionate about her, and she knew it, for he had changed everything about who he was in order to please her.

Love is not about oppression, manipulation or coercion, yet Megan, who professed to love Ethan 'more than life', wanted to oppress him, then manipulate him into proving his undying love by surrendering something that was clearly very important to him, and then she wanted to coerce him into settling down sooner rather than later.

This isn't love.

Real love is quite the opposite; it's about facilitating the happiness of the object of your affection, and about nurturing and encouraging them to be the best that they can be.

A friend whom I met whilst researching this book and have known for over ten years is a good example of this. She loves her husband very much, and when it comes to his happiness, she's his number one fan.

This lady researches, organises and, where possible, finances activities she knows her husband will enjoy—some with the family and others with his friends (I know this because I'm one of them). Don't get me wrong; they too have their disagreements, but she'd never seek to project her own insecurities onto him and, by association, seek to control him in such a way.

There's no doubt in my mind that, in this scenario, she'd be the first person to research flights and book the accommodation (assuming she couldn't go with him)!

That's because Renee believes that love isn't about suppressing her husband or compelling him to conform to her ideal. Nor does she believe that it's about ritualising terms of endearment and displays of affection—it's about allowing her partner to be the best that he can be, for himself, for her and their children.

Here's a simple but great example that most of us can relate to, especially if there's a child in your life whom you dote on.

How many stories have you heard of mothers (and fathers) who have traipsed malls, high streets, scoured deep recesses of the Internet, battled hordes, paid over the odds, threatened fellow shoppers and come close to maiming shop assistants, all in their quest to get their beloved the perfect Christmas gift?

How many times have *you* actually done this?

And ask yourself, *why did you do it?*

Love.

The reason we go out of our way to say, do or even seek gifts for our loved ones is it gives us an overwhelming sense of pleasure to be instrumental in their happiness.

Love; our compulsion to experience and express it is something that is ingrained in us. It isn't something that we consciously consider and/or elicit—it simply is.

16 THE TRUTH BEHIND CLOSED DOORS

If somebody asked you to get involved in a long-distance relationship, what would be your reaction?

By 'long distance' I'm talking about five thousand miles.

Yeah, that's pretty far.

We're talking the approximate flight path from England to the United States (depending on which part of the States you're talking about of course).

For me, whether or not to be involved wasn't a conscious decision I needed to make; it simply was. Ever since the first holiday with M, I knew I wanted him in my life. The logistics of this wasn't something either of us even discussed.

Besides, we had email.

Remember, this is back in the late 1990s, early 2000s (or noughties), so cross-platform (and thus continent) communication technology wasn't even a twinkle in its creator's eyes. In fact, the current leader in this technology, WhatsApp, subsequently purchased by Facebook, wouldn't come to be until 2009, many years after our relationship took place.

So, emails and rudimentary emoticons were the best form of communication for us, and they worked just fine, along with the aforementioned (in previous chapter) video and chat applications.

We'd meet online nearly every night and chat, among other things, about our day, taking into account the fact that there was a five- to six-hour time difference.

But we made it happen.

It wasn't a pain or a hassle, but was actually something we looked forward to. We did it because we enjoyed connecting.

It was a way of life that actually worked. When peppered with frequent trips of course: roughly four per year with the odd special occasion thrown in.

Where we'd meet for each trip was subject to discussion, but we never argued over it. Generally speaking, we'd tend to alternate; one trip in England and the next in the United States and so on.

Most trips would include a series of road trips, and this is how I managed to explore my beautiful island of the United Kingdom and my first twenty of the American States: from the East to the West coast of America, from the Southwest to the North of England, Scotland and Wales.

It truly was a case of planes, trains, automobiles and boats with each and every trip being a whole new adventure, underpinned by our need to be close to each other. So close that once one picked up the other from a respective airport, what I used to call *the stopwatch* started and it was countdown until it was time to return to that hideous place again (I would eventually come to dislike airports for that reason).

For my first visit to America, I flew into Atlanta Airport. At that time, travelling transatlantic was a pretty new experience to me, so to say that it was somewhat daunting would be an understatement.

I remember my first experience of American immigration and what it felt like to be involuntarily herded by the thousand or so people, all from different flights, to converge in the arrivals hall.

The process appeared to me to be total and utter chaos. I actually remember thinking, *this is what it must feel like to be a refugee in a foreign land.*

Although I had no worries about where to go next since, like it or not, I found myself being inexorably swept forward by the crowds of people who slowly but surely, like a herd of zombies, shuffled in the general direction of the battery of immigration booths manned by very serious-looking officers.

As we inched forward, I lost count of the amount of people whose I94 and Custom forms (compulsory for all visiting immigrants) were deemed null and void by pre-screen officers and who were sent to the back of the hall, like naughty school children, to fill said form out correctly.

The pre-screen officers were as grim as their booth counterparts and spent most of their time barking orders at arriving travellers, generally about staying in line and ensuring that forms were correctly filled out.

At this stage, I started to get paranoid that I too would be sent to the back of the queue, and I even started second-guessing whether or not the instructions given to me by my flight attendant might have been erroneous.

And I think it would be fair to say that, by the time my turn came round, I was a bit of a nervous wreck!

The immigration officer, a typical burly looking man with moustache who had clearly served way too much time in the military before considering a career change, looked me up and down several times before asking, with absolutely no inflection in his tone of voice, "What's the reason for your visit today?"

"I'm visiting a friend," I croaked like some little kid who had just been confronted by a police officer.

"And what's the duration of your visit?"

"Just two weeks," I responded in my best Oliver voice.

At least, that's how I felt, and how I think I sounded. And that was and still is so typical of each and every time I visit the United States; I sound so bloody posh in comparison!

Weird but true.

I've lost count of the amount of times I've caught myself sounding so snooty in the company of Americans when in reality *'I'm just a poor boy from a poor family'*. Oh, okay, sounds much better when Freddie Mercury and his crew sang it.

Anyway, Mr Customs Man was unforgiving in his interrogation and was totally unaffected by my British accent which normally has Americans leaning in to eavesdrop on my meaningless conversation, not for the content of course, but presumably the plummy way in which I annunciate my S's.

"And where does your friend live?" The SS officer was asking.

"He lives in Georgia. He's a marine.

"Where in Georgia—what's the address?"

"He's stationed at Camp Lejeune."

"Do you know where Camp Lejeune is?"

"I'm sorry?"

"Do you know which State Camp Lejeune is?"

"Um, it's in Georgia, isn't it?"

"No, it isn't in Georgia," he said in a voice totally devoid of any expression and examining, for what must have been the fiftieth time, my passport.

"I'm sorry. I said Georgia. I meant North Carolina."

"But you're not staying there, are you?"

"No, we'll be travelling," I said, hoping that he wouldn't opt to strap me to a rack or bring out the thumb screws next.

"Where are you travelling to?"

"Florida."

This is where he paused, scrutinising me once more and comparing me to my passport. As if I'd somehow undergone some kind of metamorphosis since presenting myself at his booth what felt like an hour ago.

He watched me some more, then, "What's your occupation?"
"I'm a writer."
"What do you write?"
Just let me go!
"Books."
"What type of books?"
"Action, adventure. A bit *X-Files* like."
Then, a miracle: that big moustache of his lifted very slightly at the edges. Was that a smile? Or indigestion? I wasn't sure.
"I like *The X-Files*," he said, with characteristic monotony.
I tentatively returned the smile without being too self-assured and, in an effort to sustain the moment, said, with grave disappointment, "Oh, well, it's a shame I don't have a copy on me."
He looked at me and then suddenly and loudly smacked a stamp on the page of my passport and on my so-called green immigration card.
"Have a nice stay," he said, inserting the card into my passport and handing them both back to me.
"Thank you," I said with a big smile, but he was already looking for and waving forward his next victim.
I don't think I ever felt such an immense sense of relief as I did that day, walking away from that booth, nor had I ever looked forward to seeing M as much as I did in that moment. Little did I know that my ordeal wasn't over.
As I made my way beyond passport control through the arrivals corridor, I spotted four or five customs officers roaming among my fellow travellers and randomly yanking them to the side like some hideous scene out of *War of The Worlds*.
I groaned inwardly as my heart started to pound furiously and I had to have a word with myself. *You have nothing to hide. What's your problem?*
I had no idea what my problem was or the cause of my nervousness. What I did know is that I wanted out of that place and I wanted to see a familiar face; I wanted to see M yet I knew that the only way that was going to happen was if I ran this gauntlet successfully without being detained.
So, I stood up straight, tried to look less balding Italian, and

thus, by association, Middle Eastern and stereotypically trouble (yes, I don't know how my mind works sometimes either. Call it desperation).

I slowed my walk so as to not seem too eager, kept my head up so that I didn't appear as if I had something to hide, navigated just a smidgeon closer to the person in front of me in the hope that they'd get selected before me and generally seemed distracted by the passport still in my hand.

And it worked!

I ran half of the gauntlet successfully…

Then three-quarters…

"Sir…"

Nearly there.

"Excuse me, sir?"

NO!

My heart sank and I wanted to petulantly slump my shoulders, but I refrained from doing so and instead came to a reluctant stop.

"Sir, could I see your customs card please?"

He was referring to the other (this time white) card that all visitors to the United States are required to fill out declaring that they aren't concealing big plants, seeds or primes of meat in their hand luggage, nor are they carrying any communicable diseases on their person.

I handed him the card in the hope that my ordeal would be over.

"What's the reason for your visit to the United States today?"

Not again!

"I'm visiting a friend," I answered confidently, with the expertise of a spy now that I was accustomed to this kind of interrogation.

"And where does your friend live?"

"He's a marine, stationed at Camp Lejeune," I said with a smile.

"Sir, would you mind just following me with your bag over here?"

NO!

Over here was in one of the many alcoves flanking the corridor out of there and to the arrivals lobby where M was waiting for me. The same corridor through which many of the other travellers appeared to be escaping without hindrance.

I looked at them enviously, and then with a broad smile said, "Of course," and wheeled my way into one of the alcoves where the customs officer, unlike his immigration counterpart, had at least mastered the art of smiling.

"Would you mind lifting your case up here, sir, and opening it for me, thank you, sir."

Like I had a choice.

Of course, me being me, I would normally love the idea of some hunky American customs officer rummaging around in my smalls, only I would normally have some input into the matter!

I have to say, he was fairly respectful of the ironed folds of my clothing as he, with gloved hands, fondled his way through the contents of my suitcase eventually unearthing some traditional English biscuits (for my American readers, I'm talking about cookies and not something you'd eat with a Southern dish) made by McVitie's, called Digestives.

These particular ones had a chocolate and caramel topping, and happened to be a favourite of M's, discovered during his last trip to England.

"These look nice," the Officer said, lifting a packet out and examining it.

"They are. I said. A favourite of my friend's."

"This your American friend?"

"Yes."

"Is he here picking you up today?"

"Yes, he is."

"He lives here?"

"Yes, he's a marine."

And don't think I haven't noticed that you've already asked me that question.

"Okay," he said suddenly, pulling the lid back down on my case. "Looks like you're good to go, sir," he said with a broad smile. "Thanks very much for your patience."

"Thank you," I said, taking the case that he'd kindly zipped up for me.

"If you just go through there, sir, your friend will be waiting for you just beyond those doors," he said pointing at the automatic double doors at the end of the corridor and to freedom.

Your friend will be waiting for you just beyond those doors.

And I don't know what it was about that sentence, but that man just made me feel so much better. I don't know if it was the fact that he was friendly and reassuring (in complete contrast to his colleague) or simply because he was underlining that once I pushed beyond those doors, M would be on the other side.

Either way, note to any customs officers reading this: just a few friendly words can make all the difference to a traveller in a foreign land!

So, me and my suitcase finally rolled our way down the corridor and through the automatic doors and into the droves and the cacophony of voices, squeals of delight and sobbing of heartfelt emotion which, I must say, tugged at my own heartstrings, just as, through the throng, I saw him: light chinos, a polo shirt and the most beautiful smile.

I can't begin to tell you what a sight for sore eyes that man was that day.

It was all I could do to not jump into his arms, but that was in direct contravention of our unwritten rule about public displays of affection. That, and the fact that I probably would have flattened the poor bloke as I've never been the skinniest of things.

Unlike him, with those broad shoulders, muscular arms and the most beautiful pert butt I have ever seen on a man—and, boy, did it look good in those trousers ('pants' if you're an American reading this. By the way, if I haven't mentioned it, pants means underwear in England so you can appreciate why it would sound somewhat weird to have written that he was standing in the arrivals hall in light pants) which, by the way, he was wearing for me.

He knew that seeing him in chinos was my next favourite thing to seeing him in a military uniform.

I loved him for that.

I guess it's the little things.

"Was your trip okay?" he asked, as he paid for parking.

I was about to launch into a whole tirade about my experience, but thought better of it. I was tired and just grateful to have landed safely and to see his smiling face.

Besides, we had a long drive ahead of us. Approximately 500 miles; from Atlanta, down Route 75 through the state of Georgia to Jacksonville, and then to Daytona Beach, Florida.

M had just bought a new pickup truck and, to be honest, it wouldn't have been my preferred road trip vehicle, but only because we had to somewhat unceremoniously dump our suitcases in the back, although I wasn't particularly fussed since the important people were in the mercifully air conditioned cabin.

Yes, the Georgian sun was hot and the perfect prelude to what I was expecting down in the Sunshine State.

We were about thirty minutes into our drive south, and now that I was finally here, finally in the cabin of M's truck and had officially declared our two-week vacation together as started, I allowed myself to relax and thus travelling fatigue to catch up with me.

In fact, I remember my eyes starting to droop as I watched weathered billboards drift by us like giant UFOs. From governors to fast food, I took in everything about my new surroundings, including all promotional messages.

That was until I glanced over at M and noticed he was watching me, and he was grinning.

"You okay?" he asked.

"Should I be asking you that?" I said with a sleepy smile.

He just winked at me.

"I'm good, thanks," I said, cocking my head as I tried to figure out what he was thinking—that was until we both got distracted by what can only be described as an eighteen-wheeler mega truck that dwarfed us as M overtook it.

Trust the Americans. Even their trucks have to be bigger.

I was thinking this as I glanced back at M, who had completed the manoeuvre and was staring at me once more with that big grin of his.

I laughed, "What? Do I look tired?"

"No."

"What then?" I asked, inspecting myself.

Have I spilt something on me?

"Nothing."

"Then why are you grinning like that? You're creeping me out."

He laughed and said, "I'm sorry, it's just my jaw is aching."

"It is? What's wrong?"

"Oh no, I'm okay, it's just all the grinning," he said, looking away from me and at the car he was overtaking.

I followed his gaze and asked "What about?"

"That you're here," he said, completing the manoeuvre.

I looked back at him and he was grinning at me once more with those big hazel eyes of his.

Oh, my word.

Up until that moment, I don't think anybody, not related to me, had said anything so lovely to me and meant it.

"Oh, M…" I touched his leg and held it; he looked at me, my hand and then smiled one of his mischievous smiles whilst scanning the cars on the road around us.

"Me too," I said, winking at him and allowing my hand to drift down the inside of his thigh and then disappear between his legs.

He blushed.

(I loved that about him).

"I love you," I said with a big grin.

"You sure?" he asked seriously, with that gorgeous American tone of his, and as casually as he could, considering where my hand was.

"I'm sure," I said.

And if I could have leaned over to kiss him I would have, but that would have been extremely dangerous given the amount of traffic on the motorway.

These two sentences would become our trademark repartee when expressing terms of endearment: one imparting the expression and the other performing the validation rather than just saying, "Me too".

And I loved it.

And that journey south has got to be one of the most beautiful road trips I've ever taken. We talked, we laughed, and we flirted, since it was clear that we were both eager to get the other to a hotel room, stat!

I watched American culture slide by the windshield and my passenger window like a movie projected onto a screen. I saw endless billboards, trailer parks, rivers, wood houses with wraparound porches, giant trees, open roads, water towers, and cotton fields that glistened like snow under the setting sun.

We talked and laughed a lot about a variety of things, and listened to endless Country and Rock music. I can't say that I'd ever been a fan, although unspoken rules dictated that host and car owner would have overall control of the music mix and I was fine with that because, ultimately, it was part of M, part of our adventure.

I also liked the fact that we had diverse music tastes as it helped both of us open our eyes; mine to the seemingly endless calamities of Country music or the angst of Rock, versus his to jaw-jangling base of Dance music, which I would go as far as saying he hated.

Eventually, the scenery changed from the agricultural marvels of Georgia to the overdeveloped glamour of the beachside tourism of the Sunshine State.

I remember being very excited when I spotted my first palm tree as it meant we were close to our destination.

Here, somewhat cheesy Latin dance music was prevalent wherever we went outside of the bubble of the truck's cabin. I was fine with that, but I bet you can guess who wasn't.

M had booked a hotel right next to Daytona Beach complete with ocean view, which he knew would always be my favourite.

We'd arrived at the beginning of the rest of our time together: hotel rooms, theme parks, restaurants and assorted tourist attractions.

Fine by me.

That night, after dinner, and under a silver moon, we took a stroll on the beach, just chatting and listening to the sound of the surf.

I remember facing the warm ocean breeze, laden with the scent of seaweed, and thinking just how fortunate I was to be here, experiencing such a magical moment under what appeared to be a gigantic full moon with the surf tickling my toes and with this hunk of an American man, on the eve of a fantastic holiday.

There really wasn't anything else I could have possibly wanted.

Now, if you're picturing us strolling hand in hand, you may want to think again. That's something that we hadn't done so far and, as it turns out, something we would never do.

Yes, in all the time we were together we never held hands in public, and this wasn't something that we discussed.

It simply was.

I guess this was because, despite the fact that I knew I was gay, I wasn't actually out yet and M, well, one of the reasons I was attracted to him was he was a man who happened to be into me and, at the time, he also happened to be in the marines. So it was understood that broadcasting our relationship was in neither of our interests—although I have to say that I think I harboured some fantasy about being outed because, throughout our relationship, I always fostered my own code: I didn't care if people found out about me but I became fiercely protective of M's status as a hot-blooded heterosexual man. I don't even know why since, again, it wasn't something we actually talked about; I just felt that he'd have a much tougher time dealing with something like that, because I actually didn't and still don't believe that's where he was at.

For me, it was as if M was going through a phase the outcome of which neither of us chose to discuss. It felt very much as if we were both just living for the moment.

And that too was fine with me.

Until I started to feel like I needed more.

Something beyond the privacy of the hotel rooms and bedrooms. Something that didn't treat our relationship like some vampiric, hideous creature that should never see the light of day for fear that it may self-combust.

However, it was only on this journey that I learned that M didn't feel the same.

The next day we drove south to Kissimmee and the apartment that was to be our base for the next week or so during which we'd visit each and every tourist trap that Orlando had to offer.

It had to be done.

It was during our trip to Universal Studios in Orlando that I discovered just how illegal public displays of affection would be in our relationship, and it pretty much set the standard for the duration.

It was a hot, humid day, and we'd already visited quite a few of the so-called attractions of the theme park, including the WaterWorld stunt-packed show, based on the film by the same name.

The next disaster experience was Twister, also based on the movie by the same name.

However, just before we joined the queue into the darkness, M went off to get us some water, and it was as he was marching back to me, carrying two bottles, that I snapped a photo, which I still have to this day, and I remember thinking just how mighty fine he looked to me, and I felt a sudden and spontaneous urge to throw my arms around him and kiss him.

However, I had the presence of mind to refrain from such an action as the place was teaming with people and I didn't want to embarrass him.

Thirty minutes later, we and a group of others entered a hanger-type building and gathered on a specially built viewing platform.

The scene was night-time, and fans of the film will remember where the protagonists are happily watching an outdoor movie before all hell breaks loose.

Well, Universal Studios had recreated that very set in front of us and, before long, there are howling winds, burning cars, lots of debris and even a flying cow!

It was an awesome experience that took place in the dark but for some strobe lighting and streaking fire, and thus a perfect opportunity for me to take advantage of the tightly packed group of people and lean into M.

There, whilst everybody was watching the action unfold, I put my hand on the small of his back. He, almost instantly, twisted away from me and, although I couldn't really see his face that well, shot me a glare before returning back to the action that was unfolding before us.

I felt absolutely awful.

Mercifully, the experience didn't last more than a few

COMING UP FOR AIR

minutes, and before long we were back out in the Florida sun.

"That was cool," M said excitedly.

"It was," I responded flatly.

"Uh-oh, what's wrong?"

"Nothing," I said, not really wanting to get into a debate over it as it seemed so bloody trivial. Yet it was something that most couples do and don't even think about, yet for me required some bloody ridiculously planned strategy; in the dark, out of sight, nothing too obvious, just a connection.

"Oh, come on," he said. "I know you better than that."

"Well, it was you, in there," I responded, much more quickly than I'd intended.

"What?"

"Are you really going to pretend that didn't happen?"

"What?"

He genuinely looked as if he didn't know what on earth I was talking about.

"In there, M, I touched your back and you pulled away from me."

"Oh," he said. "Well, there were people there," he said quietly, as if the legion of holidaymakers around us gave a rat's hairy behind about our conversation.

"Nobody was looking, M."

"Well, someone may have seen us."

"Is this how it's going to be?"

"I thought we had an understanding," he said.

"Did we? Where was I for that meeting?" I asked, perhaps a tad more angrily than I'd intended and perhaps a bit more loudly, since it prompted M to look around us. And it was that act that was annoying me the most—how he seemed to think everybody was listening in our conversation.

"Nobody gives a shit, M," I said dismissively.

"Tony..." he began, but struggled to find the words.

"Oh, forget it," I said and walked away from him toward our next destination.

And that was the day I learned that anything goes in the privacy of a hotel room, a bedroom—hell, sometimes even a car—but once we were out of the protection of those environments, any expressions of affection were strictly forbidden.

Oddly, me being me, I'm the kind of guy who would flout the law just to solicit a reaction, but in this particular situation I conformed, partially because I knew it was something M disliked intensely, but mostly because I hated how his rejection made me feel, especially since I found it hard to reconcile the two people we were when alone together versus the two strangers we were out in public.

Nonetheless, this became one of the primary conduct codes that governed the lifetime of our relationship: there would be no public displays of affection.

And I missed that.

Interestingly, in line with the natural law that our life experiences shape who we become, to this day, it's highly unlikely you'll ever catch me holding anybody's hand in public, not even that of a member of my own family.

And yes, I know that's very sad but that's just how it was.

I wanted M in my life and I wanted him to feel comfortable around me for I was still very much aware of the phantoms from my days with Peppe and Co.

I wanted M in my life and this was a sacrifice I was prepared to make because, for me, regardless of this element, that holiday reminded me just how good we were together and, most importantly, how much I loved him, and it was a lot.

17 THE BEST OF FRIENDS

I once read a newspaper article about a head teacher—yes I said head teacher, as in person who is supposed to lead and inspire others—of a well-known British private school who was calling for the abolishment of the term (and I would assume practice) of 'best' friendships.

At the time, I believed this misguided madness was just one

teacher and one school in the UK—but I learned, to my astonishment, that the subject had actually been a hot debate on both sides of the Atlantic for some time.

I concluded that this, one of the most preposterous suggestions that I have ever heard, could only have been conceived by the same dimwits who suggested that the red pen should be banned from classrooms on the belief that it's 'too negative' for poor little students who I'm sure would feel much happier being told that their work was rubbish in green ink instead.

Seriously?

Apparently, the reason for such an Orwellian suggestion is because Miss Head Teacher, and her cronies believe that children should not be encouraged to 'pair up', but to bond with groups of people rather than making any one person the 'best'. Furthermore, they've found that the very word 'best' is in fact a negative as it implies that any one person is 'better' than others and thus this could potentially ostracise some and leave them feeling, well, substandard.

Fancy that; a word that actually inspires its very meaning.

For me, this is right up there with mothers being told not to cheer for their children on sports day and during other competitive events for fear that the 'losers' (yes, I'm very sorry for that, but there's no other term for a person who competed in a challenge and, well, lost) would get upset and that this in turn would damage their self-esteem.

But, wait a minute, isn't this the complete opposite to what any world-leading, reputable child-rearing manual tells you: praise your toddler's achievements when they accomplish something? Smile, be enthusiastic and engaging? Which is the very reason we adopt that baby goo-goo-gaga overenthusiastic tone every time we talk down to a little human, right?

"That's right, we do, don't we...?"

Sadly, this appears to be the kind of nanny state that we're creating for ourselves and for future generations. A sanitised, homogenous world where everybody is walking on eggshells, because everybody else is so hypersensitive that the mere suggestion of failure is enough to send someone spiralling into a pit of abject depression.

Does anybody enjoy being disappointed?

I don't think so.

Very few of us are able to proclaim a 'perfect' (whatever that is) existence. Life isn't like that. It's full of good, bad and bloody ugly. The secret to being able to cope with the last two is to have the real-world foresight and experience to tackle life in all of its colour because we're not always going to have a couple of misguided fools there to shield us from the things that hurt.

This is precisely why it's important to have a support structure made up of loyal family members and friends.

Disappointments are part of our life experience. They're part of the fabric of those things that shape who we are, help us grow our character and our identities so that we're better equipped to face future disappointments.

They give us perspective.

When I first started writing, I remember having a conversation with one of my friends who was rightly fed up because she was unable to find a job. She had applied to several places, had been rejected from a few of them, and was having a hard time dealing with that rejection. I asked her exactly how many rejections she'd received, she told me, "About three or four".

Three or four?

I left the room and returned seconds later carrying what looked like a ream of paper but was really a collection of rejection letters from publishers. I dropped the pile in her lap and said, "That's rejection!"

It's all relative.

Life can be tough, for some more than others, and it's at times like these that you do need a best friend, somebody with whom you have an affinity; a kindred spirit who truly knows and understands you, sometimes more than you know and understand yourself. That special someone who says "tell me what's troubling you" even after you've said "everything's fine." These rare and precious human connections are forged over time via shared experiences and not in a school-ground collective.

How many people have told you stories of being in a crowd and still feeling lonely? How many times have *you* been in a crowd and still felt lonely?

I consistently talk about how unhealthy I believe it is to focus all of your energy on any one person: my lover, my friend, my everything. It's somewhat impossible to get the perspective you need from any one person. It takes multiple people to form a healthy support structure, and that consists of family members, lovers (normally one, at least one at a time) and a group of friends, and it's from this group that we'll naturally form a closer connection with one or two 'specials'.

These become our best friends; those in whom we confide the most. The subject matter may well be topic-specific but we instinctively know what kind of thing to discuss with whom. And it isn't always in a collective; that's because we don't always feel comfortable or simply are not ready to share what's happening to us with the general circle. It's nothing personal, but more about survival; it takes a certain level of energy to cope with something that's troubling us, and it takes even more to field thought-provoking questions from multiple parties when we're busy processing the ones already in our head.

Actively seeking and nurturing a variety of friends is not only good, but it's healthy, because each person brings something different to our lives.

Actively seeking to discourage 'best' friendship is lunacy because it's what we're programmed to do as a species; it's the first step to understanding relationships and experiencing the joy, disappointment and pain of loving another human being but, most importantly, of understanding what it's like to make a meaningful connection with another person as opposed to stumbling through a series of meaningless encounters.

On the other hand, maybe we should scrap the term 'best' friend and replace it with something more suitable, say 'super' friend. Because, in my opinion, that's more indicative of who these people really are. They're the ones who don't need a diary to know if they have time for us; they're architects who build our self-esteem by supporting our dreams; they're the therapists who listen yet never judge, the police officers of our conscience, the gardeners of our happiness, the shoulder for sorrow, and the colourful clowns in the circus of life that sometimes reveals itself to be as grey as it is uninspiring.

With that in mind, maybe I misjudged our misguided school head. Maybe the term 'best' friend is wrong after all; maybe best simply isn't 'best enough'.

"A good friendship is like standing in wet cement; the longer you stay, the harder it is to leave, and you can never go without leaving footprints."

When our doorman Ethan was still in high school, he and a group of school friends, went on a road trip to Mardi Gras in New Orleans.

As you'd expect, from a gang of young, cocky lads, they were rowdy, loud and out for a good time. And this is exactly what they found, along with some food and a lot of alcohol.

So, it won't surprise you to read that halfway through the evening, spurred on by the drinking, the party atmosphere, and the peacock-like strutting in front of some girls, our boys ended up locking horns with some of the locals.

Eyeballing, name calling and threats were shared and the two opposing forces were moments from an all-out brawl before some bystanders stepped in and defused the situation.

And so the night continued.

Two hours later, Ethan found himself standing outside one of the bars, leaning into and chatting up (or hitting on) one of the girls when he spotted a member of the clan with whom he'd had the earlier altercation; he was coming out of the opposite bar.

Maybe realising that he had been out of order or maybe because he wanted to impress the girl he was with, Ethan stepped out in front of the lad with the intent of apologising to him.

However, he'd barely uttered the first few words when a beer bottle was smashed over his head, the shock of which sent him staggering backward into the street. Then, as blood trickled down his face and into his eyes, blurring his vision, he received a punch to his stomach which caused him to double over, and then an uppercut to his chin that sent him reeling backward onto the cold tarmac of the road where, to the hysterical screams of the girl he'd been with, he received further kicks to his legs, ribs and face.

After what felt like minutes, but was really seconds, Ethan heard and recognised the sound of one of his friends; his best friend whose voice was loud, angry and anxious.

What do you think happened next?

A)   Ethan's best friend single-handedly took on all three of his attackers and in turn was hurt and sent to hospital.

B)   Ethan's best friend ran to the nearest police officer and bullied them to go save his friend.

C)   Ethan's best friend saw what was happening, but chose not to get involved.

Well, there are a couple of so-called obvious choices here but neither changes the reality of what actually happened, and that's the fact that Ethan's best friend witnessed what was happening, but turned on his heels and went back into the bar.

He chose not to get involved.

Now, you may well think that he actually did the right thing. I would have most likely, and probably wrongly, thrown myself in there and got myself taken to the hospital. Yes, probably not the best move but it's that impulsive Italian side of me as well as an overwhelmingly strong sense of justice; it turns out that it was four against one.

That isn't fair.

I would have at least gone for option B.

But nonetheless.

And, once again, it's probably easier for me to make that judgement now, since I wasn't actually there.

Maybe, but Ethan's friend chose to do nothing.

That's inexcusable.

His inability to take action not only questioned the strength of his friendship with Ethan, but also the absence of basic human compassion—to be able to witness something like that and do nothing.

Ethan received stitches to the head as a result of that incident and hopes he never loses his hair for fear that the scars will be revealed.

So, what happened afterwards? Did Ethan talk to his friend about his 'betrayal'?

No, he didn't.

In his mind, his so-called best friend already knew what he had done and would have to live with that for the rest of his life. For Ethan, this was enough. And they've since found themselves playing rugby together without any recriminations.

Will things ever be the same between them again?

In Ethan's own words, "No, they can't."

Even if he could forget the betrayal, the biggest casualty here was trust. And without trust there isn't much of a friendship left.

Like most rational human beings, I think I can quite safely say that to be wronged by somebody is a painful experience, regardless of the situation. Each will, in its own way, carry its own degree of hurt depending on the scenario. In this case, Ethan learned, most painfully, mentally and physically that the person he believed was his best friend did not care for him enough to intervene even when his life was in danger.

That is a pretty tough lesson to learn.

And learning is the key word here. Did Ethan learn from that experience?

He told me he did.

But I have my doubts.

I know I couldn't stand by and see my best friend hurt, somebody I cared deeply for, being hurt.

Could you?

Best friendships are born out of at least one mutual interest as well as love, trust, devotion and a series of other essentials. They are not appointed with a metaphorical badge.

I couldn't help but wonder if Ethan had learned anything at all from that experience.

Here is a guy who, as a child, received hardly any attention from his feuding parents. He then lived through two more of his mother's failed marriages, during which he and his brother received little or no consideration.

So, what was the result?

Ethan sought attention elsewhere.

It started off with the girls at school and then grew with him into adulthood. He then sought a job in the one place that affords him even more attention; a doorman at one of the hottest clubs in Oklahoma City. In that world, he had a very powerful position; he decides who can and cannot enter the premises with or without their friends, with or without a pass and with or without paying. Hundreds of young people from all walks of life, from all kinds of careers, from equivalently powerful positions owe or know Ethan.

What better way of reclaiming all that had been denied him as a child?

And reclaim he does.

In an almost biblical way, every time he walks into a room, people clamber to hug him—both men and women.

So, that's a good thing, isn't it?

Well, normally, the obvious answer would be yes. But on this occasion, and after spending some time with him, I cannot help but wonder. If ever there was a warning of the side effects of not forming meaningful relationships, then that tragic trip to New Orleans was it.

There is no doubt that Ethan is a very likable guy with an average sense of humour and a great smile for all who care to be captivated by it. However, what I witnessed in the time I spent with him was a classic case of *buying;* Ethan is buying this adoration that he was denied many years before. This is very much in keeping with the comments he has made about his trip to Colorado and Australia where he is concerned about being a stranger amongst strangers.

He told me that if things 'got really bad down under', he would take on a job similar to the one he had in Oklahoma—the nightclub gatekeeper.

Rinse and repeat.

What Ethan fails to see is that these people he refers to as 'friends' are not friends at all; they are acquaintances, people who know him and have often been obliged to him.

As I started writing this book, I too became 'obliged' to Ethan, only I had nothing more to offer him than the unvarnished truth and maybe, of course, real friendship had the circumstances been different.

The truth is that Ethan is very ambitious. To him, being 'liked' is part of that process—and who *doesn't* like being popular? However, he places way too much of his self-esteem in the hands of strangers and doesn't stop to think that he already possesses enough talent, charisma and commitment to achieve much of what he wants to achieve, without the need to seek the adulation of others.

Be comfortable in your own skin.

We are all the by-product of our own history.

It's the events of our past that shape who we are in the present and who we will be in the future. Whether or not these traits are deemed good or bad is subject to how we approach each and every circumstance and the impact this has on both our lives and the lives of those around us.

I truly believe that we often forget what people *say to us* but we seldom forget how they *made us feel*.

As you'll discover later, Ethan will go on to remind me of this.

18 EXPECTATIONS FOR MASOCHISTS

We often feel wronged by others, be that because a friend pulled out of a special occasion last minute or our boss gave the job we'd been coveting for so very long to a colleague we believe does not deserve it.

But do these people truly deserve our wrath, or are we to blame for putting ourselves in such vulnerable situations in the first place?

Okay, so if you've been wronged lately, you're probably spitting over this book right now.

Fear not, I know what it's like to feel wronged.

God knows, I have had my fair share of scenarios where I've felt let down, put upon, and quite simply abused. The thing is though, upon reflection, I found that in many of these instances, it was I, albeit with good intentions, who kept placing myself in situations that had a good chance of yielding disappointment.

More later, but first, here's a story.

The story of a close friend I once knew. His name was Dale.

We both had ambitions beyond our current professions— Dale wanted to get into the army and I wanted to become a published author—and it was through this common cause that we became very close friends.

But things were about to change and one of us would be left very disappointed.

It was lunchtime on a working day in one of Cambridge's many restaurants. This place was a favourite haunt of ours; it was often uncrowded and the food was good.

This day, not unlike the others, we sought out our window seat from which we watched shoppers bustling to and from their cars with trolleys and bags loaded with groceries.

Dale was tucking into a baked potato whilst I picked at a Caesar salad.

"So did you get them?" I asked.

"Yes, they arrived this morning."

"And, have you filled them in yet?"

"Well," Dale paused his eating, "I was thinking that maybe I should wait until the New Year."

I frowned. "What are you talking about?"

"You know I don't have any leave left and if I send this application form in and am accepted, they will want me to go down there for a three-day physical test."

"And?"

"And I don't have any leave left."

I put down my fork and asked, "You can't afford to take a few days' unpaid leave to realise your dream?"

I looked at him expectantly.

He hesitated.

"What is it?"

"Oh, I don't know. I'm just scared."

"Of what?"

"Well, what if I don't get accepted? I'm pushing thirty-one

and they stop accepting new recruits into the army at thirty. I mean, they're recruiting bloody eighteen-year-olds! If it comes to a decision between a young whippersnapper and me, who do you think they're going to choose?"

"The one who qualifies…"

I stopped eating again and leaned forward. "Dale, I can't guarantee that you won't be disappointed, but what I can tell you is that you won't know unless you try. Unless you fill in that bloody form and send it off, you're never going to know if they're going to consider you. Now, how many nights have we spent talking about this? It's something you've dreamed of ever since you shacked up with Queen of Darkness."

The somewhat unaffectionate name had been given, by Dale, to a girl he had decided to move in with five years before. As you can tell, he wasn't completely devoted to the relationship, but somehow managed to allow himself to be swept along by the moment.

Dale had actually shared details of his ambition to join the army with his girlfriend, but she told him, in no uncertain terms, that this clashed with her ambition of setting up a home and being with him.

It was the army or her.

He chose her.

Four years later, and after an exhausting three-day stint at an exhibition in London, Dale returned home one day to find Queen's suitcases waiting by the front door. She then proceeded to tell him that she had changed her mind and that she no longer wanted to set up home with him, but with one of his friends instead.

She left.

Needless to say, the whole experience left Dale rather bitter and, whilst not being totally devastated by the Queen's decision, he still had to come to terms with the idea that four years, hundreds of pounds and giving up his dream of joining the army had been rendered meaningless by one cold sentence: "I'm leaving you."

Yes, that's cold.

Especially when he started to think about what he could have done with that time—the people he could have dated, the dreams he could have fulfilled.

Luckily, and I use that word loosely, Dale was not 'in love' with this girl; it seemed to me that he was merely being pulled by her gravity. I mean, what more could a man want but a beautiful girl, a home, a beautiful girl and a home, a beautiful girl and a home?

No, it isn't a typo; I am merely pointing out the two main things that Dale saw in the whole relationship.

Sometimes we do that.

We settle.

Remember Timothy and Aubrey?

Settling is something that we all consider in the absence of anything else: a wife may settle for a 'bad' husband as long as he is capable of providing for her and her children; an individual may settle for a 'bad' job because it is close to home.

Is this wrong or right?

Well, to say that would be to 'settle' for quite a hefty generalisation.

Relationships are about compromising. Life is about compromising. Each case is assessed on its own merits. How many times has someone told you to weigh up the pros and cons of any situation? The wife may have compromised for a man who doesn't show her much attention or doesn't make an effort to make her feel special simply because she is content with the fact that she and her children have a roof over their heads and food on the table.

Personally, I am not a settling kind of guy. Let me rephrase that. I *used to think* I wasn't a 'settling' kind of person—until it happened to me. You won't think that you are a settling kind of person until it happens to *you*.

How will you know?

You probably won't until it's too late to do anything about it.

You will find more about settling later on in this chapter... um, actually you will find more about settling throughout this book because, ultimately, it is something most people have done at least once in their lifetime.

And yes, even you. In fact, you may well be settling as you read this.

Now, where were we?

Oh, yes, Queen of Darkness…

"Don't remind me of her," Dale said with a grimace.

"Well, my point is that you've already lost this opportunity once before—do you really want to lose it again?"

He thought about this as I munched on my salad, which I have to say was quite boring, but I knew I had said enough to make him stop and think and, right then, I could almost see the cogs turning in his head.

A few moments later: "Okay, then. I will fill it in tonight and send it off tomorrow."

I smiled.

"What about you?"

"What *about* me?"

"Any news from the publishers?"

"Not yet."

I had submitted one of my manuscripts to one of the big publishing houses and was now waiting for a reply. Like many authors, I knew that a yes verdict from them could literally change my life.

And now, more than ever, the pressure was on.

If Dale did get accepted into the army, he would leave and I'd be stranded without a best friend and, very selfishly, this was a situation that I did not want to find myself in.

For days thereafter, the two of us would share the same conversation many more times. Sometimes at the same restaurant and others at Dale's home where we'd both stay up until the early hours, talking.

In fact, you'll never guess which subject, beyond getting into the British Army, was Dale's favourite?

That's right.

His ex, the Queen of Darkness herself.

How is that possible? You may be asking? If he didn't care for the girl, how could she have wounded him so?

Well, to say that Dale didn't care for her would be untrue. He cared enough to want to set up a home with her; he just wasn't emotionally engaged in the relationship and was suffering from a severe case of settling. Once he had made the decision to live with her, he was committed to that decision and thus her.

However, having opted to give up his dream to be with her

only to find out, four years later, that she no longer wanted him was very difficult to come to terms with. Furthermore, he had been dumped and, as you will read later, becoming a *Dumpee* isn't, well, nice.

And to add insult to injury, she also told him that one of the reasons she was leaving was because he was dull and that there was another man who was much more exciting.

(Yes, she actually said that to him).

And now you're probably wondering if she was right.

I couldn't possibly tell.

The bottom line is that Dale had received multiple strikes on two different levels; one being the attack on his personality and the other that someone else, some other man, would be, and already had been, sharing a bed, and a couch and numerous other places (at least that's the kind of thing that went through his mind) with the woman he had dedicated himself to and, yes, you've got it, given up his dream for.

This was the syndrome.

Dale was hurting and the very thing that had aided him in the decision to be with Queen of Darkness in the first place was now killing him emotionally: his ego.

In his lifetime, Dale had not experienced this kind of humiliation, and furthermore, his upbringing by a father who was already in the military had taught him not to share these feelings with anybody, not even with his family or friends.

Hugging, crying and outpourings were attributes not worthy of a man, and a male caught succumbing to these emotions would almost certainly be ridiculed, or, more accurately, ostracised.

Was this the truth? Would Dale's father and indeed his mother and his sister have disowned him for allowing them to see he was hurting?

Probably not.

Did he think they would?

Without a doubt.

I was the only person Dale could 'really talk to'.

And talk we did about another favourite subject of Dale's: a pretty blonde who went by the name of Lisa.

Dale and she had been friends for many years and it was

during this time that he developed very strong feelings for her yet was unable to declare these for two reasons: one, he was going through the usual tongue-tied, palms-sweating turmoil we all go through when we like someone very much; and two, the simple fact that she was already living with his best friend (yes, not best friend enough for him to be able to share his feelings about Queen with. Go figure).

It was the latter minor detail that made everything much more complicated.

However, Lisa's relationship with her boyfriend wasn't without anguish.

Why?

Well, because he was a bit of a philanderer.

Angus was a northern lad who was blessed with the gift of the gab and, not unlike Timothy, he was able to woo girls simply by using a seemingly endless repertoire of wit and charm, since he wasn't a particularly attractive young man (are you seeing the pattern?) with greasy shoulder-length hair, a stubbly complexion and tasteless sense of style, one couldn't help but wonder what exactly girls saw in him.

Yet they flocked—which didn't help relations with Lisa, who spent many evenings sobbing on Dale's shoulder about how she could no longer put up with Angus's infidelity, yet was unable to leave.

At this stage, you may well be thinking, "Well, it's her own fault if she chooses to stay in that situation".

Well, as usual, for us people on the outside, it's always easy to say that she should just leave him. That appears to be the most sensible thing to do. And, in the long run, it probably was. However, Lisa was unable to do so because of that *crazy little thing called love.*

The paradox was that she loved the very thing that was breaking her heart.

Angus was a rogue; he had that element of danger that many women find very attractive in a man. The cynics among you would translate that into "some women enjoy being treated like crap." Well, so do some men for that matter. Okay, maybe not as many.

The point being that, with this in mind, Dale was unable to

declare his undying love for her, thus he was forced to suffer in silence, since making a move on his best friend's girl would not only destroy their friendship, but could potentially damage the very close bond he shared with her, for, in Lisa's own broken words and as she wiped tears from her eyes, "You are such a great friend, Dale. I don't know what I'd do without you."

You can't get much clearer than that.

Therefore, the only time Dale could actually verbalise his feelings for Lisa was when he was with me; I'd sit patiently listening to his angst whilst offering whichever words of comfort one can in such a situation.

But then I threw a somewhat radical idea into the arena.

I suggested it first as a fantasy, a daydream conceived with the aim of provoking laughter. However, the more we talked, the more Dale loved it.

What if he was accepted into the army and then, on the day he boards the train to boot camp, he stands on the platform step and declares, in front of everybody, his undying love for her.

There's safety in numbers, right?

It's the perfect romantic gesture, albeit the most cowardly one.

Dale fell in love with this fantasy, for it intrigued almost as much as it terrified him; facing Lisa, telling her that he loved her now and always had, as the steam envelops them, the train whistle goes and everybody cheers…

"…No, I can't do it."

"Okay, how about a letter then?" I asked.

He considered this too.

A letter sounded much easier. He could even post it just before his departure so that she would read it whilst he was in basic training and too far away to suffer the humiliation of rejection.

Minutes of procrastinating, followed by literally hours, and Dale finally made a decision.

Which decision do you think he made?

A)   Dale decided to write to Lisa and posted the letter just before his departure.

B) Dale declared his love for Lisa one night after he got drunk.

C) Dale did none of the above.

Three months later and about three years into my relationship with M.

It was M's turn to visit the United Kingdom. This time, I chose to rent a holiday cottage in the South East of Wales, an area known for its outstanding natural beauty (yes that does sound like an ad).

The cottage décor may have been somewhat drab, but it nonetheless suited the occasion since our intention was to escape the stresses and strains of everyday life and simply retreat to a place where we could relax, play PlayStation, eat and, um, enjoy each other's company.

However, after one and a half weeks, I for one began to suffer from a mild case of cabin fever, and consequently boarded the car and plotted a course north towards the mountainous region of Snowdonia in Wales.

We were halfway there when the trouble started.

"There are plenty of mountains in the States," M griped, whilst rubbing his sleeveless arms as a clear indication that the air conditioning in the car was up way too high.

"Well, M, in case you hadn't noticed, we're in the UK at the moment and our purpose is to explore this region."

He sighed.

"What?" I asked, mildly irritated.

"Nothing."

So I repeated the question.

"Well, after all the travelling I have done to get here, I'm really not in the mood to sit in this car for four hours there and back."

"Hey, M... has it crossed your mind that maybe this trip isn't all about you?" I snapped.

The marine didn't reply; instead he pulled my jacket from the backseat and wrapped it around himself. He then fiddled with his seat, grimaced, and closed his eyes to nap, leaving me to consider whether or not I had the heart to continue in the face of such fierce opposition.

It was as I pondered this that my phone bleeped; it was a text message from Dale and it read:

Private 1ˢᵗ class, reporting for duty, SIR! ;-)

Dale had been accepted into the army.

My heart sank.

I was feeling particularly despondent because of the recent M episode in the car and, just before we'd left for this vacation, I'd received another publisher rejection letter.

Now, I was about to lose my closest friend to a dream that I had helped realise.

I looked across at M who was huddling under my jacket, eyes closed, and head shaking with the movement of the car.

He was asleep.

I felt alone.

I pushed on the accelerator. Snowdonia beckoned.

The next update I had about Dale wasn't actually through him, but through a mutual acquaintance of ours. Dale had sent her a text message saying that he was having a great time in the army and, oh, he had sent a letter to Lisa detailing how he felt and hoping that they could be together.

She accepted!

What the...? I have to confess that last piece of news knocked me sideways, and it hurt.

Why?

Well, because this had been something that the two of us had discussed for months, ad nauseam. This had always been something that he had been afraid of doing yet, when he finally did, when he finally plucked up the courage to confront Lisa with his feelings and she had actually accepted, I was the last to know.

So, you're probably thinking, all's well that ends well, right? If Dale finally got the girl of his dreams, then what's my problem?

Well, the simple fact that Dale didn't deem me important enough to share this information with me made me feel somewhat 'betrayed'.

Why?

Because I'd set myself up.

However you may feel about this particular situation.

Whomever you may think is right or wrong, the result remains the same; my so-called hurt was limited only by how much I projected, what I believed would have been the correct way for Dale to behave in this situation.

For example, I had endured, for want of a better expression, Dale's agonising about actually applying for the British Army. But for the fact that I bullied and cajoled the guy to fill in the forms and stop being a baby, he wouldn't be enjoying that career today.

Fact.

Was it right for him to disappear from my life as soon as he was accepted into the army, after three years of us knowing each other?

That's optional.

Should I have been the first to know that he had actually written to Lisa and that she had accepted?

What do you think?

I was, after all, the one who had sat, night after night, listening to his tales of unrequited love and to his anguish at how the object of his desire was being mistreated by her current boyfriend, his friend.

On the other hand, there is also the argument for the fact that the real person at fault here was me. My disappointment was defined only by my own expectation, because the cold facts of the case were that we'd never discussed that Dale would keep in touch after he joined the Army.

I may have felt that it was the decent thing for him to do so, since we were supposed to be friends, and you would have thought they'd be some kind of loyalty, yet we hadn't exactly made a blood oath.

I was simply there for Dale at a time when he needed me the most, but after that he moved on.

I was hurt as much as my projection dictated I be.

Here is a very quick story for you.

There is an office worker who is always on time, does her work impeccably and gives one hundred per cent to her job and her team.

In three years, she learns the ins and outs of her industry as well as company policy and procedures. She is well respected by her managers and her peers and is a prime candidate for promotion.

Three years later, a management position becomes vacant in her office. Naturally, she believes that, because of her experience in the role and her impeccable work record, the position is pretty much hers.

Makes sense, right?

She was passed over for someone else many years her junior who had no experience with the company or indeed the role in question.

The reason for this?

The other candidate had a simple piece of paper called a degree. Our dedicated worker didn't.

Was she mad? Too right she was.

Why?

Well, that's a pretty silly question. She was mad because she wasn't given the job. In her eyes, she had all the experience because she had already been doing the job for three years. She should have been awarded that position and thus she resented her company, but most importantly her boss.

It was only when she found herself in conversation with a friend one day that her eyes were opened.

"So, when did your boss say he was going to give you the job?"

She thought about this for a few seconds. "Um, well, he didn't."

Her friend said nothing else.

As much as we may feel that our office worker was wronged on this occasion, it doesn't remove the fact that she only had herself to blame for her disappointment.

She had set herself up.

She had assumed, albeit based on her experience, that she would get the promotion—but at no point was she promised this by her boss or anybody else in the company for that matter.

The secret to avoiding disappointment is to not assume anything, regardless of what you believe you may or may not have earned, or you may or may not be entitled to, because your happiness will more than often depend on it.

What may seem right for you isn't necessarily right for me.

What you may see as fair, I may think is unfair. What is important to you may well not be as important to me.

And so on.

Ultimately, how much others disappoint and/or hurt us is often limited by our own expectation. Recognise that your expectation is precisely that—your own—and that it may not necessarily be shared by those around you.

19 SWEETS & SOUR

Germany had been a very trying time.

Kayla had missed the United States, her life back home and her family, and was very excited to be back Stateside now that Al had received orders to transfer to an Air Force base in Georgia.

Al was also happier to be back home, albeit somewhat troubled; he was about three years into his marriage to Kayla and they'd been through some pretty troubling times and Al was worried that his marriage was on shaky ground, the potential consequence of which he couldn't even bare thinking about..

He loved Kayla and adored their children, and the thought of losing them and following in his parents' footsteps terrified him. But it wouldn't turn out that way; he vowed he would never give up on his family, no matter what.

It was a Monday evening and they had just finished eating dinner. Al started to clear the dishes from the table when Kayla stopped him.

"What are you doing?"

"I'm clearing the dishes," he said.

"Why?"

Al forced an incredulous laugh. "Why do you think?"

"I don't know. You tell me, Al. Is it because you think I'm incapable? Is it your way of telling me that I'm not pulling my weight around here?"

Al sighed. "Look, Kayla, I'm not going to argue with you about this. I just thought I would help you with the dishes. But if you don't want me to, then that is fine," he said with a smile, depositing the dirty plates back on the table.

"No, I'd rather you didn't. That's my job," she said.

He held his hands up and grinned, "That's fine by me," he said, grabbing his son from his chair and carrying him off onto the couch where he proceeded to tickle the toddler until he was shrieking with laughter.

Emily didn't hesitate to join them and add her own unique shrill to the cacophony whilst Kayla eyed the aftermath at the dinner table and tried to rub away the dull ache that was forming in her temple.

The next day, Al returned from work to find that the dishes from the night before were still sitting in the sink.

He was gawping at the mess when his thoughts were interrupted, "Daddy, are you going to watch TV with me?" It was Emily and she was tugging him towards the couch.

Al looked at the encrusted dishes and then at his daughter's eager face. "Um, no, honey. Daddy needs to clear away the dishes first."

"Can I help?" the girl asked excitedly."

"Sure, I'll pass them down to you whilst you load up the dishwasher. Does that sound cool?"

"Yeah!" she squeaked.

They moved over to the sink and Al started running hot water over the dishes before handing them down to his daughter, but noticed that she was distracted by something on the side—a packet of Toffee Buttercups. He then turned to see that the little girl was looking up at her father with imploring, saucer-like brown eyes.

Al shook his head. "No, honey, you know they're Mommy's."

"Oh, Daddy, please."

"No, they're Mommy's."

"But Mommy doesn't like them because they've been there forever."

"I know, sweetheart. I'm sorry. But you know what Mommy's like about her things. Why don't you have a cookie instead?"

"Because I don't want a cookie, Daddy," she said with deep disappointment.

Her voice tugged at his heartstrings.

The candy had been left out on the counter for over a week now. But Kayla had given strict instructions that it was not be touched by anybody, especially the children. It was hers and Al knew better than to allow either of the kids to disobey her wishes. If he gave in, he knew full well what the consequences would be for Emily. They had been in this situation many times before and it simply wasn't worth the agro.

This despite the fact that it annoyed him that Kayla would leave candy about the house knowing full well that the kids would want it.

Emily was feigning interest in the open cavity of the dishwasher as if it were the mouth of a monster.

"I tell you what, boo," Al began, placing a plate in the machine and crouching down until his face was level with that of his little girl. "How about, after we've finished the dishes, we go down to the store and buy our own candy?"

Emily looked up, eyes wide with excitement once more, "Really? Really, Daddy?"

"You bet, sweetheart," he replied with a big smile.

"Oh, thank you," she said, hugging onto him.

"You're most welcome."

And so they finished the dishes and went down to the store.

Kayla was home by the time they returned.

"Hey, how are you?" Al asked, walking up to the breakfast table where Kayla was sitting.

"Hi," she replied.

"Mommy, look what Daddy bought me. Just like you," Emily interrupted as she held up a packet of Toffee Buttercups.

Kayla looked at the candy in her daughter's hand and then glared at her husband,

Al lost part of his smile. He recognised that look. "What's the matter?" he asked.

"What did I say to you? I told you I didn't want her having candy."

Al frowned, "No, you didn't. You said you didn't want her to have *your* candy. She's been asking for it, so I thought I would buy her some of her own."

"There is a reason I didn't want her to have any."

"Yeah, and what's that?"

"Don't try and be smart with me!" Kayla yelled angrily.

Emily's head lowered and Al noticed this.

"Do you really want to get into this now?"

"Yes, yes I do, Al, because I am sick of being taken for granted."

"What are you talking about?

"You know perfectly well what I am talking about!"

Al was about to reply, but stopped himself. Instead, he bent down to his daughter and said, "Emily, honey, why don't you go play in your room?"

The little girl nodded, glanced at her mother and then scuttled off.

As soon as she was out of earshot, he spoke. "What is your problem?"

"You! My problem is you, Al, because it seems to me that you care more about them than you do me."

"Now you're being ridiculous."

"Oh, am I?"

"Yes, you are. You know that isn't true."

"No! No, I don't!"

Kayla's voice was getting loud once more.

"I told you I didn't want her having candy."

Al sighed. "No, you didn't. You said you didn't want her to have *your* candy."

"I've got to tell you, Al. I can't live like this anymore. It seems that no matter what I do, you are always trying to make me out to be the villain."

Al sat down. "Kayla, nobody is the villain here; we're a family…"

"Why did you clear away the dishes?"

"What?"

"Why did you clear away the dishes? It's a perfectly reasonable question."

"I cleared them away because they were in the sink, as were the ones from the day before…"

Kayla pointed a finger his way. "No. I'll tell you exactly why you cleared away those dishes. You did that because it's your way of telling me that I'm an unfit wife, that I'm not even capable of taking care of my own home. But I've got news for you; I'm more capable than you'll ever be."

Al shook his head with exasperation.

"Don't you shake your head at me! Don't shake your head!" Kayla's voice was a manic shrill.

"I just can't believe you; I don't know where you are getting this crap from."

"It's not crap, Al. It isn't crap and you know it. It's no different to that time my parents came down and you were all watching that movie that I bought *for us* as a family and you couldn't even be bothered to wait for me. Sometimes, it's like I'm not even part of this family."

"You seriously bringing that up now? As I told you then, we wanted to wait for you. It was your parents who said it would be okay and that you wouldn't mind. Shows how much they know you. I, on the other hand, knew you would come in and pitch a fit, which you did. They, like most people, thought it wasn't that important. I'm sure that if they knew you would have come in, slammed down the six pack of coke you were carrying and stomped off to the bedroom for an argument with your dad, they would have reconsidered it!"

"You're an asshole!"

Al was going to say something, but thought better of it. His feelings were a mixture of rage and resignation. He knew that no matter what he said, good or bad, Kayla would find her own unique way of twisting it to her detriment.

And he was tired.

He simply couldn't do this anymore with her. Every day there was something.

He felt emotional. He loved her so much. Why couldn't they just get along as a family? Was all of this stuff really that important?

His eyes filled with tears.

"I can't do this anymore, Kayla."

"Do what?" she snapped.

"This." He held out his hands to her as an example. "I know you're mad at me, but I swear none of it is to hurt or make you mad. I just thought it was the right thing to do."

"Well, you thought wrong," she retorted.

He shook his head. "I've got to tell you. Unless we get this thing sorted out, I don't know how much longer I will be able to put up with it."

"What are you saying? You saying you want to divorce me now—is that it? See what I mean? All of this, all of this was just your way of leading up to an excuse to dump me."

"No," Al said angrily. "No, Kayla, it isn't that and you know it."

"All I know is that no matter what I do, in your eyes, it's never good enough for you." Her voice began to falter.

"You really think that?" he asked.

"Yes, I do."

"Then help me, Kayla. Help me make us better."

"And how do I do that?" she asked with a quivering voice.

"Let's book an appointment with a counsellor. There must be something we can do to make this work."

"We've already been to see three psychiatrists and God knows how many counsellors. None of them were any good."

"Kayla. Do you at least want to try?"

"Of course I do," she said, completely discharging any emotion from her voice and adding petulantly, "if there is anybody out there who can help you, then I'm all for it."

Al nodded.

The next day, he phoned various places in a desperate attempt to find somebody who could make sense of all of this, someone who could make sense of everything that was happening to his marriage.

Then he stopped to consider, could *he* actually be responsible for making Kayla the way she was? He didn't know, but was determined to find out.

Eventually, he did find someone who was prepared to see them. However, not unlike the other four counsellors and psychologists, the session ended somewhat abruptly when Kayla didn't agree with what the therapist was, in her mind, insinuating.

It wasn't Al's fault; it was hers.

They didn't go back.

Now, I know there's a good chance that you're wondering what on earth Al was thinking. And I have got to be honest with you; me too!

Yet, before we apply the cool logic of detachment, let's take a few seconds to look at the overall picture here.

It's always very easy to look into the drama of a relationship from the outside, without any of the emotional attachment, and form a judgement.

I don't know about you, but the first question I asked myself and Al was, "Why didn't you end it? The woman obviously had issues."

Well, yes, maybe Kayla needed help—but, in a way, so did Al.

He was still carrying the scars of the disintegration of his own parents' marriage. He knew how much it hurt him and he vowed not to put his children through the same heartache.

As human beings we feel various emotions, and one of the strongest is the parental compulsion to protect your offspring from harm. In this case, it was Al's paternal compulsion that made him want to do whatever was necessary to make his marriage work. He couldn't and wouldn't allow his children to suffer the same way he did: separate homes, weekend visitations, separate holidays and the spiteful rivalry that this can inspire.

If his marriage failed, he in turn would become a failure.

And Al couldn't deal with that.

Furthermore, despite their problems, he adored his wife. He genuinely wanted them to be together forever as a family unit but, frustratingly, something wasn't working. Something that Al could neither explain nor understand.

And Al, *the fixer,* would do anything to try and fix the situation, to stop his family from hurting. Sadly, what he didn't realise is that *fixers* are often perceived by the so-called beneficiaries (who are normally the dominant one in the partnership) as weak, and all too often they are taken advantage of.

And things only got worse.

It was Valentine's Day and the family was in Florida, visiting Al's father.

Whilst there, they discussed the fact that they owed $20,000 (approximately £12,300) to credit card debt, plus two vehicle loans and a mortgage.

Needless to say, the man who had hardly been there during Al's adolescent years was shocked yet he listened patiently to his son's predicament and even went as far as intimating that he may well help his son back to solvency, but that it wouldn't be a hand-out, nor would it be to enable them to go away and repeat the same mistakes once more.

It was with these thoughts in his mind that Al found himself at the shopping mall with the rest of the family. The excursion was more of a family day out than a shopping trip.

Or so he thought.

It was February, a few days before the 'day of love'. The mall was very busy, and this included the pet store where Al, his son and his daughter were looking at puppies, whilst directly across from them, in a jewellery store, Kayla was looking at diamond rings.

It took her minutes to select one she *really* wanted.

Shea and Emily were looking at a batch of adorable black Labrador puppies. Both of the kids' eyes were wide with excitement at the thought of taking one of them home.

"So what do you think, you two? Think if we got one of these you'd be able to take care of him?" Al asked, beaming a massive smile at them both.

"Oh, Daddy! Yes! Yes! Daddy, oh yes!" came the squeals of excitement.

"Hey! Hey!" Kayla said, rushing up to them. "Al, what are you doing? Come and see this. Come and see this with me, real quick." She grabbed hold of his arm and pulled him away from the puppy's enclosure.

"Kayla, what do you think to us getting a dog?"

"You kidding me?" she asked with a frown.

"No, I think it would be cool."

"Can we afford one of them? And who's going to take care of it?"

"I will! I will, Mummy," Emily interjected anxiously.

"Al, come and see this! Come see," Kayla said.

Al, noticing his daughter's disappointment, paused for a second and winked at her, "Don't worry, boo, we'll come back. I promise," he said, taking his daughter's hand.

Kayla led them to the jewellers where it was now her turn to be excited as she pointed out a small solitaire diamond ring.

The ring was on special offer and now available for the eye-popping offer price of just $1,000 (at least that's what the sign said).

"Isn't it beautiful?" she asked, adoringly.

Al nodded and said flatly, "It's great."

"You don't like it?" She asked sharply.

"Well, it's not that I don't like it, Kayla. It's just really expensive."

"What? You don't think I'm worth it?" Kayla asked, forcing a smile and suppressing a rise in the tone of her voice.

"No, I just don't think we can afford it," Al replied as discreetly as he could for there were other couples milling around the store.

"Really? Well it seemed to me that a few minutes ago you were perfectly happy to spend God knows how much money on a stupid dog—yet on Valentine's Day, on *our* day, you don't think you can afford to buy me a gift."

Kayla's voice was a loud whine and it had attracted the attention of the nearby shop assistant who quickly busied herself when she received a glare.

Al recognised the look. "Can we talk about this outside?"

"No, we can't!" Kayla snapped. "Why bother taking it outside when the truth is obvious for everyone to see. You don't care about me. You've never cared about me and that's why we're even having this conversation."

"Of course I care about you," Al said calmly.

"No you don't. If you cared about me you would buy me that ring," she said petulantly.

"Kayla, we have just got through talking to my dad about helping us out of debt."

"Yet it didn't stop you wanting to buy a dog!"

Now the other people in the store were taking time out of their excitement to look at the commotion whilst a tall thin man, dressed in tailored black suit, smiled at them somewhat apologetically and quietly willed the noisy couple to either part with their cash or take the argument outside.

"Fine! Well, I don't have to ask your permission, anyway. The credit cards are in my name too, you know," Kayla said, rummaging inside her bag for her wallet.

"Kayla, don't do this," Al warned.

"I have to. I have to, Al—because I know I am worth it. You obviously think money is more important than my happiness."

He took a deep breath. "Honey, please, let's…" he began, taking her arm. He wanted to take the conversation outside because he could see the potential flashpoint up ahead and he didn't want the world to witness it.

"Get your hands off me!" she shrieked, slapping away his hand and causing everybody in the store to look up and the kids to bury their faces into Al's leg, while he wished the floor would just open up and swallow him whole.

The store manager had reached the end of his rag and was about to say something when he noticed the noisy woman, who must have been drunk, take out her credit card and strut over to the counter, looking back at Al as she did so.

"That one there please," she said to the manager as she beamed one of her best grins.

The man acknowledged her instruction with his own smile that failed miserably in masking his contempt for the woman—although he soon recovered at the thought that she was about to spend nearly a thousand dollars.

It took a few minutes for the man to place the ring in a box, put it through the till and produce a credit card slip and a pen for signature, all with yet another of his best fake smiles.

Kayla took the pen and turned to Al, who could only watch on as the kids clung to him. "If you want to prove to me that you never loved me, then let me buy myself this ring for Valentine's Day," she challenged in a tense, heart-stopping one liner that would have had Hollywood executives scratching each other's eyes out to cast her.

Al paused.

He was torn between what was sensible and trying to please his wife. And now, more than ever, the pressure was on, seeing as she had so publicly thrown down the gauntlet, and it seemed to him that, albeit discreetly, the whole shop was waiting for his reaction.

He signed for it.

And so, Valentine's Day arrived three days after the mall incident, and Al presented Kayla with yet another gift, one that he had been short-changing his own bills for.

It was another ring.

Kayla was furious, and questioned his motives for not saying anything and allowing her to embarrass herself in front of a bunch of strangers. Was his sole purpose in life to humiliate her?

And so on…

Ironically, they never did buy a puppy that day which is something that was inevitably impressed on his children.

Indeed, teenage Emily would eventually go on to ask her father if he remembered that day at the mall. Clearly, Al did— but what he hadn't realised, until that conversation, was that his daughter did too.

That was the day he bought a ring for his wife, but didn't have enough money to buy a pet for her.

At least that's what she remembered.

And it made him sad.

When Al apologised, the teenager's reaction was, "No problem, Daddy. If it had been me and all the people were watching, I would have bought Mummy the ring too!"

And so, we're back to that old chestnut about the fact that we will often do or allow things to happen that may affect the people around us for the rest of their lives.

In this case, Al's children were, once again, subjected to a situation where their happiness had been clearly compromised for that of their mother. And whilst, in perspective, this particular incident wasn't that traumatic for the children, it nonetheless left an indelible mark.

So now take a few seconds.

What do you think my answer is when I'm asked if couples in a bad relationship should continue to stay together 'for the sake of the children'?

You've got it.

20 THE IMPORTANCE OF BEING SELFISH

Love may well be selfless, but in order for a relationship to thrive, *both* protagonists need to be selfish.

Yes, I know that sounds like a contradiction—but here's why: selfishness has such a terrible reputation, as it seemingly equals our disinterest in the wants and needs of others, and there's a lot of truth to that. However, there is also a lot to be said for the fact that, in order to make others happy, we must first learn to please ourselves.

I once saw an advertisement that demonstrates this point beautifully.

The ad, for a tourism company, was glossy, colourful and depicted a typical family of four. They are all human but for one, Daddy; he's actually not human—he's an ogre!

However, with each day, each fun-packed, relaxing activity, Daddy transforms from an evil, ugly ogre to a human being once more.

The stresses and strains of life, as we know it, turn us into different people, since we often find ourselves having to 'perform' not out of choice, but out of necessity and/or obligation: work, chores, family visits and generally keeping up appearances. We all do it because it's life, but what we don't realise is that, like the proverbial frog in the pan of boiling water, each and every one of these things is slowly but surely taking its toll, turning us into a completely different creature until we're cooked!

I, like millions of others, am a completely different person when dealing with the demands of a very busy career than I am wiling away the hours on a sandy beach with my feet in the sand. Some, I'm sure would go as far as saying that I'm much easier to be around (although I couldn't possibly imagine who).

We all know that life isn't a permanent vacation (at least not for most of us), and that's why it's even more important to fit in, the best way we can, the things that make us happy. And by *us*, I mean *you*—not your partner, not your children, not your family and not your friends, but you.

I was reading an article about this very thing the other day.

In the article, the author (a psychologist) talks about how, when embarking on a relationship with his wife, he brought to it one of the fundamental beliefs instilled in him by his parents and their parents before them: family comes first.

He, like most people, wanted to do right by his wife and his children and so he always put them first.

However, it was his wife who explained to him that he was mistaken; to do right by them, he would have to put himself and not them first.

Yes, I was surprised too!

Not necessarily by the concept, but more by the fact that somebody else was writing about the very same theory as my own, and that this theory came from the other side not only of the world, but of the relationship; it came from his wife.

But how could this be?

In order to be righteous, surely one must put others before oneself? No?

Well, again, all good things in good measure.

The man's wife explained that the quality of her husband's life was no less important than that of the rest of his family's lives. And that if he didn't take care of business in his own personal life, one way or another, then he would inevitably burden others with his stress and his concerns.

"I don't want a husband—and the children wouldn't want a father—who feels unhappy or burdened… the greatest gift you can give us is your own happiness," she said.

How about that?

He then went on to explain that he had to hear that speech a few hundred times before he actually understood what his wife meant: a husband who felt happy and fulfilled in himself was a better husband and father. It is his responsibility, and not that of his wife or anybody else, to ensure that his needs are met and that he experiences fulfilment in his life.

I couldn't have put it better myself.

It is true that many go into a relationship with the intention of getting something out—companionship usually, although it could be argued that many go in seeking sex, and a relationship just happens to be a by-product of that. But that's way too cynical a statement to make.

Oh, well, I guess it's out there now.

You can only be the best that you can be for others when you feel content with yourself. Do the things that please you by nurturing relationships with people of similar interests; for example, if you love football, but your partner doesn't, then make a point of enjoying football with a friend who does. If you enjoy spa days, but your partner doesn't, then it's crucial that you make time to enjoy these activities without your partner as it gives you the opportunity for your own introspection and/or to share, discuss and explore other topics with friends.

There's no doubt that it is in your significant other's interest to encourage individual pursuits not only for the fact that they please you, but also because you are satisfying urges, working out frustrations that enable you to successfully process everyday occurrences, which in turn enables you to reach an equilibrium that truly completes you.

That's right—because, contrary to popular belief, it isn't the physicality of our partner that completes us but their commitment to protecting, preserving and nurturing who we are, because that's who they fell in love with in the first place, right?

Now, it would be easy to mistake this for the usual psychobabble since it is something much easier said than done, as it violates basic social protocols: being selfish is wrong; being selfless is right. This is what has been programmed into us for centuries.

Yet the flight attendant will tell you to, *"Ensure your own mask is securely fastened before helping others with theirs."*

Why do you think that is?

During the many years I've spent taking a keen interest in

human behaviour and researching relationships for this book, I've come to learn that the happiest people are those who are happiest in themselves and with themselves.

Yes, I know this too sounds like a cliché, but the sad thing is it has become such not through practice but through rhetoric. It seems that many people talk about and applaud those who seek out and demand self-happiness, but only if it's a Facebook poster or bumper sticker. Many are actually afraid of pursuing self-satisfaction for fear of being branded 'selfish'.

Being selfish when it comes to fulfilling our needs is just as important as respecting the needs of our partner, providing it isn't to their detriment. And taking time out for yourself isn't at all to their detriment, although it does seem that way to some (oh, okay, many that I've encountered): socialising, going out with friends and/or family without your partner is almost sacrilegious.

Many take the fact that their partner does not choose to spend every minute of their free social time with them as some kind of insult.

For me, the real concern here is not the fact that one element of the partnership actually chooses to spend quality time with their friends and/or family, but more the fact that one element of this partnership does *not*.

To me, unless this person has spent most of their life living in a jungle, being raised by wolves, there's something very unhealthy about the fact that they are either unable to spend time alone and/or with people who do not happen to be their partners, such as friends.

In the UK, one of the most common sentences I've heard time and time again from brow-beaten men on the possibility of a night out without their friends is, "I'll have to check with the missus to see if she'll let me out."

Seriously? Since when did choosing to be in a relationship become an automatic prison sentence?

"Well, it just avoids all the hassle, doesn't it?"

But what is this so-called *hassle* these men are talking about? (And, yes, I'm sorry to say it, girls, but the general data says that men—younger to middle age—more than women tend to be involuntary prisoners in these scenarios. That's not to say that it doesn't happen to you girls, too, but it tends to be more of an infantile case of tit-for-tat rather than a control thing. (As you're about to discover further down the page.)

What's up with that, girls?

Why is it that you don't like 'letting' your men out for an evening down the pub, a long weekend away with their friends, or to go on holidays without you? Is it because you're afraid that they might discover that they can actually have fun without you?

You do realise they knew how to do that before they met you, right? It was just a different kind of fun. After all, your man knows there's no fun like the fun he has with you, right?

The 'hassle' that these imprisoned men are terrified of tends to be a lengthy argument about why they should stay at home with their partner rather than be out with their friends. And should they actually pluck up the audacity, as well as the balls, to go out regardless, they can, at best, expect a Siberian cold shoulder for the next week, or worse: sustained exposure to after-shock style acid bombs at every opportunity about something totally unrelated.

Yes, come on girls, you know you do that so well.

And for men, it simply 'isn't worth the hassle'.

I have to say that I have lost count of the amount of men (yes, it's men again) who have shared the fact that they'd like to do something, but that their partners/wives 'won't let them'.

Won't let them?

Did I write *men* above? I think I meant boys.

The other day I found myself on a fishing boat on the North Sea (as you do). I struck up a conversation with my sixty-five-year-old skipper by asking him about his past. He was very candid and told me about how, in his youth, he used to be a rally car driver for fun, and how he trained as a car engineer before that. He also shared that the very boat we were floating on was made by his bare hands.

I was naturally very impressed and told him so. He thanked me and then went on to share his next ambition: to go deep-sea fishing for a week in Florida. Apparently, this had been his dream for several years, but one he hadn't yet managed to realise.

When I asked the skipper why, he told me, "The missus won't let me."

"What do you mean she won't let you? Is it dangerous or something?"

"No, it's just fishing like we are now."

"Then why won't she let you?"

"She doesn't want me going."

"Did you ask her if she'd like to go also?"

"Oh, yes, but it's not her kind of thing."

"Then why doesn't she want you to go?"

"I don't know."

"What does she think is going to happen?"

"I don't think she thinks anything is going to happen; she just doesn't want me leaving for a week."

Seriously?

This man is sixty five years of age; he, with all due respect, isn't a teenager, you know, likely to get into some kind of trouble—which I assume is the only reasonable explanation for why somebody would be so arrogant as to think they have the right to oppress their partner in this way.

Obviously, we don't know all the facts in this case, but I have to say that the skipper's story is not alien to me; it's one I have heard time and time again, both whilst researching this book and in my own personal life with my own friends.

Giving your body to and choosing to spend the rest of your life with somebody else is precisely that: it's a choice, not a sentence.

Another story I know involves a wife wanting a child, and a husband refusing her until he needed to go on a golfing tournament on his own. Again, the wife didn't want him to go, but they agreed that he would let her have a baby if he could go to the tournament.

She allowed it.

Good Lord!

Whilst I still haven't managed to get to the bottom of why some people feel the need to control their partners, the roots of this particular compulsion appear to be entrenched somewhere in-between possession, domestic and/or parental duties.

I once asked a man why he loved his wife; he told me it was

because she belonged to him. And whilst that may sound somewhat controversial in principle, it actually isn't. There are many singletons and songs out there that talk of *'someone to call my own'*. It wouldn't be such a leap for partners to consider their 'other half' (I dislike that expression) their possession, like something they'd won at auction on the eBay of relationships.

"My partner could have gone to so many other people, but I managed to outbid them all and therefore he or she is mine. And now I no longer feel that I am missing a piece of the puzzle because he or she 'completes it'."

Here comes the technical bit: it is a basic rule of life that, as animals, we're biologically programmed to seek out a mate, the other ingredient in our lifelong mission to perpetuate the species. In this case, a man needs to possess his female partner's womb so that she may conceive his child and not that of another man.

And whilst a woman is prepared to surrender her life-spawning vessel, she requires one fundamental thing in return: total commitment to her and no other. And in theory, this should be the case: man, having conquered a womb and thus the ability to conceive his offspring should, in theory, become disinterested in another.

Yet you and I both know that it doesn't always work out that way, don't we?

The very thing that led the man to seek this woman in the first place is still present and active and thus a constant and present danger.

Another theory, at least for couples with children, is that the female of the species has naturally been responsible for 'nesting', and subsequently the nursing and welfare of her offspring. Now, in the wild, this would be a relatively straightforward process, but in civilised society it's a whole different story.

As gender equality has gathered momentum throughout the decades, the role of women has undergone a massive shift; the majority may have joined their male counterparts in the workplace, but they naturally tended to retain their roles as mothers and nest-makers too. Now, these life warriors are doing it all: earning a living, running a home, giving birth to and raising the family brood.

(Stay-at-home mums look away now).

The net effect is that her day is one perpetual cycle of chores: career, home, children (not necessarily in that order), whilst the man's role is mainly that of the hunter-gatherer family provider.

Well, he was doing that anyway.

So, whilst women will now put in a full day's work, just like their male counterparts, they also have to come home and worry about homecare as well as that of their children.

Men, generally, just worry about what's for dinner.

At least, that used to be the stereotype, and may well still be true in some households.

However, what I've personally witnessed multiple times is a massive shift here too, with brow-beaten males often returning home to perform house chores even in cases where their female counterpart has been at home all day but 'busy'.

This tends to be particularly prevalent in younger couples.

That said, if you are female and have been at work all day then come home, find the house in disarray, the kids hyperactive and a husband/boyfriend who tells you he's going out for the evening without you, you're going to be somewhat miffed, as you would be if you'd been stuck at home all day charged with the perpetual care of a newborn and in desperate need of some support.

Cue: *"Let me check with the other half (there's that hideous saying again) to see if I'm allowed out"*.

Of course, the above is a just a theory.

However, the issue of whether or not women will 'let their men out' and the subsequent somewhat popular tit-for-tat behaviour is well and truly alive today.

I have witnessed it many times, be that because one partner had decided to go out without the other or sometimes even when the two have been out together.

The latter often starts with something fairly innocuous; one partner wanting to stay out for a few more drinks whilst the other wants to go home.

The general expectation is that if one partner goes, then the other must too.

However, that isn't always the case, and when it isn't, rather than just kissing and saying, "Okay, see you when you get home", the anti-party animal sees this as a slight, an act of disrespect: "What could possibly be more interesting than me?", but says nothing. They simply trudge home knowing full well that they'll deal with it later.

Thus the cold war (and the sulking) begins.

The sulking follows into the next day and maybe even the day after. Eventually, if not before, these sulks turn into full-blown arguments and a lot of agro and discontent.

Now, as annoying as it may be to hear, girls do have more of a reputation for being somewhat adept at this type of behaviour. Nobody masters the art of cold war as well you girls, and there are a multitude of reasons for this that I don't have to explain. But boys are powerless in the face of them, so they'll do absolutely anything to avoid them, including telling the odd 'white' lie.

Sometimes, they even fight back.

This is when you get the case of tit-for-tat. "If I wasn't 'allowed' to stay out with friends on that occasion, then why should you?", or "If you can go out with your friends without me then I'm going out with mine."

Then it becomes a basic rule of fairness.

The result, however, is that neither party does (or is allowed to do) anything without the other.

And some are more than happy with this arrangement, the result of which is often; friend alienation.

Really?

Whatever happened to love, trust, honour, and respect?

There isn't much love in treating your partner as a possession. Nor is there trust in trying to keep the person that chose to live with you on a leash. And there certainly isn't any honour or respect in becoming their life warden.

So, at this stage I'm almost feeling as if I should apologise to partners of young couples; you guys have been receiving a particularly tough time in these chapters. But there is good news: you *can* break the cycle!

I'm not saying it's going to be easy because once you get into a syndrome with something—a habitual way of behaving or speaking to each other—it's really difficult to break the cycle. But if you really want a healthy relationship, it's quite crucial that you do.

Look to your own individual requirements, those activities that you enjoy, the things that please and make you happy, and seek to fulfil them, but be sure to extend and encourage your partner to do the same.

Then, arrange for regular quality time with each other.

Trust me, you'll be amazed with the result.

Remember Sting once sang: *"If you love somebody, set them free."*

21 THE HASSLE

So, something I already touched on in previous chapters is something that I've personally been exposed to multiple times. By *exposed* I mean I have met people, generally men, some of them friends of mine, lamenting about the very same thing: *The Hassle.*

If you're a regular reader of my blog, you'll know that I often host dinner parties for my friends and family, each of which has its own theme and is meticulously planned and executed like a theatre production by yours truly.

Over the period of a couple of years, and especially before each event, my electrician would visit to carry out new installations, fixes and routine maintenance.

He's a really friendly man, in his early forties, married with children, and we'd always enjoy a good chat.

Given the fact that most of his visits would take place on the lead-up to an event, he'd always ask about the latest theme and about what I might have in store for my guests.

Each time, I'd explain and extend him an invitation, adding my belief that he'd fit in well with the fifteen or so other guests.

Each time he'd decline.

Now, I should point out here that the invites went to him personally and nobody else. There are rarely any 'plus ones' with our invites and that's because the event tends to be very popular and, with each and every one tailored to each guest, there are always limited spaces.

Anyway, the ritual of invite and decline continued for two or three events until, suddenly, one day, he accepted!

I was naturally delighted as I knew he'd fit in well— although, considering his reluctance to attend other events, I was somewhat apprehensive that he may not turn up on the night (this particular event being a murder mystery in which he had been assigned a fairly important character).

However, my fears were misplaced since, come show night, he showed up with the rest of the guests—and, as suspected, a fantastic time was had by all.

So?

Well, as is customary at all of our events, official photos were taken and published to the Facebook page the next day, and, as was customary at the time, each guest was tagged in each one of their photos.

So, now you know exactly where I'm going with this, right?

He didn't comment on any of the photos—which, for reference, didn't depict much other than him posing (*à la* red carpet) with other guests.

That was it.

We didn't hear much from him until…

…a week or so later, one rainy evening in early May.

There was a knock on the door and when I opened it, who do you think was standing there in the pouring rain?

You've guessed it, our friendly electrician.

So, I ushered him inside, expressed how happy I was to see him and wasted no time asking if he'd actually had a good time. I added that I was worried, since I hadn't heard anything and wondered if he had actually enjoyed himself.

He told me that he had, and went further by presenting me with a thank-you card and a gift. He'd even taken the time to pick up a birthday card for my sister (her birthday was in a few days).

So, I asked if he liked the photos from the party as he hadn't interacted with them. He explained that he couldn't say much on social media because his wife and other people he knew would be watching everything he said.

I was naturally confused, and that's when he explained everything.

Apparently, as soon as his wife learned that I had not included her in my invite, she launched a campaign of doubt that questioned my motives.

Motives?

"Don't you think it's odd that he's inviting just you?"

Well, him and fourteen other men and women.

Apparently, they even discussed the situation with their circle of friends, each time questioning why the invite had not been extended to both of them.

Really?

I was naturally unaware that this was taking place in the months and weeks leading up to the event, but it was something that he had had to deal with each time the subject of him attending the dinner party was raised.

I can only assume his wife felt shunned—but the reality is that, in light of the fact there is often a waiting list for these events, if I invited couples from each household, many would have to wait over a year to get the chance to attend!

It simply isn't practical.

Furthermore, to be perfectly frank, I had become acquainted with him and felt comfortable introducing him to a dinner table full of my friends.

I'd never met his wife.

I explained this to him and questioned why he believed she felt the way she did.

He said he didn't know, although I had an idea.

I had overheard a couple of her phone calls to him whilst he was working for me. Both times she sounded irate and both times she was asking (or demanding) when he would be home.

Now, I should stress that I've never met this lady, but if I were to hazard a guess, I would say that I've probably met 'the type'.

Here's why:

I believe that she is a controlling person. How do I know

that? Well, the frequency of calls made to him whilst he was working at my home. She'd regularly check in with him.

Not enough.

How about the fact that her tone was angry, insistent, borderline petulant about the fact that his not being at home is an inconvenience to her?

No?

How about the fact that in conversations with him, he'd shared that there were things in his life that he'd like to do, but 'couldn't'.

Still not convinced?

How about her overreaction to the fact that her husband had received an invite, but she had not?

Or the fact that he was unable to comment on any of the images of himself from the party for fear of reprisal. It's not that he didn't want to; he was not 'allowed to'.

I believe he was unable to because there were other women at that party and he knew his wife would be very upset if he made any comment about these ladies, the majority of whom, including my own sister, had spouses.

Still all hearsay.

How about this?

I asked him if his wife knew where he was that rainy night. He told me that she did not. When I questioned why he hadn't told her, he told me that it was just easier that way. When I asked him where she believed he was, he told me that he'd said he was going out to assess and estimate a job in a nearby town and that she could expect him home in a couple of hours.

Why was she expecting him home in a couple of hours?

Well, she knew the time it would take him to get to his destination and back with a factor of time to actually talk to the prospect and give them an estimate.

Now, you tell me, does that sound like normal behaviour?

This man had to lie to his wife so that he could come out visit me and say thank you for being invited to a dinner party. Furthermore, he had to furtively stop off by a store, purchase thank-you cards and a bottle of drink, write the cards in his car and then come over.

Really?

We're talking a thirty-something-year-old man.

Now, you might think that I was surprised, if not shocked, by the revelation—but I wasn't. I have seen this type of behaviour, worse in fact, in other relationships. I have heard of instances where a girl has literally flung herself onto a bonnet of a car to stop her boyfriend from leaving, and another where she locked them both inside the house and hid the key so that her boyfriend couldn't leave.

This was not a random stranger, but one of my good friends who called me in a stupor once he had managed to 'escape'!

Seriously?

I should stress my total and utter belief that there are always two sides to every story, and most of the stories you will read in this book don't have the benefit of perspective from the angle of both parties. However, what we do know is the symptomatic behaviour of the protagonists in each and every story, including this one.

I told the electrician that I was deeply sorry for any inconvenience I was causing him and I contemplated saying that, had I known, I would have tried to extend an invite to his wife. But then I stopped short of making that statement since I don't believe this type of behaviour should be indulged and/or rewarded.

To me, rewarding this type of behaviour is tantamount to rewarding a child for throwing a fit in a supermarket.

Remember that favourite story?

The more you reward that child, the more they'll keep repeating that behaviour every time they are out with you. It's simply because they believe it is acceptable.

It is not acceptable to treat your partner like your possession or your prisoner.

Now, it would be easy to read this story and see 'the wife' as the evil villain here. The evil queen bitch who is jealous and controlling of her husband, someone who doesn't allow him to live his life or be the person that he could be.

What do you think? Do you think she's the evil protagonist here?

The reality is, like that aforementioned child, it isn't necessarily her fault.

From day one, this woman has clearly been indulged; she's been led to believe that this type of controlling behaviour is acceptable, and is only comporting herself in that vein because she can.

It's natural human behaviour for the dominant to dominate the weak.

Here, my electrician has enabled his wife by the very thing he did that night. Rather than 'growing a pair' and telling her where he was going, he opted for an 'easier life' without 'the hassle' and chose to lie rather than be true and say, "Babe, I'm going round there to drop off a thank-you card."

Yes, I know what you're thinking, especially if you're living this kind of relationship: *that's way easier said than done.* The moment he confessed to his intentions, war may well have broken out; since this woman didn't want him coming to the party in the first place, she's certainly not going to endorse his going out of his way to return and shower his hosts (my sister and I) with gifts.

Tough.

She'll get over it.

"I love you, but this is the right and proper thing to do and, yes, it means I'm going to start another cold war and some arguments, and I am really going to hate that because life is unbearable in those circumstances. On the other hand, you need to understand that I should be able to do what I believe is right without you beasting me about it. You also need to understand that, whilst I am totally devoted to you and committed to our relationship, this does not give you the right, nor do I feel it's acceptable, that you treat me with such disrespect. I am not a slave or a possession; I am the man who loves you. I am your husband."

In this case, like many men, the electrician chose to avoid 'the hassle' because it 'makes life easier.'

I told him how sad I was that things had turned out this way. I shared my belief that he and I could have been good friends, but that I naturally didn't want to cause him any more hassle.

And just in case you're wondering why I didn't extend some kind of olive branch to his wife (despite what I said earlier about indulging this behaviour), you should know that I did.

When I subsequently held a major launch party for a business of mine, an event where partners were more than welcome (because there was plenty of room), with all expenses paid, including overnight accommodation, I extended an invitation to both of them—yet, despite his attempts, she refused to attend.

I haven't seen him since.

By now you'll have noticed a somewhat common theme throughout this book, including the part where I say that, over the years, I've discovered that the happiest relationships appear to be those where each partner has retained their own independence, their own identity; financially and socially—couples who do things for each other *and* themselves.

These relationships appear free from angst and drama and have an abundance of trust and mutual respect.

Whilst writing this page, I know of two couples who recently made the decision to accept jobs located hundreds, and in one of the cases, thousands of miles from each other for a period of years.

Now, I can't say that this is necessarily something I would recommend since, ultimately, relationships need regular interaction. However, the fact that both respective partners are supporting the other's career for the ultimate benefit of them both is nonetheless impressive.

There's no doubt that both of these couples are in for some challenging times ahead, but that's what life is all about.

After all, long-distance relationships may well be tough but they *are* possible.

I would know.

22 RALEIGH

In January 2003, M, who was stationed at a base in Georgia at the time, had orders to his now least favourite place, Camp Lejeune, on a Sergeant's training course that would see him marooned there for more than a month, which included his birthday.

I remember talking to him and hearing just how miserable he sounded at the prospect of 'doing time' there.

"It's not that bad, is it?"

"No, it's worse," he said. "You've never been to this place; it's like being confined to hell."

"So I take it you won't have any plans for your birthday then," I laughed.

"Not funny," he said miserably.

I didn't say anything to him at the time, although the idea had crossed my mind, but I decided that I would buy a ticket and go visit with M just for the weekend.

Was it extravagant?

Yes.

Did I have loads of money to throw around at the time?

Of course not, but I had a credit card.

Was it worth every penny?

Of course it was; love knows no value.

I booked the ticket and flew out of London Heathrow the next day, Friday 10th January, late morning, which put me in Raleigh, North Carolina early evening the same day.

It was the day before the Sergeant's (my new pet name for him) birthday.

Like most marines, he had physical fitness nearly every day, and that Friday was no exception; they were kept out in 'the yard' in the freezing cold (yes, well, marines are tough) for longer than he hoped so he was unable to come and get me from the airport. But that wasn't a problem; I kind of liked the idea of getting to the hotel before him, settling in and waiting for the knock at the door before seeing his smiling face.

And that's exactly what I did.

Needless to say, the novelty factor soon wore off as we exchanged text messages once he'd managed to leave the base, but was slowed by icy roads out of Jacksonville. The weather wasn't terrible, but there was some snow on the ground and that snow had frozen over.

I must have waited in that hotel room for over five hours. I was starving, but I refused to eat without him.

Finally, there was a knock at the door. I rushed over to open it and revealed his weary, but smiley face. He seemed so genuinely excited to see me, which in turn accentuated my excitement.

Now, if I was a girl, I probably would have jumped into his arms and kissed him passionately but, as you will have gathered by now, I wasn't the lightest of things; it would have been the equivalent of a pony jumping up at him.

Not a good look.

Instead, I pulled him into the room and reminded him just how much I'd missed him.

So, Raleigh wasn't exactly a major tourist attraction.

The hotel I booked was functional, but not necessarily in the centre of a natural wilderness of any kind, but that didn't matter. There was only one purpose to my visit and it was for us to spend time together.

We went out for breakfast the next day, shopped and then spent the rest of the afternoon in our hotel room.

I remember him remarking on the fact that I had brought the sun with me. Unusual really, given the fact that I'm English and we're not known for being a sunshine nation—yet, sure enough, I remember the sun blazing through that hotel window that afternoon. It was shimmering off of the glass coffee table and dazzling the whole room with light and colour.

We sat on the couch, cuddling and just being with each other, and it felt so good. But things got even better when he asked me to close my eyes.

"Why?"

"Just do it."

"No."

"Don't you trust me? You trust me, right?" he asked.

I nodded.

He shrugged as if to say, "So? What's the problem?"

Reluctantly, and very warily, I closed my eyes.

"Open your mouth," he said.

"Seriously? M…"

"…Trust me. Open your mouth."

"If you do anything rotten to me, I promise I'll make you suffer!" I warned whilst reluctantly complying.

Then I heard some rustling. It seemed to go on forever and I was really starting to get nervous. Suddenly, I felt his warm hand on my cheek, then his fingers (they were rough enough to be working man's hands, but soft enough to make me nuzzle against them like a cat).

Then I felt his lips brush my right ear. The act made my whole body tingle, then there was the sound of his breath, and then he spoke, or more specifically, he whispered, "What's the flavour?"

"What are you…"

But my words were cut short as he placed two Jelly Belly jelly beans in my mouth.

My favourite.

I grinned as the inimitable flavours exploded on my tongue.

Eyes still shut tightly, I turned to him and found the red warmth of the sun behind my eyelids, then the softness of his skin and the power of his muscular forearms. I stroked my cheek against him as taste buds tingled with what seemed like coconut and strawberry sensation.

I shouted out my guess, but was wrong.

"No!" I laughed. "Again! Let's me try again!"

So, that's pretty much how we wiled away four whole hours that afternoon.

That and other activities that blindfold feeding will eventually elicit.

I'll spare you the details, but I will say it was beautiful, sustained and intense as we both basked in the golden rays of the now setting sun.

That night, we went out for a celebratory birthday dinner. We were both well aware that the stopwatch was ticking, but neither of us was interested in indulging the sadistic practices of time.

Sunday was a completely different day. It was grey, almost as if the weather knew that I'd be catching my plane home that afternoon, and I so hate afternoon flights as it always feels like an interminable wait for the impending doom, trapped in between enjoying the morning or feeling miserable about the inevitable.

That feeling wasn't helped by the fact that somehow, over breakfast, we started talking about the future and the potential next trip. Well, I think he raised the subject, but I felt somewhat reluctant to talk about it right then, opting instead to enjoy our last morning together.

The truth was I had no idea when our next meet would be, nor any clue about our future. M would be leaving the marines that year and neither of us had a clear understanding of what that actually meant. It was a subject matter that, rather surprisingly, we'd been avoiding.

I guess neither of us wanted to confront what we were both probably thinking: that perhaps our whole relationship wasn't anything more than just a long summer love, one that happened to last six years—or, more specifically, the time of M's Marine Corps contract.

I didn't know if it was this subject, which often surfaced at the end of our time together, or the fact that M would be returning to Camp Lejeune that made him appear particularly grim this time round. He was normally the stronger one when it came to saying our goodbyes.

"Are you okay?" I found myself asking him a couple of times that morning.

"I'm good," he'd reply with one of his sleepy, sad smiles.

"I love you," I said.

"Are you sure?" He asked.

"I'm sure," I said.

We were at the security gate now.

I hugged him tightly as I sensed something was off. Sure, it was sad; it had never been any different. If anything, it'd been worse, but this time, well, this time seemed particularly depressing. But I concluded that was probably due to the fact that the whole trip, the build-up and all of the anticipation was over in what seemed like hours.

Add to that the fact that the Sergeant was going back to Camp Lejeune; the place he had come to hate.

A somewhat mythical place to me. One that I had not managed to visit throughout our whole time together and hoped I never would, given M's description of it.

When emerged from the hug, I held my hands on the muscle of his arms and looked into his big sad hazel eyes. "It'll be okay," I offered. "You've survived that place for years. A few more weeks will mean nothing. They'll soon fly by."

He nodded with a faint smile.

I grabbed my bag and turned to leave, but had only progressed a few paces when he called, "Hey!"

I turned around.

He simply nodded and smiled once more. Code I interpreted as "I love you, but you know I can't say that in public places."

It was my turn to nod with a faint smile.

I handed my boarding card and passport to the security officer and was soon on my way home, totally unaware of the fact that M's sadness had nothing to do with my departure or Camp Lejeune and everything to do with something entirely different.

23 GAME OVER

A few pages back, I asked you what you would have done in Megan's place—could you let your partner go on a world tour for six months without you?

So, what did you decide?

Ethan decided that enough was enough. Megan's stunt at the bar and in front of his friend was the proverbial straw that broke the camel's back.

She moved out of the apartment.

Megan had gone too far. Her 'game' had backfired. She may have got the reaction that she wanted, but she drove yet another wedge between her and the man she loved and, try as she may, she was unable to fix this.

And this is the particularly interesting part. It would be easy to think that it was because of Megan's somewhat unpredictable behaviour that Ethan decided to call time on their relationship—but what if that wasn't the only reason? What if there was another driver for both of them?

Indulge me if you will.

We know the argument about the controversial trip had raged on for months without either party being able to reach an accord.

We also know that, after Megan moved out, she didn't lose contact with Ethan—on the contrary she'd actually visit the apartment daily.

Why?

Well, apparently Ethan wasn't very good at taking care of their pet cat.

Really?

Indeed. When I asked Ethan about this, he told me that it was true; he wasn't very good at taking care of pets.

Hang on a minute, but aren't these two supposed to be separated?

Well, yes, they were, at least physically.

It seems to me that the pet is just another game: Megan's to stay in Ethan's life, and his to keep her in there.

What do you think?

I think that there's a distinct possibility that these two people actually want to stay together, but just don't know how to, at least not officially. Similarly, neither was capable of reaching an agreement on Ethan's trip, so the easiest thing to do was downgrade their status as a couple.

By downgrading their status as an item, Ethan was able to go on his trip and Megan was able to accept his decision because he no longer had the obligation, and she the expectation, that he would put her first.

Both were better able to deal with the conundrum before them.

Convoluted?

Without a doubt.

But this is exactly what happened. Ethan continued studying for his degree and she kept visiting the apartment.

At least that's the stage they'd reached when I interviewed

Ethan.

In fact, the two of us spent quite a bit of time together as I researched this book. Time during which I learned much about this lovable rogue, including the fact that some stereotypes are true.

There's one more chapter to Ethan's own story later in this book, and it will detail why our acquaintance came to an abrupt and final end.

24 THINGS WE LOSE IN THE FIRE

Why it is that one bad thing can destroy the effect of a thousand good ones? And how many good things need to happen before we forget the one bad thing?"

Why is it that bad odours seem to linger and beautiful scents evaporate so quickly? Why is it that good news has an expiration date yet those troubling thoughts, the painful ones, they tend to linger on the periphery of our minds like heavy rain clouds waiting to unleash their load the second we attempt to smile?

One of my friends asked me that.

And I wondered...

I want to go have some fun... I lost my lover... I want to go out and enjoy life... I lost my job... I want to spend some quality time with my family... but somebody precious to me is no longer here... I want to stop feeling sad... I lost my home...

The things we lose in the fire of life stay with us like smouldering embers, ever ready to burn our consciousness as soon we seek change, serenity or happiness, and the only cure appears to be time; time for the burning scent of sadness to fade and make way for rebirth, renewal, and hopeful serenity.

So, with so much natural heartache in life, does it seem at all conceivable that humans would actually chase conflict, angst and drama as a child would an ice cream van? Well, as incredible as it may seem, the answer is "yes".

There's no doubt that we're attracted to danger: we jump out of aeroplanes, off buildings, off cliffs; we plunge down ravines and swim with sharks. And when we're not busy doing that, millions of us around the world (including yours truly) flock to theme parks, seeking thrills and chills on the biggest, fastest and scariest roller coaster rides—and, yes, whilst this adrenaline-seeking practice tends to wane with age, many of us remain addicted to the 'drama', be that in real life or on TV. This is one of the very reasons soap operas have remained a TV staple for decades.

In fact, you can bet your last penny that if all was good and 'fluffy' on a regular basis, TV's best-loved soaps would soon see ratings plummet—hence the paradoxical success of 'trashy' talk shows such as *Jeremy Kyle* and *Jerry Springer*—oh, and *Big Brother*. (That and the common trait that many of us have, which is to 'look down' on these poor wretches and in turn make ourselves feel superior.)

Yet, despite the negative connotations of these voyeuristic, low-budget shows, they remain consistently popular. And what does each and every one have?

Drama.

What's up with that?

Well, to give you an example, I'm going to need to call on the help of American writer Kurt Vonnegut, and entrepreneur Derek Sivers.

Why would I need the help of an entrepreneur? Well, because Derek very kindly translated Vonnegut's theory with some really useful graphs that I came across while researching this book.

I've recreated a simple version below.

Vonnegut's theory is that humans need drama in their lives because, from our infancy, we've been exposed to a myriad of fables, many of which we've experienced in multiple variations, yet are more than happy to revisit.

It's believed that it's these stories that we all often strive to emulate in our own lives.

So, here comes the science bit.

Make yourself comfortable, free your mind and take a look at the following graph.

Ready?

As you will see, the graph moves from top to bottom, from ecstasy to misery. Then from left to right, indicating the passage of time; from present to future.

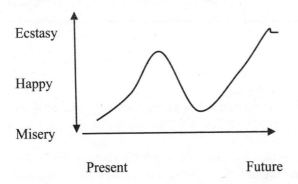

Present   Future

Now, let's add that well-known story of Cinderella to the above and you'll find that it starts steeped in MISERY. Then, over time, as we follow our heroine's story, it moves up the scale towards HAPPY, as Cinderella gets invited to the ball, and then ECSTASY as she attends—only to then plummet back towards MISERY when she has to leave. Then, eventually, Cinderella finds her prince again and the story moves back up the graph, past HAPPY to ECSTASY once more as they both go on to live ecstatically ever after.

Generations of us have watched, loved, relived and re-experienced this type of story in various guises over the years.

Now, let's try that same experiment again.

This time, take a look at the graph, but imagine it with a more sociological example based in a small town and on an ordinary day until disaster strikes: a little girl falls down a well and the town has to rally together to save her.

On the graph, ordinary life would start somewhere on, if not below, HAPPY. It would then plummet into misery as the little girl falls down the well, but then as she is rescued, the graph would climb once more towards HAPPY and then into ECSTASY as she is saved. It would then hover there until the novelty factor has dissipated before descending back to on or below HAPPY.

233

In fact, it might even linger longer on or above HAPPY due to the common cause, where everybody rallied together towards a positive outcome.

These are the real-life documentary stories that we love to read about and watch on TV.

Now, I'd like you to take a look at the chart one more time. Only this time, imagine REAL LIFE on it—just everyday life. Where would you put it on your chart?

Think about it for a second.

So where is it? Down near MISERY or just below HAPPY? Or is your life so exciting that you've actually placed it in ECSTASY?

If so, lucky you!

Generally, normal everyday life just drifts along like a faulty heart monitor around the HAPPY area, very occasionally straying into ECSTASY, which becomes the proverbial 'no man's land', whilst MISERY, subject to your kind of disposition, may well get frequent visits.

There are a few ups and a few downs in real life but nowhere near as exciting as the endless extraordinary life stories we've been hearing and continue to hear about on a daily basis. This is the very reason we crave these stories, we crave drama, and we'll even pay good money to watch these over and over again.

However, the eventual realisation that these stories are in fact intangible means that we tend to generate our own real-life drama, often to our own detriment.

But why would human beings be so self-destructive?

Quite simply, we're attracted to danger, real or perceived, and there's a strong belief among psychologists and writers that humans appear to be much happier and fulfilled during wartime than during times of peace and prosperity.

Really?

I can appreciate this concept may well connect with those of us lucky enough not to have lived through wartime, since we have no perspective against which to bounce our fortuitous existence. However, you don't have to look far in the world to appreciate the fact that, quite frankly, the citizens of some countries just seem to be much happier killing each other.

Ever since humans walked the earth, we've been exposed to persistent danger, forced to endure incredible odds in order to survive. This natural primeval instinct has been handed down for generations and remains with us even today. Although the odds of survival may have changed somewhat, the instinct remains ingrained in our genes and is very closely related to the *fight or flight, kill or be killed* theories.

In his book, *The Psychology of War*, Lawrence LeShan states that the more we accumulate wealth, eliminate dangers, and industrialise our world, the more 'miserable' humans tend to be. He goes on to say that humans and ants are the only species that 'do' organised violence (although chimpanzees have also been known to organise attacks on rival clans).

But does living in peace for too long really trigger an urge for decadence and self-destructiveness, both on an individual and societal level? By *self-destruct*, I'm not talking specifically about self-harm, but more of the need to generate drama, a sense of purpose, the need to be challenged to overcome and to succeed.

The answer may lie with the world's anarchists who often take the need for drama one step further.

You only have to look at the infamous London riots of 2011 to get what I mean: violence and destruction—but for what purpose?

Delve a little deeper and you'll find one very interesting demographic observation, if not the answer.

According to the BBC, of those arrested for the London riots, in terms of ethnicity, forty-two per cent of those charged were white, forty-six per cent black, seven per cent Asian and five per cent were classified as "other". Some ninety per cent of those brought before the courts were male and about half were aged under twenty-one. Only five per cent were over the age of forty. Some thirty-five per cent of adults were claiming out-of-work benefits.

So, how much drama is there in *your* life?

Too much, more than enough, a little, none?

Well, drama is this year's (well last year's and the one before and the one before that's) new adrenaline. It's the new must-have thing, the new boredom chaser, or so psychologists would have us believe.

Yes, I pulled the same face you're most likely pulling right now, but this theory does appear to have some legs, and if the above demographics are anything to go by; they're pretty muscly.

We've spawned one of the worst generations of teenagers ever to have roamed the earth.

Born into a world where school boards have moved to limit lawsuit liabilities and imposed strict guidelines for teachers, who are barely allowed to look at a pupil in the wrong way let alone dispense discipline, the result is a bunch of narcissistic zombies for whom adults are a necessity to be borne rather than an example to which they should aspire. Add to this an endless sociological diet of modern-day propaganda that tirelessly pontificates about how the transition from childhood through puberty and to adulthood is fraught with 'trauma', 'difficulty' and 'enormous pressure' (to get out of bed mainly) and we're left with an ever-growing crop of egocentric angst-ridden and very bored little monsters with a lot of time for drama, experimentation (in relationships and sex) and maybe a bit of studying.

Now, some experts will refute this observation as 'ill-informed and perhaps even 'reckless', but the reality remains that teens have oodles of time to dramatise everything about their lives, and if we throw in the fact that they live below the 'poverty line', well, then we're expected to accept that this somehow completely 'justifies' their shocking behaviour and the lack of respect for themselves, their own families and society.

Well, it doesn't.

"Sweetheart, could you pass me the cornflakes?"

"Why are you always on my back? Why can't you leave me alone?"

Don't worry, it's just the hormones.

So, by now, if you're a mother or a father, you're most likely chewing on this book's pages and wanting to spit it out with vitriol.

"Relax. Don't sweat it."

There are obviously exceptions to this theory. There's no

need to get all *"ghetto on my ass"*. For every group of angst-ridden, maladjusted teens who are often 'misunderstood', who enjoy nothing more than to bathe in drama, wallow in their own misery and discontent, there are at least a couple, especially those with parents who refuse to entertain let alone capitulate to their rebellious offspring, who put their nose down, study hard and live their life the best way they can in their attempt to carve themselves the best possible future.

Chances are you're one of the aforementioned parents.

Feel better now?

'Acting up' is a choice, not a requirement.

Most of us have endured hardship as teenagers and have managed to make a decent life for ourselves. History is littered with shining examples of the many who have overcome adversity and what appeared to be impossible odds to make their life and those of their children and grandchildren the best that it can be.

Don't get me wrong; we all experience and maybe even cultivate a bit of drama in our lives—but we don't always see this as a badge of honour; rather, we interpret it as a lesson on how easy it can be to become consumed with, tarnished by, the negative things that happen to us and use them as an excuse to wallow in self-pity rather than pull our socks up and make a change.

But is it true?

Does the devil really make work for idle hands? Do some of us actively solicit and seek out drama in order to complete a self-fulfilling prophecy, even beyond our teenage years?

Here's the quick story of Jane.

Jane had spent most of her adolescent (and angst-filled) years not as a rebel, but as a dreamer who would one day marry the proverbial prince at the proverbial 'fairy-tale' wedding.

Yet, it was at the mature age of twenty-three, just as Jane was starting to wonder if she'd be left on that proverbial shelf, that she met the man of her dreams, John.

John was everything Jane had dreamed of: handsome, charming, relatively successful (in that he had a job and worked regularly), committed, and kind to her and her family.

He was the perfect catch.

In fact, in Jane's opinion, John was way too perfect and possibly untrue (yes, the self-esteem eroded during her teenage years had left an impression). She'd concluded and steeled herself for the belief that it would never last between them.

That was until John asked her to marry him.

They married.

Jane fell pregnant and took early maternity leave.

John, on the other hand, took on extra hours at work because he was all too aware that he'd soon have three mouths to feed and bills to pay with just one income.

Jane, on the other hand, was 'stuck' at home all day. The few friends she did have were at work. John became her closest friend, but he was spending more and more time at the office—or was he?

Jane started to wonder.

As the days went by and she got 'fatter', Jane had nothing to do but think.

And think she did, about how she was starting to resemble the Michelin Man both metaphorically and physically (since the pregnancy caused swelling in inconvenient places). She felt very low, very lonely, very ugly and very bored.

So she started to telephone and send John text messages at work. But John was very busy and often unable to take the call or reply to the text messages promptly, which in turn sparked suspicion and arguments between them.

John, eager to keep the peace and not stress his pregnant wife, would always be the first to apologise, back down and promise to try harder. Yet, day after day, bored Jane (and her hormones) generated discontent and more drama for a weary John, especially when she began accusing him of having an affair, disbelieving that he was indeed at work and instead believing that he was shacked-up in a hotel room with another female.

John did his best to refute these accusations and comforted himself with the belief that things would get better once their baby was born.

They did not.

In fact, they got worse.

Jane was convinced John was going to abandon her and their

COMING UP FOR AIR

daughter, and a day seldom passed when the topic was not raised—to the point where John started to dread going home.

Now, you may well have heard this story before and will have some idea where it is going. The sad thing here is that it seems that Jane had decided many years before that her relationship with John was not going to last (spawned from her low self-esteem).

Add to this a lot of bored time, and Jane sought to fill her days with drama. She became hooked on living the drama, got a fix from John's surrender and then a buzz from making up.

So, what should have been a very special time for this small family became a living nightmare and, without knowing it, Jane worked tirelessly to destroy her own dream of having a loving husband, a home and a family of her own.

Her own miserable and self-fulfilling prophecy.

Jane is now alone, wallowing in the misery that she sculpted for herself. She remains addicted to drama, both the act of and the sadness that this yields, and she wears this like a shroud on a daily basis to solicit the attention and/or sympathy of family and friends in order to feed her perpetual hunger for attention, and thus she remains unfulfilled.

Now, there is much more to this story, but the basic element remains: if it isn't broken, don't try to fix it. If you feel there's something missing from your life, then take time to understand exactly what this might be and then seek to treat it either by conventional methods, such as therapy, friendship or other constructive pursuits such as a hobby, a project, or even a selfless act of kindness.

Most importantly, do not make your partner your everything. They are busy dealing with their own life challenges, which will most likely include you and potentially the family that you have together. Help them thrive by fostering their own peace of mind rather than unloading your own insecurities on them.

Don't wallow. Or let me rephrase that: take some time out to wallow—a day, a week, maybe even a month in extreme cases—but then it's time to take a shower and start facing whatever it is that is bothering you, because it is *you* and *only you* who can make the change.

Do not rely on others to make you happy, but be grateful

when others bolster your happiness.

Each and every one of us has at some stage or other of our lives imagined, rightly or wrongly, that everybody else is having much more fun. The reality is, more than often, the opposite. We simply don't know everything about everybody else.

The grass may well be greener on the other side, but it's the grass that is already beneath our feet that we should preoccupy ourselves with. It may be a bit dry, flaky and may even sport some bald patches, but it only takes a bit of nurturing, care, thought and imagination to restore it back to its lush, verdant glory.

The things we lose in the fire of life are often irretrievable, irreplaceable. They become the pain that strengthens us and the scars that define us; they are the end to one chapter and the start of another of a life that may be imperfect, but remains nonetheless a blessing.

25 THE ULTIMATUM

It's late afternoon.

Al is in the master bathroom re-laying tiles, Kayla is in the living room and Al's mother, just over for a visit, is outside in the garden.

Al was smearing grout on one of the tiles when he heard muffled voices coming from the living room; Emily, was saying something to Kayla but he couldn't quite discern exactly what his daughter was saying to his wife, although, by the intonation, it sounded as if the ten-year-old was crying.

So, he stopped what he was doing and listened in…

"I told you, I'm on the phone!"

"But Mommy…"

"I said get out of here! Can't I even have a telephone conversation without you snivelling around me?

More tears. "Mommy, please…"

"Emily, I swear to God, if you don't get out of here I am going to rip your head off! Get out of here! Get out! Get out!"

That was it.

Al left what he was doing and rushed into the living room to see his wife slouched on the sofa, talking on a cordless phone, whilst glaring at her ten-year-old daughter who was standing nearby, clutching the back of her head.

The little girl's face was contorted in pain and tears were streaming down her blotchy red cheeks.

"What the hell's the problem?" Al asked, incredulous at the sight before him.

"Daddy..." was Emily's sobbing reply as she ran to him.

"Will you tell that little brat to stop being so damn rude; I'm on the damn telephone," Kayla barked, turning her back on them both and apologising to whomever she was talking.

"Daddy..."Emily repeated as she buried her face in her father's chest. It was as she did this that Al realised what she was clutching to the back of her head; it was a hairdryer and it seemed that his daughter's blonde hair was somehow weaved inside the motor of the contraption.

"Hello? It was Al's mother, who had made her way back into the house when she heard the raised voices.

Kayla rolled her eyes.

"Mom, come in, the door's open," Al said as he tried to pacify his daughter who, responding to the warmth in her father's concerned tone, began to wail even louder.

"Will y'all shut her the hell up!" Kayla hissed again.

Al's mother threw her a look of contempt as she rushed over to her son and her grandchild. "What happened?"

"I don't know, Mom; I think she's got her hair tangled inside the dryer."

"Oh, poor thing..."

They examined the damage.

Emily's hair had indeed been sucked into the back of the hairdryer and was wrapped around the fan blade. It had pulled at her scalp which was now red in places where some of the hair had actually been wrenched from its roots.

"Can you help me with this, Ma?"

"Damn it! What is wrong with you people?" Kayla seethed as she took her phone call into the bedroom and slammed the door behind her.

Al and his mother spent the next hour liberating the traumatised girl from her ordeal and damaging her hair as little as possible.

When it was over, Kayla joined them. "Can't I even have a telephone conversation without world war two in the background? And Al, you've hardly got anything done in that bathroom."

"Your daughter got her hair caught in the hairdryer," Al's mum interjected as calmly as her emotions would allow.

Kayla looked at her mother-in-law and then at her daughter, who was huddling into her father's chest, and then let out a grunt of satisfaction. "Good. She knew the back to that thing was missing; she should've been more careful."

"I didn't know the back was missing!" Emily wailed back at her mother.

Kayla flared. "Don't you yell back at me, you…"

"It doesn't matter now. All that matters is that she's okay," Al jumped in, well aware of what would ensue otherwise.

His mother, however, wasn't going to let it go that easily. "So, what exactly was more important than your own daughter's safety?"

If Kayla detected a tone in her mother-in-law's voice, she didn't show it, and with a smile said, "That was work; they wanted to know if I was interested in a promotion," she said smugly. She waited for a comment from the others but none came.

"I don't know what ya'll are so bent out of shape about. This is just Emily, as usual, making more of a fuss about nothing," Kayla added irritably. "If anything, I should be the one upset that I had my boss on the telephone and all I could hear was her screamin' and hollerin' in the background."

"If you weren't so busy talking on the phone, you would have seen the state her hair was in and known that she wasn't making a fuss over nothing," her mother-in-law said, bluntly.

With that, she kissed her granddaughter and left the house, for she knew that if she stayed there any longer she'd probably end up doing something she would regret.

Kayla was about to shout something after, her but thought better of it. Instead, she turned to her daughter with narrowed eyes and gritted teeth and seethed, "Why didn't you tell me it was so damn urgent?"

Emily shrank back further into Al's chest and began to sob once more.

"She was standing right in front of you, Kayla, with tears streaming down her face, her hand to her head—how much more important did you need it?" Al intervened.

"I wasn't talking to you!"

"Well, I'm talking to you!"

"You yelling at me?" Kayla asked, incredulously.

"No, I'm not yelling; I am telling you this has got to stop."

"This? This what?"

Al fumbled for the words. "This, Kayla… I can't take it anymore. I can put up with all the other crap—your mood swings, even the debt—but when it comes to the kids… I'm just not having it anymore." There was determination in his voice.

"So, what are you saying, Al?" she asked, a pair of defiant hands on her hips.

"I'm saying that unless you get help, we're done." The words were said quickly.

Kayla let out a snort. "Ha! Yeah, right. You can't be serious."

Al stood up, squeezed his daughter to him and said, voice brimming with repressed anger, "Unless things change around here, you'll find out just how serious I am."

And he stood, unfaltering, his flexing jaw line the only indication of the emotional turmoil inside him.

It was then that Kayla knew her husband meant every word, and it spooked her. Yet she wasn't about to be intimidated by him. After all, it would be his loss, not hers, if they split up. So, after taking a few seconds to consider that particular scenario, she said in a cocky, defiant tone, "So what do you suggest we do, Al?" Then added, scornfully, "Mr know it all."

"I don't know… maybe another counsellor. At this stage, we could go see a priest for all I care, as long as this stops."

Kayla laughed. "Is that it? Is that all you can come up with, brainchild? You give me an ultimatum about our marriage and the best you can come up with is to suggest we go and see yet another quack or get you an exorcism? We've already been to see God knows how many shrinks and none of them have been any help. None of them have been able to see just what it is like having to live with you."

Al was about to respond to her comment, but realised there was no point. Instead, he said, "Then we'll keep looking until we find someone who can help us."

"*You*. You mean you. You're the one who needs help, Al. It is because of *you* that we're in this mess."

"Really? And how exactly am I to blame for this?"

"You know full well how. It's always like this. And when you think you aren't doing enough of a good job embarrassing me in front of your mother, you enlist her help." She nodded at Emily.

"I don't need anybody's help, Kayla."

"And here we go again. You never accept responsibility for anything. You are always trying to blame someone else. And this is the problem. And it doesn't matter how many shrinks, quacks, doctors or magicians we go to see; unless you're prepared to accept that you have a problem, then it's never going to get better."

"Me? Me? I have a problem…?"Al asked, raising his voice.

Emily began to whine once more.

"I'm sorry… I'm sorry, sweetie," he cooed to his daughter. Then he shook his head in exasperation and looked at his wife. "You know what? I don't care. I accept responsibility. There. Okay? Is that better?"

"See? And now you just get sarcastic…"

"I don't care who's to blame for what. Let's just try to fix it, right?"

Kayla shrugged her shoulders. "Well, I'm ready when you are, babe."

And so it was.

Now, at this stage, you will have either written off Kayla as a psycho bitch from hell and Al as the poor victimised husband, or you may have gone one step further and concluded that Al is indeed the one at fault here.

What do *you* think?

There is a very good argument against Al that questions why on earth he let this thing go on for so long. Why was he subjecting himself and his children to this kind of daily abuse? Why wasn't he taking decisive action?

Well, ask yourself, why does an abused wife stay with her husband (and vice versa)?

Each relationship has its own mitigating factors, but there are some typical reasons many of us will put up with a bad relationship. These tend to be: hope—that the person will change or, worse, that we can change them; responsibility—we often assume responsibility for the other person's unacceptable behaviour, believing that we are in some way provoking or contributing to it; separation anxiety—we just can't bear the idea of being separated from the object of our affection and/or our children.

The latter is a big factor in many relationships; separation from a partner inevitably means leaving the marital home and thus separation from your children (often the case if you're a man), and life as you know it.

Al was in love with his wife and he hoped that things would get better. Like many others in his predicament, all he wanted to do was share a place he could call home with the woman he loved and children who were a result of that love.

This was his only expectation.

For Al, a devoted husband and father, the grass was not greener on the other side. He'd convinced himself that, like many other couples, they were just going through a rough patch.

They just needed to find the right help.

Truth was, he was in denial (more about this later) and had rationalised his wife's behaviour. He had settled for very little, but what he couldn't see is that even that was too much to ask.

Meanwhile, his life and that of his children was passing by as each and every one of them was exposed to a situation that was as damaging as it was toxic.

As I keep saying, it's always easy to look on a situation with cool detachment and form a judgement—and, more often than not, this is exactly what some relationships need. However, when you're on the inside looking out, your perspective is somewhat skewed. We hope and settle because the unknown, like the dark, is scary; if we give up what we have, how do we know if what we will subsequently get, if anything, will be better?

We don't.

Cue some of the biggest cases of *rationalising* and *settling* ever to exist on the face of the earth.

How many times have you heard someone (normally a woman) say, "He may not make much of an effort, but he's really busy", or, "He can be really sweet when the mood takes him and we're on our own"?

When the mood takes him?

When they're on their own?

Seriously?

To that kind of woman, it doesn't matter if she is treated like a doormat the rest of the time, because *he can be sweet when there's nobody else around.* (More about this later also.)

If you aren't one of those people, you're probably thinking that that kind of life is not a choice; it's a sentence.

Don't be surprised when I tell you that many of these people are actually very happy (relatively speaking). Like Al, they've set themselves what they believe to be a realistic expectation and therefore are less likely to be disappointed.

But as you can see, this wasn't the case for Al.

That's because there's more to this story than currently meets your eye but, as you're about to discover in later pages, what Al didn't know is that he didn't stand a chance.

It would not have mattered if he'd put a big fat zero in the column of must-haves; he was fighting a battle that had already been lost many years before—the moment he met her.

26 SURRENDERED LIVES

Al surrendered himself to his wife's will to keep the peace, but there are actually many people in the world who are more than happy to dedicate their whole existence to the sole purpose of contributing to and safeguarding the total and complete satisfaction of their partners and their offspring, and these people are supremely happy for it.

That's because their happiness is not dictated by convention, sexism, social or culture shifts, materialism, power or greed; it's defined only by expectation—the one they set for themselves and that set for them by their spouses.

Whilst this may sound somewhat simplistic, there's much more to this technique than you'd think. I'm forever telling business colleagues and friends that the best route to a harmonious partnership is to set expectations and then strive to meet them. That way, customers and friends know exactly what to expect of you, and you know exactly what to expect of them.

Nobody is disappointed.

In Ira Levin's 1972 novel, *The Stepford Wives*, a young mother suspects that her neighbours' submissive and wonderfully attentive wives are in fact robots designed by their husbands to do their bidding.

It turns out that they are.

However, whilst the novel is pure fiction, there is much about it that is actually steeped in fact.

'Surrendered Wives' is a movement inspired by the book, *The Surrendered Wife,* by Laura Doyle. Fans of the book tend to be adopters of its main premise: women should surrender to what is deemed as the 'inappropriate control' of their husbands and focus more on their own happiness; this will in turn enable them to become better wives and thus retain or return romance in their relationship.

(Remember the Importance of Being Selfish?) A surrendered wife respects herself *and* her husband.

It's out with the shrew and in with a wife who is not in the least bit controlling, nagging or mothering.

This is consistent with research that suggests much of the 'controlling' exercised by women over their husbands, their children and friends originates from their youth. A time when many basic requirements went unmet: freedom to pursue a specific career, achieve a certain grade, romance the man of their dreams, as well as failure to realise fantasies born from romantic fiction.

The result is more often than not a wife (or these days a partner) who is lost without asserting control over her partner, her children and her home.

They mother their men by setting chores, telling them what to wear and how to wear it, which friends they can visit, when they can visit them, which are a 'bad influence', as well as what type of car they should drive and how to drive it (even if they themselves do not drive).

They assume a lot of the responsibility for running the home, not necessarily out of need, but out of control or for fear that kids won't get fed, bills won't get paid and beds won't get made.

They'll often correct, publicly contradict, and sometimes even deride their partner.

Thus Doyle suggests that women should learn more to trust the men they marry (or choose to live with) and show them the respect they deserve. They should abandon all preconceived ideas about how things should be, as well as the negative (often self-fulfilling) belief that 'things will never change', and actually start treating their man as an equal and not as a child to be controlled.

And she has a point.

Most of us will marry someone that is our equal with the view to setting out on the journey of life together as equals. If any partner sets down this path with the premise that they have made a union with someone who is 'beneath them', then they will have doomed the union to failure right from the start.

Kayla believed that Al was beneath her.

To redress the balance in a situation like this, Doyle suggests that women (who tend to be the most dominant in the domestic arena) learn to respect the man they have chosen to live the rest of their life with. She acknowledges that this is not an easy practice and that big and somewhat challenging changes will be required from both parties.

Respecting our partner is ultimately about respecting our self, since our partner represents one of the biggest life choices we've ever made.

In this case, respecting your man means respecting his choices—clothes, friends, acquaintances and hobbies—because to allow him to make his own decisions is to allow him to flourish and be the best he can be.

It's from here that 'surrendering' became a movement.

It connected with many women around the globe who had been in marriages for some time and who came to realise that their relationships had become somewhat lacklustre, dulled by the stresses of life, finances, the responsibility of raising children and disappointment with unfulfilled expectations.

So they resolved to make a change: either go back out to seek a career, or turn the maintenance and servicing of their homes, their relationships and their family into a career by devoting to it the time they would normally devote to a job and, albeit metaphorically, make their man their boss.

Okay, try not to choke on that last sentence.

Thus, freed from the restraints of commercial and financial pressures of conforming to modern life and social expectations, a surrendered wife is able to rediscover her femininity and vulnerability and, because she is no longer competing with her man, is able to display this.

A surrendered wife respects herself and her body for its own unique beauty. She'll dress as if a visitor might show at the door at any moment and will never allow herself to be seen without at least one layer of makeup; nor would she ever be seen in casual clothing such as a dressing gown!

A surrendered wife is house-proud; she makes her home a warm and welcoming environment for her husband and her children. She makes love to her man; she doesn't just 'have sex', and the experience is very feminine, doused in romantic touches and not just something to be satisfied at the earliest opportunity.

She doesn't pimp her partner out to work to enable her to pay the bills, but instead she lets him take care of that. In turn, she focuses on herself, on making sure she feels happy and fulfilled, thus enabling her to be a better wife to her man.

Now, I could go on here, but I know I've probably already lost you and you're also probably thinking that I've been sniffing something dubious.

The reality is that there are many variations of a surrendered wife and, whilst much of this may well seem like something out of a Norman Rockwell painting, it does have a place in the noughties, especially now, when many women are tiring of the frenetic pace and pressures of the modern world and often find themselves romanticising in the innocent nostalgia of period novels and movies.

Many couples, despite the technological and social evolution, are finding modern life, well, tough. Competition has never been fiercer both in and out of the workplace because, whilst life may well have become easier, it's also becoming unaffordable, with both forced out to work in their quest to make ends meet.

Some have even taken to working multiple jobs or moonlighting in industries that, if discovered, would make their nearest and dearest's hair stand on end.

This is the sign of our times and the struggle is getting tiresome for many women who often long for the financial freedom and thus the opportunity to spend more time at home with their children, baking cakes, readying slippers and generally fantasising about what exactly the world would be like inside a Jane Austen novel.

The life of a surrendered wife may not be for everyone, but there are undoubtedly elements of its practice that could easily be applied to many of the problems faced by some of today's modern relationships in which apathy is often allowed to set in like cobwebs in a dusty room.

We all have things in our lives that we wish we could either eradicate or change, and, sure enough, our immediate reaction is to do just that. But there often comes a time when accepting or 'surrendering' to the things over which we have no control is in our best interest.

There truly is freedom in acceptance.

And, yes, that does sound like a slogan on a religious pamphlet, but it actually does make a lot of sense to make yourself happy in the face of something that is making you feel the opposite.

27 THE DEATH OF MARRIAGE

In England, June is believed to be the most popular month for weddings.

I've always found this somewhat ironic since the motivation behind this preference is the fact that summer starts in June—but any Brit will tell you that the beginning of summer does not necessarily equate to the beginning of sunshine!

However, if you're reading this book during the summer, there's a good chance that you, a relative or an acquaintance are busy organising some aspect of a wedding—you know, that special, often very expensive, event that has many breathless with nervousness; the same that takes months (if not years) of dating, organising, negotiating, compromising and weighing so that you can live one day like a movie star with cameras flashing, people fussing and eyes watering as you legalise your commitment to your soul partner in a ceremony which for some, (generally those guests that you hardly ever see, but had to invite because it would otherwise look bad), went on a bit.

In reality, it's not long after the confetti has settled that the mass migration of guests begins and it's off to the reception that (if you took out a small mortgage) takes place at a nice hotel with an 'olde world' decor, or (if it's a wedding on a budget) will take place at an old village hall or maybe even in somebody's back garden.

Regardless of the location, most will be plied with copious amounts of alcohol and just about enough food to see it to the end of the evening when, with blistered feet but still with a smile on their faces, the happy couple will make their way to their hotel room or (if they're lucky or rich enough) to the airport and onto a flight to some exotic location to consume even more alcohol and finally the marriage.

Because that's the process, right?

Step 1—You date

Step 2—You get engaged

Step 3—You get married

Step 4—You 'consummate' the marriage

Step 5—You move in together

Step 6—You start a family

That's how it goes, isn't it?

No?

You mean this wasn't the process you or most of the people you know followed?

Tut-tut.

So, which steps did you and yours take and in which sequence?

Stop for a second to consider that. In which sequence did you follow the above steps, and did you follow all, most or hardly any of them?

Generally speaking, the more 'mature' you are, the more it is likely that you will have followed most, if not all, of the above steps albeit maybe not in the same order.

Why?

Well, I don't think it's because you didn't enjoy the liberation and the excitement of your youth, because most people do (even if they don't truly appreciate it at the time). No, there's one simple reason, and that is that the more we regress in time, the more, as individuals, we would have been expected to do what was commonly perceived as 'proper'. The above steps are 'proper' according to our social psychology—oh, and the Bible of course.

At least they used to be.

Fast forward a few hundred years and you can pretty much mix and match the sequence as you see fit without having to worry about any particular social stigma—unless you're religious, for the Bible tells us that sex before marriage is immoral.

This philosophy is true of most religious cultures where the corruption of purity and morality is still dealt with the harshest of punishments, such as the rack of personal failure, the guillotine of social isolation and the drowning weight of shame, to name a few.

This is somewhat ironic since some of the religious initiatives that purport to preserve purity have been accused of degrading it.

This is true of the so-called Purity Ring, sold directly to adolescents or to their parents as gifts to their children, which is normally accompanied by a vow of celibacy until marriage.

The purity ring initiative was, not surprisingly, started in America during the 1990s and has since been adopted into thousands of households.

Such was the popularity of the 'The Silver Ring Thing' that American organisations that promoted abstinence and encouraged teens to sign 'virginity pledges' would receive federal grants under the Bush administration to sell the rings both in America and abroad.

However, some say that the vow may as well be to have a life of psychological disorders brought on from the pressure not to fail.

Although what has drawn the greatest criticism is the idealistic belief that a ring and a vow is enough to avoid pregnancy and the spread of sexual diseases.

'The Ring' is believed to have contributed to an increase in both.

Whatever your opinion, the fact remains that, these days, sex out of wedlock is pretty much the norm and that almost mythical virginal bride is slowly, but surely, becoming the stuff of fairy tales.

The 'sacred feminine' may have been persecuted centuries ago by the church, but she came back and with a vengeance, cleverly exploiting that very thing that resides in every heterosexual male's basic genetic programming: to pursue, to woo and to conquer a woman's sexuality not only to satisfy physical and emotional urges, but to ensure the continuation of his bloodline and the perpetuation of our species.

This basic natural law has endowed woman, the so-called weaker sex, with spellbinding power over man but only for as long as she keeps her sexuality, um, sacred. This is the very thing that for centuries has fed that old belief that if a man sleeps with multiple partners, he's a stud (conquered many), but if a woman does the same, she's 'easy' (allows herself to be conquered too easily).

This power shift was—and for some still is—a sore point, since sometimes, "a good reputation is all a woman has."

And the power struggle continues with today's young women seeking equality not only in the boardroom, but in the arena of life. Man, the so-called hunter, has now become the hunted, with unorthodox females adopting sexual guerrilla tactics to lure, seduce and consume their chosen mate, and this isn't for life, but for as long as it pleases them, often just for one evening, one hour or even a few minutes.

Gone is the old adage of love at first sight; this has now been replaced with sex at first sight. Compatibility with a mate is not assessed by personality, things in common, star-sign compatibility, financial status or even blood group but on willingness to have 'fun'.

This fun generally takes place at weekends and is often initiated or fuelled by alcohol.

The same alcohol that the UK Government has estimated costs the NHS (National Health Service) an estimated 2 billion pounds a year (approximately 3.43 billion USD) in hospital admissions.

All of this is a far cry from chaperoned evenings—again, introduced to preserve the sanctity of a woman's virginity until her wedding night, a concept that today is more commonly seen as romantic yet 'unpractical'.

We're now able to 'try before you buy' most things—why not apply this principle to something as momentous as marriage?

The answer is that we *are*—and, more disturbingly, we're also applying the same rule of a money-back guarantee in the form of a prenuptial agreement or lawsuit for the purpose of obtaining a 'settlement'.

The so-called 'institution' of marriage has now become a commodity, an article, a possession that many are using for as long as is suits only to then claim a refund when it isn't quite working the way it used to when it was first acquired.

And why not?

Why persevere with something when, in true consumer

fashion, getting a bargain on a divorce is so easy, with basic 'divorce packages' starting from as low as £25 (42 USD), all you need is the Internet, a credit card and you'll have that man (or woman) washed right out of your hair in no time.

The epitome of our fast-moving, self-serving world: "Why bother spending time trying to salvage your marriage when it in itself is a waste of time? Swap your current partner for one that makes you happy."

What? No time to go out on the prowl?

No problem; with that trusty credit card and an Internet connection, you can get 3 FREE months' membership of one of the world's leading dating agencies and you'll be flirting in no time.

What's that? You don't want to burn your bridges too soon.

No problem; membership has its privileges: your account is discreet and password protected which means your husband or wife or partner need never know what you've been up to, so you can flirt to your heart's content. Then, once you've met the new man or woman of your dreams and are feeling more confident, you can break the news to your spouse (and your children if you have any) that you've decided to move on.

So, bearing all that in mind, why bother getting married? What exactly is the benefit?

It's not spending time with the object of our affection, because we're already doing that. It's not moving in with them, because we've already done that. It's not carnal pleasures, because, well, we've all been doing that. So it must be having babies.

Well, it's not that either, because more and more people are having babies regardless of their marital status, or age for that matter.

"After all, when *is* a good time to have children?"

This is a question I've personally heard several times.

Well, I don't know; let's start with you being old enough not to have to wear a school uniform, then maybe having a job and some disposable income after paying your bills—oh and you aren't still living at home with your parents.

I think that pretty much covers some of the basics.

There is undoubtedly a growing and rather worrying

apathetic approach to social responsibility. For some, it's due to the eternal struggle to make ends meet because, no matter how hard you work, money never seems to be enough, so some reach a stage where they just give up; if money's never enough, then you may as well take the plunge, give life to another human being and what will be will be.

For others, those completely devoid of any self-respect or morals, it's the belief that the world (otherwise known as taxpayers) actually owes them something, combined with the fantasy that they're rebelling against the system, against what is 'socially acceptable'.

So, by today's standard, what is and what is not socially acceptable?

Well, I conducted a basic online poll of 100 people of various ages, male and female, which may not necessarily represent public opinion but is nonetheless interesting. I asked what they believe was indicative of today's society, and here are the results:

Sex before marriage = 65%
Sex after marriage = 35%.
Babies before marriage = 83%
Babies after marriage = 17%
Living together before marriage = 67%
Living together after marriage = 33%

When asked if they supported this new culture, sixty-nine per cent voted that they did, versus thirty-one per cent who voted they did not.

If these alarming results are anything to go by, then it's clear that the institution known as marriage is slowly but surely dying (if not dead already) and many of us are quite happy with that.

So this is the message we're sending to impressionable teenagers: marriage is just a very expensive excuse for a 'knees-up' (British for 'shindig') with an equally expensive holiday thrown in for good measure, especially when considering how easy it is to get out of a difficult, angst-packed youth and into your own home.

The reality is that, like it or not, education starts at home. Good morals, a sense of self-worth and a strong work ethic must be indoctrinated from an early age by parents, backed up by the education system and not vice versa. It's this basic lack of foundation that is breeding (if you'll excuse the pun) a new generation of apathetic, self-indulgent, misguided and disillusioned civilians who, tragically, are setting the same standard for future generations.

Of course, as always, and thankfully, there are still many exceptions to this rule. Mine was very much the cynic's view. Whether or not you concur is entirely up to you.

The question remains; what would we be as a race if we lacked any kind of moral structure?

Marriage, the union between two people who are truly committed to love, honour and obey (yeah, not sure about that last part), is the legal ceremony that holds us accountable to each other, a contract that literally states that through thick and thin you're committed to take care of your partner. It's where you say, "Okay, things aren't always going to be perfect, but that's exactly why I took the time to get to know you, chose to spend the rest of my life with you and, all being well, start a family. And, if we don't, well, at least we'll still have each other."

That's why it all started in the first place, isn't it?

There's a common misconception that if you've lived with a partner for a couple of years, you get the same rights as a married couple.

This is not true.

In England, cohabiters (and I'm hoping they've woken up from this) used to believe in the fallacy of the so-called 'common law' marriage whereby couples would believe in the rights of and declare themselves married regardless of the fact that this had not been formally registered by state or church.

The reality is, cohabiters have hardly any rights compared to married couples; e.g., your partner does not have to pay you any maintenance if you gave up your job to look after the children (although they would have to pay child support). Similarly, if you live in a home that is rented by your partner and he or she asks you to leave or walks out, you'd have no automatic right to stay. This is also true if you live in a mortgaged home without any form of cohabiting agreement.

Furthermore, your partner would have the right to walk away with any savings or possessions purchased by them. You'd only have rights over your things or items you co- purchased (that's assuming you both agree to split these evenly).

And, should your partner die without a will, you'd have no entitlement to state bereavement benefit, nor any pension based on their national insurance contributions but, most importantly, you'd have no rights to their estate; this would pass automatically to their immediate (or blood) family.

Of course there have been some suggestions, but there are currently no plans to change the law nor, some would say, should there be if we want to preserve the importance of marriage.

That said, I wouldn't worry too much since unless you are truly committed to your partnership, unless you truly believe in being together, for richer and for poorer, in sickness and in health, until death do you part, then there are, as mentioned previously, a variety of 'break glass in emergency' schemes that you can call upon to save yourself.

All you have to do is decide what exactly, when it comes to your marriage, constitutes an emergency.

28 LIVING WITH THE DEVIL

Al spent most of his married life deluding himself that his family, and the home that he had made for them, made him happy.

The reality is that it didn't and wasn't—and rather than accepting that, he just kept trying to fix it. And that's not in the least bit unusual for somebody like him.

Al is a *fixer*.

And it was only after seven years of marriage, when he was T.D.Y. at an Air Force base down in southern United States and found himself in conversation with an old buddy, that he realised; the man was chattily telling him about his marriage and all the great times he had had with his wife but Al was unable to contribute to the subject.

After all the years he'd spent married to Kayla, he was finding it very difficult to think of any happy times. His whole marriage had been one perpetual battle for peace: his own and that of his children.

This was a metaphorical slap in the face—one that enabled him to seriously contemplate life without his wife, and, a few days later, he met a man who would direct him onto a road that would change his life forever.

The counsellor's offices were in downtown Savannah and the building itself resembled an enormous plantation house. The rooms were spacious and furnished opulently and, at first, it was hard for Al to understand how anybody in such a profession could afford this extravagance. That was until he learned that the fit, well-tailored man before him was actually an ex-divorce lawyer. Apparently, the man had grown so tired of facilitating separation that he decided to work on the opposite side: fixing marriages rather than helping dismantle them.

A lot of his work was pro bono or indeed financed, for a fraction of his usual lawyerly fees, by the government.

During his sessions with Al and his wife, it became clear to the ex-lawyer that they would benefit from attending one of the weekend seminars hosted by a group called the Tree of Life.

Apparently, these events, set loosely against a religious backdrop, had gained a lot of respect in the field of marital counselling, and consequently proved rather expensive. The total cost to attend a weekend seminar was four hundred dollars.

Al was honest; he said that, as much as he'd like to go, they simply couldn't afford it, whilst Kayla said that even if they could afford it, she wasn't sure she would be able to get the time off from work as it was inventory weekend.

"Is your work more important than saving your marriage?" the lawyer asked.

"Of course not!" Kayla snapped. "I would do whatever it takes to save this marriage."

"Then go to this," the lawyer said. "I will pay for it."

And so he did.

The man made all of the arrangements—the booking, the fee—and ensured that Al received all the information necessary for him and his wife to make their way to the event that began on a Friday and ended on a Sunday afternoon.

Al was comforted by the fact that the event was very well attended. He wasn't alone in this situation; there were other people struggling with similar problems.

One of the first exercises upon arrival for both spouses was to fill out a questionnaire consisting of a group of words. Each person had to circle a word and their interpretation of it. The idea was to then compare these with their partner's choices and note the difference between the two.

Al completed his questionnaire, but was unable to compare this with Kayla's because she wasn't there. In fact, she missed the whole Friday session, saying that she couldn't get away from work.

She did, however, attend the Saturday and Sunday sessions and even got into the swing of things by proclaiming on several occasions that her marriage meant everything to her and that she would do everything within her power to make it work.

But it was too little, too late.

When the session ended on Sunday afternoon, two of the organisers asked Al to join them backstage. There, they explained exactly what they had learned over the weekend. It can be summed up in one of their sentences: "Some things just aren't worth saving."

They then went on to explain to Al that it was not a failure to let this marriage go, but a sign of strength. Words that were of great importance to a man who struggled so very desperately with the notion.

There are many things in our lives that we associate with goodness, badness, success and failure. For Al, the bitter end to his parents' marriage represented failure. For his marriage to follow suit could only mean the same, and it was something that he had vowed to himself many, many years before that he would never, ever allow to happen.

However, it took a pair of complete strangers to lay it all out for him: giving up on his marriage after trying for so many years did not represent failure or success; it simply meant that he was finally able to recognise a situation for what it really was; sometimes, no matter how good your intentions may be, some things simply cannot be fixed.

This was the boost he needed to take a step into the unknown and, not long after that, he told Kayla that he wanted a separation. He stopped short of saying that he wanted to end the marriage, but explained that they would both gain from spending some time apart.

Now, if you've been in this situation or know of it, you'll also probably know that this all too often represents the beginning of, if not the end. Couples often say that they could benefit from time apart when they really mean that it's over, they simply haven't come to terms with it yet or, more commonly, they already know they don't want to be with their partner anymore, but are just postponing the inevitable in the hope that the whole mess might just go away without them having to deal with it.

It seldom does.

Kayla knew this, and her rage was unrestrained.

So much so that she called Al's mother. "Do you know what that bastard, sorry ass son of yours told me today?" she vented.

Al's mother closed her eyes and took in a deep breath.

At last.

And it was during the 4th of July holiday, when Al returned with the children from visiting his father in Florida, that his mother met him in the driveway.

"She's taken everything, Al. All the furniture. She's gone. Except for the kids' rooms; all their stuff is still there."

The news hit Al like a truck. He had known this time would come and he had even prepared the children for it. He just didn't realise it would be so soon.

Yet it didn't hurt as much as he expected and this gave him pause for thought. He considered whether or not, in some kind of perverse way, Kayla was right; he didn't care about her.

The truth actually was that Al had disconnected.

Throughout their time together, unbeknown to him, his feelings for Kayla had been degraded, leaving behind mostly a daily routine and the hope to realise his idealised view of family life.

I think the same could be applied to the majority of us; we each have a breaking point where the line is drawn and from which there's no going back. For some, this process happens sooner rather than later. In Al's case, he genuinely wanted to do what he believed was right and, of course, as is famed with many southern men, he was raised to meet a lady, court her, do right by her, cherish and provide.

So, to see Kayla upset or distressed broke his heart and he would do anything to *fix* the situation, which included giving in to her many tantrums. But all Al was doing was enabling what many would class as the *devil*.

That wasn't a metaphor; it is literally what thousands of sufferers have dubbed people like Kayla: "It's like living with the devil."

Here's a very quick story for you.

It's a sunny spring Sunday morning and the church is packed with worshipers.

Suddenly, Satan manifests himself, scaring the congregation and sending them, screaming and shouting, out of the building.

Before long, the place is emptied but for one old man who remains in his seat, somewhat oblivious to the panic that has just taken place.

Satan walks up to the man and asks, "Do you know who I am?"

"Yes," replies the old man, "I know who you are. You are the devil."

"Exactly. So, if I'm the devil, why is it that you do not fear me?"

The old man shrugs his shoulders and says, apathetically, "Because I feel like I've been married to you for the last twenty years."

Most of us would probably have had the same reaction upon reading Al's story. It seemed as if he was married to the devil. I know my first reaction was exactly that. And to be fair, I have to confess that along with that thought came my belief that, whilst a wonderful man and dedicated father, Al was also very weak; in his quest to please his wife, he gave into her every whim and, sadly, because we are human beings, the strong will always dominate the weak.

It's human nature.

But now that we've established that Al was what some of us would wrongly class as a wimp and Kayla a bitch from hell, there's another very short story I'd like to share with you.

It is about a character from Greek mythology, called Narcissus who, after peering into a pool of water, fell madly in love with his own reflection. Obviously, Narcissus' love was unrequited and he slowly pined away and perished, leaving behind only a flower bearing his name.

NPD or Narcissistic Personality Disorder was first given credence by the American Psychiatric Association in 1980. Those suffering from narcissism will often show signs of excessive or erotic interest in themselves.

Does this sound like somebody you know or knew?

I bet you're nodding your head right now.

I believe that all of us have come into contact with a narcissist at one stage or another in our lives, as I believe that we all bear narcissistic traits, albeit, I would hope, in diluted form.

The word narcissist is frequently bandied around these days generally to describe someone who is self-absorbed, egocentric, vane and downright rude.

The reality is that whilst most narcissists may well exhibit these traits, it doesn't mean that we all fit the actual prognosis.

Far from it.

A narcissist believes he or she is a superior being, a unique individual who is equalled by none and revered by all, somebody with an overinflated sense of grandiosity who will exaggerate achievements and talents, who will be obsessed with fantasies of success, fame, omnipotence, and brilliance— the cerebral narcissist; and of beauty and sexual prowess—the somatic narcissist.

A narcissist will speak just to hear the sound of his or her own voice, and will believe that he or she should only be associated with, or treated by, other 'special' or high-ranking individuals or institutions. They are egomaniacs, pathological liars, impostors of their own self; what they don't know or haven't experienced, they will invent. A narcissist is perfectly capable of looking you in the eye and swearing to something that is, often quite clearly, untrue. They will reassure you that they will not do something whilst at the same time plotting to do that very thing.

Haughty and arrogant, a narcissist will be envious of others and often believe that most people feel the same way about them. They will demand immediate compliance with their requests, and will often explode into fits of rage and frustration if denied, contradicted or confronted.

They require excessive adulation, admiration and affirmation, or, failing that, they wish to be feared and/or notorious—'narcissistic supply'.

Generally speaking, to a narcissist, the people who surround them are only as good as their narcissistic supply. In return, they will be devoid of empathy for others. Their only priority is that of self-preservation. A narcissist will do anything for his or her own gain and will generally not think twice about stepping on somebody to achieve their goal. They will select acquaintances based on status and their capability to enable them to enrich their own way of life, be that in their professional careers or in their personal life.

There appears to be no evidence to suggest that the child of a narcissistic parent will develop the same illness. It does seem, however, that narcissists are often the result of an abusive childhood, in whichever form; doting and smothering a child can sometimes be just as abusive as beating or starving one. Either way, medical research clearly states that NPD is a personality disorder. As such, it can be the fruit of a myriad of cognitive, behavioural and emotive factors.

It has been observed that children who grow up with an 'N' mother are more likely to develop the disorder than those of 'N' fathers, but overall, it seems these children tend to become more co-dependent than narcissistic. Clearly, if you were brought up thinking that, in the eyes of your narcissistic parent, you weren't worth much, then, unless external factors prevail, you are going to end up believing it and consequently will have low self-esteem or self-respect.

Now, after hearing all that, you have to ask yourself, *why would anybody want to be with somebody like that?*

Well, that is a good question, but why do we put up with any of our partners who mistreat us?

I guess it all comes back to those old chestnuts: settling and rationalising (which you'll read more about later).

I was talking to a policeman once and he was telling me about a domestic incident he'd attended whereby a girl had quite clearly been physically abused by her boyfriend, but when the police asked her to press charges, she chose to remain silent.

The policeman was somewhat perplexed as to why anybody would want to protect someone who had hurt them in that way and, even worse, want to stay with them.

Well, there are many reasons why, which would be a chapter in itself, but the bottom line is he was not privy to all aspects of their relationship; he was only aware of one facet. And whilst it is understood that nobody deserves to be physically abused by their partner, or anybody else for that matter, it is important that we consider all aspects of a situation before jumping to conclusions.

For example, this guy may lose his temper every now and then, but he may be an angel to her the rest of the time. To you and I, the emotionally disconnected, that may still appear unacceptable. To her, well, it is probably a price worth paying, just to be able to be with him, wake up next to him, share his life, his money, whatever. The end result is that some people will settle because they believe the good outweighs the bad. Often, they simply believe they can't get any better. And then, in some cases, similar to the one mentioned above, some are just too terrified to sever ties with their partners, be it for fear of losing their children, of being unable to cope alone, and sometimes simply feeling terrified that they'll be persecuted or even killed by their ex.

The emotionally disconnected will probably think that is what the police are for, and I would probably agree, but in the real world, how many times have you heard the phrase, "Unfortunately, there isn't much we can do until he or she does something."?

Well, sadly, all too often, that's too late.

Kayla was diagnosed with narcissism in extremis by two of the psychiatrists that she had seen yet, in true narcissistic style and not unlike many sick individuals, she refused to acknowledge her condition.

And, indeed, so did Al.

When he researched narcissism, he was horrified by how many of the symptoms matched Kayla's behaviour. Yet, despite this, he continued reading only for a short while because he refused to believe that anybody could be that bad, certainly not somebody he was married to.

Furthermore, he began to believe that he was using what he had learned as an excuse to leave her and to not accept the responsibility that maybe he played some part in her unhappiness. Yet, no matter how much he read on the subject, the answer was always the same: narcissists are the type of individuals you should have nothing more than an acquaintance-type relationship with.

Narcissists are among some of the most complex characters to treat, simply because of that overinflated opinion of themselves. They truly believe that nobody is qualified enough to treat them. A narcissist could sit in front of one of the world's most eminent doctors and still believe that he or she was not worthy and/or not qualified. They are most likely to sit and nod politely whilst processing thoughts such as, *"What does he know? What are his credentials? What makes him think he can treat someone as intellectual and as complex as me?"* and so forth.

So, a therapy session is pretty much a nonstarter.

Because, as we all know, one of the basic rules of therapy is that of acknowledgement. Once again, there is a lot to be said for that famous phrase, "My name is… and I am an alcoholic." You will rarely hear a narcissist tell you their name and admit to being a narcissist—simply because they can't; in their mind, there is nothing wrong with them.

So what does that mean, in essence?

Should narcissists be written off as 'damaged' creatures? Maybe be branded with some kind of tattoo on their forehead warning that they should not be approached under any circumstance?

Well, some who have been unfortunate enough to have experienced a relationship with a narcissist will probably scream for immediate legislation. Others, perhaps the most rational among us, would advise to steer clear so as to avoid being sucked dry by the endless demand for narcissistic supply.

And, of course, there are the minority, the few, easily mistaken for masochists. People who know full well the traits of their significant others yet choose to stay—or, even more incredibly, delude themselves into thinking that they might be able to change them. After all, they wouldn't be the first or the last partners to believe they have such super powers.

Serial adulterers, gamblers, etcetera.—many of us enjoy a challenge. And what better accolade, what better proof of devotion than to know that your partner changed a lifelong habit just for you?

It is an envious achievement to be attempted at your peril.

So, what about these few, the so-called masochists, those people who are actually living with and/or choose to live with a narcissist.

How does one survive it?

Well, by surrendering yourself of course (I did tell you that there were some benefits to *surrendering*).

Start by modifying your personality to a point where you no longer exist as yourself, but as a drone, an entity whose sole existence would be that of supplying your narcissist with as much supply as you can possibly muster.

Never disagree nor contradict; consistently look awed by whatever attribute matters to your partner, be that professional or personal. Never remind them that there is a life out there, a real world where they are just beings among many; never make any comment that might directly affect their self-image, omnipotence, judgement or skills.

Avoid sentences like, "I don't think you should…" "We cannot…" "You made a mistake…" These are phrases that would be perceived as rude.

Never refer to yourself in the first person; narcissists regard others as an extension of them. Listen attentively, even if you know that what you are hearing is utter nonsense; be endlessly patient, accommodating, never yell back, and remain completely unemotional at all times.

I could go on, but I think you get the gist.

Now, I ask you, do you think you could change or fix that? Narcissists cannot be fixed.

Most of us who have been in a relationship that simply isn't working will put up with it up to a certain point until one day some kind of switch is thrown and we simply shut down. And it's in this somewhat catatonic state that we're able to deal with the unthinkable.

In this case it was divorce.

That day was a blur for Al, who was emotionally drained by the whole experience. To him, it seemed to take the judge minutes to approve the dissolution of what appeared to be a lifetime's commitment for him. Yet he didn't feel anything. It was nothing like the way he thought it would be, and somehow, in some kind of perverse way, he started to believe that there might be something wrong with him. How could he possibly not feel what was happening to his marriage? Was it his fault that it had come to this?

And so the cycle continued.

In Kayla's mind, it was his fault. He had betrayed her as much as he had saved her. In her own words, "You were like a knight in shining armour; you rode up on your horse to save me and now you're gone."

It was a seemingly emotional Kayla who stood in the law courts, sobbing, hoping for a spark, a flicker in Al's eyes that would tell her that he still loved her, that he still cared, and was regretting his decision.

But there was no such sign.

And it was this that cut Kayla like a knife. In all the time they had been together, Al had always reacted to her heartache. As a fixer, he had always tried to fix that which brought her misery. But that day, well, that day he didn't seem to care.

It was over.

Shortly after, he flew out to England and was stationed at an American Air Force near Cambridge where one day he'd walk into the interview room to talk to me so that I could share his story with you.

Kayla has since remarried.

Today, over ten years later, Al is living with his new wife and, together, they now have six children: two with each other and two respectively from previous marriages. For Al, life may not be perfect, but it's the best it has ever been.

29 THE DARK INSIDE

A few chapters back I introduced you to British Air Force girl, Katy.

After nearly a decade in the Air Force, Katy had been presented with a conundrum: accept her latest orders and be transferred to a base in rural Wales or accept her boyfriend, Mark's, marriage proposal, get out of her contract and leave the Air Force.

So what do you think Katy did?

Read on.

It had been a long day at work but Katy was feeling upbeat; there were just four more weeks until her wedding to Mark.

It was now, as she watched the verdant landscape of trees, flowers and fields doused with the golden honey filter of the setting sun that she felt excited about the marriage that may well have started out as a convenient exit from the Air Force, but had now become something she was really looking forward to.

Katy had grown to love Mark. He was a good man.

Sure, he wasn't Tom nor most of the other men she had dated, but he was sound and dependable, and, she decided that she'd reached a time in her life when she wanted, needed that.

Mark's car was already on the drive when she pulled up behind it and that made her smile.

Again, this was something she loved about being with him; she had loved her independence but she also loved coming home to a man, coming home to him.

"I'm home," she said closing the kitchen door and dumping her handbag on a nearby chair.

She found Mark in the hallway. He was still wearing his overalls from work and was crouching down by the front door, scooping post from the welcome mat.

"Ooh, post!" She squealed excitedly. "That'll be our wedding RSVPs," she said, moving over to him and waiting like an anxious puppy as he sifted through the correspondence.

"Yeah, there's quite a lot here," he mumbled, distractedly, handing her everything that appeared to be wedding related and retaining all of the other mail, including a letter that he immediately and somewhat gingerly opened and began to read.

Katy, on the other hand, began ripping open envelopes and enthusiastically narrating her thoughts as, one by one, more friends and family members were accepting wedding invites.

She was beside herself with excitement.

But Mark wasn't sharing her enthusiasm; he seemed engrossed in the letter he'd just opened.

"Who's that from?" Katy asked with a smile on her face.

But Mark didn't answer.

"Mark? Who's that from?"

Still no answer.

"Mark…"

"You don't want to know," he blurted.

Katy's smile faded and she stepped closer to him. "Of course I want to know—otherwise I wouldn't be asking. Who's it from?"

"It's from Caroline."

"Who's Caroline?"

"She's just an old flame."

"Why would an old flame be writing to you?"

She waited but he wasn't giving her his eyes and this slightly unnerved as well as irked her.

"Mark?" she said, forcefully.

"It's all right, Katy, it's just a letter," he said, dismissively.

"Yeah, I got that, but what does it say?"

"Nothing much. She just heard that I was getting married and thought she'd write to me."

"And say what?"

No answer as he continued to read.

"Mark…"

But her sentence was cut short as he finally looked up at her, eyes wide with anger. "I'm trying to read," he slowly enunciated through gritted teeth.

Katy was taken aback by his sudden menacing stance and was rendered momentarily mute as he fixed her with an icy glare.

Eventually, she found her dry tongue and uttered, "And I'd like to know why she is writing to you."

"You don't need to know," he said without taking his eyes off the page.

This act riled her further, and she echoed, "I don't need to know? Of course I need to know! We're getting married in four weeks and I...."

Her sentence was cut short once more as Mark suddenly, and in one big movement, threw the letter to the carpet, dropped to his knees and proceeded to bang his head against it.

Katy's initial thought was that he had fainted.

It was only seconds later that she realised that wasn't the case at all; instead, her boyfriend was slowly and deliberately smacking his head against the carpet like some demented robot.

"What the hell are you doing?" she asked, incredulously.

There was no answer.

"Mark? What are you doing?"

Still no answer, just the sound of the sickening thud of her fiancé's forehead as it hit the carpet.

Katy had absolutely no idea what to do next. The whole scene was as surreal as it was bizarre; an orange spotlight of sun was shining through the hallway window illuminating a man in mechanic's overalls, on his knees, surrounded by post as he slowly and deliberately slammed his head against the carpet as if performing some ancient preying ritual.

Meanwhile, a woman, dressed in military uniform, was standing idly by watching the spectacle unfold whilst clutching a handful of colourful wedding invites.

That's when she realised that that woman was her, and it spurred her into action.

"Mark, stop! Stop it!" She screamed, pulling at his shoulders.

He shrugged her off, "Leave me alone."

"Mark... stop this, stop!"

"Leave me alone, Katy! Leave me alone! I need to get this out of my head. I need to get this out of my head!"

Again, she didn't know how to respond, but found herself uttering, "What? Mark, what? Let me help you."

He stopped suddenly and looked up at her, eyes wide with some kind of horror and, lips moving but saying nothing, as if some nightmarish entity was preventing him from speaking.

The vision chilled Katy, "Oh, my God, Mark, what is it? What's wrong? Tell me," she supplicated.

"I can't. I can't tell you," he said, eyes glistening with tears.

With that, he sprung to his feet and ran upstairs, slamming the bedroom door shut behind him, leaving Katy to stare after him in disbelief.

She remained where she stood for what seemed liked minutes. She had absolutely no idea what had just taken place, nor did she know what to do next.

Should she go after him?

She had no clue.

Yet, in a somewhat comical and perhaps typically British reaction to the situation, she resolved to make a cup of tea. If anything, the act would give her time to think. Time to process what had just happened here, because this wasn't just about the content of that letter. It was also about the bizarre scene she had just witnessed in the hallway that she was now staring at through the open kitchen door as if by doing so she'd be able to decipher the conundrum that had just unfolded there.

In the year she had been dating Mark, she had never witnessed anything like this. Suddenly, it was like having a different person in the house and this really scared her.

She switched the kettle on once more.

What Katy didn't realise is that this must have been the third time now; she'd let the kettle boil but forget to make the tea as she was too busy processing what had just happened and trying to decide what to do next.

She realised then, after nearly half an hour since the incident, that the only way to get answers was to confront her boyfriend.

She left her seat at the kitchen table to slowly and apprehensively make her way up the stairs where the sun seemed reluctant to give up its day and was still pushing faded red rays through the window. But to Katy the house was no longer full of colour, but had instead turned into a dirty monochromatic grey.

She knocked on the bedroom door.

"Mark?"

No answer.

"Mark? Can I come in?"

"Yes," he said faintly.

She opened the bedroom door to reveal a simply furnished room with magnolia walls and carpet and a double bed clad in a white quilt.

Mark was lying on this, still in his overalls, with his back to her whilst she, still in her Air Force uniform, slowly made her way into the room.

"Are you all right?" she ventured.

There was a long pause and then he said in an expressionless voice and without turning over, "I've got a whole load of stuff to tell you."

The sentence made Katy's blood turn cold as the whirlwind of thoughts recommenced in her mind. *Doesn't he want to get married anymore? Is he sick? Is he having an affair? Does he have a child with somebody else? What was in that letter? What did this Caroline tell him? Who the hell is Caroline?*

To these she'd then added the practical fact that she'd already handed in her notice to the Air Force and was currently waiting for her discharge papers. If the marriage was called off she would lose everything.

Had it all been for nothing?

She needed to know and found herself mumbling, "Okay... I'm listening."

She placed the mug of tea on the bedside table, kneeled on the carpet next to the bed and stared at his shoulders.

Eventually, he rolled over, and it was all she could do not to cry out; her boyfriend, her husband-to-be, now sported a dark discoloration that covered half of his forehead, the beginning of an ugly bruise.

The image in the hallway automatically replayed in her mind.

His hair, his lovely brown hair, was unkempt, his face was drained of any colour and his big brown eyes were wide with some kind of distant terror she could not decipher, as if he was carrying the world's most terrifying secret, the mere mention of which would devour him whole.

Her maternal instinct made her want to pull him to her chest and comfort him, because he resembled every bit a frightened little boy, and she yearned to take and strangle the life from whatever was tormenting him.

"When I've told you this, I don't know if you're still going to want to marry me," he said flatly with now vacant eyes.

Katy's heart was already hammering in her chest, but these cryptic lines had a way of increasing that percussion tenfold.

From her suddenly very dry throat, she croaked, "Okay. I'm ready. What is it?"

"In order for you to understand, I'm going to need to start at the beginning."

And so he did.

He began to tell Katy all about his family, and the fact that they, along with his three brothers, lived in Derby, England, which is something she already knew, but how, before then, when he was just nine years old, the family lived in Australia.

He talked about an uncle, on his mother's side, that he had out there and how this man would often take him and his brothers out on his boat, and how, one day, when it was just the two of them, his uncle had sexually abused him.

He paused here, allowing Katy to absorb this information, and then offered, "I can give you the full details if you feel you need to know them."

Katy shook her head.

She felt nauseous to the point where she thought she might vomit all over the white quilt.

Mark continued, "The thing is, Kate, I don't know... When it happened, I don't know, or I can't remember whether or not I actually enjoyed it. In fact, I still don't know."

"But you were married before," she said quickly.

"I was. But that's it, Kate; I don't know if it was because I really wanted to be married to her or if I was just trying to understand exactly how I feel about women."

Katy hesitated, "And how do you feel?"

"I don't know. What I do know is that I've gone through life dating different girls in an attempt to understand; was it abuse or did I want it to happen?"

Whilst Katy understood what was being said to her, in that it was being spoken in English, she could not comprehend nor was able to process the content and the candid way in which her fiancé was telling her that, as a little boy, he had been abused by an uncle he barely knew and that, to this day, he did not know whether or not he actually enjoyed what happened on that boat as well as what took place over the subsequent four years.

This cannot be true! This cannot be happening!

While her heart ached for the man she knew she loved, the question now had to be posed as to whether or not he cared a thing about her.

Had she become just another of his experiments or did he love her?

She asked him.

"I know I love you, Kate," he said. "I know I love being with you and that I want to spend the rest of my life with you. This is true, and you have to believe it," he said earnestly.

"What is the letter thing all about, then? Who is this Caroline?"

He sighed then closed his eyes for a few seconds. When he reopened them, he said, "Caroline is an ex and she knows everything I just told you. In the letter, she's telling me that, as my wife-to-be, I should tell you. It's why I reacted the way I did and why I was so angry. You see, Kate, it's like my past has caught up with me. No matter how hard I try to outrun, hide from what happened to me back then, I just don't know if I ever will."

His eyes were brimming with tears.

Katy wanted to reach out to him, but she couldn't. She simply couldn't. Not right now. Instead, she asked flatly, "You say you love me and want to be with me, but you're also saying you want to be with other men?"

"No, I'm not saying that, Katy. I'm saying that I don't know and that I want to be completely honest with you. I want you to know everything, including the fact that I've watched porn, but not the usual stuff, stuff with other men in it."

"Oh no, I can't have anything to do with that," Katy blurted, quickly.

"No, no, that isn't what I'm asking. I'm just trying to explain how I'm feeling."

Katy waited a few seconds as she considered his words, and then asked, "So, are you only telling me this because of that letter?"

There was a pause.

"You are, aren't you?"

"I was just hoping I could leave the past behind. I just wanted to look forward to making a future with you."

She considered this.

"Do your parents know anything about this?"

"No way," he said quickly, shrinking back into the mattress.

She understood this for she knew too well that one of the reasons why Mark was not close to his father was the fact that he'd always been a very strict man. She couldn't imagine any scenario in which his son would be able to approach him with such a story and not be absolutely petrified by the fallout.

And it was this thought that touched her heart.

The thought of a little nine-year-old boy starved of affection from his father but gorged on so-called love by his uncle, an adult, someone who knew exactly how to influence, manipulate an innocent to participate in nefarious acts under the guise that they were born of love and not a selfish, despicable compulsion.

The thought made her angry and, not surprisingly, protective of the now twenty-four-year-old man before her.

"You do realise none of this is your fault, right?" she said, slowly.

He said nothing.

"Mark? You realise that, don't you?"

"The thing is, Katy, I don't know. That's what I've been struggling with for most of my life. I don't know if I enjoyed that any more than I know if I actually like men." His voice faltered as he fought back tears.

Katy could see the struggle behind his eyes.

She said with conviction, "You dated girls, Mark. You dated girls because you like them."

"I was experimenting..."

"You got married and were married for three years..."

"But I don't know if it was love or just a test."

Katy thought about this once more. The idea of everything they had being just one big experiment. She fought back a sudden pang of revulsion. The man she was going to marry in just a few weeks was lying on the bed in front of her and he looked frightened and exhausted, and if she allowed herself to think about it long enough, so was she.

She needed time. Time to process everything she had just heard.

"Would you like a fresh cup of tea?" she asked, desperate to be out of there, if only for a few seconds.

He nodded.

She stood slowly and stopped to rub the ache from her knees before leaving the room.

She pulled the door shut behind her and then stood there, hand still on the handle, as if pausing to catch her breath when she was really trying to catch her thoughts that were flapping around in her mind like a migration of butterflies.

She felt giddy as a myriad of images, none of them fully formed and each a sickening disjointed orphan of the other.

After half a minute or so, she made her way down the stairs that were now shrouded in darkness that, like screeching flapping bats, invoked darker, seedier thoughts in her mind as she recalled all of the intimate moments she had shared with Mark, which inevitably led her to question whether or not she could ever be with him again, which in turn led her to argue with herself, part reasoning that the human shell inside her bedroom was still her fiancé, the man she had chosen to marry, the other that he was only the man she thought she knew and not the damaged creature that had just been revealed to her.

How could she ever be with him again?

How could she ever sleep with him again?

How could they ever have children together?

She'd always wonder if he was with her because he loved her or if she was just another experiment, another social cycle in his quest to establish whether he was a heterosexual, bisexual or homosexual.

And it was the last word that she struggled with as she busied herself with the tea, the process of which she drew out to the last possible moment so that she could have time to consider everything that had happened in her home today.

And so, it was nearly twenty minutes later before Katy returned to her bedroom, the room that in some inexplicable way had now changed and, like the scene of a crime, most likely would never be the same.

Mark was now sitting up on the bed.

He watched her return to the room and place a mug of tea on the bedside cabinet. She could feel his eyes as if scrutinising her to read exactly what might be going through her mind, but she avoided making eye contact with him until she sat with her own mug of tea on the side of the bed.

They looked at each other for a few seconds until he prompted, "So… now that you know everything about me, do you still want to marry me?"

What do you think was Katy's reply?

A) Try as she could, Katy could not come to terms with the details of Mark's revelation and was terrified of what might happen after they were married; she called the wedding off.

B) Katy resolved that Mark was a young boy and that what had happened to him was beyond his control and that she loved him and, no matter the risk, decided to go ahead with the wedding.

Katy already knew the answer to Mark's question.

She'd done nothing but think about this and everything else he had told her during her time downstairs.

She was horrified and disgusted by what she had learned today, especially since she was unable to shake the imagery of Mark with other women, worse still, other men, and what exactly this entailed.

If she stayed with him, there was a distinct possibility that she'd spend the rest of her life wondering if she'd made the right decision and second-guessing whether or not he was seeing other men behind her back.

And what about her?

He said he loved her and that he enjoyed sex with her, but what did that mean? Did he enjoy sex with her whilst thinking about other men?

The thought was just too grotesque to even contemplate and the problem was that each and every time she did, it made her skin crawl.

But then homosexuality wasn't exactly something she'd been exposed to, understood—and nor did she want to.

On the other hand, this was her fiancé she was talking about, the man whom she had agreed to marry in just four weeks. The guests had been invited, the venues were booked and deposits paid.

She loved Mark, at least she loved the man he was now, and whilst she didn't know the boy back then, she could sympathise with what he was subjected to. It was nothing less than a horrendous ordeal that no child should endure, nor be tormented by for the rest of their lives.

It was clear to her that Mark was already carrying a heavy cross of guilt and confliction, and struggle as she did, she didn't have the strength to forsake him now that he had exposed his heart to her in such a candid and brave way.

She loved him.

The past was the past and she didn't want him to hurt anymore. In fact, she would do anything to take away that hurt.

"Katy…?"

She looked at the dishevelled, vulnerable and terrified man before her and then, without hesitation, she placed her cup of tea on the side, threw her arms around him and sobbed.

They remained that way, in each other's arms, for over an hour before eventually emerging, and Katy, true to form, decided that the time for wallowing was over and that they should go out to dinner and finalise any last-minute wedding plans.

And so it came to pass that, four weeks later, Katy married Mark but, unbeknown to her, this union spelled the start of a chain of events the culmination of which would change her in ways she could never have imagined.

30 LOVE HURTS

It was late spring, and summer had signalled its imminent arrival with one of the hottest weekends England had experienced in months.

The streets of London were teaming with people as they made the most of the sunshine and spring sales.

Sarah and Steve were no exception.

They had spent most of the morning shopping in London's Oxford Street. The trip was meant to be a treat for Sarah who, up until now, had only dreamt of visiting so many designer stores all in one day. She certainly couldn't have afforded to shop in any of them, but Steve took care of that with his credit card.

Sarah found the process as scary as it was exhilarating, especially when Steve kept insisting she could choose whatever she wanted no matter the cost.

Her first reaction was to laugh. It was only when she stopped giggling that she realised, and then asked, "You're serious?"

He nodded and winked at her in his trademark sexy way.

"Oh, my God!" she had squealed in response as he took her hand and led her from one fine store to the next.

It had been a fantastic day and Sarah didn't want it to end. Occasionally, in the few moments when Steve wasn't by her side, she found herself wondering what life would be like without him, and she absolutely hated the thought, but she just loved being with him.

It could be anytime, anywhere—out shopping for designer clothing or watching soap operas on television—any place was a great place, as long as he was by her side.

There was something about Steve that made her feel safe, warm and good inside. It wasn't just about how he was with her or what he did for her; it was more about how he made her *feel*. For the first time in a long time, Sarah felt good about herself. She felt as if she actually existed in the world.

Nobody had ever made her feel this *complete*.

That's why now, at the end of the day, as London was cast in the shadows of a setting sun, and to the soundtrack of children laughing and playing in a nearby park, she felt a sudden compulsion to express her love for this man.

So, she uncharacteristically dropped her bags in the middle of the street, spun him to her and kissed him long and deeply on the lips.

If only her sister could see her now.

Maybe she could; maybe she was watching from one of the upstairs windows.

It had been nearly a month since their conversation, and during that time Steve had been the epitome of the ideal fiancé.

Now more than ever, she knew she wanted to be his bride.

"I love you," she said, when they finally emerged from the kiss.

Steve smiled his cool smile and said, "Wow—and I love you too, babe."

"How much do you love me?" she asked in a giggly, girly tone.

He thought about the question with lingering seriousness and then said, "I'm not quite sure about that, but leave it with me."

"Oi!" she complained as she playfully smacked his arm, and was about to kiss him once more when a car horn demanded her attention.

She turned, smiled and waved at the driver as the car sped by.

"Oh, hi Geoff!" she waved enthusiastically.

"Who was that?" Steve asked.

"Oh, it's just Geoff," she replied, still waving and smiling after the car.

"Who's he?"

"Oh, he's a family friend."

"What kind of friend?"

Sarah looked at Steve and smiled, "Just a friend." She paused and then added in a teasing tone, "Ooh, are you jealous?"

Steve didn't respond. He just looked at her.

"Well, are you?" she continued with a big smile. "Are you jea—?

The rest of the sentence was knocked out of her as something smashed into the soft of her belly with such force, it took her breath away.

She clutched her midriff, sank to her knees and then collapsed on the cold concrete pavement, gasping for air.

Around her, the world continued to spin as she tried to process exactly what had just happened.

Across the street, somebody was laughing, whilst nearby the car engines sounded so close she thought she had fallen into the road.

She breathed in carbon monoxide as a shadow fell over her.

Steve? What happened? She thought she had spoken the words, but they were only inside her head. *Help me, Steve. Help me.*

Sarah squinted into the sun as she tried to discern the person looming over her, but he or she was a dark blur.

"Steve?"

It couldn't be.

With that, the shadow turned and walked away, leaving her to struggle with the incredulity of the moment.

Sarah lay on that concrete sidewalk, just metres away from her home, for what seemed like half an hour but could only have been several minutes, as she struggled to reconcile what had just happened.

Had Steve, her fiancé really punched her?

Her Steve?

That was impossible.

And it was as she was working through this that voices distracted her. A young couple towering over her. They looked anxious and were talking to her, but she was having a hard time hearing what they were saying. She could see their lips moving but no words were coming out.

Or were they?

They were.

The duo was asking if she was okay and also what had happened. But Sarah couldn't tell them what she herself was still struggling with. Instead, she told them that she'd tripped and fallen, but that she was okay now.

When they offered to call an ambulance for her or get her home. She thanked them politely, while picking up her shopping bags, explained that she lived in one of the nearby houses and reassured them that she was fine.

Steve was on the phone when Sarah entered the front door.

He seemed very angry and she overheard the words "police" and "delivery" before his tone calmed suddenly and he said, "Anyway, listen, I've got to go," he said, quickly, and then added, "Keep me fucking informed..."

He hung up and instantly turned to Sarah, but she had disappeared into the kitchen with the shopping bags.

He followed her.

"Where have you been?" he demanded.

"Where you left me", she responded, avoiding eye contact with him and busying herself packing away the few grocery items they'd picked up on the way home.

"Sarah, listen," Steve began apologetically. "I'm really sorry about what happened. I don't know what came over me. I just… lost control."

"Lost control?" she echoed, finally turning to meet his gaze. "Is that supposed to make me feel better?"

"I said I was sorry."

"Yeah? Well, sometimes just saying sorry doesn't make it right, Steve," she said dismissively, as she turned her back to him and faced the cupboard once more.

There was anger in her voice. Something he hadn't witnessed before.

A few seconds went by, then, "What happened? What possible reason could you have for doing that to me?" she asked incredulously, turning suddenly to face him once more.

"I don't know. I don't know what came over me. I just saw you waving at that bloke and I lost it."

He moved over to her to take her hand, but she shrugged him off and moved to the opposite side of the room where she crossed her arms.

"I'm sorry," he said, in a whiny, imploring tone. "I'm so sorry, Sarah. I just… well, just the thought of some other bloke around you. I got scared that you might love someone else over me."

"What?" she asked with a frown.

"I know it sounds pathetic and maybe I'm a pathetic guy who is hopelessly in love with you and I really don't know what I'd do if I didn't have you anymore. I know it's hard for you to understand that but," he sighed, "look, Sarah, I know I was out of order and totally understand if you want me to leave. I know I don't deserve you anyway, especially after what happened."

He paused for a few seconds, allowing the words to sink in, and then slowly turned to leave the kitchen.

"No, wait!" Sarah reacted instinctively, clutching at his arm. "Don't go."

He waited without turning.

Seconds ticked by.

She tugged at his arm, "Steve…"

Eventually, he turned to face her with a sad, guilt-stricken hanging of the head.

Sarah felt that, paused a few seconds and then, "You silly thing," she said, sliding her arms around him. "I love you, Steve, you and only you. I'm not interested in anybody else. Do you understand that?" she said, holding his face and looking into his eyes.

He nodded like a chastised child.

"But after what happened today…"

"It will never happen again," he interrupted. "I promise, Sarah, it will never happen again. I mean, I don't even know why it did today. It's nothing like me."

Sarah rubbed the ache that was still in her belly and considered the humiliation of that couple towering over her.

Was his reaction so bad?

She rationalised that Steve must love her a lot to not be able to bear the thought of another man even looking at her. She had never experienced anything like this before.

Was this true love? Of the kind where one heart simply can't bear the thought of being without the other? She certainly felt that way about him. She didn't know if she would have reacted in the same way, but she hated the idea of being without him and couldn't even contemplate the thought of another girl putting her hands on him.

So, what do you think?

Again, with complete detachment, unless you've experienced this kind of relationship, you will have already formed an opinion about this story, cast a judgement, especially about Sarah.

She must be crazy, right? Who on earth would want to get married to someone like that?

Well, I think the simple answer is: somebody who is in love.

Whichever way Sarah approached this thing, she would always have the 'handicap' of being in love.

Now, I call it a handicap simply because love, not unlike drugs or alcohol, impairs our ability to think rationally and to confront things with the lucidity necessary to make choices that are best for us.

Most understand that to drive under the influence is wrong for a multitude of reasons, yet thousands around the world still do.

Sarah was well and truly driving under the influence, and consequently she would have done anything to rationalise Steve's behaviour. Rather than concluding that he couldn't possibly hurt someone he loved, she concluded that he loved her so much that the fear of losing her drove him to hurt her.

Make sense?

Well, it did to Sarah.

She was in love and already in denial against that which threatened everything that appeared perfect in her world. Consequently, she *denied* what had actually taken place and then *rationalised* Steve's behaviour as an act of love because she wasn't ready to even contemplate anything else at this stage, although what came next would make her wish she had.

31 I'M DONE TALKING

It had been a few months since the weekend in Raleigh, USA.

M and I were having a telephone conversation during which we discussed the next trip, although we stopped short of making any firm dates as M said he was unable to commit given that America had just declared war on Iraq.

It was March 2003.

I don't know what exactly it was, whether I was having a bad day or simply having a hard time dealing with the uncertainty of my future with him, but I lost it.

Don't get me wrong. The *hurry up and wait* mentality of the American military was something I struggled with throughout the years we were together but, as much as it frustrated me, I understood it.

But this time it wasn't just about the Marine Corps; this time I was picking up something from M that had me unnerved, a certain reluctance that I hadn't noticed before and, quite frankly, it made me feel very vulnerable and, in turn, it scared me.

So, I overreacted.

I told him that I was sick and tired of living my life at the whim of the U.S. Marine Corps, that it was he and not I who had enlisted and thus had a contract to fulfil. I then went on to question him about the real motivation behind his reluctance to commit to this next trip. Was it really because he believed the military had initiated *Stop Loss* (all leave cancelled, all personnel required for duty) or was it simply because he didn't want to make the journey for other reasons?

He then completely broadsided me by quoting something I had said in the heat of an argument I didn't actually remember over a year before.

He told me that he couldn't see any point in making the journey since I had already intimated at the fact that, should there not be any further commitment of a future between us, after he had left the Marine Corps, I would start dating other people.

Of course, this only added fuel to the flames.

I stated that he had confirmed my suspicions, and I accused him of unearthing a throwaway comment in a cynical attempt to hide his real reason for not making the trip.

We argued some more.

I told him that I was no longer interested in debating the issue and that if he wanted to make the journey then he should get the leave approved and only contact me again when he had, and I slammed the phone down.

Yes, I know, sounds very dramatic and somewhat infantile but, if you will have gathered anything from this book so far, it is the fact that when emotions are involved, rationale often becomes the first casualty.

The truth is, I was actually very upset, frustrated that, once again, my life was being subjected to a force over which I had no control whatsoever as well as what appeared to be a clear and present danger of losing the person I happened to love—topped with the fact that, worse still, I was the one who had just initiated that.

Although, I need not have worried, because, just a few days later, M called me and told me that he had managed to get two weeks of leave approved for the beginning of May 2003.

We agreed to meet in England once more.

I was ecstatic.

Not only because of the actual journey but because of the fact that he managed to apply for and get leave so quickly regardless of the military climate at the time. I had no idea how he managed to swing that one, and I did not care (I guess it was due to the fact that M's unit had more of a service backup role; I don't think he'd actually been deployed the whole time we were together). All I cared about was that he managed to get the leave approved; we were good after all.

And I was going to repay that in kind; I was going to make this trip the best ever and spared no expense in doing so.

I booked a hotel near Windsor Castle, London, and a beach apartment in the Southwest of England. From there, I'd plotted an itinerary that would see us explore most, if not all, of the castles and other places of national interest in the South and Southwest of the England (yes, not unlike quite a few Americans, M had a thing for history and castles).

I was determined; this would be the trip to remember.

And it was but, as you'll discover, for all the wrong reasons.

It started with the fact that M and I managed to get into yet another argument just days before he was due to fly to England, and, I dare say, it was of my own making.

Somehow (do you like the way I put that? As if I had no part in this), in conversation, I told M that I had befriended someone in the UK. I stressed that he was just a friend, but nonetheless a nice guy.

M wanted to know if this 'friend' was more than that. I told him that of course he wasn't, and casually missed out the fact that he wasn't even gay.

Remember that chapter about the games we play? M had been so reluctant to schedule the new trip at the beginning that I had good reason to wonder. I needed to know that he still cared. What I didn't expect was for him to fly into an instant rage. And, much to my own detriment, that's all I remembered rather than the moment and the information that I was receiving from my little game.

Technically, it had backfired, and I remember being somewhat taken aback by his overreaction to my revelation.

"You're overreacting," I said, and then added the all-important element, "The guy isn't even gay."

But it was too late.

M told me he was calling off the trip stating there was no point if I had already started seeing somebody else. The whole trip had become a farce.

"It's like asking somebody out to dinner to tell them to fuck off!" he said.

And, regardless of my protestations, he told me it was over and hung up.

I remember sitting there for a few seconds, struggling to reconcile what I had said versus M's reaction to this. We'd never been like this before, but these past two telephone conversations really had me wondering—although it was kind of irrelevant now.

I felt awful.

It was just two days before the holiday was due to take place. I had booked everything—hotels, the apartment, entrance fees to theatres, tickets to some top attractions—and yet now, thanks to one stupid phone call, everything had changed.

I was heartbroken.

That night, no matter how much I tried, I could not sleep as I processed how exactly my biggest fears had turned into a reality, through my own doing.

Eventually, I must have fallen asleep because I remember being awoken in the early hours by the vibrating sound of my mobile phone.

It was M.

He was sorry and, if I was still up for it, he wanted to make the journey after all.

"Are you sure?" I asked blearily.

"Yeah, I am, and I promise that I am going to make it the best trip we've ever had," he said, excitedly.

But the reality couldn't have been further from that promise. When M landed in England on the 1st May 2003, he was nothing like the man I had known for the past six years. Yes, the big smile was there, the eyes and that man hug as I greeted him at arrivals, but something wasn't right.

He seemed distant, haunted.

"Are you okay?"

"I'm good," he answered, "just tired."

But his so-called tiredness continued well into the next day and the day after that.

The man I knew wasn't the warmest, most demonstrative man (certainly not in public), but he was nothing like this guy who was distant, irritable; a stranger who appeared to be in a perpetual state of discontent.

Of course, me being me, I wanted him to just snap out of it as I was actually feeling somewhat irked by the fact that I was constantly trying to 'perk him up' when, in reality, it was I who needed some kind of reassurance, some kind of reconnection after all of the recent and somewhat constant tension between us.

"M," I said as I drove us out of London.

We had just spent our first night together in Windsor and to say that it had been somewhat underwhelming would be an understatement. Not the location, not the hotel, nor the changing of the guard viewable from the comfort of our private balcony, but us, our first night together.

"Is there something you need to tell me?"

"What do you mean?"

"Well, something's not quite right and I'm worried. I want us to have a good trip, but I don't think that's going to be possible if there's something bothering you. What's wrong?"

He considered what I had just said for a few seconds, and I actually thought he was going to spit out what was bugging him, but instead he said flatly, "You know what's wrong with me."

I felt a sudden wave of anger, "Actually, M, I don't know what's wrong with you. In fact, I don't even recognise you. Who the hell are you? You are nothing like the person I've known all these years. I mean, you've been here for over a day, yet it feels like I'm alone."

"Well maybe you should invite your new friend to come along and keep you company."

I sighed, swallowing some of my frustration. "Is that really what this is about? Is all this attitude really about some friend of mine, or is there something else you want to share with me?"

He didn't reply. Instead he just turned to look out of the window.

"M?"

I looked at the back of his head for some time and was going to press him further, but got distracted by the fact that I'd actually taken a wrong turn and we were going in the opposite direction.

Eventually, we arrived at our beach apartment on the Southwest coast of England.

I remember walking into that place and exclaiming, "Wow!" The first thing I spotted as soon as I opened the front door was a wall of washed-out blue. I thought it was the décor but soon realised it was actually a picture window with a view of the ocean.

Our apartment was built on a peninsula, which meant that when the tide was in we were almost surrounded by the Atlantic Ocean, and the view from the balcony was simply stunning.

I instantly felt my spirits rise and injected my enthusiasm into the moment by hugging M and building up my excitement for the place

If M was impressed, he didn't show it but, then again, it never was about the location for him; it was only ever about us.

At least it used to be.

So, the days came and went and he would hardly say a word. We'd spend most of our time watching DVDs or playing video games, but even they were nowhere near as exciting and/or as competitive as they used to be. His excitement would last only as long as the game we were playing and then, as soon as that was over, he'd don that same haunted look that I had come to loathe.

Truth is, I missed him.

I missed that brooding American who'd hardly be the epitome of romanticism, but then he'd say or do something to make me think, *wow, he does care.*

Yes, I realised in hindsight that I too had settled.

Given that M actually fed affection to me like proverbial scraps to pigeons in the park (or at least he did towards the end), I had probably read much more into each word, each act than it actually deserved.

On the other hand, at least there had been *something*.

Now there was nothing. An affection or even an acknowledgement drought; it's almost as if I didn't exist. Every action, every word appeared to be initiated by me, and I began to resent it, finding myself locked between the two emotions of sadness or anger.

One day, I decided to change that.

I told M that we'd never worked together on a photo shoot in all the time I had known him and that now we had the perfect opportunity to make that happen.

He, or more specifically his body, would be the star talent and the room, the balcony, the view would be the perfect backdrop. I enthused the whole event by telling him that he'd be the first photo shoot with the brand-new digital camera that I'd purchased specifically for the trip, stating that it would be a good opportunity to put it through its paces.

Of course, M, didn't share my enthusiasm—not that he'd ever loved the lens—but me being me, I concluded that if he wasn't particularly fussed either way, that he may as well indulge me.

I added that I was going stir crazy in that room and that he must be too. I didn't include that the reason I felt as if I was going insane was that I felt I was locked in some kind of hideous film noire where the main protagonist knows that something isn't quite right, but nobody else believes.

His attitude was draining and I was starting to think that I wanted out of this holiday, but I'd invested too much to give up on it just yet.

The inspiration for the shoot came from the sun shining through a set of flowery red net curtains that adorned the balcony doors. I loved how they would glide up and down, billow in and out of the room on the ocean breeze creating a pattern on the oatmeal carpet.

I instantly imagined M having an afternoon siesta on the rug as the patterns and shadows tattooed his naked muscular body—and that's exactly what I shot.

Needless to say, I was surprised when M, albeit reluctantly, complied with the pitch. I say *complied;* he didn't really say much, he simply looked at me with those troubled eyes of his whilst slowly stripping down to his well-filled briefs, and I remember thinking, "Damn you!"

The photo shoot went well, but if I said that M didn't smile for the whole of the two-something hours it took for me to get the shots that I wanted, I wouldn't be lying. And even today, when I look at the photos, I don't necessarily see somebody engaging with the camera. Sure, he posed for the photos as instructed, but he always appeared to be somewhere else. In fact, when I gave him the option to go 'freestyle' (a common section of my photo shoots where I tell the subjects to just move and pose as they see fit and I shoot the image that I like), he'd often opt for poses where he was not looking at and often looking away from the lens or, in this case, me.

Conversely, when I looked through the lens, I was searching not only for the best subject for my pictures, but for the man I once knew. What I found was the epitome of masculinity with the muscular embodiment of Michelangelo's David but, sadly, with an equal heart of stone.

I think I realised then, with every click of that shutter, that the man I loved, for reasons unbeknown to me, was gone.

And I missed him.

That night, I remember waking with the belief that somebody was shining a flashlight into our bedroom window, momentarily forgetting that wasn't possible as we were in the penthouse, but realising that it was instead the full moon making shadows out of furniture and a stage of the double bed on which I sat upright. Next to me, sleeping soundly, was the naked form of a man, but it wasn't M; it was a stranger, a shell left here by the body snatchers.

And I sat there for I don't know how long contemplating this thought before I literally ran, as quietly as I could, from the bedroom and out onto the balcony where I gulped in the fresh ocean air as if it were a medicine for heartache, and drew comfort in the rhythmic pounding of the waves on the rocks below.

And I'd love to be able to tell you at this stage that, like some movie scene, it's as I stood, resting against the balustrade, crying into moonlit gloom that I heard the balcony doors slide open and felt M put his arms around me, reassuringly, and tell me that everything would be okay, but he didn't. That was just a fantasy that I played over and over in my head.

I spent the next hour or so alone and, during that time, I made my decision.

At breakfast the next morning, I told M that I didn't believe the trip was working out anywhere near as both of us had intended and that I thought it would be in both our interests that he leave early.

By early, I meant one whole week.

He agreed!

Yet, when it came to actually making the phone call to the airline to try to reschedule the tickets, we both found ourselves talking about how ridiculous this all was and agreeing that it was foolish to give up on another week together, and that we should try to make the most of the second week.

And whilst we went into the weekend with the best intentions—cinema, dinner out—the second week, slowly and gradually, turned into a grotesque twin of the first, complete with warts of petty arguments, scars of recriminations and the saggy skin of weariness.

After a while, I started to believe that M was genuinely upset about his suspicion that I was cultivating a relationship with someone else. And it was in those moments that I cursed myself and started to truly believe that, but for the fact that I had told M about one friendship and that I had led him to think, at least in the first instance, that it might be more than that, we wouldn't be in this tainted time together that was marred by constant conflict.

This was all my fault.

The arguments, the mood swings and the disengagement with intimacy was due to just one thing: my stupid game.

But it was too late now. The damage had been done.

And so that's how I came to spend the last few days of our time together accepting that which I had created. I didn't argue, try to change, motivate, or initiate; I just went through the motions.

We visited castles, old monuments and drove many miles with just a few words. In fact, to this day, I couldn't tell you exactly which places we actually visited because everything became such a blur as we made our way towards the end of the week.

Everything but the day before The Marine was due to fly home.

I remember that day very well.

We visited the white cliffs of Dover, England, and the so-called secret World War II tunnels that had been carved out of the cliffs during the conflict.

The tunnels, which feature tiny portal windows looking out onto the English Channel, stretch for miles and are set on different levels (apparently to maximise space). They feature communication rooms, hospital wards (where many of the wounded were brought during the Battle of Britain), strategy rooms for intelligence officers and temporary training quarters for secret service spies before they were sent on their way across the dangerous waters to France.

And, no, I didn't miss the gigantic metaphor displayed before me. The conflict M and I were having on multiple levels was something that had indeed inflicted its own wounds and left me truly shell-shocked for a couple of days, and I had indeed become a metaphoric walking wounded, a dishevelled shadow of my former self.

But I enjoyed my time in the tunnels.

In fact, I think I *found* myself again down there: the fighter, the leveller.

How could I not?

I'd just visited a place where people literally fought for their lives, those of their colleagues and those of a nation. In fact, it was as I walked through one of the infirmaries where discreetly placed speakers played re-enacted dramatic scenes of life down there that I felt as if some of the phantoms of history gave me a swift kick up the backside and a stern warning about wallowing.

When we emerged topside and somewhat gratefully into a fine mist of rain, I asked M if he enjoyed himself.

He nodded.

"I did!" I said excitedly, "I thought it was great! Those poor people lived in those awfully cramped conditions to serve the nation. I found it inspiring," I grinned. "So inspiring that I think we should climb to the top of the hill and take a look out over the White Cliffs of Dover. What do you think?"

He made a show of squinting into the mist of rain and then said flatly, "It's raining."

"So what?" I said. "A bit of rain never hurt anybody."

And off I went, knowing full well that M didn't have keys to the car and that he'd have to follow or wait for my return like a sulky school kid.

We walked to the top of the cliffs and took in the view. Well, as far as the mist would permit, because I remember it being a particularly dreary day.

I also remember asking M to pose for a photo.

"It's raining," he repeated with that sulky child demeanour once more whilst reluctantly posing for the camera with his hands thrust into his jeans, hunching his muscly arms and looking darned miserable.

I ignored him.

"Bloody hell, smile. What's up with you, man?" I said cheerfully, ignoring his sulky face and secretly enjoying his obvious discomfort.

"It's cold," he said, flatly, blinking at me as if to say, *"Have you finished playing crazy now?"*

And I remember looking at him in that moment as he stood there in his jeans, white T-shirt, short (but now fluffy) military haircut and goatee, specially groomed for me (as he loved to be clean-shaved but he knew I loved him with a beard), and thinking he looked so damn handsome, and I realised I still felt so much love for him. It was unconditional love of the kind felt by parents when their child is behaving like an absolute brat yet looking cute with it.

"Try smiling," I said, laughing.

"It's cold," he repeated.

"Yeah, I heard you the first time. Remember, I did tell you to wear a jacket, but you chose not to?"

"Yeah, but I was in the car at the time. I didn't know you were planning to go trekking up a hill."

"Oh shut up and smile, you miserable git," I said with my own smile, in an attempt to encourage him.

He sulkily yet somewhat deliciously posed for the photo, but just to get my revenge for him making me feel so damn crappy over the past two weeks, I said I needed to take a few more and then added, "I thought marines were supposed to be tough."

"I'm on vacation," he retorted.

"Oh, I see. So when a marine's on vacation he becomes a wimp—is that it?"

He rolled his eyes. "Are we done with the photos?"

"We're done," I said, once again drawing comfort from his discomfort, but equally eager to get back to the car since the mist had become a drizzle that was rapidly becoming rain.

It's odd; even now, as I look at that image, I feel love for that moment as I considered that, despite all of his weirdness, the guy was still wearing a beard for me.

I guess sometimes it's the little things.

I realise now that I was rationalising.

In the absence of anything truly tangible, I was latching on to whatever made me feel better or diluted the terrible way I'd been feeling for the last two weeks.

But I was done being the victim.

By the time we got to the car, we were both rain drenched. M was truly irked, but I wasn't going to let a minor detail like that get in my way. I proceeded to lay down the law about when we'd be eating dinner tonight.

Allow me to explain.

Our whole relationship had one fundamental constant—and, no, it wasn't necessarily love, total devotion—but it was when and where M would be getting his next meal. And, no, I'm not talking about the average three square meals a day; I'm talking about good, hefty, protein-filled snacks in addition to those meals.

This was more than often a bone of contention for us as most of our time together was spent travelling and it wasn't always practical to stop for a man-size snack. In fact, this was so important that if we were on a trip in the UK, I'd often make sure that the car was loaded with water and snacks just for him. The only problem with that was that dry snacks weren't necessarily the protein he craved.

The reason M needed such constant and regular sustenance was that he worked out a lot (back home) and anybody who knows somebody who trains regularly will understand that diet is a very important factor in the regime to keep the proverbial body beautiful.

And, struggle as I did in the beginning with such a distracting focus, I learned to respect it (not just for M but for my own selfish reasons of course) and planned for it accordingly.

But not tonight.

Tonight, rather than dump all our stuff in our room and rush to dinner, we were going to get my car cleared of any debris and of M's belongings as I did not believe it made sense to do so later, when it was dark, nor did we have time first thing in the morning before I drove him back to the airport to catch his flight home.

M grunted his acknowledgement but, given the drops of rainwater that were falling from the tips of his fluffy hair, I don't think he gave a toss either way.

So, we arrived at the hotel.

And, in accordance with another fairly popular tradition, I left the car and went straight to check in and pay for the night's accommodation. As I was doing so, M arrived in the lobby pulling both his suitcase and mine.

So, we checked in and dumped the bags in our room, and it was not long before I heard the proverbial line in that lovely American accent, "Are we gonna' get something to eat?"

"Not yet. I told you. We need to clear the car out first as we won't be able to do it properly later as it'll be dark."

"Yeah, we will."

"No we won't."

"We will."

"M, I'm not arguing with you. We're doing the car first. If we both get it done now then we'll have it done in no time."

And that's when the angry purse of the lip came which, for some obscure reason, didn't annoy me anywhere near as much as it normally would.

"We're clearing out the car first. Now, you can help—or, you've seen where the restaurant is, you can go by yourself and pay with your own credit card."

With that, I left the room, went back to the car and started pulling the boot (or trunk) apart, throwing out garbage and taking out anything that didn't belong in there.

M lingered nearby, clearly contemplating whether or not to go to dinner without me.

Then, albeit reluctantly, he decided to help.

The car was sorted within thirty minutes and I felt happier for it. It was something else that I didn't have to worry about.

I wasn't even hungry; I just felt like I wanted to go to sleep. I was so exhausted. It had been a horrendous two weeks and I just felt like all of my energy reserves had been depleted

I told M that I wasn't particularly hungry, but knew that wasn't going to fly with him.

We went to the restaurant, which was very busy, but we managed to get squeezed onto a small table at the centre of the place that very much resembled a steakhouse.

It was a stone building with rustic furniture, log fire and countrified memorabilia, with old cart wheels, copper pots and pans adorning the walls.

But for the fact that I felt like I was walking around in some smeared-up camera lens, I would have actually appreciated and enjoyed the décor.

The waitress took some time to come over and take our order as the room was busy with other diners who were chatting animatedly. In fact, rather than focussing on the menu in front of me, I remember drifting off and wondering what exactly these people, whose dissonant babble I could not actually decipher, were actually saying to each other. Were they happy, sad, mad at each other? Were they out celebrating a special occasion or were they weary travellers like me?

The waitress reminded me, "What do you fancy?" as she hovered nearby.

Nothing looked particularly appetising, but I think that was more a reflection of how I was feeling than the menu. I ordered a chicken salad and M opted for the safe protein that the house steak promised.

And it was then, not long after the waitress had left our table that he spoke.

"And you're welcome, by the way," he said, leaning back in his chair.

I focussed on him and squinted equivocally.

"For bringing your bag in from the car."

It took me a few seconds to actually absorb what he had just said. There was something about the smug way in which he delivered that line that really annoyed me, but I said, with all the restraint I could muster, for I was well aware of the other diners who were literally surrounding us like Indians around a wagon, "Thank you so much for bringing my bag in, M."

He nodded satisfactorily, as if he'd just saved me from imminent danger.

But I added, "It was really nice of you to bring my bag in while I was busy paying for our room."

"This isn't the first time you haven't thanked me for doing stuff, though."

And that was another cattle prod.

I looked around the room and said, as quietly and as calmly as I could, "I have no idea what you're talking about, but I don't think now's the time…"

The waitress returned with our drinks and a smile.

"Thank you," I said, forcing an equally enthusiastic smile until she disappeared once more.

Neither of us said anything for a few seconds, but it was only long enough for the words to burn their way to my tongue.

"So what exactly is it that I haven't thanked you for?" I asked as I simmered with resentment at the injustice of his remark.

"It doesn't matter," he said dismissively, sensing the tension that was building across the table.

"Oh, no, it does matter; it obviously matters, M, otherwise you wouldn't have mentioned it." That line was delivered slightly louder than I had intended.

He leaned forward in his chair, looking around the room, "I said it doesn't matter…"

"And I said it does! I want to know how exactly you feel wronged by me. Is it the way I've put up with your shit for the past two weeks, or maybe it's the way I've driven you all over England when all you've done is bitch and moan about either being hungry or cold…?"

Now I'd actually made the couple next to us, the ones that had been scoffing as if they hadn't seen food in a month, pause from their bounty of fish and chips to look over.

"Now's not the time…" M said calmly whilst keeping his eyes locked on mine, as if by doing so he could erase the fact that next door were still staring inquisitively, wondering what the raised voice was all about.

"You're right, I said," spotting the voyeurs. "Now's not a good time."

I took a swig from my diet Coke and made the process last as long as I could in the hope that it would calm the raging beast that was suddenly and inexplicably clawing at my throat, desperate to be set free.

But it didn't work.

I slammed my glass down. "Where the hell do you get off?" I snarled.

M put his head down and took a deep breath as if bracing himself.

"You show up here, empty-handed, and you lecture me on not being grateful? For what? For cow-tailing to you? For putting up with your body-snatcher bullshit?"

My growl was low and menacing and, even now, thinking back, I don't actually remember it as me speaking those words, but as some kind of alter ego, some beast that had been gestating inside me for those two weeks, ready to be born in that very restaurant in that very moment.

"Who the fuck do you think you are? Presuming to lecture me on so-called etiquette, gratitude. You want to know about gratitude... let me tell you about gratitude. You cried about me not thanking you for bringing my bags in from the car? You didn't even bat an eyelid on my spending thousands of pounds on this trip. Where's *your* thank you, M? Where's the gratitude? And what about thanking me for the fact that you've become so damn complacent that you actually board a plane to another country without so much as a penny in your pocket?"

My voice was getting progressively louder and I could sense eyes on me, but I simply didn't care. It's as if a damn had broken somewhere inside of me and all of the frustrations, all of the heartache and all of the rage just came roaring forth like a pride of lions.

"You don't thank me for that, do you? *Do* you? Come to think of it, you don't actually thank me for *anything*. And why is that, M? I'll tell you why; it's because you're an ingrate, a parasite whom for the duration of the past two weeks, if not for the whole time we've been together, has done nothing but take and give whatever scraps you deem fit in return! You lecture *me*? You're so bloody self-absorbed you haven't a bloody clue how you've made me feel ever since you arrived two weeks ago—but, just in case you are interested, LIKE SHIT! M, you've made me feel like shit! Like I don't exist, that I'm some kind of leper, something to be endured rather than the person you're supposed to love! In the meantime, I've put up with your sulks, your mood, your empty-shell, out-of-body bullshit, your hot, your cold, your ups and your downs—and for what? For *what*?"

I stood up.

I didn't realise at the time, and nor did I care, but the room had gone quiet. Everyone was looking in our direction with curious yet lowered eyes—you know, that kind of wanting to know what the hell was going on, but at the same time dreading the moment that I might glance over at them and actually make eye contact.

My eyes were starting to water at this stage, but I don't think it was sadness but rage. That's all I felt, complete and utter rage.

I didn't notice it then, but I realise now that it was without a doubt the culmination of a myriad of things. Frustration—the man I loved had, for whatever reason, changed and I could do nothing about it. Exhaustion—I felt so tired and my nerves were truly frayed from the constant emotional struggle and the relentless quest to please in an effort to restore some equilibrium to what we were together. Wronged —I felt wronged by M's accusation about being ungrateful when, all this time, it was I who had suppressed my belief that he was ungrateful, and that I felt that he had in some way taken advantage of me, at least financially.

Don't get me wrong—only in so far as I *allowed* it to happen, as it would be unfair to say that M didn't finance in part, if not wholly, all of our American trips. Most of all, I guess I just felt guilty that I may have, in whatever way, contributed to how M was feeling, and that there was something I had said or done to make him fall out of love with me, because that's how I felt, that I'd been discarded so what was the point in trying?

"I'm going back to the hotel and you can pay for your own fucking meal," I yelled.

With that, I turned and left the building. And although I didn't notice them at the time, some of our fellow diners reacted to the recent performance; some wolf whistled, others thanked God, and somewhere I think somebody actually clapped.

I didn't go back to the hotel. I took some time out, went for a drive. I didn't know where the hell I was, but just needed to get away for a while and clear my head.

Good Lord, I had just made such a spectacle of myself. And I didn't know if it was this I was trying to deal with more than the actual content of my tirade. One thing is sure; I did feel better for it.

When I eventually returned to the room, nearly an hour later, I was fully prepared for round two as I didn't think there was any way that M was going to let me publicly humiliate (and technically out) him like that, and get away with it. At best, I expected him to have actually left the room and checked into another or for him to have made his own way to the airport.

And, to be honest, my heart sank when I thought of the latter because that wasn't how I wanted it to end between us. That wasn't it at all, but it was too late now—the damage, however great, was already done and there was nothing I could do about it.

The hotel room was in complete darkness but for a very small lamp on the bedside table, which meant I didn't see him immediately and I momentarily did think he'd left already as I doubted he would have stayed in the restaurant any longer than he needed to.

He was sitting in an armchair, partially illuminated by the lamp.

I sat at the foot of the bed.

We didn't speak for what seemed like a very long time, neither wanting to be the first to break the silence.

"You left me," he said softly and maybe even with a tone of incredulity.

"What? You mean you actually noticed?" I said.

He didn't answer and I thought he'd gone into a sulk, but then I realised from the sniffing sound that it wasn't that at all, but that M, the hardnosed marine whom, despite his faults, I adored, was actually crying!

It took me a few seconds to take in this detail and I angled myself on the bed casually to get visual confirmation of what I believed I was hearing.

Sure enough; M was crying, not in a boo hoo kind of way, but there were certainly tears streaming down his face.

And I, whilst still somewhat stoical about the whole ordeal on the outside, melted. I just wanted to run across the room, throw my arms around him and tell him how sorry I was, but instead I asked, somewhat seriously, "Why are you crying?"

It took M a few seconds, but then he said, almost in a whimper, "Because of what you said."

Another tug at my heartstrings. Well, what do you expect— my boy was hurting.

I sighed. "M, I didn't say that stuff to hurt you. Nor to throw anything back in your face. You know I care about you; I love you, and would do anything for you but recently, recently, M, well, you simply pushed me too far."

I went over and knelt on the floor next to him, placing my hands on his knees.

"You've been so cold. So distant. I mean, you keep telling me it's nothing and then when you aren't saying that you're being mean and saying it's because of this friendship I have with this guy. But I don't believe it, M. I don't believe this whole change of personality is nothing. It's something. It's something and it's been eating you and I just need to know, M, I need to know what it is. Please tell me what it is."

He said nothing; he simply leaned forward and pulled me to him, squeezing me so tight I almost felt the life choked from me.

We must have stayed that way for minutes, neither of us willing to move. I could have fallen asleep in his arms right then and more than welcomed temporary amnesia in relation to recent events, but that wasn't possible.

Eventually, M's hug turned into a kiss. But I pulled away.

"What's up?" he asked.

"Nothing," I said, forcing a smile.

"Come on now. I know you better than that."

And he was right. I could seldom say no to this handsome man who, in this case, pulled off his T-shirt revealing those beautiful pectoral muscles. I gently traced their contours with my fingers and gradually migrated to his biceps and his arms.

Then I kissed him and stood up.

"This," I hesitated. "It's just all too little, too late."

With that I left him and made my way to the bathroom where I shut the door behind me.

I heard him call out, "So I guess you are just going to dump me outside of the terminal tomorrow and not even bother seeing me off?"

I didn't respond. I was done talking.

32 A MOTHER'S CHILD

Mark and Katy's wedding day went ahead as planned.

It was a gloriously joyful day, accentuated by summer sunshine and the good wishes of the whole congregation. Even Mark's father managed to crack a few smiles. In fact, families from both sides couldn't have done more to celebrate the day that nearly wasn't.

For bride and groom, that day wasn't just about the celebration of the union between man and woman, but it was also to consecrate a secret that, whilst harrowing, somehow brought them closer.

Not that they ever revisited the details of Mark's confession—they didn't need to. There was now a subliminal understanding between them, especially on the occasional 'dark day' when Mark found himself haunted by the events of his past.

These days, these 'moments', started as transitory and were normally dealt with via a knowing look or a touch of the arm but slowly, over time, they became more frequent, sometimes two or three times a month.

It was during his 'moments' that Mark would retreat into himself; he'd become mentally withdrawn, by going silent, avoiding eye contact and/or engaging in any type of conversation, and physically withdrawn, by hiding himself away in a dark room where he'd sit or stand quietly in the corner.

The first time he had one of his moments, Katy sought to understand and 'help', as she had tried that day in the corridor, but she soon learned that the best course of action was to actually let Mark work through it in his own way. And he would; he'd emerge hours later, as if nothing had happened.

It took a while for Katy to get used to the ritual but, over time, it simply became a way of life.

One day, she plucked up the courage to suggest counselling, but the way Mark looked at her, with that silent gaze of his, told her that it wasn't something he was prepared to entertain—which in turn made her feel guilty that she may have, in some tactless way, made him feel bad about himself, that he was in some way defective and thus abnormal.

She didn't mention it again.

Instead she focussed on her new career as a secretary. It wasn't necessarily her profession of choice, but money was tight and every little helped. Ironically, she went on to enjoy her new career, which was cut short since, within their first year of marriage, she fell pregnant.

Mark was delighted with the news that he was going to be a father, although something changed in him the day the news was announced. It was if somebody had flipped a switch.

He became clingy and very possessive. He started dictating what Katy should and should not wear, what she should and should not eat and whom she should and should not talk to. He began dictating what groceries she should buy as well as what she should eat.

Whilst Katy accepted this and explained it as a side effect of money being tight, she did struggle with his frequent jealous inquisitions at the end of each day when he would interrogate her about whom she had spoken to, sometimes going as far as asking for specific names in order to establish whether or not there was a pattern of regular interaction.

This and money, or the lack of it, became common flashpoints for arguments between them, which eventually led Mark, regardless of his ambition to become self-employed, to take a job with Sky Television as a satellite dish installation engineer.

The job signalled a change in the family's fortunes, but also in Mark's self-esteem. He started to question life beyond the birth of their child and whether or not he'd become relegated to second place, at least in the eyes of Katy, who tried her best to allay his fears, but was already struggling with the exhaustion of being pregnant and having to keep her job which meant she didn't have time to mollycoddle her husband—the result of which was an increased frequency of his so-called 'moments'.

These escalated from a few a month to once a week and they were starting to wear on Katy, especially when she returned home from work after a particularly busy day and found the house empty.

"Mark?" she called when she entered the house.

No reply.

Then she went to the foot of the stairs. "Mark?"

Still nothing.

She assumed he'd gone out and, somewhat wearily, she willed her heavily pregnant body up the stairs.

First she visited the bathroom and then she made her way to the bedroom which, for some reason, still had the curtains drawn and was, but for the sun peeking in through the side of the curtains, in semi-darkness.

She ignored the gloom, eager to get out of her work clothes and into something more comfortable, when she was startled by the sound of a growling cat on the other side of the room.

She leaned against the wardrobe and gingerly peered into the gloom but couldn't see anything at first. Then, slowly, she craned her neck in an effort to see beyond the bed, expecting the creature to jump out at her at any second.

But she couldn't see anything.

She stepped closer...

...another step...

Slowly, something came into view, and that's when she saw; it wasn't an animal, it was her husband.

Mark was naked, on his knees, and was rocking himself backward and forward as if praying to the wallpaper god.

"Mark?," she called to him, but he didn't answer, as was always the case during one of his moments, and she resisted the urge to march over there and smack her shoe across his head.

She was tired, swollen and not in the mood for this, not today. Instead, she changed her clothes and left the bedroom, closing the door behind her.

A few weeks later, and with just a few months before their baby was due, Mark won a contract in Ireland.

They needed the money and so they jumped at the opportunity.

He left.

Katy was still working as a secretary.

The two kept in touch via regular handwritten letters.

And it was these that would prove the last straw for Katy, who reached a point where she dreaded actually hearing from her own husband.

The letters were full of graphic sexual content.

They started out as typical couple flirtation, today's modern equivalent of sexting, but they soon became scripts for would-be sexual scenes with her. It seemed to Katy that the letters were the written account of Mark's deepest and darkest sexual fantasies, which went beyond conventional intercourse between a man and a woman and became what appeared to be the preface to some disturbing scenarios better suited to a demonic orgy of men and women.

Katy was horrified.

It was as if her husband had read every dark thought that had entered her head after she had learned his secret; every disgusting act she dreaded that he may have performed and/or ask her to perform was contained within these handwritten pages, which read more like the journals of a sexual deviant than the love letters of a husband to his wife.

When Mark came home, the subject of the letters was raised. Katy told him that she never wanted to receive those types of letters again. Mark downplayed her suspicion that these were actual real-world fantasies of his, explaining that he knew she would never participate in such things and these were just the horny ramblings of a man who had been separated from his wife for a long period of time.

But Katy knew better.

To her, these were the real thoughts of a man scarred by a traumatic adolescent sexual experience, and that man happened to be her husband.

She felt dirty, and she could no longer bring herself to be intimate with him. Luckily, she was very heavily pregnant and she would attribute her unwillingness to be close to him to that.

But, eventually, their son was born, and Mark was in awe of his little boy, although it was clear to Katy that, amid all of the excitement, there was clear and present pressure for him to deliver as a father. But the pressure wasn't only on Mark; it started to weigh heavily on her too.

But it wasn't just about providing for her son, since she already had this in hand—she had applied for and won a role as a dispatcher for the local police station, and would start work there immediately after her maternity leave—no, the pressure for her came from questioning whether or not she had made the right decision in marrying Mark.

These thoughts weren't new; they'd obviously been planted there ever since she'd learned the truth about him, along with her own torturous 'what if' thoughts.

She'd heard the stories. She'd read the statistics about the abused becoming the abusers.

Was she safe?

Was her son?

These were questions she'd asked herself time and time again, questions that she'd managed to suppress until those letters, which, like a tractor's plough, brought everything to the surface once more.

They'd now been married for two years, and by this time Mark's controlling ways had gradually become worse.

Katy had to seek permission before she did anything, and, on the rare occasion where she did not, the result would trigger a reaction in her husband that culminated in him either having one of his moments or, worse, the re-enactment of that performance in the hallway.

These were the things, along with the gradual fade of her own identity, the sex with a man she no longer desired, and the directive to submit to her husband's every whim in order to avoid one of his episodes, that Katy had learned to endure and accept as part of her life.

What she couldn't endure, though, was a threat to the safety and well-being of her baby boy, and it was this very thing that was tested one night not long after she had started working as a 999 (911 in America) operator at the local police station.

It had been a gruelling day, as Katy was still acclimatising to both protocol and the emotional complexities of manning a telephone line where her actions could literally result in the life or death of a fellow human being.

Unlike most evenings, Mark wasn't waiting for her by the front door with a battery of questions about her day, what she did and whom she did it with.

And she actually breathed a sigh of relief, as she really wasn't in the mood for him tonight. The last thing she needed was an interrogation the moment she walked through the door.

What she *did* need was the sight for sore eyes that was her eight-month-old boy who stopped roaming around the lounge in his baby walker the moment he spotted her.

"Hello!" she said, beaming a big smile and rushing over to her little boy. "Hello, my lovely. How are you? How are you today?"

She crouched down so that she was at eye level with her son.

The baby boy with pale blonde hair and big brown eyes just gawped at, and eventually cracked what his mother interpreted as a big smile just for her.

"Are you smiling?" she asked in an affected voice. "Are you smiling for mummy?"

She looked around the room. It was empty, yet she'd noticed Mark's car in the driveway, which meant he must be home— which explained the fact there was no sign of the babysitter.

"Mark?"

No answer.

"Mark?"

Still nothing.

So she stood and walked into the kitchen. Mark wasn't in there either.

She grabbed a banana from the nearby stand and began to peel it. "Where's Daddy?" she asked her son, who just blinked at her as if to say, *why are you asking me?*

She didn't wait for a reply, but instead placed the peeled fruit on the tray in front her of her son and stepped into the hallway.

"Mark?" She called when she reached the foot of the stairs, pausing only to wait for a reply, but none came.

She turned to her baby, who was still watching her, and said, "Don't go anywhere; Mummy will be right back."

With that, she climbed the stairs, as an ominous gloom fell over her.

Surely not.

She headed straight for the bedroom where, much to her rage, her fear was realised; the curtains had been pulled shut, the room was shrouded in darkness and Mark, her husband, was sitting in the corner of the room with his knees pulled up to his chin. He was naked and he was rocking himself backward and forward.

"What the fuck?" she breathed.

Her expletive wasn't necessarily because of the condition she found her husband in, because she had already witnessed this state several times before; it was more because he had left her baby boy unattended to do this.

"You are unbelievable! My son is downstairs on his own and you're up here doing your rocking shit!" Her whole body was shivering with rage. "If you can't fucking cope, and can't take care of my son, then you may as well get out of here. You may as well get out of here now!" she yelled.

"You don't understand," Mark whimpered from the corner of the room.

"I don't understand?" She echoed, walking up to him, "I don't understand?"

She kicked his leg, "Get up! Get up!"

She kicked him again.

He didn't respond at the first impact, but at the second, he met her gaze, and with that, he rose to his feet in one movement.

The fluidity of the action startled Katy, and the glare that accompanied it made her reconsider her proximity; Mark was *back in the room* and he was angry. This was evidenced by the fact that his eyes had turned black, to the point where his pupils appeared to have disappeared. This was normally a prelude to his either banging his head or him pummelling his fist against something. Katy knew that it had never been her, but there was always a first time.

She backed out of the room and hurried down the stairs where she re-joined her son.

Moments later, she could hear the slamming of the wardrobe door and then something being repeatedly smashed against it.

She looked up at the ceiling, as if she was able to see through it, to the event that was taking place up there, but that's when the sound stopped and was shortly replaced by that of footsteps coming down the stairs.

These prompted Katy to retreat into the kitchen where she feigned interest in the saucepan cupboard and the preparing of dinner but she was sure to casually glance into the lounge where she could see her son being lifted out of his walker by his father.

She rushed in. "What are you doing?" she asked.

But Mark didn't reply; he just watched her with his black eyes.

"Give him to me!" she ordered, waving at him to hand her son over. But he didn't. Instead, he clutched the boy to his chest, left the room, climbed back up the stairs and disappeared into the bedroom from hence he came, slamming the door shut.

"MARK!"

Katy raced up the stairs after them.

"MARK!"

She pushed on the door, but it wouldn't open; her husband had somehow barricaded it behind him.

"MARK! Please! Mark! Give me my son! Mark! GIVE ME MY SON!"

She pounded on the door with both her hands.

"Mark! Please! You're scaring me! Please! Mark," she tried to reason as her heart hammered in her chest almost as hard as she pummelled the wooden door. She was now gripped with terror, fearing for the life of her baby.

"MARK! PLEASE! Please Mark, please don't hurt my boy! Please don't hurt our baby! MARK!"

Her eyes filled with tears and her heart with rage as she tried to kick the door in with her bare feet.

"MARK!"

No reply.

She looked around the landing for something to break the door down with but there was nothing.

"MARK!" She screamed.

She stopped temporarily, listening for movement inside but none came.

She rapped on the door once more, "Mark? MARK!"

But he wouldn't come out of that room, not for an hour or so, and only after Katy had called his doctor. It was she who had to talk him out of that room and to deliver a somewhat bemused toddler into the arms of his hysterical mother.

And that's the day that Katy knew that her marriage was well and truly dead. But the question was how could she tell her husband and how exactly would he react when he found out?

Only time would tell but nothing could prepare her for what happened next.

33 EYES WIDE SHUT

It had been a few months since the incident on the street and Sarah was starting to feel the strain on her relationship with Steve.

She continued to rationalise his behaviour, which she now attributed to depression due to the fact that his business had slowed to the point where he actually stopped going and instead signed on for unemployment benefit.

This was in complete contrast to the 'wide boy' that Sarah had first met, who would flash his cash at every opportunity.

When Sarah asked exactly what had happened, he'd just brush it aside by saying sales had simply fallen through the floor.

But she knew better; she knew because she heard it that fateful shopping day, when she had come back into the house to hear Steve talking to his friend, John, about the police taking everything, and things hadn't been the same since.

Steve withdrew.

The shine had also faded from his trademark cheekiness that she loved so much, and this made her sad. She missed him and did everything in her power to cheer him up, including conforming to his will.

This meant going to John's wedding. Something she simply wasn't in the mood for.

And as much as she refused to acknowledge it, Sarah knew that one of the reasons why she wasn't particularly keen to attend this social gathering with Steve was due to the fact that, most of the time they were out together, she'd end up doing something that would displease him. Be that wearing something he didn't particularly like—since, in his opinion, everything was too revealing—or the fact that she'd get overfriendly with other men. If you class thanking a waiter for his service as overfriendly.

Sarah was unable to relax when out with Steve, and so she'd try to avoid it as much as possible. Not too much of course because he would start to question why she didn't want to be with him which, in turn, would force her to find excuses, like they couldn't afford it, which in turn would push him into another sulk.

"Why don't you want to go out with me? Are you ashamed? Is it because I don't have, I don't have a business anymore?

And that's how she found herself sitting in the kitchen as her best friend, Zoe, who was a hairdresser by profession, worked on backcombing and styling her hair.

"So, this John, is he the bloke that was with Steve the day we met him in that pub?"

"Yes, that's the one," Sarah replied.

"Oh, that's nice. So he's finally tying the knot then. Yeah, he wasn't such a bad catch that one. Of course, he's not a patch on your Steve though. It'll be you two next. I can't wait. I already know what I want to wear. Depending on what you end up deciding for colours of course. Are you still thinking ivory?"

No answer.

Zoe waited a few more seconds and then stopped what she was doing. "Hello?"

"I haven't really thought about it," Sarah said.

"What do you mean you haven't thought about it? That's all

you've been banging on about ever since you met the guy."

"I know, but Steve's business isn't doing that well so we've kind of slowed things down a bit."

"Yeah? Oh that's a shame, but it makes sense. You know, I was doing this girl's hair the other day, and she decided to marry her fella and they didn't even bother having a do or anything. They just got married at a registry office and then went down to the local takeaway! I couldn't believe it! But still, you know, at the end of the day, it's about you two, isn't it? What you want..."

"Oh, Zoe, why won't you come? You know we'll have a good time."

"Where? To your wedding? I wouldn't miss it for the world, silly!"

"No, I mean this one, today."

"Oh no, I told you, I can't. I have a hot date of my own to go to. Besides, I don't even know the guy."

"Hasn't stopped you going to a wedding before."

"Ha ha, very funny," she said sarcastically, as she pulled at and vigorously combed a clump of her friend's hair. "So what's up, anyway? Are you not looking forward to it?"

"Not really," Sarah said glumly.

"Blimey, why not? I thought you loved showing off your stud of a man."

"I do. Just things have been differently lately."

"Different how?"

"Oh, it's a long story."

"Well, I've still got a few more minutes before I'm done."

"Zoe, please come."

"I told you, I can't. And anyway, don't change the subject. You were about to dish the gossip on why things might not be that rosy."

Silence.

"Sarah?"

"Well, it's just that...."

"All right girls...?"

Steve appeared in the doorway. He was dressed in a morning suit. His black hair was slicked back and his goatee neatly trimmed.

This wasn't lost on Zoe, who wolf-whistled. "Bloody hell, you scrub up all right, don't ya?"

"Thanks. Are you coming out with us tonight?"

"Oh, I wish! I actually have a date."

"See, Zoe? Steve wants you to come too."

"I told you, I can't."

"But you know you'll have a good time…"

"…She said she can't make it, babe," Steve interrupted. His voice was calm yet forceful.

"Blimey, I don't know what's wrong with her. She's been trying to convince me to go all night."

"Is that so?" Steve asked, his right eyebrow rising inquisitively. "Anybody would have thought you don't want to be seen alone with me, babe."

"It's not that," Sarah said, quickly.

"Then what is it?" Steve asked.

Sarah didn't reply. She just stared ahead, waiting for Zoe to continue.

But Zoe was done, and, taking her cue, she said, "Anyway, I'd best be going. I'll leave you two love birds to it."

She hurriedly packed her hairdressing tools into a pink vanity case.

"Actually, why don't you hang around a bit longer and then we'll walk with you," Steve suggested.

"Are you not taking the car then?"

"No; you know what weddings are like, and we're bound to end up having way too many beers."

"Blimey, you're always so sensible. This guy I'm seeing and his mates don't have a brain between them."

And that's how, three hours later, Sarah found herself sitting on a scuffed metal chair at a mismatched fold-out table draped in a throwaway white table cloth at a local community hall.

The small room smelt dank with a hint of perspiration, a result of the many other activities that took place in here, including the weekly sunset dancing classes aimed at over seventy-year-olds who still had the time and the mobility to shuffle a waltz around the dance floor. At least that's what the centre of the hall became at 2:00 p.m. every Thursday afternoon.

Tonight, the room was smothered in darkness, but for the strobe lightning and flashing colours of the mobile disco that had camped out at one end of the rectangular room while the DJ, a middle-aged man with thinning hair, a black-and-white shirt that looked like it'd been stolen from the wardrobe department of *Saturday Night Fever*, played some seventies classics that had many of the assembled guests busting a groove on the dance floor.

Steve was at the bar, otherwise known as the kitchen with a temporary liquor licence and a serving hatch, and appeared to have been detained there by some old school friends, while Sarah sat alone awaiting his return.

It had been a good evening so far, much better than Sarah had expected. Steve's suit had brought on some kind of transformation. He seemed much more relaxed, less concerned with what everybody else was doing or thinking and much more interested in her. He had been attentive, affectionate, and fun.

Here, with a few drinks inside him, surrounded by his old gang, he had even roped her out onto the dance floor where he proceeded to cut shapes in the air, causing her to erupt into fits of laughter. He then caught her in his arms, leaned her back, admired her for a long lingering time before pulling her close to his body and kissing her with such passion it made her giddy.

She loved this man so much, and he loved her.

And that felt good, especially when she'd spot other girls admiring him from afar, and he was with her. Oddly, it was the very sight of their admiration that was making her feel so good since Sarah would never in a million years have dreamed to have landed such a handsome man.

However, the furtive glances of others, and even the occasional glare reminded her that all of this was real: that he was real; that her being in love was real and not just another of her adolescent daydreams.

"Is it okay if I take a seat here for a second, love?"

Sarah looked up to see a woman in her sixties with wavy grey hair and a cobalt blue frock looking down at her.

She looked at the empty chair. "Well, I'm waiting for my boyfriend…"

"Only my husband insisted on us having a dance and I now I feel as if my ticker's going to give in any second," she added, taking a seat anyway.

"Oh, are you okay?" Sarah asked, competing with the loud music.

"I'll be fine; just need to take a few minutes. I'm Eileen, by the way. I'm the groom's aunt."

"Oh, it's nice to meet you. I'm Sarah."

"Steve's Sarah?"

"Yes," she said with a laugh, surprisingly embarrassed.

"You know, I was just telling my husband that you must be the new girl in that boy's life and how he's done well for himself."

Sarah flushed. "Oh, thanks."

"Just saying it how it is, love. How on earth did you end up with him?"

Sarah heard the question, but wondered if, due to the loudness of the music, she had misunderstood the tone in which it was delivered.

"Do you know Steve then?"

Eileen let out a short cackle and then, feigning interest in the flower still affixed to the lapel of her dress, said, "Do I know Steve? More than anyone should. He and John were inseparable as kids and were often round mine, as I lived just a few doors down from his mum."

"I bet they were a right pair of tearaways when they were kids," Sarah offered with a smile.

"They were. A real pair of shits. Always in trouble with the police," Eileen responded, bluntly.

Sarah took a few seconds to try and gauge the skinny and somewhat diminutive woman in front of her who may have had traditional young granny looks but, Sarah had just noticed, had very keen eyes that were scrutinising more than looking at her.

She suddenly felt awkward.

"So, are you two married yet?"

She forced a smile. "No, not yet."

"Oh, so maybe you're not as dumb as I first thought you were."

"I'm sorry?"

If this woman was going out of her way to spoil what had been a good evening so far, she was doing a good job, and Sarah wasn't having any of it. Who did she think she was?

"Look, Eileen, I don't know what you think you know but..."

"Don't get yourself worked up, darlin'. I'm just telling you how it is."

"Well, so far it seems you've just been slagging off my boyfriend, and me, and quite frankly I don't like it."

Eileen broke into a smile. "So, you're a fighter. Good. Good. You're going to need it."

"What?"

"So, what does he do for a living these days? Found himself a job in a nice little factory or is he still robbing purses from little old grannies?"

"Actually, he has his own business," Sarah retorted, leaving out the fact that Steve was actually claiming benefits.

"What's that, selling gear off the back of a lorry? His dad was just like him you know. Always wheeling and dealing. Had no end of trouble with the Old Bill. That's why he took off, left little Stevie and his mum, then he jumped bail, didn't he, selfish bastard. Left Anne, to bring up the little monster all on her own. Of course she did all that she could which meant she was out all hours, working. I've lost count of the amount of times she asked me to babysit."

"I thought she worked at a bed and breakfast in exchange for food," Sarah said, reluctantly engrossed in the story.

"They did. Until that little shithead decided to pinch money from the landlord's flat. Then they ended up in a hostel until Anne could get a little council flat of her own. He doesn't deserve a mother like her. He treats her like dirt after all the sacrifices she made for him."

Then, noticing Sarah's somewhat horrified look. "I'm sorry, love. Me and my big mouth. I didn't mean to run him down like that. I'm going to shut my mouth and not say another word about any of the other stuff."

Sarah knew she was being manipulated, but said, "Oh, no, it's okay. It's good to hear about his past. Steve doesn't say much about it."

Eileen shook her head and then looked across at the

makeshift bar where, through the crowd, Steve had just said something funny to the men he was with and the group burst into laughter. "There are things I could tell you about him and his father that would make your hair stand on end."

"Then tell me," Sarah said, decisively.

"I think I've already told you more than enough," the woman said.

Sarah thought about this and then added, "Yeah, you certainly have, but I think he's changed. You knew Steve, the boy, but I know Steve the man."

"Does that crap fool any of your other mates then, does it?" Eileen said flatly.

"I don't think Steve is as bad as you're making him out to be. Sure, he's got a temper, but he's not exactly…"

"…Has he ever hit you?"

"Sorry?"

"You heard. Has he ever raised his hand to you?"

"No, he has not," Sarah lied instinctively, acting somewhat affronted that the woman should even ask.

"Good, because he used to beat his mum. Probably still does."

"Eileen, I'm really starting to get fed up with this. Steve wouldn't do that to his mum; he loves her."

"How do you know? Did he tell you?"

"Eileen…" She was about to protest, but the woman put a reassuring hand on her leg.

"Don't get upset, love. He isn't worth it. I just wanted to open those lovely eyes of yours," she said seriously, as she leaned in and held the young girl's gaze, then added with a smile, "Now I really must get on. This racket is giving me a headache. It was lovely to meet you."

"And you," Sarah murmured. Then, just as the woman was about to leave, she called to her, "Eileen?"

The woman turned around.

"Is what you said really true?"

Eileen paused then said, seriously, "I may be getting old but I'm not going senile just yet."

She gave a reassuring smile and then disappeared into the crowd, leaving Sarah to contemplate exactly what she had just learned.

However, before she had a chance to process any of the information, Steve returned with drinks.

"All right, darling?" he said with a big smile.

He was drunk.

She smiled at him. "Hey, there you are. Where have you been? Feels like you've been gone ages."

"I got talking to the lads." He placed Sarah's drink on the table in front of her, but didn't sit down; instead he stood, holding a pint of beer in his hand and looking into the packed dance floor.

"So, what have you boys been talking about?" Sarah asked, looking up at her boyfriend from her seated position.

"Oh, you know, we've just been catching up on old times."

"That's nice."

"I also got talking to John. He's been telling me about Martin."

"Who's Martin?" Sarah asked.

"You know, Martin," Steve said, still not giving her his eyes.

"Um, no, I don't know a Martin," she said with a perplexed smile.

Steve turned suddenly and towered over her. "Don't fucking lie to me!" he said, through gritted teeth.

The act startled Sarah, who shrank back in her chair.

"Steve, I don't know what you're talking about," she said, quickly.

"Tell me the truth…"

"I am."

"Tell, me the truth, Sarah. You want to fuck Martin, don't you? Don't you? Tell me the truth."

Sarah was both scared and irked by the sudden attack, all of which was exacerbated by Steve bearing down on her, so she moved to leave and that's when she felt the smack on her nose. It felt as if somebody had pushed her, face first, into a brick wall.

The lights seem to dim and there were white flashes in front of her eyes, closely followed by nausea and the coppery taste of blood in her mouth.

Steve had head butted her in the face.

The blood dribbled down the front of her pastel blue dress, dying it crimson, not that she could see this, for her vision had become blurry, both from the impact and the blood that had now smeared across her face and into her eyes as she held her head back in an attempt to stem the flow.

She could hear voices: Steve's concerned voice and another familiar to her.

"What the hell happened?"

"I don't know, I think it's this floor. I leaned over and I must have slipped…"

"You didn't slip, you little shit! Who are you trying to fool? Get away from her!"

Sarah felt paper towel or napkins being applied to her face, which she instinctively held there.

"Who the fuck are you?"

"I'm the woman who's going to kick you in the balls if you don't step aside, you piece of scum."

"Stop," Sarah murmured. "Stop."

"Why don't you piss off? Go back to polishing your broomstick, you old hag."

"Oh, I see nothing's changed then—just like your nasty-piece-of-work father…"

"Stop it, please, stop..."

"What kind of a monster, are you?"

"I told you, woman, it was an accident…"

"It wasn't an accident—you hit her, on purpose!"

"Just piss off you old hag, it's none of your business."

"Or what? You're going to hit me too?"

There was a pause, then, "Come on, Sarah. We're leaving."

Sarah felt tugging at her arm, but she wasn't ready to get up yet; she was still seeing stars in front of her eyes.

"Sarah, come on," Steve insisted.

"She doesn't want to go with you, you big bully!"

But she could feel Steve pulling at her, almost yanking her to her feet, so she allowed herself to be lifted and guided through the throng of people that, to her, were just white blurry faces.

She could hear gasps as she drew close despite the fact that the music was still belting out. Various members of the assembled guests even paused from their merriments to stare at her and her bloodstained gown as she approached.

It was only as she was about to exit the hall that she heard a familiar voice somewhere in the distance yell, "Get out of there! Get out of there, love, before it's too late!"

34 THE CONFESSION

Monday, 19th May 2003.

It was M's first day back in the United States after those famous two weeks and my infamous meltdown in that restaurant.

We were having the somewhat customary telephone conversation during which whichever of us was traveller would tell the other about his journey home and the week ahead.

"You seem down; was it a bad trip?" I asked.

"Yeah, it was pretty bad. My car didn't start when I got to the airport; the battery was dead. I had to get my brother to come over and give me a jump start."

"Oh, that's rubbish. But was the rest of the trip okay?"

"Yeah."

His voice was flat. There was obviously something more to his state of mind than just jet lag.

A long pause.

"M, are you sure you're okay?"

"Yeah, just tired."

"Are you sure that's all it is?"

Another long pause.

"Well, actually, I have something to tell you."

Now, I don't know why, but as soon as I heard this sentence my stomach lurched.

"Okay, what is it?" I asked.

"I have something to tell you."

"Yeah, I got that." I sat down. "What is it?"

"Do you remember the times I'd go home to Atlanta and you'd wonder why I went so quiet when I was there?"

"Yes…"

"…and you asked if I was having an affair with somebody?"

"Right…"

There was another long pause as I could feel my heart pounding against my rib cage and the blood literally pulsing in my ears.

"Well… I was."

I remember thinking, *blimey, these words were delivered way too casually for my liking*—although I was still processing what I'd just been told. In fact, my reaction was to tell myself that I'd actually misheard him, yet, in some bizarre kind of way, my brain was telling me that there was no point in denying what I'd just been told, because I had understood it perfectly.

It didn't mean that I still didn't go through the question in my head.

Could it be true?

Had M, the man I had been having an intimate relationship with for the past six years, really just told me that he'd been seeing somebody else? And had he delivered such devastating news in a casual tone, almost as if he'd been relaying the day's weather forecast?

"…she's a girl from South Carolina," he continued.

A girl?

"The wife of a marine who's deployed right now… and, um, she's pregnant."

I actually didn't know which elements of that revelation hurt the most. I didn't know if it was the fact that he'd been having an affair with a female, the fact that she was married, that she was carrying his child or my sudden and asphyxiating sense of inadequacy.

Okay, so time out.

Just telling you this right now, even after all these years, I can still remember how it felt.

Talk about shock and awe.

M had delivered enough emotional ordinance to decimate me.

It couldn't have been more than a minute, but it felt as if it was hours of silence on that line as I took in the news that changed my life, as I knew it, and would never be the same again.

Now, given the somewhat strained last two weeks, some of you may well be chanting 'good riddance to him', and you would probably be right—but then, in that moment, that was the last thing on my mind.

I just felt crushed, rejected and, once again, inadequate.

This stranger, this female, had given M something I could not, ever, and that alone weighed on me like a giant boulder. As did the fact that this stranger had, at times when I least suspected it, received M's affections. Meanwhile I, like a complete fool, had monogamously devoted the past six years to him.

That's a long time, especially considering the long-distance aspects. Aspects that I believed proved that we had something special, because if we could survive that then we could survive pretty much anything.

Or so I thought.

The sound of M's sobs brought me back to the telephone—I would say 'conversation in hand', but it was more like a collection of silences.

He started apologising and then went on to explain that he could no longer live the lie and that the truth had to come out, especially now that he had responsibilities.

This is coming from a twenty-something-year-old man, still pretty much a boy himself, who was on the verge of being honourably discharged from the United States Marine Corps in just four more months, after which he'd collect $1,400 monthly scholarship from the USMC to study, along with all the other added benefits that Ex American military enjoy as standard.

But now things had changed to such complexity that you cannot help but wonder what kind of an idiot would sabotage such a future just for a leg over?

By having sex—I would use the term 'sleeping', but I think that sounds rather naïve given the circumstances—with another marine's wife, M not only risked her husband's wrath, but that of the Marine Corps that does not look favourably on infidelity.

Furthermore, he was to be a father; thus, all of the options available to him after his military service had just been withdrawn. He would no longer have the luxury of studying, but would have to get a job. His could no longer enjoy the weightless spirit afforded to most single people, but was now laden with the responsibility of raising another human being.

So, what happened here?

Well, it would be easy to conclude that M was a stereotypical military meathead whose compulsion to spread his seed overwhelmed that of common sense and the moral values that this southern boy was brought up to believe in—although you could say they went out of the window the second he embarked on a relationship with another man, as did the code of the USMC, which is to not bring shame on yourself or indeed the Corps.

Now, whilst M's flagrant violation of the latter may well have been condemned by many of his peers and maybe even have resulted in a reprimand from his commanding officer, he could not be dishonourably discharged.

No, there was only one way that could happen.

Enter me.

Lesbians and gays had been denied the right to serve in the American military ever since its origins because lesbians, gays, bisexuals and transgender (or LGBT) people were deemed unfit for military service.

This policy evolved independently in each military branch until eventually being unified and coded as standard policy across all military branches in 1949.

In this case, *"Homosexual personnel, irrespective of sex, should not BE permitted to serve in any branch of the Armed Forces in any capacity, and prompt separation of known homosexuals from the Armed Forces is mandatory."*

One of the policy directives actually ordered that gays be committed to hospitals, examined by psychiatrists and then discharged.

However, the mass mobilisation and deployment of troops for operations in World War II meant it became impractical to convene court martial boards for homosexual-conduct offences. Command opted instead to issue 'blue charges', a form of administrative discharge, to gay personnel.

The blue discharge, which was also issued disproportionately to African Americans, was neither honourable nor dishonourable. However, blue-discharge holders faced difficulties in civilian life, since it carried with it a negative connotation.

So blue discharges were discontinued in 1947 and replaced with two new headings, "General" and "Undesirable".

A General Discharge was considered a discharge under honourable conditions, though distinct from an Honourable Discharge. An Undesirable Discharge was under conditions other than honourable, yet distinct from a Dishonourable Discharge.

The American Army also changed its regulations to ensure that homosexuals would not qualify for General Discharges. Under this system, a service member found to be homosexual, but who had not committed any homosexual acts while in service received an Undesirable Discharge. Those found guilty of engaging in homosexual conduct were Dishonourably Discharged.

In 1993, DADT, or 'Don't Ask, Don't Tell' was established by President Clinton. The act prohibited any homosexual or bisexual person from disclosing his or her sexual orientation or from speaking about any homosexual relationships, including marriages or other familial attributes, while serving in the United States armed forces. The act specified that service members who disclose that they are homosexual or engage in homosexual conduct should be separated (discharged).

DADT ended in 2011.

Persons who are openly gay or bisexual have been able to serve since (with the exception of those who exhibit "Transvestism").

However, the year was 2003.

If M's six-year affair with me were to come to the attention of his commandant, he would be Dishonourably Discharged, just months before his contract was up, which would also mean the forfeit of post-service financial benefits, of which M stood to receive many. This is one of the reasons many Americans serve in the military; it enables them to train for and achieve the skills and the qualifications to win new careers upon re-entry into civilian life—in M's case, a police officer.

Needless to say, the thought of jeopardising this horrified

him.

So, if *"hell hath no fury like a woman scorned"* What about a man?

What do you think happened next?

I had a choice. What, in your opinion, should I have chosen and what do you think I chose?

A)   I cut my losses. I accepted that what happened was meant to happen and moved on.

B)   Enraged, I took pen to paper, or fingers to keyboard, and fired off a letter to M's Commandant detailing everything about our relationship.

C)   I considered my options and demanded a meeting.

Wow, some pretty tough choices here.

Nobody likes to be wronged. Whether it's somebody cutting in line, burglarising your home, getting paid more than you do for doing the same job or simply getting a larger serving than you!

There are varying degrees of injustice and our reaction to each and every one of them is defined only by our state of mind and our take on the world. What may not have bothered you three months ago could really grate today, and what used to mean everything means absolutely nothing now—and that's because we're humans, organic creatures, and as such we're constantly growing and evolving through life experiences.

Which means the choice you make in the above case, be it A, B or C, will vary depending on how many times you've been subjected to the same or similar experiences. This is also true of all of the other stories in this book.

For some of us, life's conundrums often yield clear solutions; for others, solutions are more than often mired in our own preconceived disposition—hence the reason it's nigh on impossible to be objective and thus rationally approach a situation or make a decision on something we have a personal, emotional investment in.

One of the reasons doctors tend to avoid performing surgery on their own.

This is the very reason fools will rush head-on into

something, whilst emotional cowards will opt to put it off, procrastinate or downright avoid uncomfortable personal conflicts and/or realities, often with the help of recreational substances.

Then, rinse and repeat.

We avoid the harmful side effects of some truths because they hurt. The reason they hurt is they're yet another stage of our evolution; they're seeking to change, to modify the very fabric of who we are, contorting our personalities, metamorphosing our tolerances, and fracturing the bones of trust until brittle.

I, on the other hand, was very much aware of the truth and, at first, I was simply shell shocked. I had just come out of the most hideous two weeks' holiday with somebody who seemed like a stranger to me and I didn't even know why, until now.

However, my decision, as much as I didn't want to face it, was pretty obvious.

Now I just needed to act on it.

35 THE UGLY TRUTH

The things we think and feel but hide are plentiful, with countless motivations.

There are white lies, black lies, lies to spare the feelings of others, lies to spare ourselves, lies because 'it's best' and lies because we're cowards.

Yet, run as we may from it, the truth, like the proverbial tortoise, sits and waits with unfaltering patience for the perfect opportunity to reveal itself—and all too often wreak irreparable damage.

Indeed, a common reaction to a bad or uncomfortable truth is to deny its very existence as well as develop a particular dislike for the bearer of such ill tidings.

Don't shoot the messenger was a phrase first coined by William Shakespeare in *Henry IV* and, most appropriately in his *Antony and Cleopatra* where, upon receiving news of Antony's new marriage, Cleopatra threatens to use the messenger's eyeballs as play balls, invoking the line, *"Gracious madam, I that do bring the news made not the match."*

Yet just because we deny a truth, refuse to acknowledge its existence or bring a sudden and dramatic end to its bearer, it doesn't make it any less true.

For as long as I can remember, I have been on some form of a diet, and have even been prone to the odd early morning workout, with varying results. Even as I write this, I'm considering yet another state of dieting penance because my belly looks like I've just swallowed a baby seal. I've simply lost count of the amount of times I've starved myself in my quest to discover the 'new me'; you know, the one that diet clubs and supermarkets keep talking about, generally just after Christmas and always in time for the New Year resolutions. And it's absolutely nothing to do with the fact that the buttons keep pinging off my shirt like fleas off a dog or the fact that, no matter how hard I try, however subtly I try not to lean forward, I keep failing that damn 'Genitalia Test'!

What, you haven't heard of the Genitalia Test?

Sure you have—but just in case you haven't: the test involves standing up straight and then looking directly down your chest, belly and navel; if you're able to see your 'forbidden land' without having to lean forward or heave that blubber curtain to one side, then you're safe; you're not a BIG FAT PIG. On the other hand…

…Hold on—did I just say 'big fat pig' out loud? How rude. I actually meant 'aisle blocker', or 'lard ass', or maybe 'fatso'?

No?

How about fat person?

Still no good?

How about overweight person?

The reality is, no matter the adjective (however right or wrong it may sound), the reality will always be the same: if you are overweight then you're overweight regardless of whether or not you acknowledge it, say it out loud or somebody points it out to you.

Just because a truth is not spoken, it doesn't make it any less true.

I often find myself having this conversation, and it could well be because I have a propensity for pragmatism or simply because my tolerance levels have changed as I get older, but I'm a strong believer of 'don't ask a question if you don't want to hear the answer'.

Does my bum look big in this?

Well, actually it does.

Yes, that definitely sounds cold but if it's a truth, then it's the truth no matter how much I dress it up or sugar-coat it.

For example, if I had a basil leaf or something similar stuck between my teeth, I'd much rather somebody close to me tell me the truth than allow me to meet with others and expose them to the green bling of my every smile.

I should be able to trust those closest to me to look out for my best interests and save me from making a fool of myself. I should be able to feel 'safe in the space between us'.

The truth is often perceived as cruel or unkind, but I find this rather ironic considering that society conditions us to believe that honesty is the best policy. If that's the case, then why are we selective in what we do and do not share with others? Does our withholding of the truth make it any less real? We'd all be very comfortable telling a paedophile that his practices repulse us. But we'll more than often avoid telling our partner we don't love them anymore.

The truth simply *is*.

The only difference is who is holding it, how it makes them feel, and the impact they believe it will have on others and themselves if spoken.

Ghandi said, *"Your beliefs become your thoughts, your thoughts become your words, your words become your actions, your actions become your habits, your habits become your values, your values become your destiny."*

Most animals deceive each other, but it appears that only humans are genetically programmed to deceive others *and* themselves. The root of this appears to be in that old favourite, self-esteem. We can be so absorbed with how we're perceived by others that we're often unable to tell truth from fiction.

Psychologist Robert Feldman believes that people lie reflexively: *"We're trying not so much to impress other people, but to maintain a view of ourselves that is consistent with the way they would like us to be. Most of us strive to make ourselves 'agreeable' to others, to make a social situation 'easier' by not overtly or inadvertently saying something that may be perceived as 'disagreeable'."*

Feldman also conducted a series of experiments that involved putting people together in a room to observe how they interacted with each other. He videoed these sessions and later asked each person, individually, to watch their recording and to objectively identify things that they had said that were inaccurate or untrue. Most of the subjects were actually surprised to learn that they hadn't been entirely truthful with some of the things they had shared. Lies ranged from pretending to like someone they actually disliked to falsely claiming to be a rock star.

The study, which was later published in *The Journal of Basic and Applied Psychology*, found that sixty per cent of subjects lied at least once during the ten-minute conversation, saying an average of 2.92 inaccurate things.

The study also found that men lie no more than women—although they tend to lie to make themselves look better, while women tend to lie to make the other person feel better—and that extroverts tend to lie more than introverts.

Self-esteem and threats to our sense of self are also drivers when it comes to lying to co-workers, rather than strangers. Humans tend to show themselves in a positive light when in the company of others (especially those they care about) and will do anything to protect their self-worth, hence the saying *'cramp my style'*.

Which brings me right back to the fact that we may think something about somebody, but we may not necessarily verbalise it. But does that make it any less true or untrue?

"Does my bum look fat in this?"

What's your answer?

It would be safe to say that it actually depends on the type of person you are and whom you're interacting with.

If you're a woman, subject to how well you really know the

other person, you'll most likely lie to spare their feelings (if they do look fat).

If you're a man, again, subject to who that person is, you'll most likely lie to save yourself!

The truth hurts, sometimes but not always.

Some truths are beautiful, such as the negative and sometimes positive result of a medical test; the revelation that the object of your affection feels the same way as you, and learning that you're not alone in the world.

Ultimately, our acceptance of the truth in its various guises is subject to who we are: optimist, pessimist, depressed, or emotionally affected.

I had heard the truth and, in hindsight, and without a doubt, it was right for M to finally reveal it to me. What wasn't right was the fact that he had withheld it for such a long time and that he allowed me to suffer and crash in the face of his indifference.

Cruel but, sadly, not such an unusual practice in relationships where one party has fallen out of love with the other, be that an intimate or even a professional relationship.

As described earlier, many will put off facing the moment of truth because they don't want to deal with the fallout of their revelation and choose, wrongly, to hide that which they know will cause hurt.

What many fail to realise, time and time again, is that by the very act of 'falling out of love' with someone, they are already revealing the truth. Not overtly but in small subtle ways: the frequency of their communications, tactile actions, expressions of endearment, general routines. All are affected by their revised state of mind.

In my case, M's 'symptoms' were acute: his behaviour, his expressions of affection, which were very limited, picking fights for no apparent reason, his moodiness. These were all telltale signs and typical.

What was also typical was my reaction to this.

Whilst I may have continuously questioned his behaviour, asked what had happened to the person I had loved for so long, I, like many, don't think I actually lingered very long on the suspicion that there may indeed be somebody else (it was a truth I did not want to face).

Yes, I flirted with the idea, as you know; I even questioned him—but merely accepted his 'lie' that he was not.

Regardless, I was sad; my life partner had abandoned me for somebody else.

And I was angry; I felt betrayed, lied to and humiliated.

I was very angry.

And unbeknown to both of us, M's betrayal had set in motion an extraordinary chain of events the likes of which I could never have possibly imagined.

36 VENGEANCE

The prelude to exacting revenge is delicious. Well, they do say that *revenge is a dish best served cold.*

The thought of inflicting pain on the person who hurt you can certainly make you feel all warm and tingly inside and such is the rush from this newfound emotion after such acute sadness that, like a drug, it certainly isn't recommended whilst operating heavy machinery.

Being the Dumpee (or getting dumped) from a relationship is very disempowering, but revenge, retribution returns that power to us, albeit temporarily—but however long it lasts, it's enough to restore a world of multicolour in place of the one that had become dull and grey.

However, like most drugs, it's important to follow the directions printed on the packaging since there's a distinct risk that, try as you may, there'll come a time in your scheme where you will overdose because you decided to follow through with a dastardly, vindictive plan or because your drug is confiscated and you are banished to the dingiest, darkest dungeon.

For example, a mistress may hold terrifying power over an adulterous husband until she either follows through with the threats of telling his wife, or until he plucks up the courage to make his own confession.

Either way, the moment the revelation is made, the power is instantly withdrawn, leaving the vindictive to crash and burn in their own self-consuming resentment.

Yep, that does sound somewhat dramatic and that's because it is. If you've ever been in love and unfortunate enough to be betrayed by your partner, you'll know exactly what I'm talking about.

Being in love and feeling loved is like feeling the warm, velvety kiss of the afternoon sun on your skin. It's a delicious, honey-drenched feeling you simply can't get enough of.

That's, of course, until the day when your beloved, the person you planned to spend the rest of your life with, imparts the horrendous truth that they are leaving you because they plan to radiate somebody else with their warmth, whilst consigning you to the institution for Dumpees, a place where it's dark, miserable and downright depressing, a baron planet devoid of the verdant splendour of optimism and the orange glow of contentment. Instead, it's a place where you've been unceremoniously dumped and left painfully to realise that there isn't a word you can say, not an act you can do, not a supplication you can present for your ex to rescue you until...

... you realise that you actually have a weapon, a ticket out of misery and into the good graces of the one you love.

Most delectable is the fact that the ex you inherit isn't the complacent creature you once shared a life with but one who cannot do enough for you.

Suddenly, nothing is too much trouble, no loving is enough. There's an immense power shift and it's intoxicating.

Of course, what we don't always stop to consider is the fact that this whole new setup is a fake, an artificial world that we've created which bears no resemblance to the real world. Worse still is the fact that, whilst we retain this need for retribution, we also retain our ties to the very thing we are trying to avenge.

Rather than accepting what is, commencing the grieving process and moving on with our lives, we keep ourselves locked in the past and at the very place and moment that caused us pain.

Like any recovering addict, if we want to heal, we need to accept. *My name's Jack and I am an alcoholic* becomes synonymous with *I hurt, but it's over.*

Although it was pretty clear to me that my relationship with M was over, I could not get over the fact that 'power' had been taken away from me, that M had betrayed me. Furthermore, The Marine had added more insult to injury by cheating on me with a woman, another marine's wife, and making her pregnant.

I just couldn't reconcile this thought and nor did I want to accept it.

Not only was I dealing with my loss, but I also had to deal with a crushing sense of inadequacy (that she could give him something I could not), as well as contemplate the idea of somebody else's gain. The messages of affection, the embraces, the spontaneous touches, the kisses; everything was taken away from me and it was given to somebody else.

But it was mine!

I was bruised, hurt and burning with resentment. I wanted— no, I *needed*—an anaesthetic of some kind. I needed retribution.

So you can already see where I am going with this.

I chose option C.

I contacted M and informed him that unless he did some serious repenting, I was going to write to his commandant and detail everything about our six-year relationship. I then sat back and basked in the glow of the panic that was clearly present in The Marine's voice.

Yes, yes, all right, you can stop reading me with those judgemental eyes; it was an awful thing to do, but I believed his betrayal was equally awful, no?

Take a second to consider.

Remove all preconceived morality triggers and consider: if you were in so much pain, if somebody hurt you deeply and you had the opportunity to give them a taste of their own medicine, would you do it?

Yes? No?

If your answer was yes, then rock on! If your answer was no, then congratulations, you're a much better person than me.

I did it.

Power was restored and I loved every minute of it, especially when M asked what exactly he could do to make it up to me.

Would begging help?

Is that what I wanted? Did I want him to beg for forgiveness, was that it?

Maybe not just that, but it was a good start.

But would this truly help? Would it really ease my pain?

Well, long term, I didn't know, but short term, it sure as hell felt bloody good!

I did tell M that I didn't want him to beg, but what I did want was some acknowledgement.

M didn't want anybody to know and nor did he want to run the risk of anybody ever knowing about us. Our relationship was not allowed to venture beyond the threshold of closed doors.

In fact, it was pretty clear to me that if anybody found out, it was over.

That's when I realised what I craved: not to see M on his knees, begging, but to see him acknowledge that which he had denied all of our years together—that I existed.

So, I came up with the idea of having him meet me stateside where I was planning to go, of all places, to heal and to recover. I asked, well, actually, no I *demanded* that he buy his own plane ticket to meet me for a long weekend so that we may both 'bury' this thing in person as well as have the proverbial 'closure'.

At least that's how I felt; I believed that if I met M in person, talked the whole thing through, looked into his eyes, saw the remorse, then I would be able to put the whole thing behind me, and move on.

What do you think?

Do you think that seeing M again after what had happened between us would help me put the whole thing behind me or do you think it was some desperate attempt to keep M in my life as long as possible?

Of course, you think it's the former, don't you? Go on, admit it.

No?

Well, I convinced myself it was, and after one hour and a half of hearing M's humble voice, I was on a high—hell, I was buzzing with all of the power that had been restored to me.

The question was, just how long it was going to last.

The next day, I checked my email and received another injection of energy; M had sent me the itinerary for potential flights and was asking if these were suitable.

Of course they were!

All of the humbling, all the promises and, of course, the *pièce de résistance*, the fact that M would spend his own money, and quite a lot of it, to buy a plane ticket to meet with me in America for all of four hours was more than suitable.

I considered this.

Four hours?

Was this good for me? Was it long enough to get closure or would it simply prolong the whole thing? Of course not. It would help and I'd get to see him one more time.

But something was wrong.

Although I'd just received another injection of power, something didn't feel right. Somehow, something had changed. The energy boost didn't quite feel the same; it felt somewhat diluted, like a sauce with no seasoning. It suddenly tasted somewhat bland.

But I couldn't work out why and nor did I care.

That afternoon, I met a friend for lunch.

He was an old colleague of mine, a salesman. A regular guy, married with a toddler, and, like most in his profession, a straight talker with smooth articulation that had helped sell many a product.

For convenience, we actually met in the restaurant of a local supermarket.

The salesman was tucking into a jacket potato and a salad, whilst I, true to the way I had been feeling ever since the split with M, wasn't feeling hungry and sat watching shoppers come and go through blue-tinted sun glasses.

"So, how are you doing, then?" the salesman asked, pausing momentarily before forking potato into his mouth.

"Oh, you know, I'm alive," I said, shifting my focus to the man in front of me.

"It will get better, Tone, I promise."

"I know. It's just that, right now, it feels like crap, and with this other stuff I am starting to wonder if I am doing the right thing."

"What other stuff?"

I sighed.

For some inexplicable reason, I was suddenly feeling somewhat depressed when I should be full of beans, given my newfound power.

"Well, I spoke to M last night."

"Oh, Tone," the salesman lamented, wiping sauce from his lips with a paper towel.

"I know. I actually did something stupid too."

"Yeah, well, calling him was a stupid."

"Yeah, I'm starting to wonder. But that's not all. I actually threatened him last night too."

The salesman was about to shove salad-cream-smeared leaves into his mouth, but stopped. "What do you mean?"

I paused since it'd suddenly occurred to me that, for all my blustering about wrong and right, and despite convincing myself that M deserved everything coming his way, I was actually somewhat reluctant (or was it ashamed?) to articulate the details of my actions.

Eventually, I blurted, "I told him I was going to write to his commander and tell him all about us."

"You what?" The salesman's eyes widened as if I'd just told him I was going to kidnap his baby.

"I know. I know," came my instinctive defence. "When I think about it now, I feel like such an idiot, but I can't help but imagine I'll get some kind of closure if I see him again."

"See him?"

The salesman put his fork down; he was ready to hear the whole story.

I accepted the invitation.

"I told M that I wanted him to repent for the crappy way he's treated me. I told him that unless he met me in Oklahoma, I would send a letter to his commandant, telling him all about M's extracurricular activities, including his six-year *affair* with me."

"Why the hell would you do that?"

"Why do you think? I want him to bloody pay for what he has done to me. Not just now, but also for being such an asshole during our time together."

"And you think ruining his career and possibly his future is going to make you feel better?"

"Yes," I said decisively.

"You really think that?"

"Of course I do."

"Do you?"

"I said yes!" I snapped angrily.

And that's when it occurred to me.

In all the time since the breakup, I had never felt this way. Never felt this angry. Never felt this sudden need for revenge.

So what had changed?

Not much.

This was a natural reaction to what had happened.

I was angry.

Angry because I felt as if I had wasted six years of my life with somebody who didn't really care for me, angry that I had allowed myself to be drawn into the revenge game, angry because I had sunk to M's level, and angry that the salesman had pointed out exactly what I already knew, but was choosing to ignore; the meeting with M was a terrible idea and would only serve to prolong the agony, and this was all just some desperate, terrible attempt to keep him in my life.

I felt a lump in my throat; suddenly everything was all too, painfully, clear.

"What are you doing, Tone?" The salesman spoke smoothly and softly, as if trying to coax me off the ledge of a tall building. "Do you really think that seeing him for a few hours is going to change anything? Do you really think that you are going to get enough in such a short period of time that will justify all the build-up, all of the anticipation and the general emotional crap you're going to experience both before and after you meet with him?"

The delicately delivered rationale was infused with such overwhelming sensitivity that I could almost feel it plucking at my heartstrings.

It caused my eyes to well with tears.

"I know it's hard," the salesman continued, unabated, "but, Tone this isn't going to help how you are feeling. If anything, it will just make it worse, just delay what is inevitable. Tone. Why put yourself through more of that shit?"

The tears broke free.

"You have got so much going for you. Don't do this to yourself. It's over. You need to move on with your life. Find someone else who is going to care about you as much as you care about them."

The tears broke the cover of my sunglasses and streamed down my face.

The salesman smiled.

"I'm sorry. I didn't mean to make you cry," he said softly.

I shook my head, conscious of the fact that I was in a public place and probably making a fool of myself but nobody cared, everybody was too busy living their own lives to care about some weirdo at the corner table.

As always, when we're going through a crisis, the world doesn't stop just because we have; it continues to turn, people will continue to laugh and eat, and shoppers will continue to shop.

I shook my head. "It's not you. It's just, it's just," I wiped away tears, "what you said is right. I suppose I just needed to hear it from someone else. I just don't want to let go."

"I know. But you need to. And, as I said, it will get better, I promise, but this is the worst thing you could do right now. Trust me."

He handed me one of his paper napkins and smiled.

So what was it that the salesman said that made me break down? Well, just two words.

It's over.

And it's not as if I'd heard something I didn't already know.

I had woken up the next day—hell, even minutes after I spoke to M—and I knew that something about the agreement wasn't right. It was obvious (although I didn't want to admit it at the time) that the only reason The Marine was prepared to fly to Oklahoma was because he was afraid—no, he was *terrified*—of being 'outed'.

So, after my meeting with the salesman and my confrontation with some home truths, what do you think I did next?

A)   I left a message on M's voicemail to call me as soon as possible. Then, when M did, I confessed that I had no intention of writing to his commandant or anybody else, and we agreed that that telephone call would be our last?

B)   I thought carefully about everything that had been said, but I still felt that a meeting was the best thing because at least at the meeting I'd get the chance to see him one more time and get closure.

C)   We did meet in Oklahoma. At that meeting, M realised that he had made a mistake and we agreed to give it one more try.

It was a difficult decision. I knew what I *should* do, but the question was, did I have the strength to do it?

Now, this is the part where I tell you that I turned to my brother and mentor with whom I was very close and I asked for his counsel, and that he told me what to do and all was well.

Not quite.

At this stage, I was still very much in the closet as far as my family was concerned. All they knew was that I'd fallen out with my best friend of six years and was devastated by it.

I was lost, and I felt like I needed to get away—but the question was to where?

My older sister, Francesca, with whom I am very close, lived but a few minutes' drive from me, yet I chose to go to the one person I believed was most unlikely to be able to sympathise with my plight. The heterosexual, the man's man, married with teenage children of his own, and someone who, until then, I'd only spent time with during public holidays and special occasions: my eldest brother, Renato.

I telephoned him and asked if there was any chance of me driving the two or so hours west, cross country, to see him, and if there was any chance of me spending the night.

Both he and my sister-in-law said they'd be delighted to see me.

And so I loaded myself and a CD compilation into my car and set off on my mini adventure into the unknown.

I don't know what I expected from this trip, but what I did know is that the simple act of climbing behind the wheel and driving on the open road was a prospect I was looking forward to and it was already making me feel better.

Like me, and millions of others around the world, you're most likely a music fan. As such, your mood is also likely to be influenced by a great song, just like mine.

That evening, whether a song could be associated with a particular time and place with M, or simply because it contained lyrics to which I could relate, I listened to it. I cranked up the volume and sang as if my life depended on it, and, like cold compressions on a sore, it was as painful as it was soothing.

The melodies made me angry, they made me laugh, they made me happy and they made me very sad, but most of all, I felt as if each beat, note, lyric and melody was, like a discretion of priests, performing an exorcism on my soul.

I could already feel my heart being liberated from the demons of melancholy who seemed to have already taken up residence there.

And it was then that I realised why exactly I had chosen my brother over my sister; she was geographically too close. My mind yearned for the time and the freedom to process what had happened and what I expected would come next.

When I arrived at my brother's house, I was welcomed very warmly, but also somewhat warily given the fact that, despite regular invites, I hadn't actually made it over to see them in their new home, until tonight.

And, it probably took less than ten minutes and a cup of tea for the question to be raised. It was quite discreet—more a question of how things were in general rather than a direct, "So, why are you here?" Which would not be beyond my brother by the way—he is a Marturano after all.

And that's when I paused.

It was now or never.

My mind kept saying, *"No. You have no idea how he is going to react!"*

343

He, being my brother, the no-nonsense regional manager of a well-known British wholesale grocery chain who made no bones of asserting himself as a dominant alpha male both when managing the thousands of underlings in his charge as well as his own family.

But I couldn't help it.

Like a blushing bride on proposal night, I became the blushing groom, one that collapsed into a shower of tears at the mere mention of the fact that something was obviously troubling me.

You think?

It took my six-foot-something brother—you know, the scary one—but a few seconds to scoop me into his embrace and coo to me to reveal exactly what the problem was since it couldn't possibly be that bad.

Then, as if to make matters worse, my sister-in-law joined in the love fest and put her arms around us both so that we were an emotional love sandwich, the warmth of which melted me into a soggy, blubbering mess.

Eventually, I'm sure much to their relief, I emerged from the cocoon of arms to the realisation that my brother, the one I'd pretty much feared for most of my life, was actually quite cool and a bit of a softy!

Thus, buoyed by this new realisation and the couple's inquisitive eyes, I wiped the embarrassment from my eyes and concluded that there was no going back. I was committed.

So, after a few more seconds of recomposing myself, I said, "Well, you know my friend, M?"

They both nodded.

"Well, he wasn't just my friend."

"Right…"

"We were more than just friends."

"And?"

I remember thinking, "What do you mean, *and*?" I actually wondered if they'd understood what I was saying, so I sought clarification.

"Do you know what I mean?"

"You were an item?" my brother said casually.

I nodded as an enormous sense of relief washed over me. I

COMING UP FOR AIR

don't know if that was due to the fact that members of my family actually knew the truth, or if it was more to do with the fact that I'd actually 'done the deed'.

And so I proceeded to give them an outline of everything that had happened, including the fact that I had left a message for M to call me that night as I needed to talk to him and that he promised he would do so.

When he did, they both left the room to give me some privacy.

That phone call was one of the most painful and difficult telephone conversations of my life. That's because I had come to terms with the fact that to try and keep M in my life by forcing him to meet me in America would be a terrible mistake.

It would cause more damage than it would ease pain.

I confessed that no matter how much I felt betrayed, I still cared for The Marine and probably always would, but that I understood that we no longer had a future together.

And, whilst sobbing at the end of the line, M said nothing to contradict that. Instead, he explained that he was also coming to terms with a future that he had not planned, and the fact that a woman carrying his child meant that he had all new responsibilities as a father.

He shared with me his plan to become a police officer in order to support his new family.

For some odd reason that last comment really affected me. I just had this vision of his future as a cop, a future that did not include me.

With that, the half-hour conversation drew to an end with me verbalising, somewhat symbolically, that once we disconnected from that telephone conversation we'd also be disconnecting from each other's life.

We did.

It was over.

I fell to my knees and sobbed, oblivious to the fact that that would not be the last time I spoke to M and, moreover, I had just set my life on a somewhat destructive course from which there would be no return.

37 SPLIT: BREAK FORCIBLY INTO PARTS

There's nothing more heartbreaking than watching the distance between you and the love of your life grow wider. It's like being an astronaut without a tether; suddenly and helplessly you find yourself drifting further and further from them and slowly disappearing into some deep, black void where the only thing that responds to the sound of your screams, the sobs of your tears is the echo of the hollow where your heart used to be.

The Oxford dictionary's definition of the word 'split' is: *'break or cause to break forcibly into parts, especially into halves or along the grain.'*

The two parts in this case would be the *Dumpee* and the *Dumper.*

There are no prizes for guessing that to be the Dumper in a relationship is to be empowered; you are the one who has taken control of the situation, and you are the person who hitched a ride out of a bad place (by *bad* I mean a situation that wasn't working for you) towards an assumed better future, probably with someone else. And thus, by the fact that you took this initiative, it means you have everything going for you that you aren't afraid of the future, and are in control of your destiny.

Being the Dumpee, on the other hand, is the far worse position, as you find yourself in a state where you've been stripped of all rank, entitlements, power, and often dignity. You are the person who has been left behind.

That fateful January trip to Raleigh when I first started considering whether or not I had a future with M, I was actually leaning towards the role of Dumper, but as soon as M revealed his infidelity, I suddenly and unexpectedly became the Dumpee!

The result?

Devastation.

I had become the person dumped at Depression Central, whilst M took the next train out, maniacally grinning and waving at me through the carriage window as he sat next to 'Miss Thing', holding a newborn baby in his arms.

His baby.

This wasn't some competition about who was best in the sack (of course I knew I was); we were talking big, life-changing stuff: the ability to make him a father.

I couldn't compete with that.

Accept who you are. *Accept* your limitations.

As a Dumpee, it's easy to view yourself as *the discarded, the damaged.* Otherwise they would never have left you, right?

Wrong.

As strange as this next section is going to sound; it isn't all about *you.*

Sometimes, people just move on.

It used to work, they did feel a certain way about you—but now they don't. It's how we evolve. It isn't always you. Sometimes it really is them.

"It isn't you, it's me," used to carry a lot of truth.

Sadly, this phrase has a much more negative connotation now, since it's been adopted way too often by the cowardly who fear a confrontation and seek to limit the potential fallout of a breakup by cynically masking it as their culpa.

Becoming the Dumpee in a breakup doesn't automatically mean that there is something wrong with you. There may not necessarily be any specific reason—nothing you did or how you looked; sometimes they've just moved on.

Accept.

And, yes, I appreciate that this is much easier said than done. There are so many mitigating circumstances that don't make a break clean and that's often because even the simplest things become an obsession: *Why did they break up with me? How did they do it? Was it before or after a special occasion? Was it before or after a particularly stressful event in my life? Before or after we had sex?*

This absurd list goes on as you try to rationalise what and why it happened.

Accept that it just *happened.*

Why, when, how is pretty much academic, isn't it? The result remains the same.

Remember? Truth is truth

No matter when or how you were told. Yes, you could argue that how you were told may well soften the blow, but the end result remains the same.

I remember having a debate with my sister once about one of our mutual friends.

This lady had been with the love of her life for a little over a year. It had been a great relationship (for her) and she was exceptionally happy. She and her boyfriend spent most of their spare time together. They'd travelled England and the world, visited some of the finest hotels and resorts.

She was happy and was ready to move in with him.

He, on the other hand, much to our complete astonishment, actually broke up with her, just weeks after they had been on an exotic holiday together.

And so, after my sister and I recovered from the shock of what had just taken place and the heartache that we knew our friend was enduring, we began a debate over the 'cowardly' way in which the deed was done.

"What do you mean?" I asked my sister.

"Well, fancy taking her on a holiday only to dump her days after they got back. He used her."

"What do you mean he used her?"

"Well, he took her on holiday, had his wicked way with her and then dumped her. I think that's deplorable."

"Well, it could also be that he didn't want to upset her before the holiday. That he felt the right thing to do was not to spoil her vacation, but instead allow them (her) to enjoy one last trip together."

And so the debate continued.

What do *you* think?

Should he have told her before the holiday; laid the proverbial cards on the table and then allowed her to make up her own mind about how to proceed?

Whatever your thoughts, whatever your preference, it doesn't change the fact that the man felt the way he did.

There often isn't a 'good time' to tell somebody 'it's over'.

Some people tell me there's never a 'good time' to have a baby. I don't necessarily subscribe to that, yet many still go ahead and get pregnant regardless of their financial and/or housing situation.

Truth is truth, remember, no matter how you dress it up, how you sugar-coat it.

Reality bites.

I've often been asked an excellent question by people (and it's one I've often asked myself): if people knew—and by *knew* I mean *really knew*—the pain they were about to cause, do you think they'd still go ahead with the distasteful deed of breaking up with someone?

The simple answer is: some don't.

But isn't that how affairs are born?

Cheating behind someone's back then going home and acting as if nothing is going on.

Would you rather live in blissful ignorance? Or, angst-filled suspicion?

Acceptance is part of grieving, and grieving for a love you lost is part of the process of moving on. Accept what has happened and allow yourself to grieve. However, remember that you're not going to wake up tomorrow and it'll be a case of *all change,* but more a case of rinse and repeat.

Accept that it will take time for you to heal and that the longevity of that time is strictly subject to a complex formula of variations that are unique to you, such as how much you love/d him/her, how much you felt/feel they love/d you, how long you'd been together, what plans you'd made, how the split took place, what kind of support structure you have, how happy you are with the rest of your life, how confident you are about yourself, and the list goes on.

Nobody is going to give you an estimated time of departure from *Depression/Heartbreak Central.*

Certainly not me.

The only person who can earn a ticket out of there is—guess who?

That's right, *you.*

Yes, I know. It does sound like some hideous self-help group cliché, but it just happens to be true.

You see, with affairs of the heart, there's only so much external forces can do to ease your suffering and that's because at night, when the dark smothers the sun, the shadows grow and the demons come, there's only one person they're coming for: you.

What, you don't know about the demons?

The demons are those shadowy thoughts that lurk in the deep recesses of the mind. You know, the painful ones that loiter on the periphery of consciousness just waiting for a song, place, smell or taste to order them to the fore and remind you just how much you miss someone.

These evil demons are very patient creatures, but they do have a vulnerability; distraction is to a demon what Kryptonite is to Superman. The only problem with distraction is that at some point it will end and you can be sure they'll be waiting, ready to spring into action and cause hurt once more, sometimes to the point of making some want to go to sleep and never wake up.

I spent time with family and friends for distraction from my demons and took every opportunity to bore the pants off them with tales of my heartache.

I also took every opportunity to feel sorry for myself since I wrongly believed that what I was going through was something that nobody else could truly understand and so I often felt alone, even when with people, which only perpetuated that feeling of loneliness.

That's right. If you've been in this situation, you'll recognise that feeling of being alone even when you're in a crowd.

But then, there are many who feel that way even when they're in a relationship—but that's a different chapter.

As odd as that may seem, many seldom make time for introspection and thus much of what they know about themselves is a mere distilled projection, courtesy of others, be that good, bad or ugly.

If you're someone who always needs someone, now's your chance to toughen up, to stand on your own two feet and get to know yourself.

Don't be afraid of your own company. You could be the best companion you'll ever have and it is you, not your family, not your friends, who are key to your own recovery.

In this particular case, take a trip to discover yourself.

If you are a driver, block off a day or, if you're feeling adventurous, a whole weekend.

Load the car with supplies, the naughtier the better. Comfort food and drink is the dish of the day, and don't forget music—lots and lots of music. Make sure it's a good eclectic variety: happy, sad, vocal or instrumental, from rousing classical music to pounding dance anthems. There's no good, bad, right, wrong, cool or cheesy. Anything goes on this trip because this is your journey and you're the captain.

And don't you be afraid of those songs that you used to listen to together. You know, that favourite song that was playing when you met, or those songs that played as you made love, and even the one that was in the background as they drove away leaving you in a heap of misery.

Don't be afraid.

Trust me.

Now, switch off your mobile phone and head for the open road. By *open*, I'm talking about a motorway that will allow you to gain speed, then take a detour, ideally through some of the most majestic scenery your country has to offer within driving distance.

Now, get lost!

That's right.

Most vehicles have the luxury of satellite navigation, if not built-in, then in a portable device. If you don't own one, borrow one. If you can't borrow one, then turn to the trusty road atlas. We all got along quite happily with one of those for many years and still managed to find our way home.

Now, sing! That's right; sing like there's nobody watching (that's because there *isn't* anybody watching). No work, no worries, no ex, no friends.

Nobody but you.

Allow yourself to grieve in reminiscence, weep with sadness, smile with the lyrics you can relate to and pick yourself up with the dance.

This is your life. These are your seconds that are ticking by.

How do you want to spend them?

My first music therapy session started at 8:00 in the morning and ended at nearly midnight of that same day, after having driven over five hundred miles.

I drove so far, I actually reached a different country!

But during that time I allowed myself to go through a whole

roller coaster ride of emotions. I faced my demons and returned home absolutely exhausted, but so much better for it.

Luckily, being a writer, I'm not afraid of and actually enjoy my own company—in fact, it's a requirement of the job—but that day, and on subsequent journeys, I was able to rediscover myself. I was no longer a poor victim, the widow of a relationship, but I'd become the captain of my own destiny.

I remembered that this was my life, and that each and every second I spent grieving were seconds I would never get back. So I took stock of where I was at and where I wanted to be.

Oh, and just in case you were reading that whole section and thinking, "but I don't drive", know that the same rules apply to planes, trains and even buses!

Although you'll most likely want to invest in some headphones, and consider that your dulcet tones may not be as agreeable to your fellow passengers as they may well sound in your head.

Music therapy is good wherever you are, and headphones are a great way to disappear into your own private world, although I'd probably recommend internalising your emotional expression.

Of course, when the music therapy ends, your demons will be waiting.

And that's okay too.

Accept them as you would irritating bugs in summer since they'll be with you for some time because, believe it or not, testing your demons (since, at the end of the day, they are part of you) is part of your healing process. A bit like continuously prodding that sore to see if it still hurts.

My introspection led me to conclude that I needed to get away, but I decided I was going to go further than a road trip; I decided that I was going to leave my beloved England and board a train for a whole new voyage of adventure, one that would introduce me to a new life beyond anything I could have ever imagined.

38 ALIVE

Every car, every pedestrian was a frustration as Katy attempted to drive herself, as quickly as she could, to work. She was already running late and rush hour wasn't helping.

Cars, buses, schoolchildren and even cats seemed to want to pull out in front of her today of all days, and now, as she waited at the crossroads for an opening to join the busy motorway, even the morning sun, normally a joy to her, was irksome.

She snapped down the car's sun visor and moved her head out of the sun's powerful rays, and that's when she noticed it; up ahead, on the other side of the road, a police patrol car was parked in a lay-by with headlamps facing her and they were flashing intermittently.

At first she thought she'd imagine it but, sure enough, the cop car was actually blinking its lights at her.

Oh, what now?

This is all she needed.

She looked at the clock on the dashboard. It confirmed that she was indeed running late for her shift.

She didn't really have a choice; she pushed the car into gear, drove over to the vehicle and parked behind it, all the time trying to work out who exactly the occupant was and what they wanted, as it was bound to be somebody from the station.

She definitely hadn't been speeding and, to her knowledge, hadn't made any illegal manoeuvres.

Still, she got out of her car and, as she made her way to the passenger side of the patrol vehicle, peered in through the reflection of the glass, and that's when she broke into a smile; it was Richard, a police officer, a colleague from work.

She opened the door and grinned, "Good morning. What are you doing here?"

Richard didn't smile, but said, "Katy, get in the car."

"Why? What's up? I need to get to work. What are you doing here anyway?"

"Katy, please just get in the car," he repeated.

"Oh, all right then," she said, somewhat perturbed

She took a seat, pulled the car door closed behind her and turned to him, "What's up?"

"Katy, I just wanted to have a chat with you away from work."

"What about?" she asked, slightly apprehensive now, as she couldn't help but wonder if this somehow had something to do with Mark.

"Well," Richard started, somewhat gingerly, which unnerved her some more, "there's no easy way to tell you this so I'm just going to come out with it."

"Okay."

She pulled a puzzled expression and discreetly glanced at the dashboard clock. *Yes; you're even later now,* it blinked.

"Katy, I'm in love with you," Richard said suddenly.

She turned to him, "What?"

"I'm in love with you, Katy."

The sentence prompted her to burst into laughter.

"Yeah, that's really funny, but did you need to stop me on my way into work to tell me? I'm already late for my shift and you know that…."

"Katy, Katy… please just shush for a second. I'm in love with you."

"What do you mean you're in love with me? You can't be; you have a wife and children. You can't be in love with me…"

"I'm in love with you, Katy, and I'm prepared to leave my wife and family if you're prepared to leave your husband."

She thought about what she had just been told.

"Come on, Katy, you must have realised. All of the banter. The way we are together at the station. It just works. You're adorable and I just love you."

"You can't be, Richard."

"I am."

"You can't be. I don't want you to be," she said more forcefully.

"Katy…"

"No." She'd lost her smile now as thoughts of Mark flashed through her mind; him seeing them in the car together, her leaving him, her son, her family, and it panicked her. "I don't love you, Richard. What we have at the station stays at the station; it's just banter, nothing else."

Then, seeing the look of sadness darken his face and the water in his eyes, she added more tenderly, "Richard, you're a lovely, lovely guy, but I just don't feel the same, and I won't, I couldn't and wouldn't leave my family for you."

He said nothing, and just as she thought things couldn't get any worse, he started to cry.

"Richard, please…"

"You don't understand. I really love you."

"Yes, I do understand, Richard, but I don't feel the same. I'm sorry. Please, don't do this."

"It isn't a choice, Katy, this is how I feel and it kills me that you don't feel the same," he continued as more tears streamed down his plump red cheeks.

Katy's reaction to this wasn't sympathy or empathy but more confusion, numbness.

This is the last thing she'd expected and the last thing she needed right now. In any other year she may well have allowed herself to enjoy the moment, the flattery, but right now, at this stage of her life, it felt more like an inconvenience, a catalyst that could spell more unnecessary drama for her, and she didn't want it, need it, and nor could she deal with it right now.

She was late for work.

Richard was crying when she refocused on his face and the image of the twenty-six-year-old portly man whose sobs caused convulsions in his pot belly that was trying to escape his tucked-in shirt.

It made her want to put her arms around him, but she couldn't.

"Richard…" she was about to apologise, but thought better of it. "Richard, look, I'm going to get out of the car now and get to work. Please, just go back to your wife, and let's both go back to the station and pretend this never happened, okay?"

His reply was just sniffing and backhand swipes of the tears from his face.

Katy climbed out of the car and firmly shut the door behind her.

She returned to her car as a spring breeze brought welcome cool air to her face, cleansing the moment from her mind.

She sat in the car and sighed.

What the hell was that all about?

She considered this for a few seconds then started the engine and drove away, watching Richard and the patrol car disappear in her rear view mirror.

It was incredible.

She really had no idea that Richard felt that way about her and she wondered if she had encouraged him somehow. She concluded she hadn't.

Yes, they did have banter at the office and yes, perhaps there was the odd joke, but they were both married; it never even occurred to her that someone like him would actually be prepared to leave his family for her.

At least, not now that she was nothing but a mother, a wife, a shadow of her former self. She was the empty grey space for an online profile picture. At least, this is how she felt; this is how she saw herself these days.

Just empty.

Mark had seen to that.

She felt a pang of something. She wasn't quite sure what. Was it resentment? Anger? Or was it acute sadness?

She had become so far removed from the person she used to be. The young girl who'd sped through her time in the Air Force as if it were some youth's hedonistic daydream but now, now she was just a wife, just a mother whose sole ambition was to take care of her family.

But then, was that so terrible?

Maybe not, but was it what she wanted for the rest of her life? Didn't she want more? Didn't she *deserve* more?

And that's when she did it. That's when she actually allowed the thought to enter her mind. What if she did leave Mark for Richard? He may well represent the key out of her own self-imposed prison.

But you don't love him, she argued with herself.

I know, but I could learn to love him.

And ruin a whole family in the process? What are you thinking?

She had no idea what she was thinking. All she knew is that this couldn't be it. This couldn't be the full stop at the end of her existence on this earth. She couldn't go on living the rest of her life walking on eggshells, terrified about doing or saying something that might trigger another episode in Mark.

On the other hand, who the hell would want her now?

But that's when it occurred to her: somebody *did* want her. In fact, somebody wanted her so desperately he was prepared to give up his wife and children for her.

Wife and children, for *me*?

Maybe she hadn't changed after all. At least, not outside of her home. She was the same person, a bit more repressed perhaps and incapable of making her own decisions without consulting her husband and, quite rightly so, she was married to him.

Rightly so?

Was it right for one person to control another in such a way? Was it right for any one person to control how the other should dress, shop, think, as well as who to see, when and for how long?

She thought about this as she manoeuvred her way through traffic to the office as quickly as she could, and, like her car, her thoughts continued to race around the emotional detours in her head, navigating their way to one conclusion: she'd spent the past six years in some sort of mental purgatory, allowing herself to be conditioned, manipulated, enabled and controlled by a man who purported to love her, and perhaps, in his own way, did, but this love was nothing but a shroud, a hair blanket smothering and suffocating the life out of the vitality that used to burn like an ardent flame within her chest.

What the hell happened to me?

It felt as if she'd spent the majority of her married years as a spectator, a watcher, the result of someone who had undergone some kind of out-of-body experience and had watched life pass her by without ever participating in it.

It was as if she had died already.

Richard transferred out of the station within weeks and Katy wouldn't see him again until many years later when she'd discover that he had indeed left his wife for another woman and that he had abandoned her also.

Everything happens for a reason.

Katy knew this. She also knew that, but for the encounter that morning, she would never have found the courage to take the next step.

Meanwhile, Richard's departure spelt the arrival of another man. A forty-year-old detective who went by the name of Peter—someone who turned Katy's head as he did her heart.

Not that she could act on it of course, but Peter's interest in her proved to Katy that she still existed, that she could be loved and, most importantly, that she was still alive.

The change became much clearer to her one day when she told Mark she was going to go out to a club with the rest of her team from work.

"I'll drive you," Mark said.

"No."

"Why not?"

"Because Jan has offered."

"Then I'll come and pick you up."

"Mark, no."

"Why not?"

"Because Jan will bring me home."

"Why don't you want me to pick you, up, Katy? What exactly do you have to hide?"

"I don't have anything to hide, Mark," she said, measuring her words carefully so as to avoid another potential outburst. "I just want to go out with my work colleagues. I want to enjoy an evening out with just them. Surely I'm entitled to that, surely I've earned it. Right? Right?"

After many reluctant seconds, Mark finally nodded. "Yeah, I'm just wondering why you wouldn't want me to pick you up."

"Because this is one thing I want to do on my own. Just one bloody thing, all right? These are the people I work with. You have nothing to worry about."

It was in no way unclear to Mark that Katy was serious and, most importantly, determined, and thus he had no choice but to concede.

What he didn't realise is that he had just endorsed an event that turned out to be one of the best Katy had had for a very long time.

And it was during that evening, as she drank and danced with her workmates, including Peter, that she realised she wanted more. She wanted to be the person she used to be again. She didn't want to just to be happy, but she wanted to be alive, and maybe even fall in love.

Yes, there was no doubt that her new dancing partner, Peter, not only encouraged the rhythm in her feet, but he stirred the rhythm within her heart, and she knew in that moment that she wanted to be with him, she wanted to be with him more than she ever wanted to be with Mark, her husband.

And she knew that there was only one way that could happen: she needed to leave.

And that's what she vowed to do, unaware that it was this very decision that would set in motion a train of events with tragic consequences.

39 UNFAITHFUL

Anybody who has been involved in amateur dramatics will most likely have played 'the game of trust'.

The game is often played as a 'warm up' before rehearsals and is normally played by two people: the catcher and the faller. The faller being the person who has to turn their back on their catcher, close their eyes and then allow themselves to fall backwards whilst hoping the 'catcher' isn't busy admiring themselves in the studio mirror.

This very same game is played at team-bonding events around the world and is supposed to encourage 'trust'.

So who would you trust to catch *your* fall—is it your partner? Yes? No?

We place (or feel) trust in another person when we believe that they have our best interests at heart, and they consistently reinforce this belief (through actions and words).

Our diversity as individuals means that the length of time it takes for us to trust and to earn trust differs considerably and is subject to a complex formula of self-esteem and other human experiences versus the amount of 'reinforcement' we're exposed to over a period of time, as well as whether or not our trust has been broken once, or several times, previously.

Naturally, the more our trust is broken, the harder it becomes for us to trust again. This is a sad yet inevitable side effect of us abusing the trust of others as well as allowing our trust to be abused.

And so, like dominos, each cycle affects a new relationship to the point where trust is either seriously eroded or absent.

Cue some of the most suffocating and corrosive relationships imaginable.

A famous actress once said "marriage doesn't need sex", but experts would beg to differ, and so would I. For humans, sex isn't just about pleasure; it's about intimacy, about satisfying a need and making a 'connection' with someone else of our kind.

In relationships, this reinforces a strong or a fraying bond. In casual partnerships, it fulfils a basic need to engage with another human being, which is something that is ingrained in our biological makeup. And whilst this compulsion may fade over time, it remains one of the basic staples of life's necessities.

You will have noticed, above, that I talk about sex 'reinforcing a fraying bond', which does sound a bit strange; how can sex reinforce something that is damaged or no longer exists?

It doesn't.

What it does is maintain a connection, an illusion, not necessarily in the mind, but in the body. This is because many of us view sex as the ultimate intimacy, although some would question that. I'm not talking about one-night stands, where it's pretty clear from the start what the two protagonists are out to get; I'm talking about an established, 'comfortable' relationship where, after a period of time, sex is actually bartered over, like a division of chores, or given as a reward for good behaviour!

In existing relationships, our willingness to give of our body, to be up close and very personal with our partner sends a very strong message, since the antithesis of this is to not be able to stand the sight of each other.

Thus sex in a damaged or broken relationship doesn't necessarily fix a fraying bond, but it does fulfil the basic need for intimacy. Also, it doesn't require a hell of a lot of talking, and has a mutually satisfying result.

It's win-win!

Well, not quite.

'Sex for convenience' in a broken relationship simply slows down the effects of the relationship essentially being over. You may be through with your partner and might even be seeing somebody else, but whilst you are still having sex with your partner, you're actually sending the completely wrong message; you're substantiating the lie, prolonging the inevitable, and maybe even shoring up the fact that, when you finally pluck up the courage to confess, the event will be doubly explosive.

It's bad enough discovering that your partner doesn't love you anymore. It's worse if they cheated on you—worse still if they've been cheating on you and then had sex with you, and worse *still* if others knew of it, thus making you the proverbial 'last to know', compounding the humiliation.

…etcetera, etcetera.

All of these permutations will have a bearing on just how devastating a breakup will be.

But not always.

I actually told myself that, in this book, I was going to try to avoid what the media has been talking about for years: recessions, shifts in the economic climate and so on and so forth. But there really is no way of getting around the fact that these events have had an impact on the economy and life as we used to know it.

Now, more and more, we're seeing couples, who can no longer bear the sight of each other, trapped in a property together because they simply can't afford to move out or, incredibly, choose to stay together as the arrangement means that they can continue to split the cost of the household bills— at least that's until they 'hook up' with somebody else, move in with them and start the cycle all over again.

The generalisation, regardless of economic factors, is that men tend to do this more than women and are often likened to primates who refuse to let go on one branch before they've latched onto another.

Other couples, actually living together, continue to pay rent to each other as communal lodgers.

I received an email once from a couple in the US Air Force who purported to have the perfect marriage; they had been together for over forty years and they rarely fought.

Naturally, I agreed to meet them since I was intrigued to learn exactly how this couple managed to achieve such marital bliss.

The interview started fairly well as the wife talked me through the marriage, told me about the home and how they spent a lot of time in the same house.

However, alarm bells started ringing when I learned that they slept in separate rooms (okay, not so unusual), that he had his own lounge, sofa, TV and that she had the equivalent, that they had separate bank accounts, and bills were split evenly down the middle.

Suddenly, to me, they were no longer a married couple, but a pair of lodgers. Forget joint mortgage or even adding both names to a lease agreement; they opt instead for this practical, albeit somewhat unromantic, arrangement.

Many unmarried couples are adopting this same marriage of convenience, but without the whole hassle of actually getting married.

Yes, this is, very sadly, yet another sign of our times. But this isn't the worst part; the worst part is the impact that living this type of relationship has on us and our whole perspective on love, romance and trust.

Here's a quick story.

I know a couple who have been together for four years now. She comes from a turbulent relationship out of which she had a son. More specifically, her ex mismanaged his and her funds, and was generally an unlikeable person who eventually left her, thus obliging her to become a single mother, working in her job in sales and generally using that killer instinct to savage everything and everyone that threatened her and her baby.

He comes from a similar setup, but without any children.

They moved in together.

She, like many, has had some very bad experiences and has the emotional baggage to prove it. He, a much more laid-back yet practical kind of person, came from a similarly disastrous relationship, but with half the emotional scars.

Both of them share his rented home as well as their inability to trust again. To the point where she pays him, her current fiancé, rent.

Fair enough.

However, he feels, like many devoted couples, that they should have a joint bank account for the household bills. An account into which they both pay and out of which all of the bills are automatically debited.

She doesn't. She feels much happier splitting the cost of the bills, like lodgers, but she doesn't feel comfortable sharing a bank account with him.

Why do you think she doesn't want a joint bank account?

She doesn't trust him.

Why do you think she doesn't trust him?

Because of what happened in her previous relationship.

What kind of message do you think she's sending?

That's right. *"I don't trust you; you're just like my other boyfriend".*

Although he isn't. He's just paying for the ex's sins.

And whilst she may not be verbalising this, her actions are doing all the talking for her.

Meanwhile, she's been somewhat bent out of shape that it's taking him, with regular cajoling from her, over four years to actually propose to her.

She pays him rent, she doesn't trust him, doesn't trust any of his advice and hates the fact that he thinks he's right all the time.

Not exactly a match made in heaven—or even in a church for that matter.

So, by now, you're probably thinking, *why the hell are these two people even together?* And if you're not thinking that then you're wondering what the big deal is with her wanting to keep her independence. That's not so terrible, is it?

Of course not.

However, what you don't know is that there's much more to this story.

The aforementioned lack of trust is further exacerbated by a severe lack of respect; she doesn't like hearing, nor does she trust his advice or his opinion, they do not consult on major expenses or purchases such as furniture or cars, and nor do they even discuss career choices.

As long as the rent payment is there at the end of the month.

She won't be told.

He knows it all.

Never the twain shall meet.

On the bright side, considering the imminent marriage, they sought counselling. Unfortunately, they abandoned this after the first session because they don't need it anymore.

Seriously?

Trust is an absolute must in any partnership. Instilling and receiving reinforcing messages of trust reassures our partners that, "no matter the history, you can rely on me". Our words, our actions carry enormous power since, like a radio mast, they are constantly sending our partners a stream of information.

I send you a text during my working day = I'm thinking about you.

I bring you flowers = I thought about you and I care about you.

I leave you notes on the kitchen fridge that tell you how much you mean to me = I love you and love thinking about you (depending on the type of message of course)!

Everything we do or say substantiates our love and our trust.

Equally, everything we *don't* say or do erases that and will undoubtedly inspire distrust in somebody who is used to receiving all of the above, but suddenly doesn't anymore.

That's because, as human beings, we're inclined to respond to the familiar and draw comfort from the reinforcement of it. It tells us that all is well in our galaxy, everything is spinning as it should, and that the main anchors of our life—love, work, home and friendship—are all holding up well.

So, what about those 'perfect' relationships? You know, the ones where there's constant reinforcement and everything seems to be working fine. The touchy-feely, vomit-inducing ones where each person is constantly, often in public, expressing their affection for the other. These people appear to share the perfect home, have well-established careers, look handsome together, and so on and so forth. How on earth do these people end up on the scrapheap of broken trust and betrayal? Worse still, how on earth could anybody in the 'perfect' relationship look for that proverbial 'connection' elsewhere?

Why, that would be because of that overused and underestimated phrase "perfection is subjective".

There are a multitude of reasons partners stray from each other, too many to list here and each and every one simpler or more complex than the other, but I'm going to highlight just some of the ones I've been 'exposed' to over the years.

Seeing:

So, outside of a family member, who do you trust the most?

Is it your dog?

Your cat maybe?

Or is it your partner?

If there's one person we expect to look out for our best interests, it's our partner. Good or bad, thick or thin. You know, there's that whole vow thing. So, when we dream and/or we achieve, the first person we'll generally turn to for validation is the person who is supposed to have our back, right? The one person who is supposed to really care about us making a mark in this world.

But what if that person is disinterested, be that because they are genuinely not interested or they're busy taking care of the family or they have career pressures of their own? Or what if they just suddenly appear incapable of 'seeing us' because they're too wrapped up in themselves?

Most relationships tend to be conceived in the same way: boy sees girl or girl sees boy one day and thinks, *"Wow, I want to be with that person."*

With a bit of luck and sometimes a bit of cajoling, they manage to realise their thought, and with a bit more luck, hopefully love, and cajoling they actually manage to move in together (I won't say *get married,* because we've already covered that).

Nonetheless, we'll still call this the *honeymoon phase* and, during this time, our happy couple are still 'seeing' each other like the view through freshly washed glass. They'll perform romantic gestures, leave romantic notes, send text messages, voice messages, change social media statuses and generally declare their undying devotion for each other whilst showing an avid interest in what's happening in their partner's life— work, family, friends, and whether or not they're happy, sad, inspired or generally depressed.

They'll genuinely 'see' their partner, every day.

The thing is, our need to be 'seen' by the object of our affection does not stop as soon as we're in a committed relationship, but continues throughout the life we share together.

The need to be seen is perpetual.

Make time to 'see' your partner each day. Any gesture, big or small, is enough to let them know that, no matter what life may bring, "I see you, now and always".

The flame:

Where did all the passion go?

Do you remember what it was like to meet your partner for the first time? (Yes, go on, even you must be able to remember that far back.) Your mutual passions probably burned as hot as the sun (okay, some artistic licence here).

How about now? As hot as a match? Or is it dead as a doornail?

Passion is such an important factor in any relationship because it's not just about the obvious sexual gratification, but it's more about that all-important trust affirmation; telling your partner that you are still burning hot for them is telling them that you still need and want only them. Without passion, the opposite message is being transmitted.

In time, as part of the normal biological progress of ageing, there's a distinct possibility that those flames may well turn into smouldering embers. That's okay too, but that's when the consistent trust reinforcement of words and actions becomes key; your partner needs to know that they're still special to you above anybody else, regularly and consistently. This is particularly crucial in those who are contemplating greeting or waving goodbye to middle age because this, as we've discovered, is a very delicate and vulnerable time in all of our lives. It's that delicate, insecure time in which we're contemplating not just our own mortality, but the fading of youthful beauty. A stage where we're craving a lot of 'reinforcement' to believe that we aren't anywhere near as old, and that our looks haven't faded anywhere near as badly as that pathological liar of a mirror keeps telling us. It's a time when we, effectively, need to trust our partner to support us the most, and though we may subconsciously know that they have a vested interest in telling us what we want to hear, sometimes premeditated patronisation makes all the difference and is most welcome.

In the arts they call that 'suspension of disbelief'!

The alternative, of course, would otherwise take us full circle right back to that good old *seeing* thing again; if a stranger sees us, when our partner has become distracted and we're feeling particularly vulnerable about our existence on this earth, then, like moths to the flame, we're going to crave that attention— and this, more often than not, leads to other things, with devastating effect.

But what about self-restraint?

Seriously?

Let's just take it as a given that I've said that people should be loyal to their partners and not decide to jump ship just because they aren't hearing the right words anymore.

You have my total support on that.

But ask yourself one simple question: as idealistic and virtuous as that may seem, how often is it not practised and how often has it been proven ineffective?

Humans need to be noticed.

And this is the part where another smartass will pipe up and say, "I don't; I'd much rather not be noticed".

There is always going to be the exception to the rule. Many will pretend they don't need it, whilst a few will learn to live without it but, ultimately, as humans, we need and enjoy recognition, be that at work (by your boss), socially (by your friends), at home (by your partner) or by members of your family.

We all seek validation, we all seek to 'be seen', because to *not* be seen is to not exist.

So, let's say you did become somewhat remiss and your partner decided to stray elsewhere to 'get noticed', you found out , were devastated, they were disinterested and dumped you and left you festering in all of your pain and resentment (see how I made that sound really crappy—because it is).

You were betrayed!

The result is a potential emotional basket case with trust issues.

Yes, thanks for that.

Now you're having a hard time trusting the next person that comes along. Moreover, you'll be looking for the signs. Is there constant 'reinforcement', is there 'passion', and all that stuff?

You're not seeing that?

Oh dear.

They must be having an affair—that's the only explanation. This is what happened to you before and it's happening all over again.

Hang on a minute. Really?

Yes, really.

This is the neurosis suffered by many with low self-esteem and/or who have experienced betrayal. It's self-feeding and self-destructive because it eats away at the proverbial trust and where there's the absence of trust, there's a hungry 'attention seeker' with a very inquisitive demeanour and, often, what you do not tell them, they'll just need to find out for themselves, and the best and easiest way they know how.

So, before we proceed any further, ask yourself; should your new partner really be held responsible for the wrongdoings of your previous partner?

Don't answer that.

Secondly, should your new partner be responsible for any low self-esteem you may have fostered over the years and that perhaps was compounded by your previous disastrous relationship?

Don't answer that either.

Both of those questions are potentially incriminating.

Just ignore them and proceed with your plan. If you need information, there's just one place to start. No, I'm not talking about your partner. That'd be too obvious—and if they *are* cheating on you, they're not just going to admit to it, are they?

No, there's only one thing for it; you're going to have to 'snoop'. You're going to have to search through your partner's phone, email and any other device you can get your hands on to make sure he or she is not covertly communicating with Mr or Mrs Sexalot.

But that's crossing the line, isn't it? Not only is it an invasion of privacy, but it's also an outright betrayal of trust.

Who cares? The means justify the end. (Or should that be the other way round?)

And that is very much the case in many partnerships these days—but does it make it right?

There is an argument for the fact that your partner should not hold any secrets from you; what's yours is theirs and what's theirs is yours. And, if they weren't doing anything untoward then they shouldn't mind you snooping through their phone.

Right?

That's subjective.

The real thing to look at here is the fact that you are being compelled to do it. It means there are serious trust issues between you. Something is so wrong in your relationship, be that lack of 'attention', 'affection', or 'passion'.

Or something is wrong with you. You have such a lack of respect for yourself and your partner that you've resorted to snooping through their personal stuff. And where does it stop?

Today it's their phone; tomorrow it's a spy.

We're all entitled to our own thoughts, our own privacy, and this shouldn't have to end because we're in a relationship.

Remember that familiar example about venting?

Say you did have an argument with your partner and you're really angry with them, so you text a friend and tell them all about it; you may even use a few expletives and, whilst venting, say some things that you don't actually mean, but that, in the fog of rage, escaped nonetheless.

These things can be very damaging when read out of context.

And that's just a basic example.

Each and every one of us has the right to privacy or to share our thoughts with whomever we choose. It's the very reason many keep a journal or diary. There is much that is said in these records that the writer does not want shared with everybody else.

My thoughts be my own.

The thing is, we all know that when we're emotionally affected it's really easy to jump to the wrong conclusions. This is the very reason many couples seek therapists: because it's much easier for somebody who is impartial to be able to dispassionately review the evidence in a case and reach (or enable the couple to reach) a conclusion.

This is exactly what happened to me once.

A friend of mine asked if I would consider meeting his brother-in-law and his girlfriend, who were going through a 'rough patch' in their relationship, with the view to helping them 'work through' their issues.

I agreed to meet the two twenty-something-year-olds-primarily because I already had an idea of what the problem might be.

The following is a transcript from part of that meeting, which I'm hoping will enable you to form your own opinion about this duo whose names have been changed to protect their identity.

The three of us were alone in my friend's dining room. I was sitting to the side of them, at the dining table.

First impressions didn't really tell me much; the couple looked pretty good together. I noticed she was 'holding onto' him, but not vice versa. Jamie, with his arms folded in front of him (defensive gesture); Jane with her arm around his as if united in the face of my potentially probing questions.

I started the interview by asking, "So, I hear you work at a gym, Jamie?"

"He does, but he's looking for another job," replied Jane on his behalf.

"No—you *want* me to look for another job," Jamie said, avoiding eye contact with her.

"Why do you want Jamie to find another job, Jane?"

"Well, it doesn't pay enough and we're looking to start a family…"

Jamie scoffed.

"What's funny, Jamie?" I asked.

"It isn't funny," he retorted. "It's tragic," he said, forcing a smile.

"Jamie," Jane warned, as if trying to not 'spoil' the conversation.

"What don't you want Jamie to say, Jane?"

"She doesn't want me to work at the gym anymore because she doesn't like me talking to the other girls," Jamie said and then added, "which just happens to be part of my job."

"Yeah, well, flirting with 'em ain't part of your job, is it, babe?"

"I don't flirt with them."

Jane just smiled knowingly, letting go of her boyfriend's arm, allowing him to shift in his seat.

The tension was revealed.

"Do you flirt with the girls you work with, Jamie?" I asked, breaking the silence.

"It's part of my job to be friendly…"

"That isn't what I asked. Because there's a difference between being friendly and flirting, right?"

"I don't flirt," he insisted. "Sometimes they flirt with me, but that's just part of the job."

"Okay, so you wouldn't mind if Jane visited you at work to see for herself?"

"I do now, after last week," he answered quickly.

Jane shook her head, rolled her eyes, and now it was her turn to fold her arms and look away.

"What happened last week?" I asked, already knowing the answer.

Silence…

"What happened last week, Jane?"

"Ask him," she retorted. "He's the one spilling his guts."

"Hey, guys, you asked me here," I said. "I'm just talking this through with you. I'm just trying to understand. Nobody's trying to trip the other up. There are no right or wrong answers. We're just trying to understand what's happening."

"She threw a fit at work and embarrassed me in front of everyone. She started screaming at me in front of a client and all the way to the car. It was humiliating. The worst thing is, she's always doing that. I only have to talk to someone and she thinks I'm having it off with 'em."

Silence.

"What happened exactly?" I asked.

"Well, I was in one of the…."

"If you don't mind, Jamie, I'd like Jane to tell me," I interrupted.

He looked at her, pointedly.

"I went to pick him up from work and I walked in and found him."

"Having sex?"

She pulled a face, "No."

"Naked?"

She laughed.

"The girl was naked?" I asked.

"No."

"They were kissing?"

"No."

"Okay. So, what were they doing, Jane?"

"Well," she couldn't find the words, "they were talking."

"Talking?" I asked, and dramatically lifted my eyebrows.

"Yeah, but, you know, they were laughing and talking."

I nodded knowingly and sucked the air in over my teeth. "Right… talking AND laughing. I can see where you're coming from."

Jane laughed. "You're making me sound bad."

"I'm making you sound bad? No, I'm just listening to what you're telling me," I smiled.

So, what do you think to the story so far, then? Was Jane right to 'throw a fit'?

The reality is, I'd already been briefed about the incident at the gym before I'd even agreed to the meeting, and I already had an idea of the type of person Jane might be.

She was indeed an insecure girl who had a relatively handsome man as a partner. He happened to work in a gym where he did receive a lot of female 'attention' and he did use this to increase bookings for personal (one-on-one) coaching sessions, because for each booking he'd earn an additional commission. He was putting this additional revenue into a separate 'wedding' bank account so he could marry Jane.

Was he just being friendly? Yes. Was he flirting? Possibly. Is that such a bad thing in this particular scenario?

I'll let you decide.

The big question is, can flirting with somebody other than your partner be deemed as being unfaithful? Or just talking for that matter?

Ultimately, they are nothing but words.

But then, I guess this all boils down to intent. Flirting could be construed as intent to perpetrate the crime, yet it clearly is not conclusive evidence of the crime, and is certainly nothing upon which a conviction can be obtained.

To prejudge such an innocuous action is more a reflection on you than it is on the suspect.

I'm using the legal analogy because I tend to base a lot of my decisions on facts and evidence rather than on supposition and innuendo.

Yet, I'm often told that the world isn't a consistent legal black and white, but that it's made up of various shades of grey, and I can tell you, when it comes to affairs of the heart, I would have to agree with the exception of one thing: *trust is earned, not given.*

This is the ultimate fact of the case and it is undisputed.

40 THE LIBERATION

If I said that waking up the next day was like being reborn, I wouldn't be exaggerating.

As had been the case since M's revelation, my first thought was of him—only today it wasn't with anguish, sadness or intoxicating power, but more a bitter-sweetness for what was. And whilst this held none of the exhilaration that having power over another human being can afford, it was nonetheless liberating since I no longer felt the need to cling to and gather together all of the strands of my broken relationship.

Instead, I'd simply let go, and it felt good.

My next thought was about me and, like a person who'd had a few too many drinks and ended up in that awkward morning-after bed of a stranger, *what the hell did I do?*

I had driven over to my brother's in some kind of a stupor and revealed for the first time to a member of my family the truth about my sexuality. And, in the nicest way, it appeared to be received not as a major revelation but more of a *"what took you so long?"*

I'd think I'd almost go as far as saying that, oddly, and somewhat mercifully, it was a bit of an anti-climax.

I'd also discovered my brother, the one I thought I never had.

I'm not talking in the physical sense of course, since I was obviously very much aware that I had an older brother. In fact, you couldn't help but be aware of his stoical presence at family gatherings. He was the first of all the siblings to carve a very successful career for himself. As such, he automatically became revered and somewhat respected as *the elder* who imparted wisdom whether you wanted to hear it or not. A man who attempted to rule family as he did those who worked for him.

Add to this the provincial, somewhat archaic yet ever-present Italian custom that the eldest man (or husband) tends to 'assume' the role of alpha male, the primary breadwinner, the one who must be respected and to whom others should kowtow, and you've bred all of the egotistical personality traits to spark some of the most explosive family conflicts.

However, given the sporadic frequency of our reunions throughout the year, it had become an unofficial yet universal family practice to approach each meeting with the premise of getting through it with no, or as little as possible, controversy, and this meant agreeing to much of what the man said (which only enabled that ego).

The result was generally light-hearted and somewhat meaningless conversations and thus the absence of an opportunity to bond.

Until now.

We were both much older and I'd only just discovered a whole new man who could be as warm as he was self-centred, as sympathetic as he was arrogant, but most of all, a man who was capable of deep compassion.

Last night, I laughed and cried with my brother, and when we weren't doing that, we talked, not as older brother to younger sibling, but as equals. And it was through this process that I came to the true realisation that, no matter what, family is family, and it was time that I stopped lying to them, time to accept who I was and make changes in my life, for good.

And it was this warm and giddy feeling that stayed with me, well after we shared breakfast and I declined the kind offer to stay another day, when I emerged into the morning sunshine.

It was a beautiful spring morning with chattering birds absconding in the myriad of verdant leaves in nearby trees and the fresh grass-scented prelude to summer on the breeze.

I boarded my car and knew exactly what I needed to do.

41 THROUGH THE BEDROOM WINDOW

It had been three months since Peter had walked into Katy's life.

During this time the two of them developed a closeness that neither could deny. It's not that they had behaved inappropriately or anything like that, since they were both still married—although he made no secret of the fact that he had become somewhat estranged from his wife.

But, most importantly, Peter reminded Katy that there was more to life—or, more specifically, there was *much* more to life than what Katy had allowed hers to become.

It was time for action.

Needless to say, the reality of what that entailed absolutely terrified her. There was no telling what Mark's reaction would be, and it was the very notion of this that made her stomach churn. It's not as if Katy wasn't aware of just how unpredictable and volatile Mark's episodes could be. There was no telling exactly what he might be capable of.

But it was something she had to do. She'd been downtrodden for way too long. And it's not as if she didn't care for him anymore, she did. She just couldn't contemplate living the rest of her life this way.

And so the next evening, as they sat at the dinner table, the words that Katy had struggled to even assemble in her mind actually escaped her mouth. They contained no emotion, no preamble, just a simple and calm, "I'm leaving you."

Mark remained reactionless for a few seconds and then he looked at her as if he hadn't understood the statement.

She repeated it, bracing herself for a reaction, "I'm leaving you, Mark."

"Why?" he asked with eerie calm.

"I just don't think there's a future for us. And, to be perfectly honest, I can't spend the rest of my life living in fear."

"In fear of what?"

"Of you!" she said with astonishment. "I just have no way of knowing what the hell you're going to do from one moment to the next."

"You know exactly why I react the way I do, Katy; it's because I love you and I'm afraid of losing you."

"Maybe, Mark, maybe you do, but I don't love you anymore," she said with conviction and she could see the words visibly register on his face.

Seconds went by as they both simply stared into middle distance, each contemplating what had just been shared.

"What about our son?" he asked, suddenly.

"What about him?" she said.

"I suppose you think he's going to live with you."

And there it was. The one thing she dreaded about ever being in this situation. And she wanted to scream at him, but instead she said, with all of the restraint she could muster, "I know we have a son together, Mark, and this is something we're going to have to talk about."

"Talk about it? There isn't much to talk about…"

"We're going to have to talk about it," she repeated, not

wishing to bow to his threat despite the fact that her fear may be realised that her son may well be taken away from her regardless of what she knew about the law.

"You realise that you're ripping us apart, right? You are going to rip this whole family apart."

"I'm not setting out to rip this family apart, Mark. I'm just doing what I believe is right," she continued in a low, calm voice.

"What's right for you, you mean," he retorted.

"What's right for all of us."

"For you!"

She lowered her eyes, as one would when confronted by a rabid dog, and said with determination, "There's nothing else here, Mark. There's nothing left."

And so it began; several weeks of moods, arguments, supplications and threats. As well as a cancer scare.

Mark told Katy that a bruise that had formed on his face was actually cancer, and whilst this did get Katy's attention for a short period of time, it soon became obvious that this was simply another desperate attempt to make her stay, and she knew that she could not yield to that, not anymore. She had made a decision and she needed to follow through.

This prompted her to actually move out of the marital home and in with her parents.

However, it took but days for Mark to show up there and demand that she return home, insisting that she must do what was right for their little boy.

Katy informed him that she was actually planning to find her own place. Mark laughed at this and told her that finding a place for her to live on her own would mean she'd be on her own with nothing for she would have no money, no husband, no son and, most importantly, no family.

It was a risk she was willing to take.

She told Mark that there was nothing he could say to change her mind no matter how hard he tried, and that they should both now look to selling the house and dividing it equally.

This enraged him, albeit temporarily.

After he had taken a few seconds to compose himself, he spoke calmly, as if coaxing a child down from a tree, "Katy, just come home, please." She was about to answer, but he held up a hand as a signal to let him finish. "I know how you're feeling and I accept what you're saying, I do," he forced a smile, "but it doesn't mean I have to like it, right?"

The question was rhetorical.

"Just come home. It doesn't mean anything has to change, and if this is really what you want then we'll do it. But please just come home where we can discuss and plan everything properly. For example, Florida—we've paid a deposit and everything, what's going to happen to that? Just come home, Katy, please, I'm begging you."

They had booked a family trip to Florida months before when a mutual friend had invited them to attend a wedding there. They'd originally decided not go, but then both agreed that it would do them both some good to get out of the country and enjoy a change of scenery.

It was because of this subject, the idea of one last family outing, plus an additional hour of cajoling and reasoning, that Katy found herself back in the marital home the next evening.

She agreed to return only on the understanding that they would be able to rationally discuss a way out of the marriage and the cash-strapped situation that they both found themselves in.

It was this discussion that had dominated dinner for that evening and Katy resolved that it was probably one of the most rational conversations they'd both had for months. So much so that it led her to conclude that maybe her husband could be reasoned with after all and that maybe, who knows, they could actually work on building a future together, and she verbalised this.

Florida was about a month away.

"I tell you what, regarding Florida, let's do it. Everything's paid for anyway. Let's go on holiday and see how things go. And I promise, hand on heart, to give the whole thing some thought whilst we're there. Let's face it; it can only make us rather than break us, right?" She said with a smile.

Mark was ecstatic.

If anything, this gave him hope that if this split did happen, it could be done in a way that would benefit them all.

"So, what do you think?" she asked Mark again.

"I think it's a great idea," he said with a big smile.

"Good. Now, how about we clear away the dishes, put this little boy to bed," she said, ruffling her son's hair and putting on an affected baby voice, "then we can have a nice cup of tea and talk about the details?"

"Sounds good," Mark said.

So they cleared the dinner plates away to the kitchen and Katy left Mark to clear up whilst she put her son to bed.

When she returned, fifteen minutes later, she was expecting Mark to be clearing up, but instead pretty much found the kitchen as she had left it.

"Mark?" she called out but there was no reply. She looked in the lounge, but he wasn't in there either.

"Mark?"

Still nothing.

She looked through the kitchen window; he wasn't in the back garden, but she did notice that the garage door was shut and, since it was getting dark, she could see a slither of light all around it.

"Oh no," she said under her breath. She thought it was too good to be true. Mark had absconded in the garage, which was a common MO when he was having one of his 'moments'.

At least that's what he did when he wasn't stalking the bedroom.

She felt a weight settle in her stomach once more and it made her feel sad. She'd truly believed that they'd moved beyond this, and she'd hoped that they'd be able to draw this thing to a conclusion in a reasonable way and not in the usual way.

She felt deflated and somewhat annoyed that it was all going so well and he'd had to ruin it once again.

But she wasn't going to be beaten.

She resolved to give him some time to get whatever it was out of his system and then she'd take him a cup of tea in the hope that the peace offering may well get him back to the reasonable man she'd seen at the dinner table.

So, she busied herself with washing up the dishes, drying and packing them all away and clearing down the surfaces. She then turned to look out at the garage door; it was still closed, the light still on—he was still in there.

So, she boiled the kettle, made tea and then carried the mug outside into the night.

She tapped on the garage door. "Mark?"

No answer.

She waited a few seconds.

"Mark, I've brought tea. Let's talk."

Silence but for a bird's fluttering in a nearby tree and the low hum of traffic on the motorway several miles away.

So, she held the mug of hot tea in one hand as she crouched to pull the garage door up and over her head with the other.

She did so in one movement, but nothing could have prepared her for the sight that was revealed: Mark, her husband, the father of her child, was hanging by a rope from one of the beams.

His head was lolled to one side, his face was pale, and bulging bloodshot eyes watched her vacantly as his tongue protruded from his lips like a macabre taunt.

The mug slipped through Katy's fingers and smashed loudly onto the concrete floor spraying hot liquid over her legs and nearby walls.

But she stood there, motionless, for seconds, that seemed like hours, transfixed by the horror before her as the blood drained from her face and her heart hammered like a pneumatic drill, pumping adrenaline around her body that made her feel giddy whilst at the same time urging her to move, compelling her to lunge forward, making her DO SOMETHING!

She dashed over to her husband and put her arms around his body in an effort to hold it up and loosen the strain on his neck.

"MARK! She screamed. "MARK!"

She scrambled with her arms around him, trying to assume the impossible weight of his limp body, but her efforts were futile.

"HELP!" She whaled out to the open garage door as tears of frustration streamed down her face. "SOMEBODY HELP ME! HELP ME SOMEBODY!

But nobody came. No sound of voices, no sound of approaching footsteps.

"HELP ME!" she screamed as she tried once again to hold her husband's body, but it was impossible.

So, after hesitating, torn between staying and leaving him, she eventually ran out of the garage, down the side of the house, screaming through anguished sobs, "HELP ME! SOMEBODY HELP ME!"

She reached the next-door neighbour's front door and pounded on it as if it were her life that depended on it.

Eventually, after what seemed like an eternity, the door opened, "Help me, please! Mark is in the garage! Help me! Help me!" she screamed.

The next-door neighbour raced back to the garage with her where, astonishingly, he immediately took action to hold the weight of Mark's lifeless body as Katy cut the rope that had gauged an ugly purple bruise around her husband's neck.

She half fell with the body to the ground as her training kicked in and, after demanding the assistance of the neighbour's wife, she immediately began CPR (cardiopulmonary resuscitation).

"MARK! Wake up! MARK! MARK! Stay with me!"

She looked into the fixed and dilated pupils of her husband's eyes. The eyes that for years had contained so much expression, but were now lifeless, locked in a cold state of bemusement.

"MARK!"

She cleared the saliva that was dribbling out of her husband's lips and began giving him mouth to mouth. But it wasn't lost on Katy that her efforts were in vain.

"MARK!" she screamed in frustration. "MARK!"

Bizarrely, and rather than asking her neighbour to call an ambulance, she took it upon herself to stop what she was doing to race out of the garage once more and into the house where she dialled emergency services and cursed them for asking her too many questions; she needed to get back to her husband…

"JUST SEND SOMEONE, NOW!"

She abandoned the phone and returned to her husband to begin CPR once more as the neighbours stood by, aghast.

Katy was still doing this when the ambulance arrived some ten minutes later, but it may as well have been ten hours as far as she was concerned.

She fought, swore and clawed at the policeman, a colleague from work, who tried to pull her off the father of her son.

"Get off me! Get off me! I have to save him. I have to save him!"

"Katy…"

"Get off me!"

"Katy… he's gone!"

"NO! NO! I have to save him! I have to save him!"

But the officer and his colleagues were not relenting, and despite her wailing supplications, the swearing, the kicking and punching, they managed to pull her out of the garage and into the night where, high above her, with eyes just about reaching over the windowsill, a five-year-old boy watched the scene unfold, through the bedroom window, with perplexed horror.

We'll never truly know what drove Mark to do what he did that night, what drove a man to such extreme lengths to rob his son of his father, his wife of her husband. What we do know is that Katy felt somehow responsible for his death.

But for the fact that she had made the decision to leave Mark, then the tragic event of that evening would most likely have never taken place.

The reality, of course, was completely different. As much as Katy felt 'obvious' guilt about her husband's suicide, she could not hold herself responsible for the decision that he made.

Some would say a selfish decision.

Others would say that Mark was mentally disturbed and therefore not in full control of his faculties.

Whatever your thoughts, Katy is now living with the events that took place that night and, while the memory may well fade, they have now been branded on her subconscious forever.

The good thing is that today, over eight years later, Katy has found someone to help her through her darkest days, and that person is Peter.

The two are not married, mainly because Katy sees no reason to marry once again, especially since they are perfectly happy with how things are.

Peter moved in with her and her son nearly a year after the events of that tragic night. He's never attempted to take Mark's place as a father to his child, but he's willingly assumed the role of surrogate father and, whilst family life may not be perfect, they're certainly making the most of each and every day, as a family.

42 THE POWER OF DENIAL

If Katy's story has taught us anything, it's the fact that life is precious and that life, as you know it, can well and truly change in the blink of an eye.

We'll never know what was going through Mark's mind in the minutes leading up to his suicide and that's because he didn't share his true feelings. Katy only witnessed the projection of what he likely wanted her to see.

So, how are you feeling today? Everything okay?

Yes?

Are you sure about that?

Have another think. Is there really nothing troubling you today? Some dark lingering thought in the back of your mind. Something that is there, but that you'd much rather not think about? Something that you were happily ignoring until I came along and made you pause for thought.

Anything?

Many of us are guilty of it. You might even be doing it as you read this. You may well go on to do it after you've finished reading—but is there really anything wrong with that?

I am of course talking about the wonderful and mystical power of denial.

Whether it's ignoring that mounting credit card bill, turning a blind eye to that suspicion that someone close may be betraying us or burying some terrible trauma that we simply can't face, each and every one us will, sometimes subconsciously, turn to a trusty friend we know will protect us, albeit temporarily, and see us through some of our most difficult and challenging life events.

If we deny it ever happened or is happening, then it isn't, right?

Um, well.

I guess this takes us right back to the chapter about truth is truth. It doesn't matter which way you look at it, say it, hide it; the truth simply *is,* no matter what we'd prefer it to be. The only difference is how mentally prepared we are to face it— and often, the present, the here and now isn't the right time, at least not according to our brain.

Apparently, it was good old Sigmund Freud who first coined the phrase 'being in denial', and that's because it was he who first suggested that human beings immersed themselves in this state when confronted with situations that were too uncomfortable and/or horrific for them to deal with. Thus, to deny the existence of the situation or event equalled not having to process the fact that it *was*.

Mind exploding yet?

Read on.

There are various degrees of being in denial. From deep trauma, such as experiencing or witnessing something horrific, to knowing you have to go back to a job you hate on Monday morning after two of the best vacation weeks of your life.

The following are classed as key types....

Denial of Responsibility: shifting the blame away from yourself and often onto others in an effort to make you look less culpable, and/or more favourable, to others.

Denial of Impact: the impact that your actions will have on the things and/or people around you. By denying impact, you're denying the assumption of a sense of guilt or remorse that acknowledging your actions would entail.

Denial of Cycle: as in denying the sequence of events that led to the eventual outcome. "I wasn't even there," is a common phrase.

Denial of Awareness: as in denying the fact that you knew anything about the event by adding some mitigating circumstance. "I didn't see what happened because I was busy washing my car." Also believed to be commonly used in a more cynical way (stereotypically) by corporate bosses, who use others to take action in their absence, thus giving them the legal stance of "plausible deniability".

Similarly, denying that you have a problem means there's nothing you need to address and/or correct; e.g. addicts who deny having an addiction. This is the antithesis to, "Hello, my name's Tony and I'm an alcoholic" (but only socially).

Denial of Denial (my favourite): a state of self-delusion that often overlaps all other forms of denial. Here, the denier actually denies being in a state of denial and sees no reason for correcting any behaviour that may well be harmful to themselves and others.

Recognise any of these?

Sure you do.

The brain's automatic defence mechanism places us in a state of denial by telling the conscious that in fact it never happened, often deceiving itself into thinking that it was our own imagination fabricating untruths. And because this version of the event is much more palatable, the conscious actually clings to it as reality.

This can also be true of those who witness rather than experience an event first-hand. Such as a mother who may well have been aware of, or even witnessed, the abuse of a daughter by her father; however, because she believed herself incapable of doing anything to stop the abuse, she'd actually put herself into a state of denial that it ever happened. In turn, this would enable her to cope with something over which she believed she had no control.

This is one of the many scenarios that's particularly dangerous for the victim, for not only will she be potentially denying that the event ever took place (and thus holding on to all of the associated feelings that come with this type of trauma), but she may well, if she becomes aware of her mother's perceived 'betrayal', develop and foster repressed animosity towards her for her inability to 'save her'.

This mindset of denial is not so dissimilar to that of a 'pathological liar' who will usually tell dazzling and fantastical stories about themselves, their achievements as well as the celebrity of their circle of friends. Stories that will more often than not bear no resemblance to reality and will always portray 'the sufferer' as a hero or indeed a victim.

Not much is known about pathological liars but, interestingly, what one study did find is that there's a prevalence among juvenile offenders, which is the average age of onset. However, most importantly, a good proportion of these subjects come from a dysfunctional home environment where a parent or family member has a mental disturbance. A disturbance which could well be attributed to their own unresolved psychological conditions, such as the denial (or repression) of a psychological trauma that is now manifesting itself in other ways.

Thus, the pathology to lie is their way of escaping (denying) an unpalatable physical environment and/or state of mind.

Similar to, but nowhere near as altruistic, as talking about somebody else's problems and forgetting your own!

So now I want you to take a second to consider the next question carefully.

How many times have you witnessed yourself or somebody you know have a verbal outburst that appeared to come from absolutely nowhere? One where everything seemed just fine, and then, suddenly, bam! *Where the hell did that come from?*

Take a few seconds to consider that.

Some men will often joke that this is pretty much the norm when it comes to their female partners.

"One minute she seems fine and the next she's flying off the handle."

Some males will (at their peril) even go as far as patronising a female by explaining away their so-called outburst as hormones or a particular time of the month. When in reality, more often than not, and as odd as this may seem, it's actually her way of trying to communicate—thus talking down to her is probably not the best course of action.

The truth is, if your partner has an out-of-character episode, then it could simply be down to them having a particularly bad day or even week. You will have heard of the proverbial straw that broke the camel's back.

However, if these episodes are becoming more frequent, then chances are that there's some other troubling or irritating thing that hasn't been, and isn't being addressed.

On the other hand, if these outbursts appear to be a perpetual state or have been present for a sustained and long period of time, then you may well be seeing the side effects of some other physical condition, grievance or trauma that has been repressed and is manifesting itself in some other way.

That or they're just inherently grumpy by nature! (Which is what most people will most likely latch onto, as it's much easier to deal with).

Remember, we're all pretty much a by-product of our own history, so if there's something eating someone, chances are it's due to a particular life experience. So don't always take it personally!

Instead, if somebody you care about is behaving out of character, then take the time (yes, you can find it if it's really important enough to you) to sit them down and have an eyeball-to-eyeball chat.

Yes, as alien as that situation may well sound, just take some time out and ask them, earnestly, "What's happening to you? I'm worried that there's something on your mind."

Ironically, many people reading this will be reluctant to subject themselves to this somewhat simplistic process.

Why?

Well, because they'll understandably be somewhat apprehensive about what they may find. Move that proverbial rock and who knows what kind of black and ugly things are going to skitter out from underneath it.

Of course, by avoiding this, you know what you'll be doing, right?

That's it; putting yourself in a state of denial. If you deny there's a problem that requires you to sit down and have a serious conversation with your partner, then it doesn't exist, right?

The power of denial is immense, but it is nothing when ultimately compared to the power of reality

For me, it was time to get real.

43 YOU CAN RUN, BUT YOU CAN'T HIDE

When I decided to flee, for want of a better expression, from England to the United States to recover from my split with M, I was very much aware of the fact that my sadness would follow me.

But they say that a change is as good as a rest, and I was desperate for a rest, from feeling sorry for myself.

Oh, the irony.

One of the things that I've been exposed to over the years (and there have been many) is the common misconception of many that they can just up, leave everything behind and outrun their demons.

You can't—remember, they are part of you.

However, what you *can* do is get out the monotony of your routine, seek out other life forms and get some perspective. But pack light because your thoughts, your fears, your memories, hopes and dreams will be coming with you, along with those ghastly shadow-dwelling friends.

I knew not to expect too much from this trip since, not unlike back home, there wouldn't be anybody there to wave some magic wand and make everything better.

I needed only to present myself at London Heathrow Airport to be reminded of that, since the last time I was there was when I said goodbye to M, and the closer I got to security, the hotter and more fetid was the demon's breath on my neck.

I stood there for a good few minutes replaying that last event over and over in my brain: the rucksack on his back, his sad face.

"I guess this is goodbye," he'd said, reluctantly.

"I guess it is," came my tired, expressionless response.

He'd turned to me. "I guess this is goodbye."

My response, "I guess it is."

"I guess this is goodbye."

"I guess it is."

Over and over again.

And it felt as if I was going to suffocate.

I seriously contemplated turning back as I watched the other passengers who, one by one, handed their documents to the balding uniformed security officer. I noticed that he made an effort to smile at each and every person who handed him their papers, and remember wondering if that was indicative of his actual personality or if that was all just a front.

Time was ticking and I half expected a hand on my shoulder by an armed policeman wondering why I was loitering with intent.

So I shuffled forward.

I handed my papers to Mr Balding Security Officer and collected my token smile.

This was it.

I had ventured beyond the inner sanctum of the departure gate, retracing M's very steps as I went through a somewhat bizarre cataloguing process. *This is where he will have walked. This is where he may have browsed Duty Free. This is where he may have got something to eat...*

And so on and so forth.

And I have to confess, just writing that now, many years later, I am thinking, *what the hell? Seriously?* It all just seems somewhat peculiar and maybe even a bit creepy, and that's because now, with cold hindsight, I'm able to think that way, but at the time, every little thing gave comfort and, somewhat strangely, made me feel closer to him.

Don't be afraid of your feelings.

Remember, each and every one of us is unique in our ability to deal with a particular set of circumstances. How you'll cope in such a situation is subject to who you are, and if it works for you, then sod everyone else.

"I guess this is goodbye."

It was as I walked among my fellow travellers that I reconciled that never had M spoken a truer word. As much as I didn't want to see it at the time, I somehow knew he would never return to England, at least not to see me.

I hated that thought and it hurt, tearing chunks out of my soul as I presented myself at my departure gate. I hoped that this feeling wasn't planning on staying with me throughout the duration of my journey

Of course, my flight was delayed, giving me even more time to savour the sights and imagine how M must have walked these very steps to reach his aircraft and fly out of the country—and my life.

It took over eight hours, with delays, for me to finally land at Will Rogers Airport in Oklahoma City.

My sister, Rosa, was waiting for me. I'd made it. I was on American soil. Now the real challenge would begin.

That evening, we dined at a waterfront restaurant, where I shared with Rosa all of the details of recent events, along with the reasons behind how I found myself back in the United States.

It was quite a momentous moment since, for the first time, I didn't break down whilst recounting the story. It was surreal. I actually felt somewhat calm, maybe even at peace.

Was it working already? Had coming to America already cured me?

I was considering this when, suddenly, the whole restaurant exploded into rapturous applause. Each and every diner was clapping, and, for a few bizarre seconds, I thought Rosa may have staged some kind of special reception, as one would a birthday celebration, but that was before I noticed that the whole dining area had been drenched in a warm orange glow; the shutters had lifted from the glass walls, revealing a spectacular sunset over the lake, and I drew a sigh of relief; everything was going to be okay.

That was Sunday.

44 LAMB TO THE SLAUGHTER

Love is blind. So they say.

And 'they' would be right.

None as blind as Sarah.

The fact that Steve, the man she loved, the love of her life could have humiliated her in that way at the wedding for no particular reason was something she could not come to terms with.

No matter how hard she tried

And the hurt wasn't necessarily physical but it was mental; the concept that the man who had treated her as a queen had now turned into some kind of violent entity.

Worse still; things didn't end when they left the wedding reception; they actually got far worse.

Steve was already enraged and Eileen's intervention had only fuelled that fire. Her 'outing' of what he had done to his fiancé was something Steve didn't see coming. It shamed him, and he blamed Sarah.

But for the fact that Sarah had been 'fucking' this other man, he wouldn't be this angry, and but for the fact that she had lied about him to Eileen, then 'the old hag' would not have stuck her nose in their business.

It was all Sarah's fault.

All of it.

The moment they walked through the front door, he spun her to face him so he could examine just how bad this so-called injury was to her face.

He looked into her tear-streaked, bloodstained face and asked her, full of concern, "How is it? Have you stopped bleeding?"

Sarah couldn't respond; she was still convulsing from the sobbing wreck she'd dissolved into when they boarded the taxi home.

Steve had told her that she was a state and that he was embarrassed to walk the streets with her, to the point where he covered her with his jacket—not to keep her warm, but to hide the bloodstain down the front of her dress; it was drawing attention to them and had even prompted the London cabby to ask questions. At least, that was, until Steve gave him a direct reply: the iciest glare, which struck the man instantly dumb.

For Sarah, just seeing that 'death glare' (as she called it) was enough to strike the fear of God into her, even in the gloom of the cab, and she had begun to sob uncontrollably despite the fact that Steve was squeezing her thigh, seemingly to reassure her, but hard enough to get her to shut the hell up.

So now, Sarah was standing in the hallway, trembling and sniffing as his somewhat concerned gaze scrutinised her.

"I'm so sorry, Sarah. I didn't mean to, but when I heard about

391

Martin, I just lost it."

Sarah began to cry once more. It would have been a wail but for the fact that she was aware that her mother was upstairs and she didn't want to wake her nor worry her. She was too traumatised by the whole ordeal to articulate any kind of denial.

Steve's face darkened, "For God's sake!"

This sudden volatile stance startled her and she began to sob even louder.

That's when Steve saw red, and he brought a backhander up to her face, the impact of which sent her first reeling then sprawling backwards, until she slammed against the kitchen doorframe.

She remained still, but for her convulsive judders, emitting a dissonant sound of hiccups, sniffing and sobbing.

She was absolutely horrified. She had never even witnessed anything like this, and her body had gone into shock.

"See? See what you made me do?" Steve hissed. "Why do you make me do this, Sarah? Worse, how can you *do* this to me? How can you humiliate me by fucking Martin and then embarrassing me in front of everybody at that wedding? Why would you do that to me, huh? Why?"

Steve's voice seemed genuinely perplexed.

However, if he was expecting a response from Sarah, he would receive none, for she forced herself to stay as still and as quiet as possible for fear of soliciting another unprovoked attack. Instead, she stared into middle distance as she shivered, snuffled and blinked.

Steve watched her as if she were an alien being he was trying desperately to understand. Then, suddenly, he turned and climbed the steps leaving her alone in the semi-darkness.

Two days later, Monday morning, the children, still recovering from the excitement of having their aunt stay for a few days, finally left the house and made their way to school whilst Sarah, complete with welted lip, sat at her sister's kitchen table, gingerly drinking tea.

Melanie was on the phone, speaking with their mother.

"Yes, Mum... I told you, she's fine... Don't worry... I'll be round in a few hours, but she's staying with me until we've decided what she needs to do… No, Mum… don't worry, if he comes round here, I'll sort it…"

And these words were pretty much on a loop the whole ten minutes their mother had been on the phone.

"She's worried about you," Melanie said, finally hanging up and joining her sister at the kitchen table.

"Oh, God, you didn't tell her, did you?"

"Sarah, she lives in that house. Do you think she's deaf?"

There was a pause and then Melanie ventured, "You know, you've been here two days and you still haven't really talked about it."

"What's to say?"

"Well, what happened for starters? What went wrong?"

"Everything went wrong. Steve finally showed his true colours," Sarah said, staring into her tea cup as if it contained the wisdom she needed to deal with what had happened to her as well as her sister's probing questions.

Her eyes began to well with tears as she recalled her sister's words. Then she added, "I should have listened to you."

Melanie reached out and touched her sister's hand.

"I just can't stop seeing his face, Mel. It's like he gets possessed by some demon, you know. It's like this thing takes over, and his face is replaced and what you see isn't Steve, not my Steve, anymore, just some demon, all angry and so full of hate."

She wiped a runaway tear from her cheek.

"Well, he can't do anything to you now, but you're going to have to decide what you're going to do."

"Well, I can't leave him," Sarah said quickly.

Melanie frowned. "What do you mean you can't leave him?"

"I can't."

"Sarah…"

"I can't, Mel. He'll just come after me."

There was genuine fear in Sarah's voice.

"Once you've spoken to him he won't…"

"He will, Mel. You don't know what he's like, what he's capable of. He'll come after me and he'll kill me!"

"Sarah, you're getting carried away…"

"For crying out loud, Mel! How much more proof do you need?" she said, pointing at her lip. "Especially now... I'm worried..." She trailed off here.

There were a few seconds of silence, and then Melanie spoke, "Especially now?"

She could see that her sister was avoiding her gaze.

"What do you mean, Sarah?"

She hesitated, then, "I'm pregnant," she said, finally turning to meet her sister's eyes.

"Oh, Sarah," Melanie said with deep sympathy as she put her arms around her.

"I'm so worried for the baby, Mel."

They remained locked in the embrace for a few minutes.

Eventually, Melanie emerged and asked, "What are you going to do?"

Sarah was about to reply, but they were both startled by loud rapping on the front door.

"It's him!" Sarah said quickly.

"Don't worry. I'll deal with it," Melanie said, getting up from her chair.

It seemed like it took minutes for her to reach the front door, which was just in the next room, during which the banging continued.

Then Sarah heard muffled then raised voices.

"She doesn't want to see you, Steve," Melanie was saying.

"Well, I want to see her. Sarah! Sarah!"

"'Ere, you, piss off out of my house," Melanie yelled.

"Sarah!"

To Sarah, hearing him call her name may as well have been fingernails on a chalkboard; it sent shivers down her spine. She wanted to ignore him; she wanted to go hide in one of the bedrooms until he'd gone because she wasn't ready to deal with him, she wasn't ready to talk. She wasn't ready to look the man that she loved so very deeply in the eyes after he had hurt her so badly.

"Sarah!"

"Get out!"

"Sarah!"

"If you don't go, I'm going to call the police!"

Sarah covered her ears like some child.

She was torn; wait, as she'd agreed, or give in and save her sister from something that appeared to be rapidly descending into an altercation at the front door.

What if he takes a swing at her?

She leapt from her seat, promise or no promise.

"I'm not leaving until I've spoken to her," Steve was saying, looking over Melanie's shoulder while she stood resolute behind a partially opened front door.

"What do you want, Steve?"

Melanie turned around and was annoyed to see her sister standing behind her.

"Sarah?"

"It's all right, Mel."

The two sisters exchanged looks.

Melanie was naturally unhappy to see her; that wasn't what they had agreed.

On the other hand, Sarah hadn't agreed to put her sister in danger either. This was her problem and she needed to deal with it rather than let others fight her battles.

It may have been that way when they were children, but not now. She'd grown up. She was going to be a mother.

"Sarah, I need to talk to you," Steve said urgently.

Sarah didn't give him her eyes; instead she glanced at Melanie, "Give us a second, will you, Mel."

"Sarah…"

"It's okay. Really."

Melanie observed her somewhat incredulously. She then glared at Steve with all the menace she could muster.

You touch her and I'll kill you was the message, but whether or not he received it was unknown.

Reluctantly, she left the hallway and positioned herself nearby. Just in case.

"What do you want, Steve?" Sarah asked, taking up Melanie's defiant position behind the open door.

Steve seemed visibly taken aback when he noticed the welt on his fiancé's lip.

"Sarah, I'm so sorry. Can we please talk?"

"I don't think there's anything for us to talk about, Steve.

Besides, the only way you seem to talk now is with your fists."

"Look, babe, I can't begin to tell ya' how sorry I am. I'm sorry, Sarah, I just, just got so jealous when John told me about Martin."

"There is no Martin, Steve!" Sarah said, reacting to a sudden flash of anger. "I don't know any Martin!"

"I know," Steve said calmly. "I realise that now. I realise that John lied to me. You see, he's jealous of us, Sarah. He's jealous of what we have so he fed me a pack of lies, knowing full well that it would drive a wedge between us. That's the God's honest truth, and you've got to believe me, babe. You've got to believe me because if you don't, I just don't know what I'm going to do to myself. Sarah, babe, please."

"Even if I believed you, Steve, which I don't, you hurt me, and there's no excuse for that. You put your hands on me; you broke my heart—for what? For something your mate told you? I can't have that. I can't, especially now. I can't put me or the baby through that."

"I said I was sorry," he said petulantly.

"Yeah, and I heard you, and I told you that saying sorry doesn't make it right, either."

"What else do you want me to say?"

She looked at him, incredulously; his dishevelled hair, and the dark circles under his eyes. He obviously hadn't been sleeping, for whatever reason.

"It's not about what I want you to say, Steve, it's about what you do, and I don't want you to hurt me anymore, or my baby."

"Your baby?" he retorted. "Don't you mean *our* baby?"

"You gave up your rights to this baby when you starting smacking me about."

"Come on, Sarah. You know as well as I do that that kid is going to need its dad"

She thought about this.

Sarah had actually considered this for a moment, as it's something that had played on her mind ever since she'd arrived at her sister's house. She had wondered what life would be like as single parent, and also what her baby would think of the fact that she'd walked out on her father.

Although this was the least of her worries.

Even if she was crazy enough to give Steve a second chance, where would they go? They couldn't go back to her parents', not now. Besides, they'd never forgive her if she was crazy enough to go back to him after everything that happened.

But what if what he said was true? What if John had drip-fed lies with the hope of splitting them up?

Sarah was aware of the fact that John did have a soft spot for her. At least this is something that Zoe had noticed and was quick to share with her.

"Haven't you noticed how he looks at you when you're in the room?"

But Sarah hadn't noticed, and there was just one reason for that: she well and truly only had eyes for the man standing at the front door right now. The man whom she had agreed to marry and whose baby she was carrying.

Steve.

Her Steve.

Could all of this just be some kind of a mistake? Some terrible misunderstanding? That whole episode that day they'd been shopping. Could that have been a result of more of John's lies? It certainly seemed to be out of character for Steve.

Could it be that Steve loved her so much that the mere thought of another man with her sent him into this fit of jealousy?

It still didn't justify his actions.

But it went some way to explaining them.

And an explanation now was more than she had a few hours or a day ago.

She looked at him again.

"I can't do this, Steve. I can't be with you and be in constant fear that you're going to throw another fit and hurt me, I can't," she said, as tears suddenly pricked her eyes.

She loved this man. She loved him and she just wanted all of this to go away.

And as if he read her mind, "I love you, Sarah. I love you and our baby more than my own life. I would sooner cut off my arm than hurt you again, babe, I would," he said, choking on his words as his eyes also began to well with tears.

"I am sorry, Sarah. I am so sorry, but I just, just the thought of losing you to some other fella, I just couldn't handle it. I need you back, Sarah. I need you back and I need you to give us another chance. Please give me another chance, please."

He was crying now, as was she. They were both hurting.

But could she, should she go back?

What do *you* think?

Well, I was going to put another multiple-choice here but you already know where this is going, don't you? And you will also have formed your own opinion but, remember, you're gifted with insight because you are emotionally detached.

Sarah wasn't.

Sarah was in love with that man. To her, he was her first love and the father of her child. She couldn't give up on him, not now, not so soon.

That's right. She agreed to get back with him.

Only now they couldn't return to her mother's house for obvious reasons, since there was a good chance that, despite her disability, she'd crawl her way to him to give him a taste of his own medicine.

So, they moved in with his mother instead, much to the protestations of her sister and her parents, but Sarah felt she had to do this; she had to give her relationship, her marriage a chance, if only for her own peace of mind.

So two months went by.

Sarah was now four months pregnant.

Steve, despite the fact that he appeared incapable of finding another job, seemed in very good spirits. In fact, it seemed that the old Steve was back. An excited Steve who was ecstatic about becoming a father as he was about their future, one that had been discussed several times over the past few weeks, specifically marriage.

Like many girls, Sarah had always dreamed of the perfect fairy-tale wedding with a princess gown, a church ceremony and lots and lots of guests.

But that was before her fiancé got put out of work and she became pregnant.

Now, overnight, she had come to the realisation that how she became married to Steve was of no consequence when compared to him actually becoming her husband and her baby growing up in a loving family home.

And so, despite his protestations, Sarah insisted that they get married sooner rather than later. Thus the fairy-tale wedding in a cathedral-style church became the grey, governmental square room of the registry office, and the reception, a small gathering down the local pub.

"I'm sorry I couldn't do better by you," Steve had told her on their wedding night.

"You've made me your wife. There's no getting better than that," Sarah had replied with a kiss.

They honeymooned for a week in Southend, England where they spent some of their gifted wedding money on a small bed and breakfast close to the seaside.

It may not have been much in reality, but it meant everything to Sarah who, despite what she called 'the blip' in their relationship, had managed to rediscover her man, her husband, and the father of her baby.

She loved them both beyond anything else in the world.

Life was good.

Not long after they returned from their honeymoon, Steve had a meeting with some of his old 'work colleagues' as there had been talks of them starting up in business together again.

Sarah, very much aware of their financial situation and the fact that they could not live with Steve's mum forever, chose to push any reservations she may have had about Steve's meeting to the back of her head with the foresight that none of it was worth worrying about until the actual detail was known.

Steve returned from that meeting with a whole new lease of life. He would soon be back in business and Sarah accustomed to the lifestyle that she deserved.

At least those were his words.

That very same night, Sarah was shaken awake by him.

"Sarah! Hey, Sarah, wake up!"

The clock on her bedside table read 3:07 a.m.

She heaved herself into a sitting position.

Steve was out of the bed and wearing just his boxer shorts. He was pacing at the foot of the bed, in darkness but for one side of his face which was eerily illuminated by just part of the streetlight spilling in through the bedroom window.

Sarah switched on the bedside lamp to reveal her husband's somewhat agitated demeanour.

He seemed troubled.

"Babe? What's up?" she asked through her grogginess.

No answer, just pacing.

"Steve?"

"I need to know, Sarah. I need to know," he said, looking around the room, as if searching for something in the shadows.

"What? What is it you need to know?" She asked, rubbing sleep from her eyes.

"I need to know about you and Martin.

Sarah's heart skipped.

"What?" she asked.

"I need to know about you and Martin. I need to know if he's been putting it in you; I need to know if that's his kid inside you."

This can't be happening again.

"Steve," she reasoned very slowly. "Steve, I told you, I don't know any Martin. I don't know anybody by that name, you know that."

"Just tell me the truth, Sarah. Just tell me the truth," he said, slapping his head as if trying to empty it of some horrendous image.

"Steve, I told you…"

"Don't lie to me, you whore!" he sneered, fixing her with that 'death stare' of his.

Oh, God.

Her heart was racing now. She felt vulnerable in bed. She glanced at the door and wondered if the best way to deal with this situation was to leave the room. But she daren't move.

"Just tell me," he started to whine as if burning from a lot of emotional pain. "Just tell me the truth!"

"Steve, I am telling you the truth, I swear."

He stopped pacing and looked at her as if the last words she'd just spoken were in some way blasphemous then he stalked over to her side of the bed as she automatically shrank back into the headrest.

"Steve, please, you're not thinking straight, babe. I love you and only you and this is your baby…"

The rest of the words were snatched from her mouth as his right hand shot out and grabbed her shoulder-length hair causing her to yelp in pain.

"Stop… lying… to… me," he said slowly, cocking his head to one side as she grabbed his powerful grip with both her hands in an effort to alleviate the pain.

"I'm not lying, Steve, I swear, I'm not! Please! Please let go! Please! Please don't hurt me! Please don't hurt us!"

"Tell me the truth, Sarah… tell me the truth."

"I have told you the truth! I am telling you the truth!"

With that, he slumped his shoulders, pursed his lips and cocked his head to the other side, as if trying to resolve another of her barefaced lies.

She'd left him no choice.

He yanked his wife out of the bed by her hair, causing her to land with a loud thump on her backside, then dragged her to the middle of the room.

By this time, Sarah was hysterically pleading with him not to hurt her.

"Tell me the truth!" he yelled, eyes wide with rage. "Tell me the fucking truth!"

He accompanied each demand with a vicious kick into his wife's ribs.

"That isn't my kid you're carrying, is it?

Kick!

"Tell me the truth! Tell me! Tell me the truth!"

Kick!

"Tell me the truth or I swear to God I'll kill it! I'll kill it!"

"What on God's green earth is going on in here? What's going on?"

The light bulb that hung from the centre of the ceiling sprang to life revealing Steve's mum, in her white nightie, standing by the open bedroom door.

"Get out of here, Mum. This is none of your business," he snarled.

"HELP ME!" Sarah sobbed from her position on floor, "HELP ME! PLEASE!" She wailed, hysterically.

"Steve, stop this! Stop it; you're going to kill her!"

"I said, get out of here, Mum! Get out!"

"No, I won't. You leave her alone. You leave her alone right now! She's carrying your baby, for Christ's sakes."

With that, in one swift motion, he leapt across the room, snatched a pint glass of water from his bedside table, empties its contents onto the carpet and then smashed it. Then, he pinned his mother against the wall with one hand and put the shard of glass to her throat with the other.

"I told you this is between me and her, and if you don't go back to your bedroom right now, I swear to God I'll cut ya."

The words were delivered with a snarl and a contorted face that his mother had seen so many times before, both in him and his father.

It filled her with deep familiar terror.

With that, he released her, and the lady fled back to her bedroom, locking the door behind her.

Sarah, in the meantime, had just about managed to pull herself into a seating position against the nearby wall when the shadow of her husband fell over her once more.

She screamed.

45 THE SINGLES

My sister, Rosa, had to work on my first Monday morning in the United States, which meant I was going to be alone in the house.

But that wasn't a problem, I was in good company. My demons awoke me first thing so I knew they'd be hanging out with me for the rest of the day.

Joy.

And, of course, they kicked off the day's proceedings by joining me in a singsong with Savage Garden's *I Don't Know You Anymore.*

I collapsed in a sniffling heap.

And that's how I started my first week of antisocial behaviour.

No, I didn't start roaming the streets swearing at people and vandalising property; I just chose not to do anything or to go anywhere. I just wanted to be left alone, confined to quarters in my sister's house.

Of course, I only realised that one week later after I'd turned down no less than eight of Rosa's invites to separate social gatherings, including a meeting of *The Singles*.

Not unlike me, my sister, after being married for many years with one daughter, was also somewhat happily single. And as such, she would meet on a regular basis for food and a chat (or commiserations) with a group of other single men and women.

"You want me to go to one of those meetings and listen to a bunch of rejects bemoan love and life? No, thank you. I have enough of that going on in my head already without hearing a group of overenthusiastic, overanalysing, self-absorbed forty-somethings bitch about it too."

At least that's what I thought. I just told her that I would rather not.

And Rosa was really good about it. In fact, she was very patient regardless of how many times the English visitor refused to, well, visit.

"A friend of mine has asked me round for dinner tonight— would you like to come?"

"No, thanks."

"I've told my work colleagues that you're in town and they'd really love to meet you."

"No."

"How about you drop me off downtown today and keep the car. Then you can go explore rather than stay cooped up in here all day."

"I have writing to do."

Who was I kidding?

I was supposed to be working on *Nimbus 2* at the time. I had already laid down something like thirty pages, but each time I went back to it, the internet seemed much more interesting or I felt tired, or I had work to do from back home, or it was too hot in the house and I had to mess with the air conditioning, or maybe I'd go back to it after just another cup of tea, some toast and maybe some chocolate.

Anything but write.

Then, one night, about seven days into my stay, Rosa started a sentence with, "Hey, listen…"

Oh no, here we go again. Brace yourself.

"…our company is having a cookout on Tuesday and, as you know, I've told them you're in town and they'd really like to meet you…"

Then, just as I was suppressing a sigh and preparing my stock answer, she added, "My boss will be there and he's heard so much about you."

I thought about this.

"It's a fairly informal thing and you'd almost be like the guest of honour."

I thought about it some more.

"No, thank you," I said.

Rosa looked at me, and if she wanted to beat me around the head with the salt mill she didn't give any indication of it; instead she just started clearing away the dishes to the kitchen.

I just couldn't face it.

And that evening I was feeling particularly depressed because M had messaged me on MSN Messenger (now decommissioned).

He just wanted to check in with me to 'see if I was okay'.

What the hell do you think?! I wanted to scream but instead, when I saw MSN say he was online and his smiley emoticon face pop up, I played it really cool and said that I was fine; that I'd been in America for seven days now and I'd been meeting all these new people and was having a great time.

The actual conversation didn't really last long as he was *on his way out,* but it was long enough to etch the fact that I was lying both to him and to myself.

I wasn't having a good time at all. I was having a rather crappy time, quite frankly, and I was ready to go home.

What the hell was I doing over here without him anyway? It was bloody ridiculous. For me, America was only great when he was with me. Now that he was gone, it had lost all of its appeal.

I was thinking about this as I rather glumly chatted with Rosa about her day as she made tea for both of us.

COMING UP FOR AIR

I felt bad.

She had been so good with me and so patient, and I'd just been a miserable git. No, not just miserable, but downright rude!

And that's when the words just fell out of my mouth, "What's this work thing you were talking about again?" I asked.

And that's how it happened.

Just there and then, in that moment, I realised that all I had done was swap the four walls of my home, surrounded by all of my things, in England, for those of my sister's in a completely foreign land.

What was the point of that?

I had been wallowing, and the worse thing is I enjoyed it. In fact, I'd actually become addicted to it. Just me, my misery and my demons. Together, we'd made a good crowd.

But it was time to venture back out into the real world.

The so-called 'cookout' at Rosa's office in downtown Oklahoma was actually an 'eat in' at the office and it seemed that everyone and anyone who worked at Sonic Drive-In was present that day.

Talk about overwhelming.

Worse still, I was the visiting Englishman so it seemed everybody was clamouring not only to meet me, but to hear me and my accent!

I always find it interesting how many of us respond to regional accents, whether these be from a different region in the same country, or actually from a different country. In this case, whilst I couldn't understand the fascination, because they were ultimately talking about little old me, I could relate to it because I know how I felt about M.

He had the perfect accent, nicely enunciated with just a subtle American drawl. He may well have been a Southern boy, but he'd travelled around quite a lot, spending time in Washington State (which happens to be one of my favourite American states, probably because the climate reminds me so much of England) and so he had just enough of an accent to make him bloody well sexy.

(Oh, I'm sorry, have I mentioned that before?)

I'm sure I didn't have the same effect on all of the people I met that day, at least not that I noticed, but they sure were extremely polite and showed a great interest in me and in my writing.

The best bit was when they asked me what I was working on, my automatic response was that I was working on the sequel to my book, *Nimbus*, but each time those words left my mouth I felt this jarring of guilt because the reality was, I wasn't writing a thing—although from my casual, "Oh, yah, yah, I'm writing the sequel and I've already laid down something like thirty thousand words," you would never have guessed.

In fact, I hadn't written anything for about two months.

Ever since M had shared *that* news, I had done nothing but wallow and feel sorry for myself, retreating into my world of seeming teenage angst and emerging only to tell whoever stood still long enough my sorry tale of betrayal and despair. And while that may seem tedious in the first instance, I understand now that it was my way of coping with my separation anxiety.

Often, our way of dealing with the loss of someone is to talk about them ad nauseam, and we're doing this because we're processing what has just happened in multiple ways; we're keeping the memory of that person in our mind because we don't want to let go, we're wallowing (for want of a better expression) in what has happened to us (licking our wounds) and, a bit like putting ointment on an irritating wound, we're constantly bathing in the soothing sympathy of others, and generally coming to terms with the event.

What we tend to forget is that, whilst this may well be our main preoccupation, it isn't necessarily that of everyone else.

What was happening to me, is happening or has happened to you, is happening to and will happen to millions of other people around the world, and each and every one will probably deal with it in a similar way—but in their own way. How they react is entirely up to their own circumstance, as it is up to you, but there are some basic things you should be mindful off.

This too shall pass, and whilst it may not feel that way right now, I promise you, it will.

It may be a week, a month, a year or years, but there will

come a time when that pain becomes an ache and that ache a bittersweet memory.

How long this process will take, again, is subject to your own personal circumstance and the protagonist involved, but, most importantly, how well you handle the separation.

Handle a separation badly, and you could be locked in a prison of misery for decades to come, seldom finding contentment in anything or anyone.

And you wouldn't want that, would you?

No.

And that's why, as terrifying and as painful as drifting into oblivion alone may seem, believe it or not, it's probably one of the best things you can do. By that I mean it is important to understand and accept what is happening to you even if you can't do anything to change it.

Remember the chapter on surrendered lives? Well, if you thought that concept was alien to you, then you may well want to become reacquainted with it because the opposite of that, the opposite to accepting that which is inescapable, is to set course for a road full of anguish, sadness, anger, rage, jealousy, incomprehension and sometimes even so-called diminished capacity (or responsibility).

Yes; the infection with, and the loss of, love is the only thing that truly has us behaving in ways we don't even recognise, it's the very reason some actually use it as a defence in court in what is more commonly known as a 'crime of passion'.

Thankfully, not everybody is pushed to such an extreme, and that's because most of us have moral inhibitors that block us from behaving with such wild and illegal abandonment, as much as we'd like to!

And thank God for that.

Because the reality is, like it or not, and as shitty as this particular situation may well be, it's nonetheless part of your life experience. You can choose to fight and rebel, or accept and learn from it.

Choose.

And, if you're anything like me, you'll probably choose to rebel.

Whatever it takes, right?

I felt that way, especially as I'm a control freak/fixer. I used to find it (and still do) excruciatingly difficult to accept anything that is beyond my control, but even I've learned (and this often comes with maturity, yes even my own) to pick my battles. There are some things over which even I have no control and I have to accept them, because to not accept would be to condemn myself to a perpetual state of discontent.

What's the point?

Understand that your compulsion to do something (try and win your loved one back or rebel against what happened) is part of your reaction to what is happening—but not necessarily the right action.

For example, when a pet goes astray, owners are able to deal with the experience better by actively seeking to find their pet, walking pavements, handing out fliers, driving in cars—just doing something, anything, feels better than sitting at home and thinking about it.

Right?

Dealing with a breakup isn't necessarily about doing something; it's about doing the *right thing*, what's right for you, not just in the here and now but in the long run.

Take an objective view (or have somebody without a vested interest take it for you, such as a good friend, as you're way too emotionally involved and thus unable to be truly objective).

Then ask, why exactly did the breakup happen?

Make that famous two-sided list of reasons FOR and AGAINST and then rate them in order of significance.

"She left me because I keep leaving the toilet seat up" may well be a reason, but on the scale of importance in a loving relationship wouldn't (shouldn't) even register.

What, it does?

Need I say more?

Some things just aren't that important—and if they seem to be, have become that way, then ask yourself why? Is it really the toilet seat that was the problem or is there something else that isn't working the way it should, and the proverbial toilet seat is just a symptom of something far more important?

(Remember the power of denial?)

Okay, enough of the toilet analogy.

Now, when I talk about having a good friend take an objective view, I'm talking about friends who aren't afraid of telling you how it is. Don't bother turning to the good-intentioned, well-wishing, misguided hopeful friends who send you "Hugz" on social media, but the one that actually gets into his or her car, comes round to your home, bangs on your door and sees you looking (and often smelling) your worst.

Ask them if you were really good with your ex. Ask them for the truth—but *listen* to what they have to say rather than interrupt and project how you're feeling onto them.

You need an objective truth as this is your best starting point. From here, you'll know whether or not you should even be *thinking* about your ex let alone doing something about getting him or her back.

What? You don't have a true friend who could do that for you?

What do you mean?

Now, you weren't one of those people who believed in alienating all of their friends when they met their ex, the one that never had any time for their friends because they were busy spending all of their free time with the object of their affection? The one with the misguided belief that their ex was their one and only, their true love, their everything, including best friend?

You wouldn't do that, would you?

Would you?

I see. So no support structure.

Support structure: network of family and friends who have your best interests at heart no matter what your life status may be.

A support structure is right up there along with your life anchors: health, home, work, family.

You will have heard me say time and time again just how important it is for both protagonists of a relationship to lead an independent life from their partner. Contrary to what you may think or feel, your partner cannot and should not be your everything, and that's both for yours and their sake, because to heap that so-called *everything* on one person would be to burden both parties with a sense of duty and expectation that strays beyond the confines of commitment and vows.

And no, I'm not talking about that commitment to be there for each other through sickness and health, for richer and for poorer—don't hide behind that. I'm talking about each other's need to express and often even vent about things that a partner has no business being involved in.

Most importantly, it's crucial for each partner to allow the other time to contemplate their own thoughts, to pursue activities and cultivate relationships with their friends free from the perpetual duty of care to the other.

Remember the chapter about why being selfish is good?

Follow this golden rule and not only will you both be better for it, but if, God forbid, you should find yourself in the midst of a breakup, you'll actually have some friends you can turn to in your hour of need.

What are you saying? It's too late.

Oh, dear.

Well, fear not; I've seen this too. Recently singled people who think, "Screw it, I'm going to meet up with some old friends and go out and have some fun."

Now you want to go out and have some fun with these friends? What have you been doing up until now?

At least that's what they'll be thinking.

However, if you're lucky enough, and managed to amass enough friendship credits, from when you were actually able to give your friends the time of day, there's a good chance they'll accept you back into the fold.

But remember, your saintly friends and family members are but mere distractions in your plight; they cannot solve your heartache for you (although some of the well-intentioned will probably try and 'fix you up' with somebody else as soon as possible, oblivious to the fact that your heart, albeit reluctantly, may still belong to somebody else).

But remember, you should not expect others to be responsible for 'amusing you' just so you don't have to deal with the inevitable. To do so will be setting yourself up for more disappointment.

This is not their struggle; it's yours. Take ownership of it.

Accept.

"My name is… and I'm heartbroken because the love of my life has left me."

I thoroughly enjoyed my day with the Sonic Drive-In team.

The best part, even if it only occurred to me the day after, was that the whole time I spent talking to these people and asking them about their lives and listening to their problems, I'd actually forgotten about my own—and it felt damn good!

Another lesson learned: don't be so self-absorbed. If you stop long enough to show an interest in and listen to the stories of those around you, you'll realise that what's happening to you is not so unusual, that you aren't a special case, that you are not alone, and, most importantly, there are people out there who have suffered far greater heartache than you.

Get some perspective! Or, in today's vernacular; #getsomeperspective!

The next day I felt like I was ready to face the world, so when Rosa asked me if I wanted to keep the car for the day, guess what I said.

"No, thank you."

I know. Looking back at that guy, I find myself shaking my head.

Really?

It gets worse; I added with a big smile, "I was actually thinking of staying in and getting on with some writing."

Two hours later, what do you think I was doing?

Staring at a blank page that said something like, "Blake and Sky boarded the train…"

Blake and Sky being characters from Nimbus, my first novel.

These two people were old fictional friends of mine who were going through their own relationship trauma, but even they couldn't manage to board a train to God knows where for their latest adventure.

Thanks to me.

But my trip to downtown HQ had not been *completely* useless because I realised now that my mindset had changed and my eyes were actually starting to open rather than being wide shut.

It became obvious to me that, if I wanted anything to change, I would have to put myself out there, meet new people and embrace new experiences.

So when Rosa told me that she had a friend in Wichita, Kansas and was thinking of visiting him and his ex-wife for a long weekend, I was ready.

To say no once more.

Amazing, isn't it?

Right off the back of my newfound interest in the lives of others, I was ready to take on the world; however, once I was back in that house, I went back to my usual recluse ways.

And that wasn't a typo, by the way; I did mean to write her friend and his 'ex-wife'.

Does that sound familiar to you in any way? It should do, as you read about them earlier in this book.

So I said no to Rosa, who by this time had obviously lost the will to live because she followed up her question with, "You're more than welcome to stay here if you'd rather not come."

"Let me think about it," I said.

Seriously?

Road trip to the next State with my sister and some serious bonding in her SUV, and I wanted to be left behind? What was I thinking?

I guess I wasn't.

I was just so lost. I wasn't writing. I felt miserable and I missed M. I'd seriously lost my life focus, and I didn't know how to get it back.

What I did know is that I wouldn't find it in her condo, nor would I find it in the blank screen of my laptop computer. I was more likely to find it out on the open road, and you would have thought I'd know that, considering I'd been through the whole music therapy thing.

Another day went by.

Still no venturing out of the house.

Still no writing. Just feeling sorry for myself.

(Are you bored with me yet?)

It's easy to feel frustrated with somebody who has got themselves into such a flunk, especially when you're so disconnected from it. You just want them to snap out of it. However, as per most depressive states, it's much easier said than done.

However, you'll be pleased to read that I, luckily, saw the error of my ways.

I think it was probably the day before, when I heard Rosa discussing the trip with one of her other friends, that I considered the prospect of being stuck in the house on my own for the whole weekend—and for what?

That night, over dinner, I said, "Rosa, you know this trip that you're going on? Is it too late to change my mind?"

She paused and then said with a big smile, "Of course it isn't."

What neither of us knew is that this trip would spell a whole new chapter in my life that would eventually lead me to talk to you today and for this book to be top of the bestseller list!

What? You didn't know I was a psychic too?

If I were texting rather than writing, I'd be <inserting wink emoticon here>.

46 THE ESCAPE

Sarah thought she was going to die that night in that bedroom in her mother-in-law's home. The same mother-in-law who had run to her room and left her at the mercy of her violent son— and while she may not have known it at the time, Sarah later came to learn that it was because she too was terrified of her offspring since, like his father before him, he reminded her that there was no alternative, but to yield to his demands.

Sarah learned this the hard way.

That night, she sustained multiple injuries: bruises to her face, where Steve had punched and slapped her, a swollen eye, cut lip and bruises to her ribs and her back where Steve had kicked her several times.

Worse, when he calmed down, he refused to take her to the hospital for treatment for fear that everybody would see his handiwork so he banned Sarah from visiting Melanie—not necessarily because he didn't want her to find out what he had done, but more because he believed they were having a sexual relationship.

"Why do you always want to be with her? Is it because you're a pair of lesbians?" he'd ask.

Everything about Steve was sexual. All of his neurosis about Sarah always had a sexual angle; she was either having sex with other men, her sister or even her father.

So instead, he kept Sarah confined to the house, to her bedroom, on pain of death. She was expressly forbidden from even answering the door before her wounds had healed.

She felt alone, isolated, yet she didn't want to involve her family because she was terrified that Steve might turn on them, especially her mum who would be a sitting duck for his rage, and she couldn't run the risk.

Instead, she'd telephone at regular intervals and tell them that she was feeling unwell, that she'd caught something, some kind of bug, that she felt lousy and didn't want any visitors, especially as there was a distinct possibility that it would be contagious and she didn't want anybody else to come down with it, especially Melanie who was the only person keeping things together now that she had had to take over the care of their mother.

But Melanie wasn't stupid. She knew the truth and threatened to call the police on Steve, but stopped short only when Sarah told her not to for fear that she would be putting everybody at risk, including her own children.

She begged her sister not to intervene and promised she'd remain in regular contact to confirm she was okay.

So, what are you thinking now?

I bet I can guess.

However, if you've suffered bullying or abuse of any kind, you'll be able to fully relate to Sarah's plight. If, on the other hand, you're a strong, independent person who hasn't suffered anything like this, then there's a good chance that you're very angry right now. Angry at what he did and angry at Sarah for allowing this to happen to her.

What you should know is that Sarah didn't allow this to happen to her—terror did. Terror for her own life and that of her family. If Steve could do this to her, then there was nothing stopping him from doing something to other members of her family, including her nephews, and she couldn't have that.

In the meantime, she became accustomed to her so-called house arrest that lasted nearly a month. During this time, she did make a very close friend, a friend that she loved more than her own life: her bump.

Sarah would speak to her unborn child at every possible opportunity. She'd spend literally hours telling her about her future, a future that didn't include her father, but another man, someone with a big heart, a prince, who had taken them both in after their misadventures, someone with whom they had made a new home, far, far away from London and, most importantly, far away from Steve, a place in the country where there was a forest, a river and wide open fields full of flowers where'd they'd fall asleep to the sound of hooting owls and rise to a house full of sunshine and to the chorus of chirping birds, a place where on Sundays she'd make eggs and bacon and the aroma would fill…

"Sarah!"

"Wakey, wakey!"

It was Steve's voice that jolted her out of the daydream and to the present, where she was standing by the cooker over a frying pan full of bacon that was rapidly being cremated. She hastily pulled it off the electric ring.

"What the fuck's wrong with you? I've been calling you for the past ten minutes," he grumbled, momentarily looking up from a copy of *The Sun* newspaper.

Sarah forked the bacon onto a plate and placed it in front of her husband who, without looking up from his paper, pushed his cup towards her and said, "More tea."

Sarah refilled his cup from the tea pot and added milk and sugar, exactly one and half teaspoons, no more, no less.

Then she pushed the cup back in front of him.

Again, without looking up from his paper, he took a swig from the mug and promptly spat the contents of his mouth all over the paper and table.

"What the fuck!"

"What's the matter?" she asked.

"It's fucking freezing! Where did you get this from?"

"From the pot," Sarah replied, regardless of whether or not it was a rhetorical question.

"You're fucking hopeless," he lamented, shaking his head. "Make another pot, and while you're at it fetch me some…"

He stopped mid-sentence when he caught sight of the bacon on his plate. "What the hell is this shit?" he asked incredulously.

Sarah didn't answer.

"I asked, *what the fuck is this?*" His words were spoken slowly without looking at her as he gingerly lifted the rashers of bacon with his fork as if they were Martian scrapings.

"It's bacon," Sarah said.

Seconds later, the plate, the eggs and the bacon were sailing inches past Sarah's head where they crashed against the wall behind her.

She flinched at the sound of the impact.

"Make some more," he growled, "and make it right."

"I can't. We don't have any more bacon."

"Then fucking go and get some!" he screamed

"I can't. I don't have any money," she said.

"Use the wedding money."

"I thought we were going to use that to get the stuff we need for the baby…"

"Just fucking go get it! NOW! NOW!" His voice was so loud, it drilled through Sarah's nervous system like a jackhammer.

With that, she promptly turned on her heels, opened the cupboard behind her, retrieved a jar of drinking chocolate, opened it and pulled out a ten-pound note (sixteen dollars). She then hurried into the hallway, pulled on her shoes and a coat, and was about to leave when Steve called after her.

"Sarah?"

She hesitated.

"Sarah!"

"Yes?" she answered reluctantly.

"If you don't come back, I'll hunt you down and I'll kill you and that baby. You hear me?"

Silence as she wrestled with the shiver that those words sent through her body.

"SARAH?" he yelled.

"I heard you," she said, tears pricking her eyes.

Then she turned and ran out of the front door, pulling it shut behind her.

So, what do you think Sarah did?

Do you think she picked up the bacon and ran back home or do you think she kept on running?

Time and time again, you will have heard stories of amazing endurance, often about people you've never met from around the world; brave, courageous people who have survived against impossible odds.

The thing is, each and every one of us has this same capacity although we're not always aware of it until it's tested, often by someone else.

Sarah had the capacity to endure because she believed her love for Steve was worth it. Eventually, her love metamorphosed into fear—that he may hurt her or, worse, a member of her family, and that wasn't a risk she was prepared to take.

However, there comes a time when endurance, perseverance and inability to accept that which is inevitable become so eroded that the decision is almost taken out of our hands.

The hammering on Zoe's door startled her and she rushed perhaps not as much to see who it was, but more to make whoever it was stop.

When she opened the door, her mouth fell open. Her friend, Sarah, was standing before her; she was wearing pyjamas stencilled with piggy faces, boots and a long anorak, her greasy hair was tangled into some fashion of a pony tail, her eyes were wide open as if she had been running from a waking nightmare, and her face was ashen, but for her flushed cheeks and a purple discoloration next to her eye that looked as if she'd done a terrible job with her eye shadow.

She opened her mouth to speak, but Sarah pushed passed her, "He's going to kill me! He's going to kill me, Zoe!"

"What the hell...? Who is going to kill you, Sarah?" Zoe asked, following her friend into the living room.

"I couldn't stay there, I couldn't stay any longer... I had to get away," Sarah babbled quickly as she stood on the opposite side of the room.

Zoe had never seen her friend like this and she was really shocked, so much so that she slowly walked up to her friend, as if she were a stranger on the street, and slowly reached out to take her hands. But Sarah pulled away very quickly, as if the mere idea of her touch terrified her.

"It's okay," Zoe cooed. "It's okay, I just need you to take a seat... come on," she said gently, ushering her to the couch. "Just calm down, take a seat, and then you can tell me all about it. Come on, sweetheart, come on... tell me what's goin' on."

"He's going to kill us, Zoe! He's going to kill me and the baby, and I can't let him do that, I can't," Sarah said imploringly as she took a seat.

"Who, Sarah? Who's going to kill you?"

"Steve! Steve is going to kill me!"

"Steve? Why would he want to do that?"

"Because he's crazy! He's a psycho! Oh, God, Zoe. I shouldn't have come here. I shouldn't have come here but I didn't know where to go, and you're my best friend, but I can't stay here, I can't."

"Look, Sarah, I need you to calm down, babe. I need you to calm down. You're safe here," she said softly, placing reassuring hands on her friend's trembling arms.

"No, I'm not; this is the first place he'll look for me after Mel's. The first place—but you were the closest and I didn't know where else to go."

Her friend was obviously as distressed as she was confused. Whilst Zoe wasn't completely ignorant of Steve's jealous streak, she wasn't, until that moment, totally aware of what that actually meant. But the jabbering state of her friend, the mark next to her eye, and her general appearance were more than enough to tell her that something particularly awful had happened.

She was also painfully aware of the fact that her friend was seriously distressed, but she didn't know exactly what to do other than make a hot drink and perhaps call Melanie; she'd know what to do.

"Sarah, I'm going to make us a drink and I'm going to give Mel a call too, okay?"

But Sarah wasn't looking at her; she was looking around the

very small lounge with just room for one sofa, a coffee table and a small TV, as if Steve was going to jump out at any moment.

"Sarah!"

She finally focussed on her friend.

"I'm going to make us a drink and give Mel a bell, okay?"

Sarah nodded as she sat, perched on the sofa, shivering and quivering despite the fact that she was still wearing her coat and they were sat in front of a gas fire.

"I'll be right back," Zoe said.

Sarah nodded distractedly, whilst watching the window that looked out onto the main road.

This was it, this was the end of her life and that of her baby, because if Steve nearly killed her last time there was no way he was going to forgive this, no way he was going to let her get away with it. After all, he had warned her. He did call her back and told her specifically to go home. He told her to get back home or she would pay with her life and that of her unborn child. But what if he changed his mind? What if he didn't come after her at all? What if he went after her family? Her mum? Her dad? Her nephews. Zoe! What if he came after Zoe—after all, she was stupid enough to take her in.

Oh, God!

"Zoe? Zoe!"

Zoe appeared in the doorway, "What? What's wrong?"

"You disappeared, I thought something had happened to you," she said, eyes wide with terror.

Upon seeing her friend's face, Zoe rushed over to her, knelt in front of her and squeezed her tight, then she added, softly, "Nothing's happening to me, Sarah. I was just calling Mel and putting the kettle on. Just calm down, babe, all right? I need you to calm down for me… It ain't good for you and it ain't good for the little one…"

Zoe may have spoken the words, but she was at a loss for what to say or do. She had never seen her friend in such a state.

That's why, thirty or so minutes later, she actually felt relief when she heard the sound of the doorbell. But it was all she could do to stop Sarah from jumping behind the sofa.

"It's Mel, she reassured her."

"How do you know?" Sarah had asked in a panic.

"Because I saw her go by the window. It's okay, Sarah. It's okay."

Melanie rushed over to her sister and threw her arms around her, then checked her, inspecting every bit of her body for damage but stifled a scream when she saw her baby sister's bruised face.

"Are you okay?" she asked.

"I'm fine," Sarah lied, instinctively switching from victim to protector.

They were all sitting in the lounge with hot mugs of tea in their hands.

"He's not gonna' stop me from having this baby, he's not! Sarah said.

"Nobody's going to stop you from having your baby, Sarah," Melanie reassured.

"You don't know what he's capable of, Mel. He's a nutcase."

"Doesn't mean he's going to hurt his own baby," Zoe chipped in.

"Don't you get it?" Sarah said, frustrated. "He doesn't even think this *is* his baby. He thinks I had it off with one of his mates or this bloody Martin bloke I've never even heard of!"

"Who's Martin?" Zoe asked.

"That's exactly it. I have no bloody idea!"

"It's all right. It doesn't matter," Mel said, trying to defuse the tension. "Look, Sarah, I'm telling you, if you really want to have this baby, you're going to need to calm down because all of this stress can't be doing it any good."

There was sisterly mastery in her tone that actually prompted Sarah to take in a deep breath. Then, after a few seconds, as the thoughts entered into her head, her face creased into a distressed frown and tears appeared in her eyes. "What sort of a future is my baby going have?"

"It's going to have a great future because it'll have a great mum," Mel said.

"What kind of great mum would put it through this?"

"You've got to stop talking like that," said Zoe. "You had no choice. It's not your fault its dad is soft in the head."

"Yeah, but I married him."

COMING UP FOR AIR

"You didn't know what he was like at the time."

"Of course I did. I just didn't want to see it. I was too bloody blind—and now, now, I'm stuck in this nightmare, and it's never going to end, never," she said as runaway tears streaked down her face, prompting her sister to put her arms around her once more. But Sarah emerged fairly quickly from the embrace with a somewhat stony look on her face. "No, there's only one way this will end."

All of the women exchanged glances as if they knew exactly what she was talking about, but it was Zoe who broke the silence. "Why? What you planning on doing, killing him?" she said casually, almost with a smile—which faded as soon as she noticed that her best friend's stony look remained.

"You aren't serious?"

"It's the only way it'll end, Zoe," Sarah said, matter-of-factly.

"I reckon that prick smacked you about the head way too many times, because you're talking shit."

"That's right, Zoe, he has, so many bloody times I've lost count. He's also punched me in the stomach in the middle of the street and left me there, head-butted me in the face at a wedding, dragged me down the stairs by my hair, kicked me in the ribs, punched me in the face and elbowed me in the stomach in the hope of making me lose my baby. He's also locked me up in his mum's house for weeks on end so that nobody would see his handiwork, including you. He's hurt me so bad, terrified me so much that I've actually considered climbing out of his mum's bedroom window and throwing myself to the road below in the hope of making it all end. It was only because I thought, knowing my luck, I'd break both my legs, which would then turn me into the perfect punching bag for 'im that I stopped myself. Now, you tell me; can you think of any reason why I shouldn't stick a knife through his neck?"

Sarah's eyes were wide with something that neither of the other women could decipher—rage? Terror? Or, even more terrifying, resignation to what appeared to be the inevitable.

"Mel?" Zoe prompted, seeking an ally, for she did not know how to respond to what she had just heard.

Sarah's sister took a few seconds to contemplate.

"So, where is he now?" she finally asked, changing the conversation.

"Where I left him, I would have thought, at his mum's house."

"Right, then you're coming back with me."

"I can't."

"What do you mean you can't?"

"That's the first place he's going to look for me. I need to disappear until I have the baby."

"What's she going to do? Go on the run for the rest of her life?" It was Zoe asking this question.

"One thing at a time," Melanie said.

"I mean, has anybody even thought about contacting the police?" Zoe asked.

"They're no good."

"What do you mean they're no good?"

"I mean, he's covered his tracks well. Don't you think I've already thought of that? He even told me. It's the reason I wasn't allowed to see anybody until the marks had healed," Sarah explained.

"Well, they haven't fully healed," Zoe wanted to retort but thought better of it.

The casual way in which Sarah delivered the details of her plight made her heart ache, and she wanted to reach out to her, but the moment was interrupted by Melanie who said, suddenly, "What about the baby? Where will you have it?"

"I'm already booked in at St Thomas's."

"Well, that's no good; he'll know to find you there. He's the father—he's bound to make enquiries."

"Yeah, but they're pretty hot about privacy. If I explain the situation, I'm sure we'll be okay."

"I don't think you should risk it though."

"Well, what's the alternative? Go private? I haven't got money for a bus let alone bloody health care," Sarah said.

And she had a point.

"Okay, I'll have a word with the in-laws—see if you can stay with them in Dagenham for a while. He won't think to look for you there. But that's only until we've figured this out. I'm not having my sister and my niece or nephew on the run for the rest of their lives," Mel said, angry that it had come to something like this.

"Thanks, Mel," Sarah said, reading her sister's face and reaching out and touching her arm.

And so that's exactly what happened.

Sarah moved in with Mel's in-laws, where she stayed until it was time for her to give birth, when she returned to St Thomas's hospital in London. There, she gave birth to a baby girl, Tina.

"I was so proud of myself. Naming Tina was about the only decision that I had made on my own in months, and it felt great."

Sarah wept, almost hysterically, the moment she heard her baby cry, and there's a good chance that the attending paediatrician and nurses would have interpreted this as the usual postnatal climax, but what they didn't know is that Sarah was weeping with absolute joy that her baby, her friend, the companion who had seen her through some of her darkest times, had been born healthy despite her ordeal.

Several months later, with the help of her sister and her sister's in-laws, Sarah actually moved into her own small flat. It was a tiny place above a shop—nothing fancy, but it was a palace to Sarah, who actually danced around the living room with her baby the very first time the two of them were left alone.

However, Sarah's happiness was short-lived because, before long, Steve actually tracked her down.

He was waiting outside her front door one day when she and Tina returned from their time at a local play area.

They'd had another fun day, which was instantly darkened by the arrival of the man she had loved more than her own life but who, on more than one occasion, had threatened to take it from her.

She was smiling as she carried Tina up the stairs, but that smile instantly disappeared the moment she spotted him, and she quickly turned to leave.

"No! Wait! Sarah, wait! Please! All I want to do is talk. Please."

She didn't want to, but she knew there was no point in

running; she wouldn't get far with Tina in her arms and she couldn't risk her getting hurt. Therefore, slowly and reluctantly, she turned to face him.

"What do you want, Steve?"

"What do you think I want, Sarah?" he said with a sheepish smile. "I want you back. I want us to be a family," he said, nodding to the baby in her arms.

Sarah instinctively pulled her daughter closer.

"Not going to happen," she said quickly and defensively.

"Come on, Sarah," he said, softly. "Won't you even let me meet little Tina?"

"How do you know her name? How did you find us?"

"How I found you isn't important, Sarah. What is important is that we've been reunited and we can be a family again. Don't get me wrong, babe; I know I've been a crap husband to you and I've treated you really shitty, but I've changed, I promise, I've changed."

"You'll never change, Steve. You don't know how."

"I want us to be together, Sarah."

"Why? So you can use us both as punching bags?" she said viciously.

He looked visibly hurt. She'd seen that look before. It was that same look he had when she'd first met him and he'd talk to her about his own childhood and his abusive father, only this time Sarah didn't feel an ache for him, as she had then, but instead she ached for her daughter and what her life might be like in a home with this man, whom she now feared almost as much as she had loved.

On the other hand, she had the presence of mind to conclude that this encounter outside of her apartment would never end the way she wanted; Steve leaving them be, to live life in the bliss that she and her baby had become accustomed to, and never darken their door again.

So, she allowed him to recite his usual routine—the apologies, the supplications, and the promises—whilst she contemplated her options.

She thought about running to the storekeeper, an elderly Asian man who had always been kind to her, as if he had known her plight from the moment he had shown her around her little palace, but he was no match for Steve.

Then she thought about the police. Even if, by some miracle, she managed to contact them somehow, they wouldn't be able to do anything for her. She had been down this road before: unless there was some physical evidence and she pressed charges, they couldn't do much.

For a fleeting moment she even contemplated trying to rile him to solicit the rage that, for all of his contriteness, she knew was still there. But how would that help? And what about Tina? He would then have good cause to keep her with him as her biological father.

She quickly dismissed that idea.

And what about reprisal?

Steve knew where her mum, her sister, her whole family lived. There was no telling what he might do to them.

No; there was only one way this meeting was going to end and it filled her with abject sorrow, not for her but for her baby girl.

So she resigned herself to everything, but one thing: if he ever so much as laid a hand on her baby, for as long as there was life in her, she'd kill him, she swore to God she would kill him.

Three months later.

"Is she asleep?" It was Melanie asking the question as Sarah returned to the room and retook her seat at the kitchen table.

"My sister, the mum," Melanie said with a smile. "You know, I can still remember when we were kids and I had to take care of you."

"It wasn't that long ago, Mel," Sarah said.

"It seems so long ago. With Mum getting worse by the day, I had to keep you with me at all times. You were my first little baby—and now look at you, married with your own kid."

"Thanks for reminding me," Sarah said, glumly.

"What did this social worker say?"

"The usual crap: there really isn't much they can do to help."

"What, even if you fear for your life and that of your daughter?"

"They said it's a matter for the police, and even then, they need evidence. Funnily enough, even that's going to be hard to get right now."

"So, what are you going to do?"

"I guess I'm just going to have to keep taking her up there myself."

"What? All the way to the Isle of Wight with a little baby?"

"What other choice do I have, Mel? Unless you want to go for me."

"No, I do not," Melanie said emphatically. "It's nothing to do with me. It's nothing to do with you either."

"Of course it's to do with me—he's her dad."

"It isn't your fault he got himself nicked! If he can't see his daughter for eighteen months, that's his problem. I don't see why you should traipse halfway across the world just so he can see her."

"The Isle of Wight is hardly halfway across the world, besides," she hesitated, "I promised I would take her to see him."

Melanie's eyes narrowed and she exploded, "Are you completely off your trolley? Why the hell would you tell him that?"

"Wake up, Mel! The bloody man has gone down for attempted murder. If I don't take Tina to see him, he's perfectly capable of paying us both a visit when he gets out and succeeding where he failed last time."

Steve was arrested just a few weeks after he showed up on Sarah's doorstep for an incident that had taken place only a few days before. He had been involved in the attempted murder of a small-time drug dealer from London's East End. Whilst it could not be proven in court that Steve was the one who wiped the blade across the drug dealer's throat, there was evidence placing him at the scene and thus he was convicted as an accessory to the crime.

The man survived, much to Sarah's disappointment.

A harsh thought perhaps, but his continued existence as one of the scumbags of the East End meant that Steve would not be incarcerated for as long as she would have liked. At least not long enough for Tina to grow older, and for her to have saved enough money to disappear somewhere he would never find them.

She was trapped.

At least that's how she felt.

In the meantime, the safest thing to do was to make the four-hour or so train, boat and bus journey each way to keep him happy and just hope that she could make enough money to take her and Tina away somewhere safe before he got out.

"Sarah," Mel continued, "listen; if you have to go, why don't you at least leave Tina with me?"

"And what's he going to say when I show up without his daughter?"

"Surely he won't mind you not taking her just the once."

"Have you not been paying attention, Mel? What does this man have to do before you wake up to what he's like?"

"Just tell him she's coming down with something, Sarah. What the hell is he going to do from in there? Worse case, you can always take her next time."

Sarah thought about this.

"You know it makes sense. That trip is bloody hard enough without having to lug a pram and all that other stuff with you."

She was right.

And as much as Sarah knew it would probably cause more hassle, the journey was rough and she hated putting Tina through that.

"Are you sure you'll be all right with all of them?" she asked.

"Of course," Melanie said, as if it was something she did every day.

Sarah forced a weary smile. "Thanks, Mel. I appreciate it."

"Why don't you give Zoe a bell? Ask her to come with you?"

"I can't. You need a permit to visit and she has to work. No, this is something I have to do alone," Sarah said as her heart sank at the thought of seeing the man who, for all intents and purposes, was still her husband.

47 THE SCREWS

It had been a long and hot journey to Her Majesty's Prison on the Isle of Wight, and Sarah was grateful that her sister had convinced her not to take Tina on what turned out to be a five-hour journey, one way, with delays.

She already felt exhausted and she hadn't even embarked on the emotional power drain that was Steve. That was about to take place and she was looking forward to it as one looks forward to a stomach ulcer.

It was now, as she sat across from him at the rectangular grey metal table, that she wished she hadn't bothered, for the visiting room was as cold as it was stark.

"Sarah?"

She looked at her husband and wondered what she ever saw in him; the handsome face hadn't changed much since the first day they met yet he may as well be wearing a mask for the effect it now had on her.

"Sarah!" He clicked his fingers as if to wake her from a trance. "I said, as good as it is to see you, I was hoping you'd have brought our little girl too."

"Yes, I heard," she said, finally tuning into the conversation. "But I couldn't. She was running a bit of a temperature last night so I couldn't risk her making the journey."

"Right," he said knowingly, nodding his head. "Did you get her looked at by the doctor?"

"Of course I did," she said, somewhat affronted that he should even suggest it. He'd hardly shown an interest in her on the outside, but now that he was in here, he was playing the role of concerned father.

Realising that she may have sounded a tad more caustic than she had intended, she added, "He said it was a reaction to her changing her milk."

"I didn't know you'd changed her milk."

"Well, she is growing."

"Are you sure?" he asked, scrutinising her.

"What do you mean?"

"Well, are you sure that her temperature is the reason you haven't brought her to see me?"

"Of course it is. Why wouldn't I want her to see you?"

He shrugged, looking around the room, taking in the other nine or so tables behind which were his fellow inmates and their respective families. He then glanced at the two nearby uniformed officers who were taking in the activity of the room, ensuring that no unnecessary contact between residents and visitors took place.

He focussed on Sarah once more and forced a smile. "You know, I had a dream last night."

Sarah didn't acknowledge him.

So he prompted her, "Do you want me to tell you what it was about?"

"If you want to," she replied with all of the interest she could muster.

"Right, well, let's see if I can remember… oh, yeah. Well, you were in it, of course—you see, I often dream about you, babe, especially in here, you know, ain't much to do but daydream about past times, you know, when we used to do it. Do you remember that time when you wanted me to give it to you in the toilet at that party? Good times, hey?"

She suppressed what would have been an obvious shudder of revulsion…

"Anyway, this dream… it wasn't just about you, it was about Tina. Actually, come to think of it, it was about us, as a family. It started with me being stuck in here. You know, day after day, with nothing else to think about but you and my little girl. So, the dream started off okay because you'd come and visit me on a regular basis and you'd bring the little one with you, but then, for no reason, you just stopped bringing her. I was heartbroken. Yeah, it was one of those typical dreams, the ones that start out great, but end up turning into a nightmare.

Anyway, I can't remember what happened next; I just know that I got out of here, came home and I found out that the reason you two weren't visiting anymore was because you decided to up and leave me without so much as a forwarding address, nothing. Well, you can imagine, I was frantic. My family had suddenly disappeared and was nowhere to be found. The good thing was that, unlike one of those nightmares—you know the type, the ones where it's like you're running in mud—I was

429

able to run really fast, a bit like superman, so fast in fact that I managed to catch you up, and I was so mad. No, I wasn't mad; I was beyond mad, so mad in fact that I can't even remember what happened next. All I can remember is you crying—no, not crying, *begging* me not to do something. I didn't even know what the hell you were even talking about until I felt the shotgun in my hand… And do you know what? I have no clue what the fuck happened next. Funny that."

He shook his head and smiled an incredulous smile, one that to any other person in that room would have looked like the smile of a husband overjoyed at the sight of his wife, but to Sarah meant something altogether different; it was that death glare that sent chills skittering down her spine.

"You know, I even told Paul about it," he continued. "I said, 'Paul, I had the strangest dream last night. I dreamt that my wife ran away and took my kid with her, you know, just like yours did.' And he told me that I needed to watch you because, before I knew it, you'd be gone.

I said, 'Fuck off, Paul. My wife's nothing like yours. She's a loyal type of bird, you know, the kind that stands by her man right until the end. She'd never dream of not bringing my kid to see me because she knows that, if she did that, when I got out of here, if it's the last thing I did, I'd track her down and…'"

He left the sentence unfinished for dramatic effect, and it worked.

Sarah was shaking.

"What's the matter babe—you cold?"

She took a few seconds and then stuttered, "I'm fine."

"How's your mum, doin'?"

"She's fine."

"What about your sister?"

"She's fine too."

Steve nodded. "Good, good. Glad to hear that the family is still nice and healthy and that nothing awful has happened to them. You never know these days. One day everything is tickety-boo and the next…What about Martin? Is he fine too?"

Sarah gawped at him and then past him at the officer on the opposite side of the room.

"What are you looking at?"

"Nothing. I'm looking at you."

"No you fucking weren't. You were looking at that screw, weren't ya? You were looking between his legs, weren't ya? Hoping to cop a feel, weren't ya?"

She squinted at him incredulously, and spat with disgust, "You're mental, you are."

"Don't fucking lie to me," he hissed.

Sarah stood up. She'd had enough.

"Sit down," he said.

"I'm going to miss my train."

"I said sit the fuck down or I'll jump across this desk and rip your fucking head off and I promise none of these screws will be able to help ya," he hissed, lowering his eyes and keeping a smile on his face so as to not draw the attention of the so-called 'screws' who were keenly watching Sarah's sudden movement.

Slowly but surely, Sarah sat back down.

48 LAMB OR LION?

"My God, he's going to have a go at me in here and nobody's going to stop him!"

Sarah was under no illusion that, if it came to it, Steve would have leapt across that table and broken her neck before those 'screws' had even noticed what had happened, and she couldn't risk it. She wouldn't have cared before, but now, now that she had Tina, everything was different; everything she did was for the sake of her daughter, and if that meant dealing with that 'nutcase', then so be it.

As far as she was concerned, no matter what, her baby girl came first.

Besides, she was more than confident that if she didn't comply with Steve's demands, he would find a way, whether in jail or out, of making sure his so-called dream came true. And she just couldn't run the risk, again—not for her, but for her family, including her sister, with whom she'd often clash about her constant capitulation, but then, as far as Sarah was concerned, Melanie couldn't possibly understand what she was going through; she'd found her knight. Sarah, on the other hand, had found her nightmare.

And so eighteen months went by.

Steve kept his proverbial nose clean—just how he did it was lost on Sarah, but he did—and so he was released. But things had changed: Sarah had worked the best part of the year through most of the night and had managed to scrape together enough money to move her and Tina to another small flat on the other side of London.

Well, it wasn't exactly a flat but more of a room with a pull-out bed that she shared with Tina, and that suited her just fine. It would mean they'd always be together.

Of course, both her mother and Melanie had told her to just move back home, but there was no chance she was going to do that and risk Steve going round there and exposing them to God knows what else.

And, when Melanie had broached the subject of care for their mother, Sarah had quickly shut her down, telling her that it would do her sister good to spend time with their mother, since she had given up a good part of her teenage years to do so.

Melanie couldn't argue with that, although she knew the subject would have to be revisited since, in her opinion, she wouldn't be able to cope with all of it, and Sarah had offered to help once more, just not before she'd got herself settled into her new place.

Sarah was very sad to have to move away from her little palace but it didn't feel the same anymore, not since Steve had pushed his way in there, albeit for a short while, as he had somehow imprinted himself not only on her memory but also on the place, and it chilled her to remember him sitting on the couch, sleeping in her bed, watching her from the doorway.

She especially hated saying goodbye to Mr Patel and the shop but that's just how it was. That was her life.

She didn't give Steve her new address, but then she didn't need to. He always found a way of tracking them down, and, of course, as soon as he'd come round, it was the usual drama, the usual threats that she was trying to run away from him, trying to take away his little girl.

Sarah always laughed inside when he talked like that. He didn't know anything about that little girl; he didn't know that she hated peas, or that she loved to have her belly tickled, or that her favourite place to nap would be on the bed, on top of her mother's rising and falling bosom. He just liked the idea of being a father—but he wouldn't have a clue how to actually be a man and behave like one, to be a provider like most decent fathers. He just wanted to possess Tina, like Sarah before her.

One small mercy is that Steve didn't muscle his way into their new home, but instead he'd show up unannounced at least once a week, and if Sarah wasn't in, he'd go absolutely berserk.

"Where have you been? Who were you with?" To the point where she would actually stop herself from going out unless absolutely necessary.

It was like being under house arrest again.

And when he wasn't there, he'd telephone and if Sarah didn't answer after the first two rings he'd start accusing her of being busy performing lurid acts on men.

"Where were you? Were you busy giving Martin a blow job? Where were you? Having sex with your neighbours? I bet you girls enjoy a good old tongue fest when you aren't picking up blokes off the street."

Everything came back to some sexual perversion. To the point where he'd consistently accuse her of some of the most 'elaborate and sick fantasies' that Sarah wouldn't even have imagined, let alone performed!

One day, he insisted on accompanying her to the doctor's for one of Tina's routine check-ups, and everything was going okay—Sarah actually thought for one split second that they looked like a normal family.

That was until they were just outside the surgery doors and, out of nowhere, he slapped her across the face and accused her of looking at the crotch of one of the men who was exiting the building.

That's why, when with him, she'd often walk with her head down, avoiding eye contact with anybody, for fear that it might trigger a reaction in him.

433

Sometimes he'd telephone in the dead of night for no particular reason other than to 'check' on her.

He'd breathe down the phone and say, "You know who this is, don't ya?"

I know who this is all right.

Sarah would even encourage her family and friends to get off the phone as quickly as possible—not that she'd tell them exactly why, she'd make excuses because she knew that if he tried to get through and the phone was engaged, he'd explode into a rage and start accusing her of talking to her 'new fella'.

Things became so desperate that she thought about going to the police and getting a restraining order. But that brought with it the complication that he was actually Tina's biological father and that he had rights, which would mean a whole rigmarole over visitation—and that would without a doubt result in him throwing a fit and threatening either her, Tina or her family, because there's no way he would let her get away with something like that.

The guy had threatened to smash her face in when he was *in jail*; there'd be nothing to stop him now. By the time the police intervened it'd be too late—and then what would happen to Tina? As her biological father, she'd end up with him, and there's no way she was going to let that happen.

No way. She'd die first.

So she'd fantasise about disappearing one night, but to do that she needed a good deal of money and she was barely managing as it was. Steve wasn't giving her any money. Not that he seemed to be short of cash these days; he'd obviously gone back to his usual tricks as she doubted he'd found himself a decent job. Regardless, she didn't want to rely on him for anything because she believed that would just make everything worse. Besides, she and Tina were a team; they always had been and she didn't need or want his help or his money.

So the weeks went by. Tina turned three.

That's when the comments started about how she dressed Tina, especially if she put her in a skirt, regardless of the fact that she was wearing tights, "Trying to bring her up like a slag, are ya? Trying to bring her up like you?"

She's three years old. How can you say that about your own daughter?

At least that's what Sarah would think. She daren't say anything. Instead, she'd often consult him on what type of clothes to dress her baby in. Anything to avoid the comments. Anything to avoid his outbursts. Anything to keep the peace, and anything to stop him going anywhere near her little girl.

Not that he cared about that. He'd rarely pick her up, play with her, or even speak to her. He wanted to have a say but had no idea how to be a father to his own flesh and blood. And it was this, not the insults, the degradation, the spying, the controlling, or any other hideous thing he could do to her, that made her feel rotten inside.

Her baby girl was missing out on the love of a father, and it made her feel so desperately sad, and so desperately guilty that she had chosen this for her daughter. She had chosen this monster.

Of course, Sarah's logic was flawed, but it was a logic that, at the time, was not challenged by anyone, since she shared her thoughts with no one. She was all too aware that getting anybody else involved could put them in danger, and/or that someone may question how she was dealing with the situation. She could only deal with it the best way she knew how, and that was to give in to his demands, to give in to the fear and the intimidation because the alternative was just too unbearable. And she was tired; she was so very weary of trying to outfox, outthink this man. There was nothing she or anybody else could do; she would just have to surrender to him.

And that's exactly what she did, until one night.

It was nearly ten in the evening. Sarah had just had a shower and was in her dressing gown. Tina was in bed next to her and so, as was often the case, she took advantage of the quiet time to open up the ironing board in front of the TV and get some ironing done.

It was only a small portable TV but she loved it as it was a gift from Mr Patel. He had given it to her the day she left her palace. When she'd asked him what he would do without it during the quiet times in the shop, he had told her that she was doing him a favour as he'd spend less time watching soaps and more time stacking shelves.

She was thinking about this when a hammering on the front door startled her.

She instinctively glanced across at Tina who was still sleeping soundly.

"Who is it?" she asked in a loud whisper.

"It's Steve. Open up."

Her heart sank and she reluctantly put the iron down in its cradle. It hissed angrily at her as if irked by the interruption in their quality time together.

She unlocked the door.

"Steve, what are you doing here?"

"I've come to see my kid," he said, barging past her and into the room.

"It's ten o'clock at night, Steve," she said as calmly as she could for she could smell that he'd been drinking. It was a familiar smell, one that made her skin crawl.

"So what? You telling me when I can and cannot see my kid now?"

"No; it's just it's late to be visiting her. As you can see, she's asleep," she said, glancing over at her sleeping child.

"Nobody's telling me when and where I can see my fucking kid, Sarah."

"I didn't say that…"

"Then what are you saying?" he asked, looking her up and down, examining the tie that held her gown closed.

She instinctively pulled her gown closer to her and tightened the tie.

He noticed the action and walked up to her, causing her to step back, but she was stopped by the open door.

"What's up? You feeling a bit frisky?" he asked, pushing up against her.

"Stop it, Steve."

He started fondling her.

"Stop it!" she slapped him away and, after a short struggle, managed to extricate herself from him and move back into the room that suddenly felt even smaller.

"What's the matter? Already had a visitor tonight?" he asked.

"You're drunk, Steve," she said, glancing back at her baby girl who was still sound asleep.

"Hell, yeah, I'm fucking drunk. You would be too if you knew you had to come home and stick it in a bird like you."

Sarah gulped down the revulsion.

He shuffled his way forward, causing Sarah to back up against the ironing board.

"Come on, babe. It's been a while so I promise I'll make it quick," he said rubbing his crotch and then unzipping himself.

He pushed up against her and pinned her against the ironing board. She had nowhere else to go; one sudden move and she, the board and the hot iron would fall, crashing to the floor—or worse, onto the bed.

"Steve, please. Stop it. Stop!"

"You know you want it. Stop pretending," he said very loudly.

"Steve, please, keep your voice down; you'll wake her."

"I don't give a fuck if I wake her!" he said even louder, "she needs to be awake anyway, she needs to see her dad."

He moved towards the bed.

"NO!" Sarah snapped loudly. "Don't you go near her!"

She was breathing heavily now as the adrenaline started pumping around her system.

He examined her closely and Sarah was expecting him to launch into a tirade about her attempt to stop him seeing his so-called 'kid' but instead he said, with a big smile, "Told you you were gagging for it."

He then proceeded to rub himself up and down her, pushing her further back into the ironing board, causing it to tip slightly backward.

Then his hand started probing the inside of her gown and he started making appreciative sounds. As his fingers touched the flesh of her belly, he gasped, expelling a cloud of alcohol breath over here.

She flinched.

"Stop it, Steve! Stop!"

"Yeah, that's it," he said appreciatively, "fight me, babe, fight me," he said, pushing her further backward and threatening to topple them, board and all.

She tried to wrestle him back but he was too strong for her.

"Stop it! STOP!" She grimaced through the exertion.

"Yeah, fight me, babe, fight me," he continued as his fingers slid down her belly, her navel and were making their way further down.

"NO!"

And that's when it whispered to her, offering a helping hand, and she accepted.

She grabbed the hissing iron and shoving it into her husband's face causing him to scream and leap back in agony.

"AAAAAAAAHHHH!"

It took him a few stupefied seconds to process what had just happened, "YOU BITCH! YOU. FUCKING. BITCH!" he hissed through the agonising burns of his nose and lips.

Sarah brandished the iron in front of her as a weapon in case he came back for more, and he did, "I'm. Goin….. To…. Kill. You!" he said through rasps of spit and excruciating pain, for Sarah had left the iron on his face long enough to melt the flesh from it in places.

He lunged at her, and that's when she instinctively pushed the iron out in front of her, repelling him back, then swung it up and under his chin, branding him once more. The searing pain and the motion of the impact sent him sprawling backwards so fast he smacked his head on the nearby wall and slid to the floor in a daze.

"Mummy," Tina murmured.

"Go back to sleep, darling, go back to sleep, now," she said quickly. "Mummy's TV was just a bit loud, that's all," she said, glancing back at the little girl who was rubbing her eyes. "Go back to sleep."

The benefits of living in one room: the girl was used to sounds and was able to sleep through anything.

Sure enough, Tina rolled over and went back to sleep.

Meanwhile, Sarah snatched a weapon from the kitchenette just as Steve starting growling, "Saaaaarah! You bitch! Saraaaaah! I'm going to kill…"

…But his words were cut short when he felt cold metal against his neck. He knew what it was for he was very familiar with this implement.

Sarah held the serrated blade of the roast knife against his throat and seethed through gritted teeth, "If you don't shut the fuck up I swear to God, I'll cut you; I'll cut you here and now and I'll chop your stinking body into little pieces," she spat, and pressed the teeth of the blade into his skin to show him that she meant it.

She didn't know what had possessed her. It was as if she'd been taken over by some demon. An angry, malevolent creature that resided deep inside and compelled her to take action.

To this day, she still doesn't know where the courage came from—and at the time she didn't particularly care because it felt so bloody good.

"You've made my life a misery for way too long, you sick bastard," she hissed. "But not anymore. I'm gonna' gut you, Steve. I'm gonna' gut you here and now like the pig you are. You hear me? I'm gonna' gut you!" she snarled with such venom it was Steve who actually started to tremble.

Sarah didn't know if that was from fear or the shock of the burns that had already bubbled and now disfigured that once beautiful face of his.

"Sarah, p... pl... ease..."

"Oh, it's *please* now?" she asked. "Not, do me, fetch me? Not, do me now, Sarah, do me? Don't you want me to do you, Steve?" she said, "Don't you want me to touch? Touch you there?" She asked, sliding the blade down between his legs. "Don't you want me to unzip you? Don't you fancy it anymore, Steve?"

"Sarah, please...." he said through chattering teeth. "Sarah..." he started to whine. "Sarah, for God's sake, I'm the father of your child..."

"Shut up!" she said abruptly, pushing the blade into her husband's genitals. "Don't ever say that to me ever again! You wouldn't have the first clue about what it means to be a father. As far as I'm concerned, you were just a sperm donor; you're not fit to be a father to my baby. In fact, you're not fit to be a father to *any* child. In fact, I think I need to do the world a favour and burst those bubbles you call balls, to make sure you don't father any other child, ever again."

The menace in his wife's voice was unmistakable.

"Sarah, please... please..."

"Please... please..." she mimicked. "Now it's *please*. Whatever happened to *do it, fetch it*, and *fetch it now*?" she mocked.

He just whined, eyes bulging with terror and streaming with salty tears that accentuated the searing pain of his face, as he felt the head of the blade pressing hard against his testicles, threatening to pierce his right one any second.

"You were going to hurt my baby, weren't you?" she asked.

"What?"

"You were going to hurt my baby girl, weren't you?"

"No..."

Smack!

She slapped her husband across the face with all the strength she could muster, "Don't lie to me! Don't lie to me!" She growled in a blind rage.

" I wasn't lying... please... Sa..."

Smack!

"Don't say my name. Don't you ever say my name, ever again..."

"I won't... I won't," he whined. "Please stop hurting me, stop hurting me..."

"Oh, you want me to stop hurting you?"

"P...p... please..."

"You want me to stop hurting you? Okay... I'll stop hurting you—but only if you stop following us. Only if you stop making our lives a misery."

"I w... il.... I will..."

"You'd better, Steve. Because if you ever, ever... so much as come near, so much as think about us, I swear to God, I'll hack these little things off so fast not even the doctors will be able to tell which sex you are—you hear me? You hear me?"

"Y... yes..."

"I can't hear you, Steve!"

"Yes!"

And that's the last time Sarah was ever that up close and personal with Steve. In fact, that's the last time she saw him.

She grabbed her baby girl, what little money she had, and fled from that house that night. Only this time she didn't go to her sister's, her mum's, her friend's or anywhere in London for that matter. She used the cash to buy herself and her little girl a bus ticket out of the city and north, to an undisclosed location miles away from her husband and her old life.

That was twenty years ago.

Sarah eventually divorced Steve and has since remarried.

Although adapting to married life with a new man wasn't easy for a woman who had forgotten what it was like to be loved rather than owned, freed to pursue life beyond her husband, rather than incarcerated, and caressed rather than manhandled.

In fact, it took nearly a year for Sarah to be intimate with her husband who, much to her astonishment, waited that whole time until she was ready to give herself to him. In fact, it was this very act that made her realise that he was the man for her.

Tina, on the other hand, has grown into a beautiful woman, and got engaged to her first love shortly before her twentieth birthday.

She remembers little of her biological father, nor is she interested in forging any new memories. She tried that as soon as she became an adult, shortly after Sarah sat her down and explained everything, since she believed that her daughter should have the knowledge to make her own decisions when it came to getting to know her 'old man'.

However, it didn't take long for the teenager to learn of her father's true colours, for he did nothing but speak ill of her mother, and nobody wants to be around that.

Besides, as far as she was concerned, Terry, her stepdad, was the best father any girl could wish for, and she needed no one else.

In fact, it was Terry who gave Tina away to the love of her life only a few years ago. A day on which Sarah broke down and wept tears of joy, because to her it wasn't just her baby girl who had grown up and was getting married, but her best friend, who had seen her through some of the worst times of her life, and that, most importantly, together, they had survived.

49 STRETCHING

It finally became clear to me that I couldn't spend the rest of my time in America in my sister's home being antisocial.

How on earth was I going to meet the next love of my life ensconced in that place?

I wasn't.

I'd forgotten my own mantra: opportunities (or potential partners) rarely come knocking on your door outside of a Hollywood movie.

If I wanted things to change, if I wanted things to get better, and to emerge from the misery that haunted me from the moment I opened my eyes to the second I fell asleep at night, then I needed to put myself out there.

I needed to stretch.

Some of the best experts in the corporate industry will tell you that when times are lean, instead of cutting funds in advertising, you should actually increase them. Not just for the obvious reason of promoting goods and services, but also to ensure that your corporate profile remains elevated among your competitors.

Sound advice indeed.

The same rule applies to your personal life.

If there are slim pickings in romance or you are feeling particularly depressed about how you look, then, rather than moan about the lack of attention, do something about it.

If those pounds are looking much heavier than they actually are, then start a fitness plan.—and no, I don't mean stay at home, put yourself on a diet so that you can't even stuff yourself happy, and pretend to follow along with some seemingly gleeful celebrity prancing around in a leotard—I mean start eating healthily and join a club, especially a fitness club (as this will have the double whammy of making you feel like you are doing something for yourself).

Get a hobby, if you don't already have one, join a singles group. Just get out a bit more, and do not pass on that party you have been invited to just because you don't feel like facing people.

(I think I did a pretty good job at demonstrating how *not* to do it.)

I met one of my good friends in the gym. We've now known each other nearly ten years or more (I'm sure he'll correct me when he reads this if I'm wrong).

He's a bodybuilder and was working as a fitness instructor at the time. He was/is cute and seemed particularly taken with me.

Without even looking, I'd made a new long-term friend. However, had I not made an effort to get out of the house, we would never have met.

I think you get my point.

I had no expectations of our weekend in Wichita.

So you can imagine my reaction when we pulled up outside this typical Americana home set back off an avenue of trees with steps up to the front door of a typical redwood-clad home with a wraparound porch and obligatory star-spangled banner waving in the breeze at our arrival.

Inside, the house wasn't anything out of the ordinary. I remember thinking that it actually looked somewhat cluttered but in a typical American kind of way (if it can be classed as *typical*—perhaps more *stereotypical*?)

I'll let you decide on that.

The house felt lived in and welcoming, but what was most welcoming was the view that could be reached through the kitchen and beyond the back door that opened onto a sprawling lawn guarded by a collection of giant trees.

And what should be at the foot of what must have been a half-acre lawn? Why, a crystal-clear lake of course, one that could easily have been mistaken for a sheet of glass, given the stillness of its surface and the way in which it reflected both the verdant forest that surrounded it and the pale blue sky above.

I was speechless.

If I said that we were made to feel welcome, that would be an understatement. There really wasn't much more our hosts could have done for us. We had a cookout, chatted about all matter of subjects, including Timothy's recent eye surgery, his ex-wife's role as a nurse, and his overall convalescence.

(Recognise them now?)

We even cracked open a beer—not something I had been particularly partial to (we both know what happened when I last tried that).

However, when in Rome (or Wichita).

After an early dinner of traditional American cookout of steak with all the trimmings, it was fishing time!

I told Timothy that I hadn't been fishing before, so he of course insisted that we take the rowing boat out onto the lake and that he teach me the craft.

Needless to say, newfound me was up for anything, including a bottle of Bud Light and casting lessons from the old pro.

That has got to be one of the most majestic experiences of my entire life. The air was warm, the atmosphere was tranquil, and the trickling of water against the boat mesmerising.

Tim was fantastic company and a patient host.

I caught my first fish that evening and you would have thought that I'd saved the world such was my excitement and pride.

But then, I don't think my feelings were exclusively about my catch but more an amalgamation of many things, including the fact that, yet again, I'd spent most of that day listening to the stories and the challenges in the lives of others and taking a break from my own.

I remember feeling absolutely exhausted that night, and really looking forward to my bed, whilst bracing myself for my usual dead-of-night encounter with the demons who enjoyed nothing more than to wake me from my slumber to claw, choke and gag me with their rotten breath.

And I expected it to be worse that night because I had had a good time and they appeared to enjoy nothing more than to remind me that fun was not permissible when I was supposed to be grieving for the love I lost, especially the love I knew was somewhere in that nation right in that moment, just like me.

Was he asleep? Was he alone? Was he with her?

I wondered about this before I faded into blissful slumber.

50 COMING UP FOR AIR

The next thing I remember was the sound of birds anxiously tweeting outside my window.

It took a while for the sound to register and for me to roll over on what felt like a giant bale of wool. When I eventually managed to prize my eyes apart I noticed, much to my surprise, that the room was full of sunshine and that it was actually daylight outside and not the usual midnight dreary.

I couldn't believe it.

Had I really overslept for the very first time since arriving in America, in a stranger's home?

The house's silence told me that this may well be the case, as did the fact that when I peeked through the kitchen window, Rosa and both my hosts were sitting on the jetty by the lake with what looked like the remains of breakfast in front of them!

I rushed to the bathroom, splashed water on my face and then calmly and as alert as I could possibly make myself appear, made my way through the screen door and joined them.

"Good morning," they all said almost in unison and with a knowing look on their faces that I was the sleepyhead who had been so sparked out I actually missed the whole of breakfast.

"I don't know what happened to me," I said apologetically.

"Well, you were obviously exhausted from your journey, honey," Aubrey offered.

"Obviously."

"Take a seat," Timothy said. "Would you like some coffee?"

"Thank you."

It was a glorious morning and it felt so damn good to be out in the fresh air by that lake, and at one with nature. (I know that sounds like a line, but it's true. That is precisely how I felt.)

Timothy poured the last dregs of coffee for me and promptly said, "I'll go make a fresh pot."

"Would you like some breakfast, honey?" Aubrey offered.

"Oh that's very kind. Thank you," I said.

"Is there anything in particular you'd like me to fix for you? Or are you happy to try a traditional Americana?"

Not sure I knew exactly what an Americana was but, again, when in Wichita.

445

"More than happy to try the Americana," I said.

"One Americana coming up," Aubrey said, flashing a smile and disappearing inside with Timothy.

Rosa turned to me and asked, "Did you sleep okay, babe?"

"Like a log," I said. "It's weird; for the first time since coming here, I slept through the whole night."

"Good," Rosa said. "You obviously needed it."

She stood up, put her hand on my shoulder and announced that she was visiting the bathroom, then, with a peck on my cheek, she was gone, and I was alone.

And that's when they came, suddenly and unexpectedly.

I thought so. I've been expecting you.

Like they knew I was taking a break from feeling crappy about myself, about life. They emerged from the very beauty that surrounded me as if they had camouflaged themselves with it, waiting for the perfect opportunity to spring forth and choke the life from any delusions I may have of normality.

The demons dimmed the sunshine and sucked the appetite from my belly.

And I thought of him.

I wondered, was he awake now? Was he awake and in bed with her whilst I was here on some pointless quest to outrun what I had become, the empty thing that had been cursed to wander the baron sand dunes of self-pity, loneliness, unfulfillment and unaccomplishment?

What was I now if not some dried-up husk of my former self? No longer the lover, the writer, the achiever.

Where do I go from here? Am I always going to feel like this?

Suddenly, everything felt so hopeless again.

It just felt like an emotional game of snakes and ladders; each time I thought I was making progress, I'd just slide right back again.

Hopeless.

And frustrating!

I felt so angry at myself; I'd awoken with such a sense of serenity and, within minutes, I allowed myself, once more, to descend into abject misery.

The truth was, I was actually clinically depressed, but I didn't understand the signs back then.

I just felt that I couldn't be in England, because it felt as if I no longer fitted in there. I couldn't stay in America, because I was a stranger there.

It felt as if I belonged nowhere—and that's because, wherever I was, I'd be forced to embrace the very thing I didn't ask for, did not want and wholeheartedly rejected: change.

Without him and without writing, I was nothing.

That's when the one tear (yes, it was that momentous) slid down my face, and it was as I wiped my cheek with the back of my hand that I noticed them: small circles on the surface of the lake.

They were everywhere.

At first I thought they were being caused by miniature bugs landing on the surface of the water but, upon closer inspection, I realised that the ripples were actually originating from under the surface of the water, often pre-empted by tiny explosions of bubbles.

It was the fish!

They were coming up for air.

And that's when I knew.

As you've read, ever since I was a teenager, there's only ever been one subject with which I have consistently been fascinated, and that's the psychology of us and our interactions with each other.

In that moment, more than ever, it made perfect sense that what I should be writing about at that particular time in my life wasn't fictional action adventure, but everything that I had learned over the years: the true story of all of us. Why, as humans, we can be so loving yet hurtful to each other.

And that's when another tear tickled down my cheek, then another and then another.

"Are you all right, honey?"

It was Aubrey, returning with a tray laden with food.

"I'm fine," I said with a smile and a quick rub of my eyes with the back of my hand.

"Are you sure?" she asked.

"I'm sure. Thank you so much for asking," I said with a broad smile and a newfound sense of purpose.

I'd found a new writing project, one for which I already had a title: Coming Up for Air.

51 4TH JULY

The premise of this book will be clear to you by now (at least I hope so), yet whilst the general theme is clear, in that it talks about relationships, there's a much more important subtext, actually, in its title, and I don't think there's any better or more succinct way of underlining this for you than to use one of today's common vernaculars; 'shit happens'.

One day you think you have it all squared away—job, house, home, family, relationship (not necessarily in that order), and then something comes along and, at best, disrupts it; at worst, takes it away.

It happens to all of us one way or another.

That's life.

And with life, it's often a case of not *if* but *when*—and it's how you deal with the so-called *when* that truly matters, since it will either expedite the learning and healing process and ship you on to the rest of your life adventure, or keep you sitting in a warehouse of perpetual grief.

You've seen how I dealt with what happened to me and, in truth, it probably wasn't the prettiest thing.

Today, after years of study and after speaking to hundreds of other people, I know I would have dealt with things completely differently, but then… I guess that's the power of hindsight, right?

I'm hoping this book, if anything, will give you a flavour of that but, most importantly, that it gives you some perspective by showing you the things that others have been subjected to either by their own hand or by that of others, and how each and every one of them coped with their own particular life challenges.

As I keep saying, each set of circumstances is unique, but one thing that is true, and I believe crucial, to a healthy recovery is to take a break from mourning or (in other words) feeling sorry for yourself; take a break from wallowing in that deep cesspool of self-pity, from the anguish, from that sense of hopelessness, and occasionally, albeit reluctantly, keep coming up for air.

Take a breather.

There's still a whole world out there, a whole life to live, someone else to love and someone else who will love you.

Yes, you were wronged and hurt by circumstance and the life you knew may have withered and died, but you did not. You are still here.

Live and love your life because, remember, these seconds are not coming back.

How would you rather spend them?

And if your instinct is to yell, "I don't care!" perhaps even delivered with a somewhat petulant tone, take no notice of yourself, that's your depression talking.

Now, pull yourself together whilst I share a very quick story with you.

I was lucky enough—I say *lucky,* but I use that term loosely—being an Englishman, to be in Oklahoma for Independence Day on the 4th July.

Rosa was always eager for me to have the whole Americana experience; we attended a baseball game by day and went downtown Oklahoma that night to see all of the star-spangled festivities.

It was a beautiful summer evening.

Buildings were draped in flags and studded with lights. There were hotdog stands on almost every corner, stalls lining the streets, flag-waving, symbolism, pageantry and a parade preceded by a redcoat marching band (somewhat ironic) that looked and played brilliantly.

The evening was awesome (in the real sense of the word)! It was pretty much everything you'd expect from one of the country's most important holidays.

My sister, her close friend, some of her friends from *The Singles,* and I were there, deeply immersed in all of the activities.

I remember being overwhelmed by the fantastic jubilance and friendliness of the crowd (as I kept discovering each time

I agreed to 'stretch' and leave the confines of my sister's home
to go out and socialise).

I'd been to numerous cookouts (or barbeques, as we call
them in England), I'd regularly attend church with her—heck,
I'd even been to a baseball game (and anybody who knows me
knows that participating in or watching sports isn't my idea of
a thrilling evening), and here I was, surrounded by thousands
of loud and proud Americans, and I loved it.

A spectacular evening was topped off by an equally
spectacular fireworks display.

Every man, woman and child stopped what they were doing
and lined the streets, the embankment and rooftops to watch a
breathtaking show of multicoloured starbursts ebb and dance
against a backdrop of a summer starry sky before returning to
earth in a shower of light reflected in the canal's water.

Awesome!

And it was as we all stood in stunned silence with a warm
summer breeze rustling the leaves on nearby trees, carrying
with it the sweet scent of sugared cinnamon and sizzling hot
dog onions that one of our group, an accountant recently
divorced, verbalised this with an absent whisper,
"Awesome…"

Nobody responded. Everybody was just simply transfixed.

"It would be so much better if we had someone to share this
with…"

Wait a minute—what?

All members of the party turned to him as if he were one of
those helpless souls from *Invasion of the Body Snatchers*.

There's nobody like you.

At least not here.

For crying out loud, man? Seriously?

Okay, he didn't say anything terrible but, come on, give
yourself a break.

The man was a member of *The Singles* clan and, I have to
say, he was one of the most, how shall I put this, verbal of the
group. Often bemoaning the loss of his beloved wife (to
another man) and how life just wasn't the same without her,
and how he'd never recover, and how he'd think of her every
morning when he woke up to the moment he went to bed, and

that she wouldn't return his calls and how it all made him very sad, but "Oh, well, I guess it's just one of those things", but then would add, "I just don't understand…"

Enough!

We'd all been there. Hell, I was still there. (You've seen that.)

But sometimes, in the interest of our own sanity, and that of those around us, it's important to take a break from all that self-flogging and remind yourself that there's still a life out there beyond what was, because to not do so is to condemn the rest of the future to living in the misery of the past.

For me, it probably would have been a much more constructive and inspiring moment if this accountant had concentrated on how next year, with a bit of luck, he would have moved on with his life and maybe even have found someone else special with whom to share that moment rather than verbalise what everybody, including me, was already thinking but trying to ignore for a few minutes.

Which brings me right back to that whole idea of getting out there and meeting people; it's all too easy to wallow, retreat into ourselves, and not feel inclined to be around people we know, certainly not strangers with whom, God forbid, we would actually have to make small talk.

Again, I demonstrated this well.

Especially when these so-called strangers have been specially selected by well-intentioned friends or family members whose idea of helping you get over your current crisis is to be 'distracted' by someone else.

You know, a bit like buying a child another pet as soon as the other one dies.

If only these things were that simple.

Meeting another person would certainly help 'distract' you from what you are going through, but it isn't necessarily the best thing for you.

Right now, your emotions are all over the place and, if you are lucky enough, this person might even be in the same place as you. But the ability to commiserate with each other doesn't necessarily make it a good match. In fact, I would go as far as saying that this is the worst possible match. Neither of you are sure about where you are at right now and there is a lot of grieving to be done before you can seriously consider 'being' with somebody else.

At least for anything more than a one-night stand.

And even then, if you're still grieving over your ex, you may well cause yourself even more misery buy adding feelings of guilt to the bubbling cauldron of your emotions.

(Don't ask me how I know that!)

Why?

Because one of the most common procedures after a breakup with someone meaningful is to compare the incoming suitor with their outgoing (or already-gone-but-don't-want-to-accept-it) predecessor as one would the upgrade to a vehicle; personalities, physical attributes, quirks, everything is up for close inspection, and that's because our need to be with our former partner is so great that we'll seek to 'replace' them.

Now, if you are a very lucky person, during the comparison process, you will find there are many improvements to this version; there may even have been an upgrade to the aesthetics, a more well-formed body, sharper looks, bolder characteristics and maybe even optional extras, such as comfort mode and more gallons to the mile.

So what's the problem?

Well, and especially if you were the Dumpee, you are not over your ex just yet!

Apparently, three to six months is a good 'waiting' time but, as you know, I believe this time to be subject to the strength of the bond with your ex, the circumstances, and severity of the breakup.

So what's the problem with finding someone new?

There's absolutely no problem.

As you know, I'm the advocate for you getting out there, stretching, and meeting new people—but it's important that you're self-aware.

Try to match yourself to someone else too soon and you're creating a new world of pain, and now it's no longer all about you. Right now, there's a good chance that you're what's more commonly known as *Emotionally Disengaged,* at least when it comes to other potential partners; you're unable to become emotionally involved with anybody else because you're still emotionally engaged with your ex.

So?

So, remember how you felt/are feeling about your ex?

Well, the potential substitute in your life may well have felt the same, but is now over it and ready to 'get serious' with somebody else.

Are you?

"I may be" (subject to the plethora of criteria branded in your preconception).

May be?

Would you like to do unto them what has been done unto you?

I know an Englishwoman who married an American after meeting him at an Air Force base here, in England. She then decided to emigrate to his hometown in America where they lived somewhat happily until they divorced twenty years later.

Rather than coming back to England, she decided to stay in America, where she eventually met another man, Harry.

Harry was a great guy but, not unlike her husband, had a serious problem with managing his finances.

This guy racked up debt as fast as she racked up her love for him.

However, it wasn't long before she learned about his increasing financial crisis, and it crushed her that she should fall, once again, for a man who appeared to have the same issues as her ex-husband, and that history seemed to be repeating itself.

They talked.

He promised to get things under control and to get help.

But he didn't.

Until, eventually, she had no choice; she had to cut him loose before his debts threatened to engulf them both.

It was one of the most difficult decisions she'd ever made, but she did it because the will to be free of debt and to avoid a return to the nervous wreck she used to be with her ex-husband was far greater than her love for this man.

And, after the usual mourning and summits on the chances of getting back together, she opted to move on, swore off men and became one of those people who were unable to see any member of the opposite sex as anything other than a good friend.

She met Aaron a month later.

Aaron was a handsome, sweet guy who pretty much doted on her from the day they met. He was the kind who'd often drop by with takeaway (takeout), a bottle of wine and a movie, but rarely empty-handed.

He was all about music, poetry, art and was all too happy to help her around the house with any DIY tasks. A man who took time for quality time with her young daughter, unlike her ex-husband, who never did anything remotely similar with his own offspring, and would chat to her about her dreams and her goals.

He was a good distraction for both of them but somehow, for her, there was something missing.

Aaron wasn't Harry.

And right now she was too busy thinking about the man she had just split up with and how they could get back together without becoming, once again, entangled in the very thing that made them separate in the first place.

Meanwhile, Aaron was patiently waiting on the sidelines and, because of his sensitivities, he was aware and made allowances for her recent breakup whilst she, although happy to spend time with him, was, guess what, Emotionally Disengaged.

Which eventually led them to have a talk, which escalated into an argument during which he told her, in no uncertain terms, that until she was able to let go of Harry, they would never be able to be together.

Not properly.

He left.

As fate would have it, that very night, Harry knocked on her door. He told her he wanted to talk. They did. One thing led to another; Harry stayed the night.

The next morning, when she went out to collect her mail from the post box she found a CD; it had been hand-delivered by Aaron for her and it featured all of her favourite songs.

Hand-delivered meant that Aaron was outside her house the

night before, and it meant that he would have seen Harry's truck in her driveway. It meant that he now knew that she had spent the night with her ex.

What he didn't know is that she woke up believing she had made a mistake and had no intention of repeating it. Furthermore, it was the mistake that made her realise just how much she loved Aaron.

But it was too late.

He phone calls were ignored, her letters unanswered.

She never heard from Aaron again and, to this day, despite being remarried, she still believes that he was the one whom she let get away.

It's really important that, when you introduce someone into your emotional topsy-turvy world, they have been well informed about exactly what you're looking for from this encounter.

Set your boundaries and (by doing so) set their expectations so that they know exactly what to expect from you and therefore are not disappointed, or, worse, hurt.

Do unto others as you would have them do unto you.

If you feel so inclined, explain your relationship background, how it had made you feel and what you're looking for in a relationship right now (without necessarily boring the pants off them—remember, this encounter is no longer just about you).

Is it okay to call and send you messages every day? Are you happy to just meet up occasionally, maybe even have some 'fun'?

Define fun!

I know that sounds awfully clinical. By all means, use your own words, but you'll be amazed by the amount of people I have met who ended up being disappointed and/or hurt by the dates they went on because both parties were completely misaligned in their expectation.

Just set your stall out—and, by association, you'll be giving them the chance to do so also.

By setting boundaries you're already laying down a common foundation on which you can both build as much or as little as your heart's desire without the risk of a potential sinkhole of miscommunication opening up and devouring you whole.

Yep, I know it sounds way too organised for messy emotions but, trust me, it can work and it will have the added bonus of making you feel good as, for the first time in probably a very long time, you'll be taking control over your own destiny.

Just remember that, while it may well be good and proper to set the boundaries for someone else, be sure to know your own. Be mindful of where you are at and consider exactly what you want from every situation before immersing yourself in it.

After my trip to Wichita and my subsequent 'reawakening', I felt as if I was ready to take on the world once more, and I guess this was mostly because, before we'd even left that beautiful house by the lake, I was already hand-scribbling (yes, actually using pen and paper) ideas for this book: topics I wanted to feature and people I needed to speak to.

First, I had to break the news that *Nimbus 2*, the genre that I was so accustomed to, would be shelved in favour of a completely new genre where everything I wrote would be one hundred per cent nonfiction.

Needless to say, it wasn't a popular conversation, since I was abandoning my own style and genre in favour of something completely new.

Authors only tend to dabble in something like that when they are well established—and even then, I can tell you, it is all ultimately down to the power of the reader.

You guys dictate exactly what you want to read and, if we want you to carry on reading our work, then we'll have no choice but to cater to public demand.

Needless to say, it was a risk, but one that I felt I had to take.

52 THE WHITE COWBOY

We returned to Oklahoma City on the Sunday and when Rosa asked her obligatory Sunday night question as to whether or not I wanted to keep the SUV, guess what my immediate reaction was...

...it was yes, of course.

(Bet I had you wondering there. I'd learned my lesson).

Regardless of the fact that I had absolutely no idea how to drive on American roads. That's right; in all my time with M, he'd always been driver designate, as was I in England.

But now, I was thinking of driving on the highway to downtown Oklahoma, sat in the opposite side of the car and driving on the opposite side of the road.

All credit to my sister; I'm not sure *I* would have trusted me to drive her brand-new SUV.

And where exactly was I planning on driving it?

Oh, I don't know, I hadn't thought that far ahead. All I knew is that Rosa kept offering and I liked the idea of having wheels. I just didn't know what I was going to use them for.

But then I remembered the road that Rosa would normally take on her way to church and that on that road, the Northwest Expressway, there was a Starbucks coffee house.

Perfect.

I have no idea how I managed to pilot the vehicle there and into a parking space, but I did.

It was early on a Monday morning so the place wasn't exactly jumping, which suited me just fine.

My laptop and I took up residence at a corner table where I set up and stared at the blank page for some time before writing the words, "That which doesn't kill us makes us stronger..."

(Ironically, following all the edits before this book got to print, that line no longer features anywhere! I guess that's because it's been somewhat overused. I'll let you decide if it applies.)

I returned to that Starbucks the next day and the day after that.

And that's how a ten-year journey to locations not even my mind could have imagined, and my immersion into the relationships of literally hundreds of people began, and how the words that you are holding in your hands today came to be.

Of course you don't know about my other journeys yet because I haven't told you about them, but you will.

Soon.

Meanwhile, my whole life had changed just because I made the decision to 'stretch'; I chose to stop feeling sorry for myself and to stop languishing in my misery and worshipping something that had died many months before.

It's not as if I didn't long for love with someone else, of course I did. I romanticised about encounters with people nearly every day—especially since, being a writer, my imagination would run wild, not necessarily with ideas for different books, but with variations of my own life/love story.

Chance encounters in partially conceived locations. Scenes where I could see a man's smiling face and I could hear him saying all of the right words. Scenes where I'd receive, once again, that first kiss that freeze-framed the rest of the world as my heart thundered in my chest, and I felt my whole being soar.

There was just one problem.

I had been locked up in my house in England.

Then I was locked up in my sister's house five thousand miles away in America.

You've got to be in it to win it.

Opportunities won't come knocking on your door.

If you truly want to move on with your life, then you need to stretch, you need to introduce yourself to life, let it know that you still have a pulse—and it in turn will introduce you to opportunities.

There's a time for grieving and then there's a time for getting on with it.

Get on with it!

Remember, your time currency is being spent regardless.

That's exactly what I said to myself the following Saturday night when I asked Rosa if I could borrow her SUV to go to a club.

Or, more specifically, a gay club.

(Yes, try not to fall off your chair if you're sitting down.)

Oklahoma isn't known for its gay nightlife and I hadn't even been to a gay club before, but I did manage to find some place just off the highway. I would love to write exactly what that place was like but I genuinely can't remember.

I couldn't possibly imagine why.

If I told you I was terrified, it would be an understatement but I willed myself because I knew I had started writing a book about this very thing so I couldn't exactly preach what I didn't practise; I needed to let the world know that I was back out on the market.

Now, I'm all about being out of your comfort zone, but this, this was a whole other thing.

It took me every last shred of willpower to leave that car that I'd parked on what appeared to be some kind of business estate with multiple giant warehouses, one of which was making the tarmac shake beneath my feet with its loud dance beat.

I paused midway across the car park as I moved towards a fairly nondescript entrance with a miniature neon sign over the door.

Blimey, I thought I was going to a gay club, not a sex club!

Then I remember adding, *"Is there a difference?"*

I was so ready to run back to the car and drive out of there and I must have considered it about ten times before I reached the entrance where two burly, unattractive guys in black suits watched as I approached and then, suddenly and in unison, flashed smiles as if programmed to do so when registering a new potential punter.

It was getting on for ten in the evening, but the place was still fairly empty, which of course did nothing for my nerves as there was no chance of me hiding in the throng.

RUN! Run now!

I made my way to the bar and ordered, thanks to my fishing expedition with Timothy, something that was even related to a man's drink, a Bud Light, but even then I realised I was actually driving tonight.

Typical when, for once, I really needed the alcohol. I didn't care what it was as long as it numbed me to this whole process.

Anyway, drink in hand, I slowly made my way to one of the many standby tables dotted around the empty place whilst being pleasantly surprised that some of the club music that was being played was remarkably Euro sounding, which at least went some way to making me feel at home.

RUN!

I looked around the room as I pretended to drink, with all of the masculinity I could muster, from my bottle while scoping out the other clientele who dared to venture, like me, into this gay Den of Iniquity.

They all looked fairly 'normal' but for the guy who was wearing a pink jumpsuit and platform glitter shoes, the girl who had clad her ample body in denim and used her face as a pincushion, oh and maybe the guy who was wearing glitter eye shadow, fake eye lashes and a white feather boa over what was actually a really sharp black-and-white pinstripe suit.

"Hello."

I turned and literally had to look up into the face of a very tall black man. From what I recall, he was fairly handsome and spoke with the very deep, honey-dripping intonation of Barry White.

It took me a few seconds to actually register that little old me, who had sought out the table furthest from the main thoroughfare of the entrance and bar, had already been accosted.

Now, I would have been flattered but for the fact that my new friend was actually wearing a white cowboy hat speckled with diamantes with matching white jump suit (kind of Elvisesque) and boots that winked at me under the flashing multicoloured laser lights.

I was struck dumb.

"Would you like a drink?" he oozed softly in that deep tone of his.

"I have one, thank you," I said in my English accent, once again sounding awfully clipped in comparison to his.

"Would you like to dance?" he then offered, glancing at the dance floor.

I followed his gaze to the still lonely dance floor to find a pink jumpsuit boy (jumpsuits were obviously the wardrobe of choice in this establishment), a tall spindly man with equally skinny jeans, boots, short blonde hair and way too much makeup, and a short dumpy girl with stereotypical Doc Martin boots, lots of denim and a face that she appeared to use as a pin cushion.

No, wait—it was her again!

I swallowed. "No thanks," I said, lifting my bottle, "I already have one."

He smiled at me, noticing before I did that I had just repeated my stock answer, which was completely out of context with his question. But the more seconds went by, the more it became too late to correct it—duh!

RUN!

Now, if I thought my sparkling cowboy would just move along after my rejection, I was sorely mistaken.

"So, you from England?" he continued.

"Yes, I am," I said, squeezing out a smile.

"What are you doing here?" he asked, sidling closer to me, clearly under the illusion that because he'd asked me about my origins I was happy to engage in conversation."

"You know what," I said, "I'd love another drink."

"Seriously?" he asked, dazzling a set of brilliant white teeth that jumped out at me in the gloom almost as brightly as the flashing disco lights.

"Sure," I said, returning his smile.

"I'll be right back," he said, as if he'd just been charged with saving the fate of the world.

Then he turned, with all of the swagger of John Wayne, and made for the bar.

The further he walked from me the more I felt relieved so please don't judge me when I tell you this next part...

I RAN!

I ran (or did I fly like a bat out of hell?) as fast as my feet would carry me, and I climbed behind the wheel of the SUV and came as close as any average Jo gets to burning rubber as I left that car park.

Good Lord!

I know. I know. I'm a terrible person, but that whole experience was just so alien to me. It was a world I knew absolutely nothing about and, quite frankly, it's one I didn't particularly want to be a part of.

Don't get me wrong. I love being gay (whatever that means)

but, for years, my homosexuality had existed only inside my head and had been expressed only within the confines of a private room.

I did not belong in that place, certainly not at that particular time of my life.

Not that I considered myself any better than any of those people—I simply wasn't ready and accepting enough of my own status to accept and engage with others of that particular brand of persuasion.

And so not my finest hour perhaps, but I learned something very important that evening: that I was still alive. That when I was standing somewhere, even in a dark club, I existed. And it felt bloody good.

I existed.

Before M, I existed as the so-called straight guy who happened to date girls in the past, but had been burned and therefore chose to no longer get serious with anybody else.

Then I existed for M, but never as the real me, not until that moment.

You'll probably have read, be it on a social media poster or a bumper sticker, that you should *never have regrets*.

Why? What's wrong with regretting something that you didn't do? A job you didn't take up, an opportunity missed? I believe that there's a lot to be taken from looking back at the events of the past here in the present as perspective for the future.

There aren't many days that go by where I don't regret not coming out when I was much younger. I'm often thinking that it would have been much easier (and much more fun) to have left my own trail of broken hearts as a younger, more handsome version of myself, to have sought and conquered with youthful ease than with a mature handicap.

Oh no, did I just write that out loud? Did I just say that it would be easier to hook up with someone as a young person than it would be as an older person?

But isn't that ageist?

It sure is.

But is someone, perhaps a misguided liberal, realistically going to say that it isn't true?

I do regret not coming out sooner, but not out of some perverse reminiscence; more as a constant reminder to appreciate the person I am now, since I'm very much aware that the youth I'm enjoying today will have aged one more day by tomorrow.

Which brings me onto my next subject, one that has been a constant topic of discourse both in, and out of, my family circle.

I'm forever being told that I'm too picky, that I should lower my so-called standards, and that I should effectively settle.

Me? Settle? Are you crazy?

But what's wrong with settling? Millions of people around the world do it, from courtrooms to bedrooms, from green cards to wedding receptions. We *settle* on many issues—so why not settle in a relationship?

He's not perfect, but he has his moments. She's a bit ditzy and can't do anything for herself, but there's something about her. He rarely shows me any affection, but he's a good man.

That old chestnut, on and on.

There are countless reasons why each and every one of us rationalises and settles in a relationship.

I've lost count of the amount of women I've met who don't feel particularly fulfilled in their marriage. The flame has fizzled, the passion has turned to exhaustion, replaced instead by abject complacency (there's that word again).

These women feed their need for chivalry, romanticism, lust and yearning through contemporary and period books and movies, whilst fulfilling their appetite for wild sexual abandonment in sexually explicit literature. This is another form of compromise; this isn't the kind of thing I'd do with my husband but I can live it vicariously through other people, albeit, in this case, fictional characters.

Not that I'm complaining of course; I'm a writer, so if you girlies are getting your kicks from books and from films made by the acquisition of rights to those books then, hey, who am I to complain?

The only point here being that whilst many women may well not feel totally fulfilled in their marriages, it doesn't mean they love their husbands any less, and it doesn't mean there's a mad rush at the divorce courts either. And there's one reason for that: on the theoretical scale of importance, these necessities, these requirements for fulfilment are ranked low when compared to other, more practical, applications such as vows, home, family and security.

So, now I'd like you to indulge me if you will, and conduct a little experiment with me regardless of whether or not you're single or partnered.

I'd like us to go back to that good old piece of paper with that line drawn down the middle—you know, the one I wanted you to draw for listing the reasons you should and should not get back together with your ex?

Same story again, only now I'd like you to draw a line in the middle of the page and at the top of the left-hand column, write SHOULD HAVE, and in the right-hand column, put MUST HAVE.

Now, what are the most important things that a potential or existing partner must fulfil in order for you to be happy? Think of the perfect partner; your ideal companion.

If you're married or in an existing relationship then I'd be willing to put money on the fact that you haven't done this exercise any time recently—and there's only one reason for that; what's the point? You're committed already, right?

All this is going to do is highlight stuff you believe you already know or don't particularly want to know, because it's pointless.

You're committed.

You've settled.

Nothing wrong with that.

But just out of curiosity, why don't you play along anyway? Remember, it's just you and me here. Even if your sheet of paper is a mental one.

Now, think about your ideal partner (not your existing one, if you have one, but the ideal partner). Then, in the column *SHOULD HAVE*, write down all of the attributes that your ideal partner should have in order for you to be happy.

Consider, is it good looks, wealth, health, physical attributes or, that age old favourite, a good heart?

You can write down as many things as you'd like, but for this exercise I'd limit these to just ten.

Go ahead. Take your time. I'll be waiting right here.

Done?

Now, out of those ten items, what are the three *MUST HAVE* things?

Go ahead and enter those in the column *MUST HAVE*.

Done?

Now, if you're single, the three items in the *MUST HAVE* column are those things you should seek, and not settle on, in a prospective partner.

These things are realistically satisfying your basic requirements from a partner. Providing they are realistic, of course. If you wrote down the fact that you'd like a billionaire who happens to be a monk with a special interest in gambling, there's a good chance that you may well have limited your options from possible to somewhat impossible.

On the other hand, if you're already married/partnered then take a look at entries in both columns and count how many attributes from each of the columns your partner actually possesses.

More importantly, how many from the column *MUST HAVE*?

If the score is high, then congratulations! You've done really well for yourself.

If the score is low, then congratulations! You're an admirable settler, but if you're relatively happy then who cares, right?

Far from cashing out, settling is something we all do and it's perfectly normal and, some would say, me being one of them, essential to a successful relationship.

There is, however, a big difference between *settling* and *rationalising*, neither of which is mutually exclusive.

In fact, I've seen many people confuse the two, especially women.

He doesn't spend much time with the children, but then he has a very demanding job. He doesn't show me much attention, but that's because he has a lot on his mind.

There's a difference between being *supportive* and *making excuses.*

The thing is, it's really easy to condemn the person for whom the rationalising is taking place when, in reality, the only guilty party is the actual rationaliser. They're 'enabling' the behaviour by making excuses.

Remember that familiar child-and-candy analogy of earlier in the book?

Deal with the issue—don't excuse it.

One seeks a therapist to treat behaviour, not to justify it.

53 TRUE COLOURS

A friend once said, "Every day's a school day."

One of mine took place on a hot July evening, back in 2003.

I glanced at my watch; it was nearly nine fifteen. I'd been waiting outside the Outback restaurant for over forty-five minutes and I was considering the idea of going home when Ethan, the doorman, finally arrived.

We ate dinner and talked on and off about this book. I asked him about his past, whilst he asked me what was in the rucksack that had become essential wear during my time in America.

I explained that it had become my writer's bag, carrying essentials such as notepad, pen, and sometimes even my laptop computer.

This evening was no exception.

Dinner was fairly short considering that the whole point of meeting there was to conduct one last undisturbed interview before I made my way back to England in a few days.

He told me he wanted to go to a club and asked if I was up for it. I told him we hadn't finished the interview and that I was hardly dressed (I was wearing shorts, a T-shirt and trainers—tennis shoes) for a nightclub.

He told me not to worry about my clothes and promised we'd talk later.

I protested some more.

He insisted.

I reluctantly complied.

We ended up at a rainforest-themed nightclub, rather appropriately called RAIN, where the music thumped so loudly it shook the leaves on the artificial plants that adorned the entrance lobby.

The place was heaving with people out for a good time.

I looked like a tourist with a rucksack slung over my shoulder; in fact, I remember thinking that I was dressed more for trekking the rainforest than dancing in it.

Since I'd met Ethan, much of his topic of conversation had been around how he was viewed by others, particularly girls, and since many of our conversations had been about him, we didn't really get the opportunity to talk about me and/or my past.

So tonight, when he kept making references to girls and asking me to contribute to that conversation, I found myself pausing for thought.

I contemplated the idea of coming clean, but I didn't think a noisy club was the type of place to attempt that kind of conversation since I had no idea how the cocky heterosexual philanderer was going to react—he might even start questioning my motives for including him in this book.

So instead I just smiled at each comment as it was flung my way.

But I was starting to feel extremely self-conscious and, as much as I desperately wanted to go over some points in the manuscript, it was as I stood there, watching the percussion of the drumbeat literally move glasses on tables, that I asked myself, *what the hell are you doing here?*

So I turned to Ethan, only to find that he was busy throwing his arms around a group of young girls and boys.

I patiently waited for the idle banter to end before I attempted to get his attention, but it was a disaster; each time I tried to say something, I was interrupted, either by the passing hordes or by Ethan's own distraction; the doorman was constantly looking over my shoulder or around the room, looking, seeking everything but the conversation in hand.

Finally, as a group of girls extricated themselves from his grasp and walked off, I moved to speak but, "They're mighty fine, don't you think?" he asked, staring at the behinds of the girls as they disappeared into the crowd.

"They're lovely," I said flatly.

"What's the matter with you?" he asked, finally glancing at me.

"Ethan…"

"I tell you, the girls here are amazing…"

"Ethan…"

"You know some of the boys here actually hate me because of all of the booty…"

"Ethan..."

"You know, if you stick with me, I can guarantee you'll be going home with some chick tonight, maybe even two…"

"Ethan… there's something you should know… I wasn't going to bother telling you because I didn't think it was relevant, but considering you keep talking about girls, well… remember, I told you about that relationship I had, the one that inspired this book? Well it wasn't with a girl… it was…"

He suddenly stopped looking over my shoulder, glanced at me, smiled and then leaned in closer to hear what I was saying, only he wasn't looking right at me, but over my shoulder once more.

"Did you hear what I said, Ethan?"

He nodded and broke into a smile. I realised then that he wasn't smiling at me, but at a duo of girls behind me. He hugged them, chatted briefly about how they should go home with him tonight and then re-emerged, but only after scanning the room once more.

I forced a smile, acknowledging the 'knowing' wink he gave me after the girls walked off.

"What were you saying?" he asked.

"I was telling you about me..."

"…Oh yeah, that's no problem… So, anyway, tell me about you. You've been asking all these questions about me, but you haven't told me anything about your life."

At last.

I forced another smile, "Well, you've never asked."

He scowled. "Jesus, you're worse than a girl, man. Girls are like that…well, you never asked… if you have something to say, just say it man!"

"I was trying to…"

"Do what?"

"I'm trying to tell you…"

"Hey…" He broke off again and slapped the back of a man who had worked out so much he carried his arms more like an orang-utan than he did a Homo sapiens.

I looked around me. The club had filled some more, it was teeming with young people. The situation was hopeless.

I just wanted to go home.

"Hey!"

I realised that Ethan was actually calling me.

"I tell you, man… there're a lot of people in here who hate me. A lot of people I've turned away from the club."

"Really?"

"Yeah…"

He looked around the room and then back at me. "So, what were you saying?"

I sighed and took a few seconds to consider whether or not I should even bother trying.

I did.

"Okay… well, you know about my six-year relationship…"

"Yeah… what's up with that? What did she do to you, man?"

"Well, actually, Ethan. She is a he…"

"Do what? She what…?"

"He…"

"She…?

"He…"

"I'm sorry, man. Sounds like you're saying *he*."

"I am."

"What…?"

"HE is in the marines."

"She is in the marines..?"

"HE, Ethan! HE is in the marines…!" I yelled so loud I thought I was going choke. I almost expected the music to scratch to a halt, the dissonant associated chatter to stop and everybody to turn to me with accusatory eyes.

Ethan frowned and visibly shrunk back on his bar stool, "Oh..."

I smiled, well aware of the change in his demeanour. "Do you want to go now?" I asked.

The doorman pulled a face, "Say what? You trying to pick me up now?"

The question seemed serious and it threw me.

"Oh, forget it," I said.

I just wanted out of there. Out of the loud noise, out of that ugly feeling of discomfort that was so familiar to me, the one I believed I had suffocated and buried all those years before.

I knew I wasn't projecting when Ethan visibly leaned back from our conversational intimacy. I'd clearly shocked this guy. And I wasn't staying in that situation—not for him, not for anybody.

I had just dismounted the barstool when Ethan caught my arm, "Where are you going?"

"I'm leaving."

"Why?"

"You just seem really surprised, almost uncomfortable."

He shook his head, seriously. "No, no man. No. Actually, I'm disappointed you think I'm that shallow," he said with mock disapproval whilst rubbing the backside of a passing girl who turned around and put her arms around him.

I knew I didn't have the guy's attention and if I didn't have it before, I certainly didn't have it now.

He gestured at me to follow as he got off his stool and gravitated towards the bar, greeting and smiling at people as he went.

"So how are you going to survive without all of this when you leave?" I asked, aware that, as far as Ethan was concerned, my conversation was over.

"Oh, it's going to be cool, man; I'll hang out with my dad. I'll make more friends—and failing that I'll get a job in a club over there." (*Over there* being Australia.)

And, I'll be honest, I don't know why—I'm assuming I was still feeling somewhat exposed by the recent conversation and wasn't thinking—but the words just came out, "Blimey, Ethan. Are you so desperate for this adoration that you're going to try and recreate this world wherever you go? Why do you give these people so much power over your state of mind?" (Yes, the irony of my words wasn't lost on me and I wondered if I was telling Ethan or myself.)

Shut up, Tony.

"You don't need them and you shouldn't let them, this adoration, become your life. It's just an illusion. At the end of the day, you don't even know these people, Ethan. They're not your friends; Christ, they're barely acquaintances. You do realise that, right?"

He looked at me as if I had just spoken another language, but said nothing. Instead, he ordered more drinks from the bar, leaving me to wonder why the hell I had just blurted that out.

I almost felt like I needed to apologise, but you'll be pleased to know I didn't.

Besides, Ethan wasn't interested in talking, at least not with me, for he was already across the room, networking with other people, slapping the backs of men, hugging and kissing the women.

I watched him and concluded in that moment that Ethan, perhaps somewhat narcissistically, was an addict; a man who could not function without the constant adoration of others. Whether or not these people felt admiration or respect for him was of no consequence. And thus, it begged the question; how could anybody else compete with this? Whether that person be a girlfriend, like Megan, a friend, anyone. How could any one person feel special in the eyes of this man?

The truth was, they could not because, for Ethan, it would never be enough.

I turned and pushed my way through the throng. The sooner I was out of that place the better I would feel. But, once again, Ethan appeared behind me and grabbed my arm.

"Where you going?"

"I'm going home, Ethan."

"Why?"

"Why? You really need to ask?" I said as he followed me. "What's the deal?"

I was about to answer, but he was already looking elsewhere, "You know, I could take her home," he said, nodding at a girl with a nicely filled bra.

"Really?"

"Yeah, man."

I stopped and turned to him, "Well, why don't you? Go on. I'll give you a hundred dollars if you end up going home with that girl."

He laughed.

"No, I am serious," I continued. "I'll give you a hundred bucks if you take that girl home tonight."

He laughed some more and shook his head, "No, no I couldn't."

"Exactly, Ethan. You couldn't because you still haven't disconnected from Megan."

He disagreed by shaking his head some more whilst looking around himself for his next fix.

I made for the exit once more.

Ethan knew he wasn't completely over Megan as much as she wasn't completely over him, and this was in line with why the two of them were reluctant to get emotionally involved with anybody else. Ethan knew that what I was saying made sense, but he couldn't face that reality right now because he would be leaving in a few months and he did not need the complication, nor did he need to think about it.

And so, by now, good or bad, you will have formed an opinion.

Yes, like many of us, Ethan may not be perfect, but he is the result of a lifelong quest to be *noticed*.

The problem is that he'd now become addicted and, like an addict, was unable to function without 'scoring'.

I concluded that Megan's rebellion may not have been entirely due to the fact that Ethan was thinking of leaving, but more to do with the fact that she felt she needed more because she never felt like she was enough for him. I accepted that, without meeting her, I wouldn't ever really know the truth but, quite frankly, at this stage, I didn't care; I just wanted out of there.

And I had nearly reached the door when he caught up with me once more.

"Hey! Hey!"

I turned to him, half expecting an apology, but instead I got, "What's your deal, man?" You just gonna' leave like that?"

I was going to launch into a tirade about his behaviour, but instead just opted to say, "Well, you seem busy so I thought I'd make myself scarce."

"So, you were just going to leave without even saying goodbye?"

"Ethan, I've tried but…"

"You were really antisocial tonight."

The music was still pounding, so at first I thought I'd misheard him.

"What did you say?"

"You were antisocial tonight. Just stood there all evening with your bag on your shoulder."

I was momentarily lost for words and remember feeling somewhat insulted. Then I heard myself saying, "Ethan, I didn't come out to meet people or dance; I came out to talk with you because I'm leaving soon."

"Still, doesn't mean you have to be antisocial."

He was serious.

"What are you talking about? I don't need these people. I'm not like you."

"Anyway, I'll give you a call, but if I don't before you leave, just want you to know that it was nice knowing you."

With that, he shook my hand, patted me on the shoulder and moved over to the bar, leaving me standing there amongst the hive of people who were either still dancing, laughing, or pushing past me on their way towards the exit.

I contemplated going after him and giving him a piece of my mind but I decided against it and I left the club without looking back.

And so it was gone midnight when my Jeep Cherokee found its way onto the empty expressway home.

Like the blurry lights of passing billboards, everything that had happened played through my mind. I felt sad, but also very foolish. I'd hung around that club all evening, and for what?

I actually remember feeling hurt.

But I had to question whether it was Ethan who'd hurt me, or whether I had hurt myself by putting myself in that situation.

I had treated Ethan like a friend, somebody worthy of my confidence, someone with whom I felt I could share details about my life, my lifestyle, when, in reality, he was just an acquaintance, a subject, somebody whose life I had discussed as research when writing this book and probably wrongly mistook for somebody with whom I had forged some kind of connection.

And I wondered if, somewhat ironically, we were both similar in this respect.

Did Ethan hurt me or did I simply mismanage my own expectation and set myself up in the process?

Had I given Ethan too much emotional power? I'd have to say *yes*. Was I wrong to do so? I'm going to have to say *no*.

In business, I'm often taking risks; it's part of the whole 'speculate to accumulate' mentality. If you don't take risks, then you're never allowing yourself to win that new deal, that new opportunity.

Friendships or relationships often follow in the same vein. We all get hurt, and in turn we're all worried about being hurt—or, worse, rejected—but life is also full of opportunity.

"There are no strangers; only friends you haven't met yet."

On this occasion, I'd struck out.

Conversely, on that same trip I'd met many other great people, two of whom remain really close friends over a decade later.

As for Ethan: *"We don't often remember what people say to us, but we do remember how they made us feel."*

Sadly, he will never get the chance to change the way he made me feel that night.

54 DISCONNECTING

I stayed in America for over a month before finally returning to England.

I was healed.

Or so I thought.

I guess this was a logical reaction given the fact that I was actually getting out of the house on a daily basis and spent the rest of my time in the United States with actual purpose; I was writing again.

I hired my own Jeep Cherokee and made the Starbucks on Northwest Expressway my new home.

Of course, Americans being Americans (unlike us snooty Brits), a day seldom went by as I sat in that coffee shop, pecking at the keys of my laptop, that I wasn't accosted by someone asking me what I was doing.

And I welcomed that interaction because each and every person proved to be more research for this book. I would talk to these complete strangers, ask them about their relationship status and situation and they'd be very generous with that information.

These people didn't even know me, which is something I asked them about. They said I was 'easy to talk to'.

Thanks, guys. (Yes, I am taking that as compliment.)

Of course, this so-called freedom of information inspired me. I knew too well that it was highly unlikely that this same writing model would transfer well to a similar coffee shop in England.

Well, what I can I say; most of us Brits simply aren't built that way. We're a seemingly antisocial bunch who generally like to keep ourselves to ourselves.

I don't think even I, despite what I know, could walk into a public place and ask someone what they're writing about. Not for antisocial reasons, but more because I wouldn't really want to intrude on their time.

And I guess this is the real reason many of us Brits couldn't just walk up to a stranger and start interrogating them on why they're ensconced, hour after hour, in a coffee shop; we're too awfully polite and afraid of intruding.

Quite frankly, I'm not sure which stance I prefer the most.
Maybe a happy medium?

Regardless, my time in the States inspired me; if complete
American strangers were happy to talk to me about their
relationships, what about American Service personnel in
England? After all, they'd make ideal candidates because they
had the additional stresses and strains of serving in the military.

I had nothing to lose.

First, I faxed, then emailed the British Army.

No reply.

Then I contacted the American Military—in particular the
Air Force (as we have two well-known American bases just an
hour from Cambridge, England).

USAFE Public Affairs office got back to me pretty much by
return, and after numerous phone calls —pretty much around
the world, including the Public Affairs office in New York who
sought approval from their superiors at The Pentagon (no
less)—I'd secured their full cooperation.

I was in business and I was bloody ecstatic!

Within weeks an email was sent to personnel on both bases
by their mutual Public Affairs office asking for volunteers.

Profiles with brief relationship synopses stated to pour in. I
was 'good to go'.

I think it was The Walker Brothers who sang, *"Breaking up
is so very hard to do,"* and they had a very good point.
Breaking up is bloody well tough! Especially if you weren't the
one to initiate the separation.

The Walker Brothers were doing the ultimate altruistic thing;
knowing that the love of their life wanted somebody else, they
actually told them to *"Make it easy on yourself"*.

Unlike The Walker Brothers, I was feeling everything but
selfless when I first found out about M. In fact, I would have
done anything to keep him in my life and, as you know, I pretty
much did, even resorting to threatening to ruin his career. Once
again, not one of my proudest moments, but it's indicative of
the fact that, when confronted with such a desperate situation,
we'll do almost anything to regain some semblance of control
in a situation where we clearly have none.

Gone were the days of dancing in our underwear, travelling to far-flung places, laughing at the inane, and watching the sun rise over Sin City in each other's arms.

And it's precisely this nostalgic romanticism that makes you want it all back.

I was fairly lucky because, as you know, the day after I let M go, I was starting a whole new chapter in my life and had embarked on the *Journey Out of the Centre of my Closet* tour which would see me perform various emotional gigs in the living rooms of family members and boardrooms of bosses.

Needless to say, I was too busy to even be thinking about getting M back, let alone acting on it. There was no time to agonise over the love I'd lost or to dream about a potential reconciliation, to the point where I'd mistaken this for having recovered already.

Seriously?

Do you really believe that?

No, you don't, because you know the truth now.

Like many, with perverse regularity, I considered making contact with M again, and each time I deluded myself that this compulsion was not necessarily a need to remain connected to him but merely a *simple* need to hear his voice—you know, make sure he was okay.

There's no harm in that, right?

Who was I kidding? I was the one who had been dumped. Why would I be checking to see if he was okay?

However, sometimes, life has a way of making things happen regardless of our state of mind.

As you know, it hadn't been that long since my return to England and I was going through my camera's memory cards and what should I find? That's right, not just photographs of my time in America, but deep inside, in a separate folder, photographs of my last time together with M.

There weren't many, but enough to stick a dagger in my heart because, despite the fact that I could see and remember the sadness behind both our smiles, I ached for a return to what we were. No matter how tempestuous, how imperfect, it was so much better to have something than nothing at all.

I missed him.

A lot.

Still.

I agonised over whether or not to share these pictures with him. Whether or not I should do what I rationalised to myself was the mature thing to do. These were pictures of his last time here in England. After all, he was in them and he deserved to be able to see them, right?

Besides, I was much stronger now. I was over it.

What do you think?

M's response to my email was almost immediate, and I can tell you that when I heard that email alert and the notification pop up with his name on it, I leapt out of my chair and pounced upon it like a hungry hound.

Much to my delight, the email was nice and lengthy, full of remorse, and didn't stop short of begging for forgiveness. I devoured every word, every punctuation mark, and each and every sad emoticon as if my life depended on it.

Did I respond to M's email?

Of course not.

Do you believe me?

Of course you don't!

I responded immediately.

M was contrite, he was repentant; he may even want us to get back together. I had to reply.

I let him know that I wasn't harbouring any animosity towards him, and I humbly added that, in the time we had spent apart, I'd managed to come to terms with the fact that it was over, that I appreciated his words, that I understood that it must be a difficult time for him since he undoubtedly had a challenging future ahead.

I stopped short of sharing just how peculiar that prospect made me feel. I don't recall being bitter about it at the time, just sad.

Cue the next email and the next and so on until M actually picked up the phone and we had a three-hour telephone conversation. Half of which was spent with M crying and offloading all the terrible things he had been through ever since our split as well as what he believed the future truly had in store for him, including prioritising his sign-up to the police academy, as he'd concluded that this would definitely be his career of choice after leaving the Marine Corps (in a matter of months).

Yes, I think I mentioned previously, that last bit hurt. For some reason, I had a hard time dealing with the fact that he would potentially be donning a uniform once more and that I would not be around to appreciate it, but I said nothing.

There was no doubt that M felt bad about what happened, but I also got a certain sense of resignation from him very much reminiscent of all Southern boys; I've made my bed and I shall lie in it (and yes, there goes another pun) because Southern men are expected to step up to their responsibilities (as are most, but these guys tend to do it so well and with such aplomb. At least the ones I've come into contact with).

And, of course, had this been any other situation I'd find these values admirable, but you'll appreciate that they stuck in my throat somewhat since I believed they were affecting my own future happiness.

But, then again, maybe not.

Because it was during the lengthy conversation with M that we actually discussed the possibility of meeting again!

Yes, try not to choke on that.

But the idea was tabled by M of all people, although it was in response to my casually delivered, "My biggest regret is that you were unable to tell me face-to-face during those two weeks, M."

"I know," came his tearful reply, "but I just couldn't. I'm so sorry for what I did to you. Do you think it would help if we met up—you know, talk through this properly so we can both get some closure?"

What do you think I said to that?

"What's done is done. What could we possibly achieve from meeting again?"

Um, no. Of course not. I resorted to a game.

Remember how we do that?

I needed to understand if his suggestion was genuine or if it was just a kneejerk reaction to the discussion we were having.

"I just think it might help," he continued.

I paused here. Whether or not this was because I was genuinely considering the possibility of seeing him again or simply for effect, I don't know.

"What difference to do you think it'd make, M?"

"It will help both of us move on," he said.

I paused again, but I was so ready to just say *yes*. Oddly, I didn't. I actually found the strength to say that I wanted to think about it.

"Please say you will. I'll cover the expense. It's the least I can do," he said.

I thought, blimey, he must be serious—that guy never parted with cash unless he really had to.

Eventually, the conversation ended, leaving me in a mixture of excitement and apprehension. M wanted to meet me in Atlanta, USA. This would most likely mean meeting him for just a long weekend. It wasn't anything we hadn't done several times before.

I thought about this.

What I struggled with was contemplating how exactly a reunion of this kind would take place. It was obvious to me that he had no intention of telling her that he was meeting me, and this meant that the whole operation would need to be conducted somewhat covertly and without her knowledge.

I'd be lying if I said I didn't like the idea of that.

On the other hand, I couldn't even begin to process what an encounter of this kind would be like. Sure, it would give us both a chance to have our say face-to-face and get that all-important closure. But would it really—or was this just some cynical attempt of his for absolution and mine to keep him in my life just that little bit longer?

What do you think?

A) Do you think I finally had the presence of mind to see reason and come to the conclusion that a meeting would only make things worse?
B) Do you think I succumbed and agreed to take the trip?

Well, I would love to tell you that I went for A because that would have meant that everything you're about to read in subsequent chapters would never have happened (whether or not that's a good thing, given the sensational nature of the future chapters of this book, is something I'll let you decide on).

I agreed to meet M and, mercifully for him, I told him that, whilst the gesture was appreciated, if I was going to travel to the United States it would be under my own steam and that I certainly didn't want to be beholden to him in any way.

I booked the tickets on the 18th of August for travel on Friday the 22nd returning on Sunday 24th August, and considering the flight was going to be in excess of five hours each way, it was certainly going to be a short but eventful trip.

55 THE HOTEL ROOM

Hartsfield-Jackson Atlanta International Airport, otherwise known as Atlanta Airport, is the busiest airport in the world. It's the base of the U.S. carrier Delta Airlines, and a major hub for international flights servicing the United States.

So, you can imagine just how busy it was on Friday evening at 17:30 local time.

In fact, the converging of no less than three international flights at immigration reminded me just how much I despised U.S. immigration procedures, although I guess there is only one way you can corral more than a thousand people, and that's treat them like cattle by positioning overweight, overzealous Latinos with thick accents and loud nerve-drilling voices at key points in the arrivals hall, and have them bark instructions at visitors, with visible boredom dressed as exasperation.

As much as I disliked the process, it wasn't alien to me given the number of times I had travelled to America, twice out of this very same airport, and, ironically, it actually felt as if this experience was better than the previous one, although that could simply have been down to the reason for my visit, which is all I could think about from the moment we landed on American soil.

In fact, as the plane came to a standstill, I remember wondering if he was out there, beyond the tarmac, beyond the arrivals hall, and the hordes of humans.

Was he awaiting my arrival with eager anticipation, dread, nervousness? Or was he simply busy texting sweet nothings to her? Reassuring her that he was about to have an uneventful weekend with his family when, in truth, he was about to embark on a secret rendezvous with me. Perhaps he was telling her that he may go dark for part of the weekend and feeding her a suitably plausible alibi for why he may not be texting as often as he normally would so as to comply with my one regulation before agreeing to take this trip: that I would not play the part of 'The Husband' and, as such, would not sit idly by as he sent messages and/or spoke with her on the phone.

I had demanded, and he agreed to, total mobile phone blackout.

You'll be pleased to know that I managed to make it past immigration with that usual apathetic wave and seemingly begrudging stamp of the immigration officer.

The stamp that told me that I had the permission of the United States Government to remain in the United States for ninety days. Ironically, I wasn't even going to be there for ninety hours.

It seemed that the more American chatter I listened to and the closer my stream of migrating salmon-like humans came to emerging from the arrivals hall, the more my throat began to dry and my heart began to pound.

I was angry at myself. Why was I the nervous one? I wasn't the one at fault here, I wasn't the one who did the dirty; I was the one…

…Bloody hell…there he was, among the throng, dressed in his trademark jeans and T-shirt.

Had the scene not been so nerve-wracking, it would have been beautiful for it reminded me very much of my arrival at Las Vegas International.

He had been waiting for me then, only that time he was sporting chinos, a black T-shirt and designer stubble—three of my favourite looks for him, and he knew that.

Also, back then, I could throw my arms around him (in the manliest possible way of course) and enjoy not only being near him once more, but basking in the fact that another human being had gone out of his way to do something he knew I would appreciate.

This time, there were no such considerations.

But he still looked good. Maybe not as bulky, but much slimmer (he said a direct result of everything that had happened). His hair was still cropped short and his hazel eyes were still big in those angular features of his, and today they looked at me with such bittersweet sorrow, and I was reminded in that very moment just how much I still loved him.

In my mind I ran up and threw my arms around him, but in real life, I simply walked up, "Hey."

"Hey," he said with a faint smile. "Is that all you have?" he asked, nodding at the small rucksack slung over my shoulder.

I forced a smile. "Yeah—the joys of jet setting across the Atlantic for a weekend."

We automatically turned to make our way out of the flow of chatter and people.

"Did you have a good flight?" he asked.

"It was good," I said, irked that he and I, after all this time, had been reduced to small talk, but at the same time grateful, for I had no idea what kind of conversation one should have in such a situation.

The small talk continued as he paid for parking and we made our way to his car, which was a far cry from the brand new gunmetal grey pickup truck he used to drive. This was some low-slung, second-hand sports thing that had a squeaky passenger door and harboured dank warm air that smelt of yesterday's fast food.

"You changed your car," I said.

He looked at me and nodded as if to say *"Needs must."*

Mercifully, he turned on the air conditioning, as it felt as if I was going to suffocate in that car—and I wasn't sure whether it was due to the situation or the Atlanta heat.

Meanwhile, my heart still leapt every now and then when he spoke with his smooth American accent; it would skip each time as random words, indiscriminate pronunciations reminded me of what was, and of how he used to be around me, and of how I missed him.

But I had to keep reminding myself that things were different now.

He was no longer mine. He had given himself to somebody else...

"Hey," he was calling out to me. "Are you okay?" he asked. "You spaced out there."

"As good as can be," I mumbled.

"We're here," he said.

It was as if we'd disappeared into some kind of time shift as I barely registered the journey from the Airport to College Park and the hotel.

"I need to get the car parked so not sure if you want to go ahead and check in while I do that."

"Sure," I said, eager to leave the confines of that vehicle in which she had no doubt sat on multiple occasions.

You have to give it to the Americans when it comes to providing value for money. The suite at the Amerisuites was, in this Englishman's opinion, very spacious and luxurious and, when considering it's aimed at the average traveller, I believed it excellent value for money.

That's exactly what I thought when I opened the door to the hotel room to reveal a good-sized lounge with coffee table, couch and an oversized TV. Beyond that was a decent-sized bedroom with the usual en suite bathroom.

I was really impressed.

Seriously?

Yes, those mundane thoughts were all I could process because everything else was just too much.

I walked into the room and the door pulled itself shut with a smooth but confident thud as I made my way into the bedroom, and that's when it dawned on me; there was just one king-sized bed. Certainly large enough for the two of us—but share a bed?

He's given himself to someone else. He belongs to someone else.

I stood motionless for what seemed like a very long time as I listened to the sounds of the city beyond the window and the hum of the air conditioning.

It seemed so dark in that room despite the large windows and my position in the orange spotlight of the setting sun that appeared to be highlighting the ridiculousness of my plight...

There was a knock at the door.

Another lurch of my stomach.

This was somewhat customary ever since the captain had told me that we would shortly be landing at Atlanta International Airport, and I have to say I was getting sick of this feeling that in turn literally made me feel nauseous.

Nonetheless, I willed my body to move and I opened the door.

He was standing there looking so damn handsome.

"Hey," he said softly but lowering his eyes in a way a child does when they've been told to *'get here this instant!'*

I didn't reply, but left the door as quickly as I could and somewhat bizarrely went to stand in the corner, on the opposite side of the room.

M walked in far enough for the door to close behind him but not too far to invade my space.

We both stood in silence for a few minutes until this was broken by M who said with yet another faint smile, "Are you planning on standing that far away from me the whole time?"

"Maybe," I said much more petulantly than I had intended.

"I know how you must be feeling..."

"You have no idea," I said dismissively, slowly shaking my head.

"Do you really think I wanted things to turn out this way?"

"I have no idea what you were thinking, M. In fact, were you even thinking at all? I had two weeks of silence and the cold shoulder. Two weeks of you making me feel like shit..."

"I tried to tell you, Tony, but..."

"You obviously didn't try hard enough."

"That's unfair. I tried the whole time we were there, but I couldn't,,,"

"Because you're a coward..."

"...Because I didn't want to hurt you."

485

I scoffed at the irony of that statement.

Hurt?

I couldn't be any *more* hurt. I was aching with hurt. I was in that very moment steeped in the excruciating agony of being denied the right to run across the room, undress and possess what had been mine for so long, but had been taken—no, worse still—*given* to somebody else.

"Tony…"

He was calling me again.

"Tony…"

I looked up reluctantly.

"You have every right to be mad at me, but please, *please* can we just try to reconnect?" He held out his arms in a conciliatory gesture.

He wanted me to hug him.

This was a common tradition in our relationship, each time we had been apart for a long time or even after an argument. We'd call the process 'reconnecting'—and God knows I wanted to, but I couldn't. I just couldn't move from that spot. And I don't think I was being dramatic, playing hard to get or just seeking attention; I just didn't know what to do. I just know how I felt.

My heart was broken.

I loved this man and I had no idea what the hell was going to happen if we 'reconnected' again.

"Please, Tony. We're here to talk this thing through."

"Then talk," I said.

"Not like this, Tony. "I've missed you."

"Yeah, well, clearly not that much," I said with a sneer.

He lowered his gaze as if my comment had just wounded him and I actually felt bad.

Stop being such an ass! Just hear him out. What's the worst that can happen?

I sighed.

"What could you possibly say, M, that will make a difference?"

He thought about this and then took one step forward, which automatically prompted me to move from my space in the corner of the room to the archway that led through into the bedroom.

"There's nothing I can say that will make a difference," he said, stopping in the middle of the room, as if to move any further forward would compel me to leap off a fictitious ledge. "What's done is done. I just want to explain to you that I never wanted to hurt you."

Those hazel eyes of his were sparkling, but not with joy, with tears.

"My whole life has changed because of this, and I've had no say in any of this. She…"

I must have visibly shuddered because he trailed off here and then continued, "She won't give up on the baby and will have it with or without me. The only choice I have is whether or not I am involved in its life."

He sounded so bloody reasonable. What could I say to that? And I have to be honest; the thought of her not having the baby did cross my mind. I did wonder, if she didn't have the baby, whether or not all of this might go away. But, even in that moment, I was surprised I had the presence of mind to think that if it wasn't this, then it would be something else; M was gone and if he wasn't gone then he was going.

There was no escaping the truth.

And that's the moment when it well and truly occurred to me; *truth is truth*. No matter how much we choose to sugar-coat it, dress it up, disguise it, or how bitter the taste, what is, is, and I needed to accept that.

Suddenly, I felt my tension, as well as all of the energy in my body just vaporise. So much so that I could have just collapsed in a heap on the floor. I felt totally drained and absolutely exhausted. I was like a warrior who had been presented with irrefutable proof that the battle had been lost and that to hold my position wasn't just futile, but senseless.

"What will you do?" I found myself asking.

"What I have to do," he said quickly. "It's my baby. I have responsibilities."

"How do you know it's your baby? Did she have a test?" I asked, meeting his eyes.

He didn't answer.

"Well?" I asked expectantly.

"Tony, come on…"

"Well, did she?" I repeated, keenly.

"I know it's my baby…"

"How?" I demanded. "How do you know? Because she told you?"

My energy was back suddenly. No, it wasn't that; it was something else. Something far scarier, and it came in just one shade: green.

"I don't want to discuss that…"

"Why? Because you don't want to consider the possibility that you may have been duped? That she may have trapped you."

He just looked at me.

"Huh?"

"I don't want to talk about her," he repeated calmly.

"You don't? But why not, M? After all, you introduced her into our lives, didn't you? You inserted her, the wife of another man, in between us—and now you've gone all coy?"

His big sad eyes met mine, he shook his head and said softly, "Don't do this."

"What?" I asked inquisitively, as if I had no idea what he was talking about, but he clearly knew me better than I knew myself.

"Do you love her?"

No answer, just more shaking of his head as his eyes began to water again. "Please don't do this," he whispered, swallowing hard.

"Answer me, M," I choked through the lump in my throat.

"Please don't so this," he chanted quietly as he fought back tears, the sight of which pricked my own eyes suddenly.

"M? Do. You. Love. Her?" I spelt out slowly as the damn burst and tears streamed down my face.

He said nothing; he just blinked back his own watery eyes.

"Oh, I see," I said slowly, realising that my secret hope—secret even to me because I had only just come to the realisation that I had been harbouring this hope—that what could have been explained as some terrible heat-of-the-moment mistake was perhaps a bit more.

No, not a bit more—much more.

He *loved* her?

My reaction to this news came seconds later, and it was unlike anything I have ever experienced or want to experience in my life again.

It was transcendent. A peculiar sense of abandonment with a complete disregard for social conduct and a total absorption in *me*, in how *I* was feeling right there in that room, in that moment: a conglomeration of frustration, anger, sadness, hopelessness, and total and utter rage.

A nearby chair was the first to bear the assault. I flipped it and its upholstered green seat onto its back. I then moved through the archway, into the bedroom where I kicked the mahogany-coloured dresser so hard it scraped across the carpet and slammed against the nearby wall causing cups on the coffee tray to chink in protestation.

Then, like a creature possessed, I hunted around the room for my next victim and homed in on the phone. But it was as I reached for the contraption that I felt strong arms on me, which I shrugged off as I lunged for the phone, missed and slammed my fist down on it sending the receiver flying in one direction and the cradle in the other as a pain shot through my finger, but I was immune, for it was nothing in comparison to the vice squeezing on my heart.

"Stop this, Tony, stop it!" M mumbled through the exertion of restraining me.

He then wrestled me and my bleeding hand to the bed where I fought and kicked against the former wrestler whilst hissing a tirade of abuse at him which he appeared impervious to, unlike me to the heat of his closeness, to the smell of his aftershave, the tensing of the muscles in his arms.

This was the man I loved, and he was gone.

It must have taken less than a minute for the red mist to dissolve, as did I into a heap of tears and shudders as his restraining arms metamorphosed into an embrace that, like a low-hanging rain cloud, had now burst into a shower of mutual tears as we both mourned what was and would never be again.

"I'm so sorry," he kept whispering in my ear as I sobbed. "I'm so sorry…"

And it was then, in that anguished moment, that our tear-drenched lips found each other. The kiss was desperate yet full of conflicted restraint; mine because I knew he had been with someone else and thus was now somewhat tarnished, and his, I can only assume, because of some warped sense of loyalty.

To her?

"I can't do this," he said, cupping my head in his hands and diving deep into my tear-soaked eyes.

"Do what?"

"This."

"Nor can I," I said as our mouths met once more and I literally tore at his T-shirt.

The sex—since, at this stage, it could only be described as that—was passionate, conflicted, angry and desperate but deeply and seemingly mutually fulfilling. We lay in a semi-naked state on the floor for what I can only conclude was a very long time, both of us wading through a quagmire of thoughts.

The irony wasn't lost on me.

How we, from an item, had suddenly become clandestine lovers, shacked up in some downtown hotel whilst she was somewhere else oblivious to the fact that she had also suffered the indignity of betrayal, as did I and her husband by her hand.

56 THE LAST SUPPER

About an hour or so later we were both showered and dressed for dinner.

By *dressed* I don't mean we donned a tux and sought out one of Atlanta's finest eateries; we simply were in trousers and shirts, and at a restaurant—as opposed to jeans and T-shirts and at one of the many fast-food joints dotted around the city.

This was supposed to be 'The Talk' dinner (as if we hadn't done enough of that already), the reason I had flown five thousand miles across the ocean for just two days.

But this was the part where we were supposed to work through what happened and perhaps even stray into discussing the events that had taken place earlier in the day in the hotel room, although I don't think either of us wanted to talk about that because to do so would be to complicate an already more than complex soap opera.

We ordered our food and sat in silence for a while. We seemed to do that a lot on that trip. I didn't really notice it at the time, but I guess it came with the need to be able to process the situation.

I felt remarkably calm but then I was somewhat exhausted from travel and tired from the emotional roller coaster that I had boarded from the moment I checked in at London's Heathrow Airport.

Why was I here? What was I hoping to achieve?

Closure?

It was more like ripping fresh stitches and gouging out a few other wounds whilst I was at it, including that of being with the only man I had ever loved, yet not being with him. It was like dining with the phantom of somebody I used to know.

There, in that foreign land, we were two people who had become the opposite of who we used be: apart yet always together. In Atlanta, we were together but would always be apart.

You would have thought I'd become somewhat adept with dealing with this state of affairs considering the disastrous two weeks we spent together in England. The two weeks during which M, unlike me, was fully aware of the fact that he had had unprotected sex with a woman God knows how many times and then found himself trapped in a beach apartment with me, a man, for two whole weeks and was unable to tell me, unable to confess to the fact that he was going to be a father.

M's going to be a father?

"Tony…"

And he, in true Southern-boy fashion would probably marry this woman as soon as her divorce from 'The Husband' became final.

And what about him—my counterpart of whom I knew nothing? How was he reacting to all of this? How did he react to the fact that his wife was carrying another man's child?

"Tony…"

Not so badly, it seemed, because M actually said, unless I was dreaming it, that such was this man's disinterest in his wife that M would actually call and speak to her on the phone while he sat in the very next room…

"Tony!"

I focussed on M's face and then his smile.

"What happened?"

"What do you mean?"

"You just disappeared again… Are you sure you're okay?"

"I'm fine," I said returning the smile.

"You sure? You looked like you totally zoned out there for a while."

I nodded. "I'm good. Just tired."

"I bet you are. Our server was trying to ask you what you wanted to drink, but you weren't answering so I just ordered a diet soda for you. Is that okay?"

"That's great," I nodded.

"Are you sure you're okay?" he asked again with yet another smile and a cock of the head.

That was my M—well, at least that was his voice speaking.

"Tell me about him," I said suddenly.

"Who?" he said, taking a sip from his glass of 7UP.

"Her husband."

His face darkened, then he set his glass down and sat back in his chair.

"Oh, you don't want to know about him."

"But I do. So he knows about you two?"

"Yeah, he knows."

"And?"

"And what?"

"What does he have to say on the matter?"

M shifted in his chair and feigned interest in the hustle and bustle of the busy room that I only then realised looked more like a traditional American diner than a conventional restaurant.

COMING UP FOR AIR

"Why are you so interested in him all of a sudden?" he asked, without looking at me.

"Well, it's only natural isn't it? He's the other party. The other side. The other," I formed speech marks with my fingers in the air, "wronged one."

"He's a nasty piece of work. That's all you need to know."

"Nasty how?"

"What is this?"

"I'm making conversation."

"But why the sudden interest in him?"

"I've already told you. It's only natural for me to wonder about him as he and I are both in the same boat. We've both been on the receiving end of this thing, remember?"

"Well, he terrifies…" he was going to say her name but instead said, "*her*, and has even threatened to kill her."

"Really? And how do you know all of this?"

"What do you mean?"

"How do you know all of this stuff about this man? Did she tell you?"

He didn't respond.

I waited a few seconds and then I added, "Has it occurred to you that everything you know about him, her, is only what she's told you? And that this is all distilled as she sees fit?"

Our food arrived much faster than I'd expected.

That or I kept falling through time slips.

We both exchanged pleasantries with the overfriendly and over-patronising waitress who eventually, after being convinced that there really was nothing else she could do for us, finally left our table.

"M…"

"I need to go to the bathroom," he said abruptly and left the table.

While he would never say so, it occurred to me that I may well have hit a nerve. Moreover, whilst it scared me, based only on hearsay from M and her, I realised that I had become more and more interested in actually talking to the other man. But the only question was how the hell would I go about that?

Not to mention how M would react to it.

Who cares?

This other man and I had something in common and the idea of being able to 'swap stories' with him appealed to me, not just because he was somebody who could undoubtedly empathise with how I was feeling, but also because he represented a sound and logical source for this book.

Oh yes, the book.

Not surprisingly, I hadn't managed to raise the subject with M. After all, unknown to him, that was one of my reasons for this dinner. I wanted us to work through whatever crap we needed to work through and I wanted to share with him the fact that I had already started writing a book about relationships and that this just happened to feature our own story.

Yet, I was fairly confident, it wouldn't matter how I pitched the book idea to him; he wasn't going to like it.

But again, did I care?

Of course I cared, as he seemed to care about me. How could I hurt him when he seemed genuinely sorry about what had happened and genuinely concerned for my well-being? Even at the dinner table just now, he had peered deep into my eyes and seemed worried about me.

And I was starting to feel bad about how I had behaved. Perhaps even ashamed. He was already going through a rough time. His whole world had already been turned upside down. The future, as he had planned it, had changed, and it must be a truly terrifying prospect for him to know that he was going to become financially and emotionally responsible for two other human beings.

So I found myself wrestling with the question of whether or not to tell him about the book—and indeed whether or not to even include us.

That was until I watched him re-emerge from the toilets (yes, if you're an American reader, I actually said that word, again), and that's when I spotted it—and I have to say, while it may not have been anywhere near the same alien feeling I had experienced in the hotel room just before I went on my demonic smashing frenzy (which, by the way, in case you're wondering, didn't result in any major damage warranting a charge to my card or a visit to the Emergency Room), I nonetheless felt a surge of rage.

M returned to the table to find me staring at him.

"Everything okay?" he asked, casually.

"Yes, everything's fine," I said, watching him. "Everything fine with you?"

"Yeah, I'm hungry! And the food's getting cold," he said, picking up his fork and digging into the plate of pasta carbonara in front of him.

After a few moments and mouthfuls, he glanced up to see me still staring at him. He nodded at my plate, "You not hungry?"

"No, I've just lost my appetite."

"What's wrong?"

Yeah, he was pretty familiar with my 'look'.

"I thought we had an agreement."

"About what?" he said, digging into more food.

"About communications whilst I was here."

"What?" he asked distractedly, as he ate more from his plate.

I smacked my hand on the table. It wasn't loud enough to draw the attention of others, but loud enough to snap him out of his hypnotic eating frenzy.

"I thought you agreed, as an express condition of my making this trip, that you would not communicate with her during my time here."

He finally stopped eating and looked up, perplexed. "We did. And I haven't."

"Really?"

"I swear," he said, earnestly.

"You swear?"

"I swear."

"So you haven't contacted her at all since I've been here?"

"Only to tell her that I'd be going dark this weekend because I was with family, all as we agreed."

"You're lying."

"What?"

"Don't even try to insult my intelligence, M. My God. And do you know, it's not even the fact that you did it—it's more the fact that it proves just how adept you've become at lying."

"I have no idea what you're talking about."

"No?"

"No," he said casually, turning his attention back to his food.

"So you didn't just use your phone in the toilet?"

He squinted at me incredulously, as if I'd just revealed I was a Martian.

I was tired with this game and shook my head in frustration, "You're such a bloody idiot. If you're going to sneak into the toilet to furtively read and send text messages without me knowing, you may well want to ensure you switch off your mobile phone's display before pushing it back into your pocket, you idiot! Because unlike jeans, the phone's display can be seen through the thin fabric of your bloody trousers."

His face instantly turned crimson.

Busted!

"I asked you for one thing, M. Just one. For you to not add insult to injury, to not disrespect me further while I was here."

He just looked at me, speechless. What could he say? He knew I was right.

"What is wrong with you, M? Since when did you become such an accomplished liar?"

"I'm sorry."

It's odd because, while I was angry that he'd lied, I also remember feeling sorry for him. He was stuck in this impossible situation; me on one side and her on the other. He wanted to please me—no, he needed to try and make amends with me—whilst, on the other hand, not having the courage to even tell her that he wouldn't be communicating this weekend.

"She'd think something was up," he volunteered, as if he had read my thoughts.

"So you're wilfully lying to her? You know there's avoiding sharing the truth and then there's perpetuating the lie. I'm writing about that very thing right now."

"You are?"

"Yes, I'm writing a book, M."

He seemed to rediscover his appetite then, but it was short-lived, "That's great. What's it about?"

"It's about us," I said, lingering long enough for the information to sink in, and I could tell it had when M's fork stopped midway on its journey to his mouth. But I continued as if I hadn't noticed, "Well, it's not exactly about us; it's about relationships, and I've already laid down thirty thousand…"

"Wait a minute, you're what? You're writing a book— *what*?"

His fork fell with a loud ding onto his plate.

"Why the hell would you do something like that?"

"I'm a writer. Writer's write," I said, suddenly finding interest in my food.

"Don't pull that shit with me," he said incredulously. He took a few seconds as the thought buried itself into his brain. "You want to ruin me, don't you?"

I laughed. "Stop being so melodramatic..."

"*I'm* being dramatic?"

"Yes, you are..."

"You're writing a fucking book about us and *I'm* being dramatic?"

"It's not just about us, M," I said with a very faint smile and secretly enjoying his discomfort. Yep, that same feeling I had back in England at the White Cliffs of Dover—remember that day?

I loved that feeling.

I sipped from my glass, as if the sweetened black liquid might wash away the bitterness that had just formed in my mouth.

"This is why I want to talk to her husband. I want to know the full story."

"I've told you the full story."

"No, you've told me what you've heard."

"Then talk to her directly."

"And get the same distilled crap that she's been feeding you? No way. I want to talk to him."

"Yeah, well, good luck with that," he said, dumping his napkin onto his unfinished plate.

He was clearly annoyed.

I wasn't immune to this, but waited a while before saying, "Look. I don't mean to upset you."

He sneered.

"I don't."

"It seems to me that's exactly what you're trying to do. It's clear you just want revenge, Tony, to make me pay for what happened."

I took umbrage. "Revenge? You think this book is about revenge? If I wanted revenge, I'd be having a conversation with her, or your family for that matter, or I would have followed through with talking to your former employer. We've been down that road, remember, and I seem to recall I was the one who came back from it."

"Yeah, you came back all right, Tony. You're writing a Goddamn book about it!"

"It's what I do, M. I write. This book isn't just about you, us; it's about everyone. Everyone and anyone who, at one stage or another in their life, has been hurt and survived to literally tell the tale."

"Fine. Just do it without talking to him."

"I can't do that."

"Why not?"

"Because he, like me, plays a crucial part in this. By speaking to him, I'd be giving this element of the story some balance."

"And what about her side of the story? Don't you want to get some balance from her?"

"Yeah, like you'd actually want me to and I'd even consider talking to her. Besides, why would I need to? You seem to be doing a pretty good job as her mouthpiece."

"Oh, I see; not so interested in balance now."

"I'm interested in fairness, M."

"Really? You want fair. How about the fact that this guy hardly shows his wife any affection? He's either away on deployment or spending his time with his weapon collection rather than being with his own wife."

"Did she tell you that too?"

"Yeah, along with the fact she's been in deep depression for months over the fact that she would never have kids. Something that she's dreamed about ever since she was a kid herself."

I don't think he planned to share that last bit so willingly.

"What was that?"

He looked away.

"M?"

Eventually, he turned back to me. "He can't have kids. He's sterile, firing blanks. She only found that out after they were married. He didn't tell her."

"Did he know?"

"He knew."

"And who told you that? Oh no, let me guess."

I took some time to absorb what I'd just learned. Was that true? Was 'The Husband' truly unable to conceive? Is that why she found M? Did she, in the most disgusting kind of way, just use him as a sperm donor? Is that why she had unprotected sex with him not long after meeting him?

The thought was horrifying to me.

"M?"

"Don't bother…"

"But you must have thought about it, surely?"

"She's not like that."

"Really? M…"

"I don't want to talk about it."

"But…"

"Tony, I swear to God." He gave me his eyes.

I knew better than to press the subject further. But I'd be lying if I said that this story hadn't suddenly taken an even more interesting turn.

"I want to talk to him, M," I said with determination.

He met my gaze. He knew what that look meant.

"You'll never find him," he said with such smug obstinacy I wanted to punch him.

But said with a smile, "I will if you help me."

"And cut my own throat? Forget it."

"You know what I'm like, M. You know when I set my mind to something I don't stop."

"Yeah. As I said, good luck with that."

We spent the rest of the evening trying to dodge that particular subject, as well as the book, and any other unexploded emotional ordinance that might end up inflicting serious injury on one or both of us. I guess that was most likely because we felt that we each had had our say, and it was clear that no further amount of talking was going to change the situation we both found ourselves in.

As M explained during the course of the evening, his life had changed beyond anything he had planned or could ever have imagined. In the Marine Corps he had often thought about what life would be like as a civilian, what he'd do for a career, but he hadn't thought beyond the grant he would receive to go back to college.

Now, he had no choice but to get a job and had, as we already know, applied to become a police officer because reality had bitten; he was going to become a father, and this was a prospect that terrified more than excited him. Not because M didn't want to be a father, but more because he no longer had a say in the matter, nor did he feel as if he had a handle on his future that was now governed by a helpless entity whom he was yet to meet, not to mention the fact that he shared this fate with some girl he barely knew. Somebody who was headstrong and was going to give birth to his child regardless. M knew that he must either make it work or spend the rest of his days negotiating visitation.

Like it or not, this was his future—and it was a future that did not include me or any of the detail of the past six years. In fact, in M's mind, the only way his future would work is if his past was buried deep in some hole at the far centre of the earth.

Now, whilst he may not necessarily have used those words (some were actually worse), the finality of the situation was not lost on me. And I guess this was exactly what M meant about closure.

Closure for him meant burying me and the past—hence why the idea of a book immortalising exactly what had happened between us was the last thing he wanted to hear about.

Nonetheless, I'm here today telling you this story, not out of malice, but out of the commitment I have to each and every one of those people who have willingly given of their time and generously laid bare their own truths to contribute to this book. I'd be a hypocrite if I chose to keep secret the very thing I purport to be some kind of an authority on. How could I possibly suggest anything to you that I had not already experienced myself?

And you may well think that M has very good reason for not wanting this book to see the light of day. I understood those reasons that night, and it was then that I came to the conclusion that if I did sit here writing about it, I'd make a point of not identifying the man whom I believe is now the father to two children and a husband to a woman who changed my life.

We returned to the hotel room that night and it was as if we both knew that this would most likely be the last time we'd ever see each other and/or the last time we'd ever be together with the same intimacy that had become the bedrock of our relationship.

This time our encounter was about love. It felt like one last bittersweet goodbye.

Later, I lay with his arms around me for what seemed like hours, listening to the hypnotic sound of his breathing as he slept, deeply. I still remember how his warm breath felt on the side of my face and, somewhat bizarrely, how it still smelt of peppermint toothpaste.

This used to be my favourite time with him. Just lying in his embrace, stroking the small hairs on his strong forearm as they enveloped me in a blissful sense of security.

Only this time nothing was real. This was all an artificial recreation, like some futuristic hologram.

It was an illusion.

I don't know how many times I kissed his arms and his hands that night, as if they were the appendages of some beatified saint with the power to grant me a miracle.

Give me back the one man I ever truly loved. The man who now had given himself to somebody else.

And it was this that played in my mind over and over and over. Each time I tried to pacify my unrequited heart with the new lesson I had learned that very day in that very room, to accept the things that I could not change, the other side of me kept rebelling against it.

I couldn't accept that I was losing him. I couldn't and I didn't want to.

I couldn't.

But I had to.

Suddenly, his arms no longer felt snug and warm around me, but instead they felt hot and suffocating.

I shifted slightly, kicked off the sheets, which caused him to murmur in his sleep, twist away from me and onto his side, giving me his back.

I sat up and swung my legs over the side of the bed. I then looked over my shoulder at his naked form in the filtered orange glow of city outside.

The city that, like me, was still awake.

Cars, buses, people, all still moving to the rhythm of life. And I wondered if there was anybody else out there who, at 1:03 in the morning, was feeling the same way as me; suddenly dry-mouthed, clammy from cold perspiration and overcome with sickness.

What's happening to me?

I left the bed and made for the bathroom where I splashed water onto my face.

It felt as if I couldn't breathe.

I drank thirstily from the running tap and then just stood in the gloom, leaning on the sink as if to steady myself from falling over.

I must have stayed there for over five minutes, staring at my shadow in the mirror as water dripped from my skin like the rivulets of dissonant thoughts streaming through my mind. What I was thinking about I couldn't really tell you, but what I do know is that they were the same thoughts that had plagued me ever since the day I learned the truth.

I felt so tired.

But it wasn't physical; it was more a mental exhaustion from the recurring theme in my head, in my life, and I felt dizzy from being on this same old merry-go-round for months now.

I just wanted to get off.

If I was a heavy drinker, there's no doubt that in that very moment I would have drained anything with an alcohol percentage strong enough to drown the life out of those demons that kept reminding me I was no longer loved.

Not by him.

And that's when I slowly picked my way through the shadows to the sofa and collapsed in a heap of tears.

And by *tears* I mean I wept—no, I *sobbed*—for what must have been an hour!

It felt as if I was going through my own exorcism, only rather than vomit the remains of my shattered heart, I cried away any hopes and/or dreams that I may have subconsciously harboured that M would ever come back to me.

It's over, Tony.

And each time I believed I was done crying my river, another wave would wash over me.

Enough already.

But I couldn't stop.

And that's when I heard a voice calling to me out of the darkness.

It was M.

Unlike that time back in England, he didn't just sleep through it.

He was aware.

"Come back to bed," he said.

But I couldn't. I just started blubbering even louder.

That was until I felt his hand touch my shoulder and, before I knew it, I was being escorted back to bed where he folded me into his arms once more.

"It's going to be okay," he whispered, reassuringly. "It's going to be okay."

He kept repeating those words until one of us, I can't remember who, finally yielded to emotional exhaustion, but not before, out of the myriad of thoughts swimming through my mind, one drifted to the fore; I'd be going home soon, yet suddenly, and strangely, I realised that I was actually looking forward to it.

But that couldn't be. Could it?

57 THE OTHER MAN

M accused me of judging his relationship with her without knowing the truth of the situation. He told me that I should establish facts before formulating my own biased opinion.

And I agreed. I should.

In my opinion, there was only one way to really find out the truth behind their affair. What drove her to so callously cheat on her husband? Was their marriage already coming to an end? Was he a bad husband? Did she not love him anymore, or did she simply not care?

I needed to talk to the other man; I needed to talk to her husband.

And so my search began.

When M challenged me in Atlanta, I vowed to do everything in my power to track down the man that I had heard so much about, but of whom I knew nothing. Not even his name.

So how exactly did I plan to do that?

I had no idea.

Camp Lejeune was a big place with literally thousands of marines. I had no way of tracking down just one specific one, and even then, how on earth would I approach this man? There was no telling what his reaction would be to me contacting him.

In the meantime, M was not at all happy with my newfound project, and I have to wonder, in hindsight, if in some kind of bizarre way, it was this that incentivised me along with this dismissive throwaway line, *"Yeah, well good luck finding him."*

He knew full well that I knew nothing about this man. Yet, he also knew that I'm famed for my tenacity when I set my mind to something.

M had no doubt that I wouldn't stop, and I would expect that this was something that chilled him; if I ever spoke to the husband, it would be a disaster for his relationship with her for I obviously knew things that could bring their whole affair to a screeching halt, and he couldn't risk that.

And so my search began.

But a few months went by without much luck, since I had very little to go on, at least in the conventional sense.

Then, I spotted and ad on an American website and I decided to give that a try.

According to the bio on their homepage, these guys had been going many years and they purported to be able to find anybody.

All I needed was a credit card and the will—apparently they had the way.

Now, remember, I had little or no clues to give these people. All I knew is that this man was a marine, and that she worked in a gym near the base, which is how she and M met in the first place.

Yes, the irony wasn't lost on me. Remember Jamie and Jane, the couple where the girlfriend didn't trust her boyfriend working at the gym? Maybe she had a point after all.

So, we had hardly any leads to go on. There was just one obvious way I could see us getting anywhere close to the information we needed, but that was the kind of stuff you only see in movies, wasn't it?

Apparently not.

Now the responsible me can't tell you exactly how, but what I can tell you is that they managed to track down her cell phone number and from that her home address and telephone number.

Finally, as summer handed over to autumn, I was in possession of the contact information I needed to reach *the other man*.

His actual name was Kevin (not changed, but you don't need to know the surname).

Now, what to do with it?

I couldn't just ring up the guy, introduce myself and ask if he was the man with the wife who was cheating on him, could I? And what if the information was erroneous? It's not like I had some way of verifying that what I had been given was accurate.

What if I contacted this man and asked him if his wife was having an affair and it turned out to be a case of mistaken identity?

But it couldn't be, I reasoned.

Was he a sergeant in the Marine Corps?

Check.

Was he stationed at Camp Lejeune?

Check.

Did he have a wife who went by her name and did she work at a gym?

Check.

Check.

I was still terrified.

I finally had the information that it had taken months to obtain, but now I couldn't use it.

Although, as it turns out, I didn't need to; my trusty investigators informed me that they had made their own enquiries. This man wasn't even in the United States at the time; he was actually on deployment and on a ship somewhere in the Pacific Ocean.

This was hopeless.

Or maybe not.

I had a brainwave.

What if I didn't try to call him at all? What if I sent him a note, one that contained hardly any information but just a contact number? Explain that I needed to talk to him and then give him the option of contacting me.

And that's exactly what I did.

I wrote a brief note to Kevin, told him that I was a writer from England and that I would really love the opportunity to speak with him if at all possible, and included my contact details.

Then I sent it all to him in a FedEx package.

Days turned into weeks.

Nothing.

The trail had gone cold once more.

Meanwhile, my interviews continued at the American Air Force bases here in Southern England, as did the rest of my research.

Oddly, M kept in fairly regular contact via emails although these had now become somewhat strained and, overall, dysfunctional, since we'd often end up right back at the counterproductive subject of recriminations.

Regardless, for me it felt good to stay connected to him. I'd realise later that the only reason he was staying in touch was just some cynical way of keeping tabs on my progress making contact with the husband, which, by this time, had become the focus of some healthy competition between us.

Of course, when I told M that I had a name and asked him to validate it, he stopped short of confirming or denying; he just kept telling me that I was "wasting my time."

I kept reiterating that even if the information I had was wrong, I wouldn't stop.

He knew this.

And so, in October of 2003, he sent me an email explaining that he no longer wanted any bitterness between us; that, from now on, he just wanted the two of us to get along the best way we could, without any arguments or recriminations—those days were over.

From now on, M was going to be an open book to me: anything I wanted to know, all I had to do was ask, and this included details about the other man.

Needless to say, I was both pleasantly surprised and wary of M's newfound peace offering. Why would he be so willing to give me such potentially damaging details? It didn't make any sense—or did it?

Suddenly, like a ray of sunlight on a cloudy day, the truth was illuminated; M's cynical attempt at reconciliation was nothing more than an offensive move at damage limitation. I told him so during a phone call.

"That was a very smart move," I said with a smile.

"What do you mean?"

"You know exactly what I mean, M. This whole thing about being an open book; you know exactly what you're doing."

"I do?"

"Yes, you do. You're not stupid. You know me. You know that, come hell or high water, now that I have decided to find this guy, there is nothing that is going to stop me from achieving that goal. So, you thought that the only way to avoid any fallout from the two of us meeting was to personally provide me with the details; you know that if you give me the husband's details, I could never betray that confidence and tell him about us."

There was a few seconds of cell phone static silence. I could almost hear M's smile at the other end of the phone.

Finally he said, "No, I told you; I am just sick of this atmosphere between us."

I scoffed. "Yeah, right." Then I added, "There is no way I am going to get that information from you, M."

"Well, that's your choice." The words were casual. "I just told you how I want it to be with us from now on. Whether or not you take me up on that offer is entirely your decision."

I knew I was being handled. I knew that M was teasing me with the information, and I was determined not to play his game.

Yet, on the other hand, I was also curious. What if I accepted the information from M right now?

The search, the wondering would be over.

I thought about this for a few seconds. It would also be nice to test M's new pledge to total transparency and openness. Would he really jeopardise his relationship with her and keep to his word?

"Are you still there?" he asked.

"Yeah, I'm here."

"What you thinking?"

"What's his name?" The words jumped out of my mouth before I even had the chance to think about it.

"Justin," was the immediate reply.

"Justin?"

M laughed as if it were a silly name, "Yeah, Justin."

Justin, not Kevin? Is he telling the truth?

I was momentarily struck dumb. This man, the other man, my counterpart, his name was Justin. No longer *the husband,* or *the other man,* but Justin; the man who had undoubtedly been through the same heartache as me, and some.

"Wow, Justin," I whispered.

"Yeah, Justin."

"I like that name. What's he like?"

"I don't know. I didn't make a point of getting to know him."

"No, I guess not," I found myself mumbling somewhat bitterly. "You must have an idea about what he is like from her though, surely."

"Yeah, I told you, he's a psycho. I mean the man collects guns and knives, for Christ's sake."

"Didn't put you off sniffing around his wife though."

"I didn't know he did at the time. I just know he's a psycho. You know, he threatened to stab her in the belly when she told him about us."

"Really? Well, I dare say that if your wife was shagging someone else, you might have reacted the same way. We all say crazy stuff like that when we're angry."

"Yeah, but I wouldn't put it past this guy. You never know what these rednecks are capable of."

"Redneck? He's a redneck then?"

"Not far from it. You wouldn't like him."

"Why not?"

"I don't know. He just isn't your type."

"M, I don't want to sleep with the guy; I want to talk to him."

"That's what I mean. The guy's retarded."

I paused here.

Justin. The name was whirling around in my brain. I was excited yet terrified. Finally, there was somebody who could truly empathise with how I was feeling. The only other person to have been wronged in this whole sordid situation.

"What's his last name?" I found myself asking.

Again, without hesitating, he told me.

Wow, he really did mean it. M was prepared to tell me anything I wanted to know about this man. Justin was the husband, the faceless, nameless man whom I had heard of and thought about so many times during the past five months.

And, as much as I was aware of the commitment my words were making, I could not resist asking M for Justin's telephone number.

I wrote it down on a Post-it note, and that is how, an hour later, I found himself admiring the yellow piece of paper adhered to the leather of the passenger seat of my car.

I was stuck in traffic; Friday evenings in Cambridge are notoriously bad.

I drummed my fingers on the steering wheel, turned up the music and glanced across; the fluorescent yellow was like a beacon in the gloom of the car. I looked at my cell phone, at the motionless traffic in front of me and then at the Post-it note once more.

It was early evening in England, which would make it early afternoon on the East Coast; Justin would be at work.

As the traffic inched forward, so did my curiosity.

I snatched the Post-it note from its place on the seat and dialled the number.

Within seconds, there was ringing on the line.

So quickly?

I didn't know what to expect—maybe an answering machine or something—but instead I heard a man's voice say, "Hello?"

I hung up as my heart leapt into my throat.

He was home. Justin was home!

The cars in front of me had moved so I hastily threw the car into gear and caught up.

The butterflies fluttered around my belly as the thoughts flapped across my mind to the rhythm of my pounding heart.

I considered whether or not to call back. Was I really up to talking to this guy right there and then, in the car, whilst stuck in traffic? What if the man started bombarding me with questions about M? And what if I forgot myself and revealed something I shouldn't?

Like me, Justin had been wronged by M and therefore, by default, he was his arch enemy. By talking to Justin, I risked revealing damaging information about my relationship with M to the one person in the world who would not hesitate to use it.

There was no doubt in my mind that Justin would call his wife and tell her everything.

This could be disastrous for M.

I truly understood the meaning of a cold sweat that day. It's weird because I knew the whole thing was so damn dangerous yet I couldn't step away from it.

Furthermore, like it or not, I was committed to M's plan; to betray him with the very information that he had provided was unthinkable.

Yet the bloody traffic had stopped again, giving me even more time to think.

I looked at my phone, at the red tail lights in front of me, and then at the phone once more.

I hesitated.

Then I picked the bloody thing up.

I concluded that I would be careful, that I wouldn't say much; I'd simply establish contact with Justin. Sound him out. The man may even tell me to go kill myself for all I knew.

Regardless, I had to know.

I pressed redial. There was ringing on the line.

"Hello?"

"Justin?"

"Yeah."

"Justin, you don't know me. My name's Tony. I am calling from England. Does the name M mean anything to you?"

A pause. Then, "Um, yeah."

"Justin, I really understand if you don't want to talk about this. If you don't, please say so and I will just hang up, but, well..."

Oh God, this is beyond crazy!

I hesitated because I knew I had to be really careful with my words "...Well, I used to know M very well; see, he was going out with my friend, Cathy...

What the hell was I saying...

"...before he started seeing your wife. Justin, I would really like to talk to you some more about this. Do you think that would be okay? I mean, I understand if you would rather not..."

"No, that's cool. It's been a few months and I'm pretty much over it now anyway," he said somewhat pragmatically.

And so the conversation continued well into the evening, with a marathon five-hour transatlantic telephone conversation in which we discussed recent events along with likes and dislikes. But, most importantly, he had felt comfortable enough, at some stage, to tell me that no matter what happened from thereon, he hoped that we had both at least found friendship.

Of course, the statement meant a lot to me. I had lived for months with M's betrayal and the subsequent isolating feelings that that kind of grief can inflict. In this case, the only other person to be able to truly empathise was this man, and I was delighted.

Yet also absolutely petrified.

I lost count of the amount of times I'd wondered what exactly this phone call would be like and what kind of reaction it would invoke in both of us. I'd imagined scenes of yelling, swearing and being told, in no uncertain terms, to never call again.

The reality was quite different.

Although clearly still affected by his wife's infidelity, Justin had tried his best to move on. And, indeed, for a few months now, had been dating a girl from California.

I naturally stopped short of lecturing him as to whether or not it was wise for him to be dating so soon!

Most importantly, this US marine sergeant was far from the redneck described by M. Instead, he impressed on me a certain warmth seldom found in most men, especially a leatherneck. In fact, he came across as a calm, perhaps somewhat naïve, individual who enjoyed playing chess and recounting nostalgic stories of back home Wisconsin where, in the summer, the landscape was green and the sky was blue, but not that faded blue—real clean blue (his words).

He told me how much he missed home and his family, now more than ever, and then went on to describe why, despite this, he had reenlisted in the Marine Corps; it was because of his wife.

Justin wanted his wife to be able to keep up college where she was studying law, and the only way she could do that was if he stayed in the Marine Corps thus retaining a wage and taking advantage of the benefits that the military provided. This included on-base accommodation at a fraction of the cost of civilian housing.

There was sadness in his voice when he added, with a sigh, that it had all been for nothing.

I hadn't known the man very long, but I have to say I had grown a natural and obvious affinity with him.

After all, we'd both received the raw end of M's and her deal.

So what really happened between Justin and his wife?

All will be revealed in due course, I promise.

58 THE MISSION

In the meantime, I'd made good progress with my interviews in England and so I decided to return to Oklahoma once more—but this time it wasn't for work; it was for fun. I visited Rosa and some of the friends I'd met during the summer at Starbucks.

And it was during this time that I received some information from American Military Command about the scope of this book.

At the time of my original application, the only military branch that had agreed to meet with me was the American Air Force. However, I had shared that I couldn't see any reason why this couldn't be extended to other branches of the military.

And it seemed that the powers that be agreed.

I was asked which other branches I would like to involve in the project. The choices were Army, Navy and Marine Corps.

I bet you can't guess which one I opted for.

That's right, the Navy.

Okay, I'm kidding. Yes, it was the Marine Corps.

I also had a choice of bases.

I asked which were the largest, and the two that were presented to me were on opposites sides of the United States: Camp Pendleton, on the West Coast, and Camp Lejeune on the East Coast.

Camp Lejeune?

Seriously?

Could it really be that, after all this time, all of these years of hearing about that place, fate would really present me with the opportunity to step foot there?

It seemed so.

Contrary to what you might think, my answer was not immediate for I was all too aware of what a potential visit there might entail.

Was I curious?

Absolutely.

Was I stupid?

I'm not going to answer that.

But, regardless of my feelings on the matter, it was fairly apparent to me which of the two bases I should select.

Firstly, Camp Lejeune was on the East Coast, which meant it was much closer in flying time.

Secondly, Justin was there. If I visited Lejeune, I would actually get to meet the man with whom I had so much in common.

Thirdly, I was curious about visiting M's old stomping ground. That's pretty much where he grew up, trained. The place where he was stationed for most of the years we were together. That somewhat mythical place that had controlled my love life for so many years, approving and not approving leave so that M and I could be together.

And then, there was this guy…

It was late December 2003.

It was actually the early hours of the morning after my birthday. In fact, I think I'd only just fallen asleep when the buzzing of my mobile phone woke me.

I didn't even bother looking at the number, I just answered.

"Hello?"

"Hello? Is this Tony?"

It was an American voice. One I did not recognise.

"Um, yes. Who's this?"

"Yeah, Tony, my name is Kevin. You sent me a FedEx asking me to call this number. I'm sorry it's a few months late, but I've been on deployment."

What?! I'd forgotten about him!

Suddenly, I was wide awake.

"Kevin?"

"Yeah."

"You're Kevin?"

"Last time I checked."

"Oh, Kevin, thank you so much for calling me but, um, I'm so sorry; when I sent you that FedEx I wasn't sure if you were the person I was looking for. That's why it seems a bit cryptic and doesn't contain much information. I didn't want to alarm you unnecessarily."

"I see."

"Kevin, as it turns out, you're not the man I've been trying to track down. We've actually found him already. And that's a good thing, by the way! Yes, I'm sorry to say, you don't have a long-lost English uncle or anything."

He laughed.

We talked for about an hour, during which I gave Kevin a summarised version of the story of how there'd obviously been a case of mistaken identity and how close he had come to receiving information from me about his wife that would have been completely false (as far as I knew).

I apologised profusely for any misunderstanding and for wasting his time. I even offered to pay for the phone call.

But he was great.

In fact, he showed a healthy interest in the story I was writing and he made me promise that if I was ever in the area I'd be sure to stop by for a coffee.

Funny you should say that.

Fate.

The chances of me getting the contact details of a sergeant in the Marine Corps were high—but the chances of that someone being stationed at Camp Lejeune?

One who happened to be on deployment at the very time that M had told me who Justin was?

I guess so.

One who had a wife who worked in a gym, and who went by the same name as her?

Um, well...

Things could have turned out much differently had I contacted Kevin and asked if he knew someone by the name of M and if he knew that this man was having a relationship with his wife!

That said, there was one minor detail that my so-called investigators missed; Kevin had two children.

As we know, Justin had none.

Life often has a way of speaking even when we're not listening.

I was listening though.

To me, the fact that I now knew two men from Camp Lejeune whom I was very curious about meeting meant that a trip there versus Camp Pendleton, on the opposite side of the country, made sense.

I called the next day and told my contact at the Pentagon that I would be interested in talking to personnel from Camp Lejeune.

And that's how, days later, an email was sent, on behalf of all section chiefs, to all those who were interested in collaborating on this book.

Many responded.

Now I was committed.

Furthermore, given that, in 2003, operations were still in full swing in Iraq, deployments were ongoing.

I was told that if I wanted to meet with all of my interviewees, then I'd need to return to the United States early in the January of 2004 to conduct my interviews; otherwise I ran the risk of most of them being deployed before I got there.

Yep, I was committed all right.

I booked tickets to fly into Raleigh, North Carolina for the second time in my life.

Only this time, everything would be different, much more different.

59 GHOST TOWN

When I stepped out of the car rental office, a small cabin on the site of the parking lot, it was as if I had stepped onto Mars; the world was filtered red as the sun slowly slid behind one of the nearby buildings.

It had been a long flight and, in typical American style, Homeland Security had me do everything but give blood.

I was already exhausted and I hadn't even started my journey south yet.

So, after finalising more bureaucracy with the rental company, I finally got to sit behind the controls of the Chevrolet TrailBlazer.

I have to say, it wasn't one of the most luxurious cars I have ever driven in the USA and the controls felt alien to me, not least because the steering wheel was on the opposite side of the car.

This always took some getting used to.

I sat behind the wheel for a second to consider; I was back in Raleigh, North Carolina, only this time my state of mind was completely different to the last time I was here.

I sighed and started the engine.

Somehow, I managed to navigate my way out of the city and eventually join I40 to begin my three-hour journey south to Jacksonville, North Carolina.

It was Sunday and the roads weren't particularly busy. Of course, this contributed to the peculiar sense of isolation that was starting to drown me, like a tank slowly filling with water. I tried to shrug it off. I'd been travelling to the US for years with no problems—why should this journey feel any different?

But it did, and a sense of being so far from home began to make its presence felt.

I felt tired, but my mind was buzzing with thoughts. I was excited, yet apprehensive, happy, but very sad.

What the hell am I doing here? What am I hoping to find?

The sun finally handed day over to dusk and, oddly, I welcomed the fact that the rest of my journey would take place under the cover of darkness. I guess I felt this way partly because I'd be travelling incognito for my secret assignment and partly because it would mean I'd be shielded from viewing my surroundings, which, from what I could barely make out, was primarily a baron, endless expanse of flat agricultural fields decorated with the occasional wooden house complete with porch and screen doors.

I stopped at a STOP sign despite the fact that the crossing was deserted and I don't think there was another car for miles. I guess it was just instinct.

I paused there for a short while as thoughts blinked through my mind like the red light mounted on a nearby water tower.

I must be on the very road that M would have travelled many times to meet me, including our rendezvous at the beginning of the year.

This was insane.

Why would I want to travel to the very place M had been stationed for many years, the very place the (now ex) Marine eventually betrayed me for another? And why the hell would I travel here alone?

It was this thought that overwhelmed me with an immense sense of sadness, and urged me to turn back, dump what appeared to be a relic from some transport museum and board the earliest flight home.

I didn't belong here.

And I seriously considered turning around on that very crossing. But told myself that this journey wasn't about M and it wasn't about me. It was about this book. I was committed and I had a job to do, so I needed to pull myself together and do it.

My decision was expedited by the sound of a loud car horn behind me. It made me jump and reminded me how easy it was to submit to road rage.

So not everybody has been abducted by aliens then?

I pushed on the accelerator and watched the headlights behind me turn and disappear in a different direction leaving me alone once more as I made my way towards the place that I would eventually dub *Ghost Town.*

Jacksonville, North Carolina is the fourteenth largest city in the State with an approximate population of seventy thousand. Demographically, it is also the youngest, with an average age of twenty-two, a figure attributed to the large military presence.

When I finally reached the city, I found myself squinting at the brightness of the place, which reminded me a bit of Vegas, but not because of the colour and razzmatazz—more because I had emerged from the dark wilderness that surrounds it like a gothic fort.

The main drag, or at least that's how I referred to the main artery that ran the length of the city, was very busy with cars that I presume actually knew where they were going. I, on the other hand, had no clue. I was simply driving and trying my best not to collide with another vehicle.

The road was more like the English equivalent of a dual carriageway (pretty much a highway) so there wasn't much time to pause and get my bearings and, back then, there was no satellite navigation to help me, just a map on my laptop computer, and there wasn't much chance of me pausing to browse that either, so I just followed the flow of cars in the hope that I'd eventually find a turning, a parking lot or somewhere where I'd be able to catch my breath.

I must have followed the road for something like five miles before the traffic started to thin and I was delighted since this meant that the stress of avoiding a collision diminished and, with a bit of luck, I may even find a place to pull over.

However, I realised, much to my dismay, that the reason the traffic was thinning was because I was actually heading out of town. This was evidenced by the fact that the so-called highway signs mounted over the road were demanding that I get in lane for *Camp Lejeune!*

The highway led directly there? Surely not.

It did.

In fact, it led directly to the gates of the Marine Corps base outside of which were some very serious-looking, heavily armed marines.

Great.

I was an Englishman lost in a foreign land and, any second now, I and my relic of a car would most probably have semi-automatic weapons drawn on us for approaching a military installation without the proper paperwork (remember, this was 2004 and paranoia was rightfully still prevalent in the US after 9/11).

And that's when I spotted the lay-by and the sign that read *Visitors' Center.* I swerved (yes it was pretty much a swerve and not a turn) into the centre and pulled up in a parking space.

Thank God!

I killed the engine and listened to it tick over as I gathered my thoughts. I knew I wouldn't be able to sit there long—not just because I ran the risk of being interrogated by marines, but also because it was January and the temperature had dropped to near zero.

What are you doing here?

Yes; that same question that I had been asking myself ever since I left the plane. I should have gone to Pendleton,

California. I had no business being in the City of Ghosts. I was tired, hungry, lost and alone.

Home was five thousand miles away. The weight of that reality pressed on me like a giant boulder.

I needed to hear a familiar voice.

I picked up my mobile phone and dialled my friend, Jake.

"Hey."

I loved his soothing Californian tone.

"Hey. I'm here."

"Where, in the States?"

"Yeah."

"Well, come on over. I'll invite Jack (Daniels) round with some ice, and we'll have a party."

"No, I'm here in the U.S., but nowhere near you. I'm in North Carolina, Camp Lejeune, to be precise."

"Oh."

Jake knew of my travel plans, but he was just being his usual self.

"So, how are you finding it?" he asked.

Suddenly, I felt emotional.

In order to dispel the overwhelming urge to start blubbering, I stepped out into the freezing cold air that, whilst chilling, smelt fresh and felt good.

"Grim," I responded as I watched the fog of my breath dissipate just like my resolve to see this journey to its conclusion. I looked around; the closed visitors' centre, the guards at the gate, the one road out of here, and trees, lots and lots of trees.

"To be honest, I'm lost," I said.

"You're lost? You didn't arrange to meet anybody there?"

"No. Well, I'm not meeting anybody until tomorrow morning, but this place is much bigger than I thought. Somehow, and I don't know how, I've ended up right outside the gates of Camp Lejeune."

"Well, that's what happens when you decide to play Christopher Columbus."

"Right. Thanks for that."

"You're welcome. But you can quit your bitchin'. You're just meters away from thousands of marines. Thought you'd be happy."

I smiled. This was classic Jake. Totally unrattled by anything. And oddly, whilst unhelpful, I found his humour somewhat reassuring.

I looked over at the guards at the gate again, whose suspicion had obviously been aroused since one of them left the warm confines of the guard hut and was pacing outside, seemingly in an effort to stay warm, whilst glancing in my direction from time to time.

"Yes, that's the irony. Thousands of marines and yet I don't know a single one of..."

I trailed off there because that's when it occurred to me. There was somebody I could call. Somebody who might come and rescue me.

"You still there?" Jake asked.

"Yes, but I've had an idea."

"You have? Good for you."

"I'll call you later."

"Okay. Take it easy."

I hung up and then dialled another number.

Justin answered immediately, and although I didn't really know anything about the man, it felt good to hear a friendly and somewhat familiar voice.

I explained my predicament to him and he, in true marine style, told me to hold tight and that he'd be right over. I hung up with an immense sense of relief. If anything, I knew Justin should be able to help me get to my hotel, at least for a hot shower and some food, and that was good enough for me.

Now it was my turn to pace to keep warm as the other marine guard, about a hundred feet from me, had left the hut and was chatting to his buddy; both were glancing in my direction now.

Great.

Luckily, just a few minutes went by before I saw a set of headlamps approach from within the base; another four-by-four Trailblazer.

I walked over as its passenger window buzzed down.

"Justin?" I asked, looking at a tall, fairly heavyset man with babylike features and crew cut.

"Yeah," he smiled.

"Thank you so much for coming out."

"Oh, no problem. Where are you heading?"

I gave him the name of the hotel and the road.

"I know where that is," he said excitedly, flashing a pair of grey eyes. "Follow me!"

That one line felt so bloody good to hear and I wasted no time resuming my seat behind the controls of the car, now with a new sense of purpose.

Before long, we were back in Jacksonville traffic, only this time I had some idea of where I was going.

I followed Justin to my hotel car park where I thanked him. During the discussion, he asked if I had eaten yet.

Music to my ears.

I locked my car and climbed into his.

The restaurant seemed more like the canteen on the set of the Twilight Zone.

It was packed with men who, whilst facially different, all sported the same Marine Corps brand; hair shaved to the scalp at the sides with no more than an inch on top. Most were dressed in their 'Cammies' (camouflage uniform).

Talk about surreal.

Once again, I was reminded of the movie, *Invasion of The Body Snatchers*, since even my dinner companion was wearing the same look.

"Where you gonna' run? Where you gonna' hide? You can't, cos' there's no one like you?"

"Are you okay?"

It took me a few seconds to stop gawping at the rest of the room and eventually focus on the man in front of me; it was Justin, 'The husband', the somewhat mythical being whom I had thought about for months, yet never dreamt of actually meeting, until now.

"I'm much better, thank you," I said with a smile as I observed him.

In the dim light of the restaurant, I could see that his eyes were not grey, but brown, and he had mousy brown hair (what was left of it).

If he was at all fazed by my arrival, he did not show it. He ordered his meal and chatted to me as if we were old pals. Topics ranged from what it was like being in the Marine Corps at Camp Lejeune, to how long it took for me to finally track him down, and, eventually, his wife.

He explained that he had spoken to her by phone only a few days ago, and that she was due to give birth imminently.

I couldn't help but be surprised by his somewhat relaxed demeanour in the face of that fact.

These two are still talking to each other?

Although who was I to judge?

One of the first things I did upon arriving in Raleigh was call M and leave a message on his voicemail. Ironically, it was his birthday, the 11th January, so I thought this would be the perfect time to call and wish him a happy day. (Of course, that was my spin on it, I'm sure he couldn't have cared less whether or not he'd heard from me).

Naturally, I also took the opportunity to let him know that I was in the United States once more and that I was on my way to Camp Lejeune to meet the husband of the woman he was with.

Remember that now famous chapter about the games we play?

Precisely.

Although, I don't know if my action was to solicit some kind of reaction from him and give myself some power, I still, to this day, believe that it was more due to the fact that I was actually in the City of Ghosts.

I felt lonely.

I tried to talk myself out of making the call, but couldn't help it. Ever since that plane abandoned me at Raleigh, his presence started to haunt me.

Yet, the former marine didn't pick up my call. Oddly, according to Justin, nor did his wife.

And that was when, in a perverse twist of fate, as I was forking some greasy battered chicken into my mouth, Justin's phone rang.

"Speak of the devil. It's her," he said casually, as he attempted to fish the mobile phone from his pocket.

I stopped chewing as if I'd just realised I was standing in the road and a truck was on a head-on collision with me, but I managed to ask, "How do you know?"

"It's her ringtone," he said with a smile.

I put my fork down, suddenly losing my formerly voracious appetite.

Now, I'm a fairly (okay, *very*) open-minded guy, but there was something about her calling her husband in my presence that disturbed me. Perhaps not as much as the candid way in which the two of them were chatting on the phone. You would have thought that everything we'd discussed so far was a figment of my imagination, like some unbelievable plot that I would never consider including in one of my books because, well, it's unbelievable!

She, his wife, M's lover (or whatever she could be classed as at the time) apologised for not being in touch with him sooner, and then went on to explain that she'd been busy giving birth to M's baby! She added that she was now at home and they were both fine. Oh, and somewhere along the way she also managed to impart the baby boy's weight.

I gagged when he relayed this to me.

The man had just finished telling me the story of how, while he was away, M and she had snuck back to the house with a trailer and emptied it of most of its contents

I had no idea that he and his unfaithful wife were still enjoying this kind of relationship. I guess that, somewhere along the way, I forgot to ask him if they were still on good speaking terms.

I felt sick.

I had overshared information with Justin, and if he was still speaking to his wife there was a good chance he'd pass it all along, maybe even editorialise a few things along the way.

What had I done?

That's when my phone beeped. It was a voicemail message from M who was returning my call so I left the table and went outside to call him back.

This time he answered.

He confirmed that he had indeed driven two hours to see his newborn son. The former marine's life had well and truly changed.

For me, this was yet another swipe of the eraser on a way of life that was not meant to be, and that was a hideous moment. Just hearing him speak those words crushed me with such an immense sense of finality it brought tears to my eyes. It seemed that everybody but me in this scenario was clinging on to somebody else and that I was the only one who could feel life, as I wanted it to be, well and truly slipping between my fingers.

And it's as I stood outside that restaurant, in the freezing cold, pacing to keep myself warm and holding the mobile phone to my ear, that I so desperately wished for M to offer me some comfort. I would have settled for any word, any trace of the affection that he once felt for me. After all, I had made the journey here, the place where I had met and lost him; surely he would be sensitive to that, surely he would offer me some scrap of sympathy.

Damn it, he owed me that!

Instead, "What? You've travelled all the way down there to stir trouble with her husband and you expect me to feel sorry for you?"

It seemed that, in true M style, he was not going to give. Not even now.

In his mind, I was in Jacksonville for one reason alone, and that was to cause more trouble for him. And no matter what I said, that was the only way he could see it.

Well, what did I expect? Once again, I'd projected onto him what I wanted him to feel and not necessarily what would be natural for most people to actually feel in his situation.

We argued.

The conversation ended.

So, this is the part where you're thinking what the hell was I thinking? Why on earth would anyone put themselves in such a situation, and how could anyone be that naïve?

Well, that would be a good question—and the honest answer is, "I don't know."

I guess my journey to Camp Lejeune started out with the objective to perform research and conduct interviews for this book, but I dare say it was also motivated by other obvious factors, including the (some would say misguided) idea that going there, facing my demons would have been medicine for the greater good.

How's that working out for you so far?

The thing is, it had been over seven months since the breakup and I was expecting all of this icky, vulnerable, ridiculous, empty, rejected, unloved, uncared for, ugly feeling to have dissipated by now.

I believed I was much stronger than that.

Anybody who knows me knows that I'm a pragmatist who doesn't stand on ceremony. Someone who deals with things effectively and moves on to the next. I'm not some simpering, lovesick puppy who can't function without a love in his life.

I wanted it to stop.

So I believed that, perhaps, if I grinned and bared the salt on that wound for a short period of time, then I'd be much better for it in the long run.

Right?

Okay, maybe not.

The bottom line is that, no matter how much we want something, it doesn't necessarily make it so, and there's no amount of projection, manoeuvring, orchestration, cajoling that is going to make somebody feel about you the same way you feel about them.

When it's over, it's over.

On the other hand, would it have hurt M to offer me one positive, anything that would release me from the black cloying negativity that had become the very frigid air around me?

Everything about that place was negative, but it was only when I was actually on the ground that I realised; I'd parachuted myself straight into depression central, otherwise known as the Demon's Lair, and there were absolutely no emotional allies to rescue me.

I was alone and weary.

And the battle had only just begun.

I couldn't refuse Justin's invite to go back to his house for tea, for two reasons; I could, quite frankly, do with the company and I was bloody curious. I wanted to see the 'marital' home, the place where neighbours had reported to Justin the presence of a stranger and his car whilst he was away on duty.

Was the stranger M?

There were conflicting reports. At first, in Justin's rage, he believed this to be so, but later, upon reflection and more discussion, it seemed that the stranger could well have been another man.

The truth is unknown.

The full moon was bright and eerie in a star-filled sky when we arrived on base.

The house was one of many identical white wooden bungalows.

Outside, next door was only a few feet away. In their garden an old bicycle lay on the floor, and a rusty car sat next to it. Opposite them, more houses lined the road, each a clone of the next, each with its own sense of poverty.

Justin jumped out of the truck and made his way up to the screen door which he held open as I surveyed the area and imagined what it would have been like a few months ago when M would drive here to visit her, the very same time he and I were in a relationship.

It was a strange, somewhat surreal moment, accentuated by the eerie silence of the place.

I turned to face the wooden steps that led up to the front door. I could see Justin standing there and, for a moment, the world felt as if it had stopped; the hum of traffic in the distance disappeared, replaced by the percussion of my heart, and I wondered did anybody even live in any of these other houses or was this actually some secret ghost town of the type used to test atomic bombs? Were Justin and I the only two humans left in the entire world, ghosts trapped between this dimension and the next, condemned to spend the rest of eternity in the purgatory of a broken heart?

"You okay?" his voice interrupted as he stood with his hand on the screen door.

I nodded, but I wasn't okay. There was nothing about me that was okay. I wanted to go home. Actually, I didn't; I wanted to throw up right there and then on the mud patch that I'm presuming was supposed to be a front lawn.

I wanted to steal Justin's car and make my way to the airport, gun the engine and speed away from that place before it was too late, before I was trapped there forever.

Stay away from the house, Tony. Don't go in there, for nothing good will come of it.

"Tony?" Justin repeated.

"Yeah," I nodded and smiled as I gingerly made my way forward.

Stay out!

The marine acknowledged with his own nod of the head and entered the house, leaving me to stare at the screen door as it smacked loudly behind him in the still of the night.

True to the exterior, the house was very small with a kitchen, a lounge area, one bedroom and bathroom. It was poorly furnished (as his wife had taken all of the furniture) and there was a strange odour in the air, the source of which was revealed to me when I felt something brush against my leg; the cat walked by to its litter tray where it casually began to dig for hidden treasure.

"He's one thing that she decided not to take with her," Justin said and then added, "Tea?"

I looked at the Marine and then at the kitchen sink that was piled with dirty dishes covered in murky brown liquid.

I nodded, reluctantly, as I took in the rest of the house and imagined what it must have been like for her living here, and for M to visit.

"Can I have a look around?" I found myself asking as Justin plucked some cups from the fetid water and began to wash them.

"Sure."

I slowly moved into the lounge where the cartoon channel was beaming animation to an empty room. I manoeuvred my way around an open ironing board adorned by a Marine Corps camouflage uniform.

"They're great," Justin said, coming into the room. "They're our new uniforms. You can fold them up, crumple them into a ball and the creases just shake out."

He demonstrated for me as if I were interested in making a purchase.

"Wow, that's really cool," I said with all the enthusiasm I could muster.

My head was numb with thoughts.

I was here.

Finally, I was seeing the inside of *her* home, the place where she and M had been together, the place where his son was most likely conceived—and it was as that thought came to me that the tour ended, rather appropriately, in the master bedroom.

Mercifully, Justin shattered the moment by picking up a state-of-the-art paintball gun.

"Guess how much it cost?" he asked.

I shook my head.

"Nearly eight hundred dollars," he said excitedly.

"Wow," I murmured again. I then politely proceeded to make a fuss of the gun and remarked on how unusual I found it that a marine would want to play with such a thing considering he handled real weapons on a daily basis.

He just shrugged and smiled. "It's fun, but it hurts like hell," he added, taking a few moments to admire his purchase and then announcing abruptly that the tea must be ready.

We returned to the kitchen where I finished off making the beverage as Justin picked up the unusually furry cat and began to pet it.

Over tea, we talked about the past and the future.

In any other circumstances, I would say that I could understand her urgency to leave Marine Corps accommodation for a new way of life. But the reality is that she hadn't moved on to another man, a civilian, a rich man, anybody who could offer her a different future, but another marine, albeit one who had already left the Corps.

Could it be that she romanticised about living with M outside of the military?

Then again, the Marine Corps way of life wasn't exactly alien to her; her father was a marine and her sister was married to a marine. Allegedly, and somewhat ironically, she too cheated on her husband whilst he was on a tour of duty in Japan.

It seems cheating is something that may well run in the family.

Justin and I talked some more, but it seemed that by the time our tea ended, so had our conversation. Besides, I was weary and the marine sergeant had an early start in the morning.

We stepped back into the freezing night where the moon was still busy making shadows of the world.

As we drove off base, I remember seeing a tall building in the distance from which a red light flashed, reminding me of a flickering hard drive, as if it was the hard drive in my head flickering as thoughts went through my mind.

I was worn out.

I'd been assaulted by legions of demons ever since setting foot on American soil and I was battle-weary.

Oddly, I felt as if I had accomplished something that day. I wasn't sure what exactly, but something—if only the fact that I had swallowed the proverbial medicine and it had indeed left a bitter taste, but I trusted it would make me feel better, eventually.

In the meantime, I waved goodbye to Justin and watched as his truck drove away from me and out of the hotel's parking lot.

I wearily brushed my teeth and climbed into bed where tears and exhaustion finally drove me into a restless sleep.

60 WHY?

I learned a lot during my dinner and the subsequent house tour with Justin.

Also, the conversation I had with M in Atlanta about how the other man's side of the story would undoubtedly add ballast to my understanding of the whole situation proved to be true.

It was March 2003 and the US/UK had declared war on the leader of Iraq, Saddam Hussein.

America was building up its presence in the Gulf and part of that presence was made up of a Marine Corps contingent from Camp Lejeune.

Justin's unit was one of many to be deployed to the region.

It was a terrifying and somewhat stressful time for the twenty-six-year-old marine who, up until then, had never even been out of the country—made worse by the idea of being in a foreign land, thousands of miles from home and the wife he loved, with the distinct prospect of never coming back.

He dealt with his imminent departure in the only way he knew how; he withdrew into himself, became isolated, spending hours alone by the beach wondering about the future and whether his wife might be better off without him.

He considered sharing his thoughts with her, but he didn't know how. Yes, they'd always been close, but these feelings, well, they were different, somehow deeper, more intimate, and more terrifying.

He thought about talking to his family, but they were far away, up north, and already harbouring their own anxieties about him going to war. He couldn't and didn't want to make them worry any more than they already were.

He didn't have any close friends since he'd alienated most of these when he married her. His only buddies were fellow marines, and, like him, they too were wrestling with their own fears.

So this was it; basic training, field ops, endless warfare video games, and weekends paintballing had let to this—war. And he was terrified.

These feeling were amplified on D-day when Justin and hundreds of other marines kissed goodbye to family and loved ones and boarded respective crafts to the unknown.

For her, it had been a surreal time, learning that her husband was about to be deployed to fight a war in a place she hadn't even heard of until recently. During this time, she had watched him become a stranger before her very eyes, yet there was nothing she could do; Justin wouldn't talk to her.

Like many men, he was incapable of sharing his feelings. She was disconnected from him, alone, and so she sought solace in the one place she could; work.

As you already know, work was in one of the many local health and fitness clubs in the Jacksonville area. There were literally hundreds of young men, marines, who frequented these establishments and it didn't take her long to befriend one of the many, who went by the name of M.

Although not stationed at Camp Lejeune at the time, M was a Marine Corps Sergeant on a training course there.

Meanwhile, Justin had arrived in Iraq. His unit was put to work immediately, taking part in many of the campaigns that the US military hoped would bring an expedient end to the war. As usual, the marines were on the front line of each conflict, and it was during this time that Justin saw many of his comrades, some of them younger than him, lose their lives, and he imagined just how devastating it must have been for their families back home to learn of their deaths.

Justin was still young but, in comparison to these boys, well, they hadn't, in his opinion, even had a chance to live their lives. And it was then that he made a vow; he promised himself that if he ever got back from the war alive, he would live his life differently; he would treat every day as if it were his last.

And as soon as he got the chance, he sat down and wrote a letter to his wife expressing his feelings like he never had before.

Meanwhile, her relationship with the new marine in town was going well. He would visit the gym on a regular basis and, as the television screens above them beamed pictures of the conflict in Iraq, the handsome young man listened patiently as she shared her grief of a husband who showed her no affection and from whom she had not heard a word in weeks.

M, in turn, explained how he too was feeling isolated from the person he had been committed to for the past six years, this person being Cathy, his girlfriend from England, who couldn't possibly love him, because in all the time they had been together, she had never visited.

And so the two found solace in each other.

She even went as far as sharing what she referred to as her maternal heartache, this being the fact that her husband was impotent and that it hurt her to think that she would never be able to have children and she wanted them so badly.

M felt for her, and what began as idle chit-chat became the emotional unburdening of two individuals. Each believed that they had found someone who could empathise with their personal turmoil. Thus, as is always the case when we share our intimate feelings with another human being, a bonding took place.

What neither knew about the other was that, despite the war, Justin's letters, although infrequent, *were* getting through, whilst M wasn't *really* a lonely soul since he spoke with me nearly every night by video chat, phone or both.

Neither of them were really neglected people, but simply partners craving physical gratification.

And so their conversations progressed from meetings at her work to those in a more intimate setting until, a few weeks after they had met, and whilst Justin and his comrades battled their way to the heart of Baghdad, she was welcoming M into her bed for unprotected sex.

The rest, as you have already read, is history.

That was April 2003, just weeks before M was due to visit me in England for those fateful two weeks.

61 SEMPER FIDELIS
(ALWAYS FAITHFUL)

I couldn't decide if the marines guarding the gates of Camp Lejeune looked more or less intimidating in the cold light of day as I pulled up outside of the visitors' centre, which I could now see was a small, unassuming and somewhat functional building.

I parked in the same place I did when I first arrived here. Only today, I had a meeter and greeter. She was a pretty, petite blonde who wore her Marine Corps uniform as well as she did her smile—and that was before I'd even left the car.

Captain Theresa Ovalle's greeting felt as warm as the early morning sun. There was something about this lady that instantly put me at ease. I remembered having felt that ever since the Pentagon assigned her to this project as 'Lejeune Military Liaison' and we shared our first transatlantic telephone conversation in the build-up to my arrival here.

Whether or not this was down to the fact that she was a genuinely friendly person or the fact that she was, ultimately, a public relations officer, I didn't particularly care; her enthusiasm for the project made me feel good and it was a most welcome reminder that I was there for a reason beyond my own personal melodrama.

"It's good to meet you at last, captain," I said with a big smile, and I genuinely meant it—I'd felt nothing but isolation since arriving in that place and now it seemed as if I had an ally.

"Likewise, Tony."

The captain asked about my journey, where I was staying and began briefing me on the day ahead before taking me into the visitors' centre and arranging for my pass.

Unlike my experience with the American Air Force, the Marine Corps believed in a different approach to security, which meant that, rather than have a meet and greet each day, I could come and go as I pleased for the week with my own vehicle pass, that—as both the corporal behind the desk and the captain reminded me—should be displayed on my windshield at all times.

I have to say I was somewhat surprised by the casualness with which the transaction was conducted considering the omnipresent terror risk at the time. I was, however, most grateful as this process was a refreshing contrast to the Air Force that appeared to begrudge issuing me with a single day pass.

I already felt welcome and found myself smiling (something I hadn't done much of since arriving the night before).

That was until we left the safety of the visitors' centre and emerged into a particularly hot morning sun that well illuminated the guards, as well as the gates to a place that had been talked about and described to me for years, but one I had never actually been to, until now.

Alas, neither the friendly welcome, nor the full might of the Marine Corps could save me from the demons that lurked inside my head. Worse still, it was something I could not discuss with anybody here, beyond Justin.

And that's when I starting thinking about it. What if I actually told the captain about my affinity with the marines and Camp Lejeune? She seemed friendly enough.

It was as I considered this that she interrupted my thoughts and told me to follow her with my vehicle.

I complied, and within seconds, thanks to my newly acquired sticker, I was being ushered beyond the barrier in unique Marine Corps style; not a smile, not a slouch, just a robotic hand gesture.

The base had a speed limit of thirty miles an hour and it was like entering another town with an array of buildings, giant masts and shopping malls cross-stitched with a network of roads that led off into infinity.

I remember driving for what seemed like ten minutes—but couldn't have been more than five—but somewhat oddly enjoying every second of it as I rolled by this other world that had played such a prominent role in my life.

I thought about M and how he must have made this very same drive for all those years, including the year before when we met in Raleigh. Now, everything had changed; he had been discharged from the Marine Corps and was desperately seeking to bury his time here, and what had taken place between us, deep in the past.

We arrived at the Public Affairs building. I parked the SUV in the nearest available space and then stepped out in the crisp fresh air, which brought with it a sense of nervousness.

This was it.

This was the part where I had to step up and deliver.

The captain had arranged back-to-back meetings with marines willing to share their personal stories with me and, not unlike in England, these meetings promised to be full-on, intensive and relentless with only the occasional break and, of course, lunch.

It was time to forget any soul-searching and focus on the job.

The public affairs office was bright and open plan. There were about fifteen marines in here, all of whom were in their 'cammies' and none of whom were wearing their covers (caps) indoors.

Many of them smiled at me as I made my way down the corridor.

I could get used to this kind of welcome. Furthermore, I was starting to see marines for exactly who they were: ordinary men and women doing, more than often, an extraordinary job, and not the caricatured, unfeeling killing machines portrayed in the media.

After introducing me to one of her colleagues, the captain led me back through the public affairs office and up two flights of stairs, past pictures of smiling men and women in uniform, to a spacious, sunlit room with a large boardroom table in the centre.

"This is your office for the week," the captain declared cheerfully. "Is this going to be okay?"

I nodded, with a smile, "Absolutely."

"Great. Just pull the door shut behind you when you're done for the day," she added with yet another of her big smiles, and then she left me to settle in, with, much to my relief, the promise of coffee in the not-too-distant future.

The room was very functional, as are most government buildings. The walls were grey and the table, which I think was just two desks pushed together, was scuffed brown and was adorned by grey plastic chairs.

I sat to one side of the desk, plugged in my laptop and positioned my cursor next to the name of my first interview of the day.

And I waited.

And that's when they came to me, drifting up from somewhere outside; voices.

I stood up and looked out of the window to see a small parking lot, my car and then, beyond that, a green where a group of marines, about fifteen of them, dressed in grey sweatpants and olive T-shirts, were jogging on the spot. In front of them, another marine was yelling something that elicited a collective response from the others.

I watched, somewhat transfixed by the vapour of their breaths in the crisp morning sun and I imagined that this may well be 'The Yard' that M had referred to on numerous occasions. I speculated, if I could rewind time whilst still standing in this very spot, would I see M appear on that green with his military crew and his bulging biceps? And if he saw me standing here, watching, would he wave at me and smile or look away in disgust?

I didn't have time to consider the response for the sound of the opening door startled me.

"Tony?"

As with the Air Force, I had been caught off guard. I was expecting to meet a corporal but, unbeknownst to me, an exchange had taken place.

"Tony, Colonel Talleri," the man vice-gripped my hand with his and then shook it.

The colonel (or Pete) was six-foot-something, in his forties with short dark hair and a weathered complexion. He looked immaculate in his uniform and was every bit the commander: tall, imposing, confident with an element of danger. There was no doubt in my mind that this man was more than capable of making decisions about the lives of men more easily than I could decide on what to wear for the day.

Conversely, he also did a very good job of dispelling the 'leatherneck' stereotype (tough, brash, with little time for pleasantries) because, in the colonel's own words, "Marines don't fight words; they fight the enemy, who is more than often trained to kill them."

"I hope you don't mind me switching interviews," the colonel said.

"Oh no, of course not," I mumbled as I tried desperately to find my place on my laptop.

"Just, I know there are going to be a lot of people who will use these interviews as an opportunity to bitch about their jobs and I just wanted to give you an early perspective."

I wasn't quite sure how to respond to that, since during my time researching this book I'd met with all kinds of people who often used these interviews as a free counselling session. There really wasn't that much I had not already heard and thus I didn't expect much to surprise me.

But then, I don't think this is what the colonel meant.

As you'll read, the American military, not unlike most governments, is committed to supporting and preserving both the sanctity and the integrity of marriage since, as you have noticed, that very institution appears to be struggling to retain its relevance in today's modern world.

More so in the military.

Many believe that the best and most effective way to salvage the importance of commitment to one another and to inspire honour, respect and decency in the intercourse of intimate relationships is for a return back to basic traditional family values.

The Pentagon's Media Affairs Department, others who have collaborated on this book, and certainly I am hoping that by reading it, if anything, you might gain some insight, some perspective on the complexities of human relationships and that you may try to avoid the emotional traps that many have fallen foul of or, at the bare minimum, limit the impact that they'll have on you and those around you.

You're not alone. All of this has happened before, it's happening now, and it will continue to happen in the future. But nobody, but you, has the power to change the past for a better future.

(As much as that may sound like a campaign slogan).

This is why, there's no doubt in my mind that the reason why the Colonel switched my schedule is because, in true leadership style, he wanted my interviews to start with a positive and constructive element rather than get bogged down in an unproductive bitch-fest about the job rather than the message.

I was under no illusion about my own mission parameters. At least I conveyed this—albeit covertly, because you and I both know one of the other reasons I chose to immerse myself in that place.

But I wasn't about to share that with the colonel even though the thought had crossed my mind.

I started by asking Pete about his own marriage to his wife, Debbie. I asked if, in his opinion, it was a good marriage. I always like asking that question of anybody in a relationship because, to me, the reply tells so much of the person I am asking and of the truth, since different people will respond in different ways.

There are those who will answer immediately and confidently with words like, "Of course. My wife (or husband) is my best friend. We do everything together and we rarely argue," and they tack a beaming smile on the end of it.

Then there are those who will actually take a few seconds to consider the question (and the potential motive behind it) and then proceed to tell me what I dub the safe answer; pause, force a smile and then say something non-committal like, "Well, you know, we have our ups and downs like most people." (My favourite as it doesn't actually answer the question.)

Then there are those who immediately launch into how their partner drives them mad for one reason or the other and are happy to tell you everything.

And those who say, "Marriage isn't perfect, but then life isn't," and maybe tack a question onto the back of it like, "Is it?" and wait for my reply.

So, take a few seconds to consider, which one of these do *you* think the colonel was?

We'll come back to that.

One of the reasons I chose to interview military personnel about their relationships is I thought that if anybody knew the stresses and strains of managing a successful relationship and/or marriage, then it had to be these people who not only spend much of their time dealing with the horrors of the world, but actually find themselves deployed there, all too often spending weeks, months and even years separated from their partners.

How the hell do you manage to nurture a successful relationship when you aren't even there?

A lot of people who actually *live together* struggle to keep it together, so how on earth do you manage a long-distance partnership?

Well, I could easily have jumped in here and said that I managed but, based on what you've read, you'd be forgiven for thinking that I was hardly a poster boy.

Of course, I could argue that there were various extraordinary elements to my relationship, the main one being that M appeared to embark on it as something that had the longevity of his Marine Corps contract, effectively dooming us before the relationship had even begun. That said, we did manage to make it work quite successfully for nearly six years. How did we manage to do that?

Well, it was all down to circumstance.

Whilst we both would have clearly preferred spending more time together, we were both also very busy with our professions. That doesn't mean that we didn't miss each other. Of course we did. But we were both busy people who were working hard on their careers—and not having the need to come home to a partner who needed our energy and our attention meant that we could focus all of our attention on being successful in our respective fields.

Yes, I know that sounds awfully pragmatic, and if I were reading this at the time I'd probably have punched someone, but the reality remains the same. We both hated the distance but, at the same time, it was the distance that enabled us to excel at what we did.

Now, I'm not suggesting for a second that long-distance relationships are great because you get to be selfish and not have to worry about the daily fluctuations of your partner's mood swings—but what I *am* saying is that time apart, time alone can often be a force for good because it inevitably allows the opportunity to consider a full perspective of all of the things that are important to us, and not just one thing, which, as you most likely will have discovered by now, can be all-consuming.

Now, that theory may well work in a situation where two people are committed to, love and care about each other. But, as is often the case with relationships, add some variables and the outcome is all too often different.

A good example of this is the affair between M and her.

Justin, her husband, had been gone but weeks, and he wasn't just busy living his life on some other sunny part of the planet; he was actually there fighting for his life and the 'freedom' of many, including her, when she chose to cheat on him.

But is this indicative of this particular marriage or indicative in general of marriage in the military?

What happened between her and Justin had nothing to do with the fact that he was in the Marine Corps (apart from the fact that his job facilitated the inevitable, but then that could happen with any profession) and everything do with this particular relationship, which was obviously struggling well before Justin was ever deployed to Iraq. This is evidenced by the fact that she had unprotected sex with a complete stranger just weeks after her husband was deployed.

If their marriage was sound, that could never have happened because, bottom line—and women might appreciate this just a smidgeon more than men—when you are truly devoted to one person, the idea of being with somebody else simply doesn't compute. Well, the idea certainly might, but the actuality doesn't, because the person we're with, to use another cliché, completes us.

Contrary to what M believed, you cannot take away that which does not wish to be parted.

Ultimately, in relationships where there is real love and commitment from both parties, it won't matter where one partner is because the other is always going to miss them and dream about wanting them home rather than how to plug up, even temporarily, the vacuum their loved one has left behind.

Why?

Well, that is simply what love is all about. Isn't it?

"Until death do us part."

There was a reason that phrase was constructed.

In the Marine Corps, the Air Force, and I'd expect most military branches and some professions, this could not be truer, only I have come to learn that the scenarios as depicted above can manifest themselves in other, more extreme cases also.

Most marines leave boot camp at an average age of eighteen. From there, they are dispatched, most of the time, across the country to a base to finish their training. This means leaving their family, friends and any life as they know it for a place like Camp Lejeune, the hub of Jacksonville, North Carolina.

Jacksonville is an isolating place where local amenities appear to be geared more towards family life with the odd establishment catering to the stereotypical requirements of the young.

I know how I felt when I first arrived there. Admittedly, I had other demons to contend with, but imagine being a very young man, dispatched to the middle of nowhere.

There isn't much on offer.

So, often bored and lonely, our marines turn to the next natural pastime: dating. Well, there is a small snag there too; the ratio of males to females in Jacksonville is staggering, something like ten to four. With those odds, you can only imagine how difficult it is for a young lad to find a partner.

On the flip side, you can imagine how easy it would be for a woman, even one already in a relationship or marriage, to find a job in public a place, such as a gym, like her, and watch the men come and go, as if they were on a conveyor belt.

All they have to do is choose.

And choose they do.

I certainly heard some disturbing stories during my time in Jacksonville but none as worrying as the so-called *Virgin Wives*.

I had my doubts when I was first told the story, but I then went on to hear it from two other separate sources and couldn't help but wonder what the hell goes through the minds of some.

There's nowt so queer as folk.

Apparently, there are some women in Jacksonville who enjoy nothing more than to frequent Jacksonville bars that they know will have a high clientele of marines (not so difficult when you consider the location) whilst their husbands are deployed abroad.

Nothing too odd about that.

No, the scary version is that these women are actually sure to remove their wedding bands in a premeditated move to appear single so as to project their availability to unsuspecting marines.

Lieutenant Wilson was such a marine.

At just twenty-six years of age, he became a victim of such a scam. Luckily, he discovered the truth before any damage was done.

For an officer, being caught in an ex-marital triangle would be considered *Conduct Unbecoming* and would have a serious adverse effect on his career since, as an officer, he is required to conduct himself in an 'appropriate' manner both on *and* off duty.

An officer is a leader and as such he is expected to lead by example.

The thing is, officers aren't the only marines to be duped. Sometimes, young marines still in training are tricked into thinking that they've actually met a nice lady, but it eventually turns out that she's a not-so-nice adulterer who happened to forget her wedding band along with her vows before leaving home for the evening.

It's for this reason that marines are advised to exercise caution when off duty.

Seriously?

Telling raging young hormones to exercise caution in the face of casual sex or the prospect of a permanent coupling is like telling a bull not to charge the red rag. So I wanted to know if there was any lenience in the face of such devious female tactics.

I asked Colonel Talleri if, when administering a punishment to a marine, he would ever take into account such extenuating circumstances. He told me that there are often mitigating circumstances, but that the law, the rule of conduct in the Marine Corps, was there for a purpose and that it should be abided by.

Marines are required to consider every aspect of their behaviour, both on and off duty and are fully aware that their actions may invoke disciplinary proceedings. There is no 'second' way or chance, for that matter.

Extramarital activities are simply unacceptable.

When Justin found out about M and her, she told him that M had already left the Marine Corps; she knew that otherwise Justin could *name* M and have him *written up* for *Conduct Unbecoming*.

It was only through his conversation with me that Justin learned that, in the three months he believed M discharged from the marines, he was actually still stationed at a different base in Georgia.

So what's with these devious tactics?

If these women know that marines can get into trouble, why do they behave in such a way?

I don't think there's any specific reason beyond an everyday selfish need to be 'seen' through fresh eyes, to be wooed, seduced and courted as if it were the first time.

Let's take an extreme case of everyday marriage.

A wife has been married to her husband for several years. The honeymoon period is well and truly over, and the only *excitement* is dealing with the intricacies of sharing a life with each other.

One if not both spouses have become complacent.

In this case, let's assume that the husband is becoming that way; he doesn't consider his wife anymore, certainly not as he did when they first started dating. He doesn't call her as often as he used to, doesn't bring her flowers anymore, and generally feels like he has nothing much to prove in the bedroom either.

Now, remove that husband and surround that lady with literally *hundreds* of other strapping young men who, in a place like Jacksonville, will most likely have been deprived of female intimacy for quite some time. Young men who are lonely and eager to shed that stigma that comes with not having a girlfriend and not 'getting laid' (at least not regularly)—and what do you get?

A bunch of men in their prime who are more than eager to please, in many ways.

Suddenly, neglected wife, whose husband hardly notices her, is being noticed by a literal platoon of young fit men who, each time they see her, behave as if she's the most beautiful girl in the world, and it feels damn good after years of so-called 'attention deficit'.

And so there's an awakening.

Not unlike thousands of frustrated housewives around the world who wake up one day and realise that, despite kids, running a home, age and the general stresses of everyday life, they're still a woman with oodles of sexuality, a woman who refuses to be consigned to the scrapheap of the mundane, the formulaic and the complacent, a woman who, not unlike the proverbial midlife-crisis male, who is eager to prove to herself (and her closest friends) that she's still got it.

For her, it's dating time all over again—only now, it has the added bonus of it being with a much younger man, which we know carries its own kudos. It's furtive, it's fresh, and it's exciting once more.

Who wouldn't literally be seduced by that?

Why would you want a diet of tired vegetables when you can have steak every day, flame-grilled to your own personal taste?

Well, because of one minor detail: you're married!

Everybody likes to feel special (yes, even those who pretend they don't care). We can all do with a bit of flattery here and there and, quite frankly, there's absolutely nothing wrong with that. The problem is when flattery becomes seduction and seduction becomes adultery and, in the case of the marines, when adultery becomes a serious black mark against your career.

But hold up a cotton-picking minute!

This all sounds so awful. This reads like all of the women in Jacksonville are a bunch of nymphomaniac, frustrated housewives who have no respect for their husbands, their marriages and, some would say, themselves.

Surely that can't be the case, can it?

Well, I didn't interview all of the women in Jacksonville but I'm prepared to put money on the fact that the majority are more than happy being married to and committed to their husbands, and that I am clearly talking about the minority, right?

Right?

In America, the latest demographics show that fifty per cent of marriages end in divorce, compared to forty-two per cent in the UK.

And the reasons for these divorces?

(Here comes the hit parade.)

At number 5, it's the one everybody's talking about, 'Infidelity'.

At number 4, that old classic of 'No longer attracted to one another'.

At number 3, it's the one you love to hate, 'Abuse'.

At number 2, it's everybody's favourite, 'Finances'.

And, at number 1, the reason most couples cite as grounds for divorce is 'Poor Communication'!

Sound familiar?

What I couldn't establish is exactly what proportion of the above figures could actually be attributed to military divorces and how these compared to militarily marriages as a whole.

However, according to a USA Today article published on their website in December 2011; military divorces were at their highest level yet. They even 'edged out' civilian divorces.

But why is that?

To know the answer, we'd have to look at some of the basics, as one would any crime, only this happens to be of the heart.

Motive and opportunity.

Well, we can quite easily deal with opportunity, because that's easy; a high proportion of military personnel spend their careers being deployed to various places around the world. These tours of duty can last months, which means that whilst the husband (or wife) is away, the mouse has ample opportunity to play.

I should point out here that I'm not just talking about the men and women left behind; I am also talking about those who are actually on tour (of duty).

Whilst I'm not going to linger on specifics, I can tell you that I've heard various somewhat shocking stories, both in the United States Air Force and the Marine Corps detailing a whole raft of activities that actually take place under the cover of one motto: "What goes TDY stays TDY", roughly translated as, "what happens on temporary duty, stays on temporary duty".

I'll leave you to draw your own conclusion as to what exactly is meant by that.

So why do many military relationships either end in infidelity, divorce, or both?

I have a pretty good theory. Let's take your typical young marine.

Why did he get involved in this relationship in the first place?

Why does any single man dress to impress and hit the town? Generally, there's one main reason: he's looking for 'fun'.

Fair enough.

But what about him, the lonely one, the guy who thinks he wants more than just a hook-up or one-night stand, the one who perhaps isn't as aesthetically blessed as his counterparts. He had to work hard to catch his proverbial fish, the one that with just one kiss transformed herself into his lifelong fantasy. What if he doesn't want to let her go again? What if he wants to tag her and make her exclusively his forever? There's only one way to do that, right?

Marriage.

During my time at Camp Lejeune, I heard about a few marital successes, but many horror stories. Granted that most of those who volunteered to speak to me will most likely have assumed that I'd probably only be interested in sensational and dramatic stories (and they'd have a point).

However, regardless of the story, when I sifted through all of the research I conducted and interviews I hosted, there was one common and unequivocal theme that remained constant, no matter whom I spoke with; marines at Camp Lejeune are lonely and isolated.

The single ones in the barracks on base more so, since home to them is being penned in cramped quarters, often with bunk beds, a few electrical accessories, a massive lack of privacy, invasive weekly room inspections as well as the stigma of actually being in the barracks

And there's only one way to break out of there.

Get married.

Married marines can qualify, if available, for on-base accommodation; hence Justin and her who had secured such a facility. These wooden places may be relatively small and may be subject to some of the base's terms of use, such as how often the lawn should be mowed, but they are homes, shared with a woman, not a bunch of men.

Most marines dream of such an arrangement and, once tasted, never wish to go back—one of the reasons Justin didn't want his superiors to know that he was still living in his on-base marital home despite the fact that his wife had left many months before. He told me that, if discovered, he would be subjected to disciplinary action and, at best, would lose his home.

But it was a risk he was willing to take.

So what if married marines don't want to live on base? What if they want to live in a house off base like other mere mortals?

Well, there's limited on-base accommodation anyway so they're actually encouraged to take benefits and live off base, provided they can afford it.

Not unlike the Air Force, the Marine Corps provides an extra allowance for partners who are married. Basically, it encourages its marines to tie the knot—although, strictly speaking, I don't think this is actually their intention; I think the idea is to encourage them to commit and stay married, not to just 'get married'.

But this is where the problem lies. Many marines marry simply to collect the allowance.

It is called a contract marriage. Not unlike 'green card marriages', marines will often get hitched just to collect a few hundred dollars extra a month, share decent on-base housing, where possible, but, most importantly, get out of the stigma of the barracks.

And thus the sanctity of marriage is diluted, with vows replaced by business clauses.

For male marines, they were going to have a roommate anyway and she may as well be female with potential benefits whilst enabling them to live either off base or away from the barracks in relative comfort and without the added pressure of weekly inspections.

Marines, not unlike most other military branches, live in a world where they are often required to 'hurry up and wait' about almost every aspect of their career. They will go for weeks with the same humdrum of PT (physical training), the occasional field ops and their daily duties but occasionally, especially in the new world of terrorism, they can receive orders and are required to leave within days.

It's a frenetic environment with most often hoping they don't receive orders when they least expect or want them, such as on special occasions that most of us take for granted.

Yes, that's what they signed up for, but remember, they're still people, and the simple fact remains that it is always difficult to plan your life when you don't even know where you will be from one day to the next.

I know I couldn't live with that uncertainty.

Because of the fluidity of their jobs, marines don't often have time to consider the long-term consequences of their actions, will often act on the spur of the moment and hope for the best.

That's why marriage is seen as a sensible solution to an unpredictable problem.

If a marine is married, he or she can rest assured that, whatever happens, their partner will be taken care of in terms of accommodation, marital allowances and, most importantly, GI insurance.

"If something should happen to me, you'll be taken care of."

Basically, he or she can't be there, but the money, the benefits may go some way to helping that.

This is absolutely true.

The civilian world isn't much different. Most partners will want to make sure that if anything happens to them, their significant other will financially be taken care of.

But in the civilian world, we are most likely talking about two people who have dated for some time, were actually engaged in a relationship and subsequently married. We are not talking about two people who may have met and known each other but for a few weeks.

They then receive orders.

What do you do?

Weather out your time apart and hope that you both survive it, or make a commitment in order to 'secure' your partner and benefits status in your absence?

Remember, in places like Jacksonville, if you aren't prepared to commit to your partner, there are many others who will and hence why some marines are married after knowing each other only weeks. Many separate within a few months.

So, amongst all of this cold and dispassionate commercialism, is there any hope for any of these marines— since they have the motive, the opportunity and the disinterest to lie and cheat their way through these so-called sham marriages with impunity?

Absolutely.

Colonel Talleri and his wife are a good example of that.

He and Debbie were subjected to the same stresses and strains of many other marines, yet they are still together after decades of marriage and have raised three successful children.

So what sets them apart from the others?

Debbie and Pete dated through college and, not unlike many teenagers, had their ups and down and even broke up a few times.

Debbie excelled in her field as a speech therapist as Pete was forging his career in the Marine Corps.

Bearing in mind everything else I had learned about marines at Camp Lejeune, I asked the colonel whether or not he'd ever strayed. "I don't think there is a person in this world who hasn't had temptation," he said.

(Yes, Pete, don't think I didn't notice that you didn't answer my question.)

Oscar Wilde famously said, "I can resist everything but temptation." A cheating spouse is often divorced because he or she could not resist temptation.

Debbie and Pete didn't survive this long because they were never presented with temptation or with the wants and needs of most other people, but they simply worked at it. They made a choice to be together and they focussed on that, come what may.

Similarly, Debbie was presented with a choice: pursue her career as a successful speech therapist or devote herself to her husband and her children?

She chose the latter.

It wasn't easy—nor was uprooting their children every few years as they followed the career progression of their father from base to base, country to country—but it's the choice they made, as a family.

The marines at Camp Lejeune may well have it rough, especially when it comes to navigating the minefield of courtship.

Similarly, the spouses of marines deployed to fight for their country may well suffer in the vacuum left behind by their partners but, ultimately, each and every one of them, like Debbie, has choices, the selection of which will go on to make or break their lives and the lives of those they purport to care about.

They'd do well to consider that the next time an opportunity presents itself.

62 THE RECKONING

If I told you that my week at Camp Lejeune was gruelling, it would be an understatement; early morning interview starts, and late evenings alone.

Alone but for my demons of course.

Every moment I wasn't busy interviewing somebody turned into an opportunity to question myself, my motives for even being there. What was I hoping to accomplish? What was I trying to achieve?

I got my answer about halfway through my week of penance.

It was during a coffee shop meeting with one of the marines from base. You'll remember him. His name was Kevin.

He was the man I sent the FedEx to, the man I nearly asked if he knew if his wife was having an affair with another marine!

Justin joined us.

We talked and laughed a lot about the situation, and I remember being somewhat comforted by the fact that these two men had become friends, as well as learning that, far from our suspicion, Kevin was actually happily married.

"As far as I can tell," he told me with a smile.

"So, what about this guy, this M? Where is he now?" he asked.

"He's gone," I said without thinking.

"Gone? As in left the Corps?" he asked.

And I thought about this question for a while, and was reminded of my rendezvous with M in Atlanta and how absolutely helpless everything seemed to me that night on the sofa. My sobbing, the hollow inside, and then M's comforting embrace. The same embrace in which I finally fell asleep, the one that I believed gave me the strength to make my way to the airport the next day without so much as a watery eye.

I felt numb.

No, not numb, that was how I felt after those two weeks. I didn't feel numb; I felt relieved, as if somebody had finally lifted some gargantuan burden off my shoulders. And I remember wondering if there was something seriously wrong with me. As if I had undergone some kind of mental breakdown and therefore was unable to feel anymore.

But then I realised, it wasn't that I was no longer able to feel—I was just no longer able to feel lousy, and I was finally at peace.

I had accepted.

M had made his decision about his future and it obviously no longer included me.

I had to accept, and that's exactly what I was doing that night on the sofa; I was coming to terms with and mourning that which I had lost.

That's why I was able to ride to the Airport with him one last time without any of the angst, any of the anguish, but just the time for one last game; would M actually walk me to the departure gate or would he just drop me off at passenger set-down outside the airport?

Of course, rather than ask or him share, we chose instead to avoid the subject the whole way to the airport until the truth was revealed.

What do you think he did?

Set me down or walk me in?

The idea of him walking me to the gate that one last time is certainly romantic, but it wasn't how it happened; he set me down.

"I guess this is goodbye," I said through the passenger car window, echoing his words in London, after retrieving my bag from the backseat.

"I guess it is," he said with what I read as deep sadness in those beautiful hazel eyes.

"Take care," I said, and with that I turned and made my way into the terminal as he drove away, and by the time I turned to actually look, he had disappeared out of sight and from my life.

So, how do you think I felt after being abandoned there on the pavement?

Don't fall off your chair, but I felt okay.

A bit sad, perhaps, but I was okay. At least that was the result of my analysis as I mentally checked myself—you know, just like a doctor would physically inspect a patient for wounds, I checked myself for emotional scars. But I, somewhat remarkably, felt okay and I checked in with a smile on my face!

Everything was going to be fine, and my thoughts turned to this book and to the new chapter that may well have just written itself.

And I was still thinking about that when I stowed my bag in the compartment above my aisle seat on the aeroplane about an hour later.

It had been a somewhat emotional trip, but M had been right. We'd both had a chance to draw closure on what may well have been a somewhat turbulent relationship—but one that was undoubtedly very special to me, perhaps even to both of us, and I was content that we were able to draw the whole thing to a close in such a constructive way.

I smiled to myself despite the fact that my fellow passenger seemed to be deaf to the persistent ringing of their mobile phone. It was only several seconds later that I realised that it wasn't theirs, but mine!

Months before, I had purchased the pay-as-you-go device in an American store as it made it much easier and cheaper communicating with my American contacts whilst in the United States. The only thing was I didn't always tune into the ring tone, which was alien to me.

I hastily pulled the thing out of my pocket and snapped it open, without checking the caller ID, and put it to my ear where I heard static—no, it wasn't static, it was the sound of a moving vehicle and air rushing by an open window.

"Hello?"

"Tony?"

I couldn't identify who it was; the voice seemed muffled.

"M, is that you?"

"Yes, it's me."

I recognised the voice; it was him, but he was crying—no, he was sobbing.

"M? Are you okay? What's wrong?" I asked, thinking he'd had some kind of accident.

"I'm so sorry, Tony. I'm so sorry. I don't know why I just dumped you at the airport like that. I should have come in. I'm so sorry," he said through sobs.

"Ladies and gentlemen, the captain has turned on the 'fasten seat belt' sign at this time. If you haven't already done so, please stow your carry-on luggage underneath the seat in front of you or in an overhead bin provided."

"That's okay, dopey. No need to work yourself into a state over it. We'd already said our goodbyes yesterday," I said with a reassuring smile.

"I handled all of this so badly, and I hurt you. I'm so sorry, Tony."

"M, what's this all about?"

"I don't know. I just feel so lousy. I saw the look on your face when I dropped you off. You seemed so disappointed, and I'm such a dick!"

"It's okay, M…"

"It isn't, Tony, it isn't. I treated you so badly. I'm so sorry. I'm gonna' turn around…"

"No, M!"

"Why not?"

"It's too late; we've already boarded the plane."

"What? No!"

"We've already boarded, M. It's too late," I repeated.

He was really sobbing now.

"M? It's okay. Really. It's okay. I've accepted it now. I have, honestly. I guess this is how it was always meant to be."

"Ladies and Gentlemen, at this time, please make sure your seat backs and tray tables are in their fully upright position, and that your seat belt is securely fastened. Also, we advise you that as of this moment, any electronic equipment, such a cell phones and game consoles, must be turned off. Thank you."

"…I never wanted it to turn out this way, Tony."

"I know, M. I know. But it has."

"There are so many things that I should have said to you, but I didn't. I even wanted to cry, but I couldn't…"

"Hey, you are, *were* a marine, soon to be a police officer. It simply wouldn't do for you to blubber like a girl."

He laughed and sniffed.

"We had some good times, didn't we?"

"We had some great times," I said fondly.

"Sir," it was the flight attendant, "I'm going to need you to switch your phone off."

"Just a few more seconds?" I whispered, desperately.

"We need to push back, sir," is all she said before walking off.

"Tony?"

"I'm here. I need to go, M; they're asking us to switch off our mobile phones."

"Already?"

"We're actually a few minutes late."

"Do you remember the last time we were in Atlanta together?"

"I do."

"I was so happy," he said, struggling to control more tears.

"Me too. I remember when…"

"At this time, we request that all cell phones, pagers, radios and electronic toys be turned off as these items might interfere

with the navigational and communication equipment on this aircraft..."

"I have to go, M," I said sadly.

This was the first time in a long time that he was opening up about his feelings and I was learning that perhaps I hadn't imagined everything, and that he actually cared about me, that he cared about how things had turned out, and that he hadn't callously moved on without so much as a second thought about me.

"Tony…"

"It's okay, M, it's okay, and I'm okay. I am. Thank you so much for calling."

"I love you," he said.

"I love you, too."

"Bye."

"Bye."

The rushing sound stuttered and then disappeared.

M was gone.

That was in the August of 2003.

It was now January 2004.

"He's gone," I said to Kevin. "He's gone from the Marine Corps and for good."

Kevin nodded as I finally came to the realisation why my time in Ghost Town had been so shockingly miserable.

What did I expect?

I was still grieving for my loss, but I (or some would say fate) took me to that place of history and shadows for the metaphorical funeral.

I'd been living the eulogy of my relationship with M by visiting the place where he had pretty much grown up, the place I had heard so much about and that had featured so heavily in my life. The place where I had found, lost my love and learned about his future that did not include me.

I was mourning only he was no longer there to put his arms around me and, albeit temporarily, put a plaster on my heart.

I just had to bleed—and I did, for that whole week, until it was time to finally drive out of that place, but not before digging that metaphorical grave and burying my demons deep inside.

Little did I know that I was too late since my visit had already attracted a curse that would follow me all the way home, and would ensure that M and I would never speak to each other, ever again.

63 HER

How many times have you said or heard someone say, after a breakup, that they'd still like to be friends?

A few times? More?

And what do you think about that? Do you think it's possible?

Well, by now I think you'll probably have gleaned from the rest of these pages that it's a fallacy to think that two people who used to be involved in an intimate relationship can then go on to enjoy a beautiful, platonic friendship.

Okay, so hold on; don't start chewing the pages just yet. Allow me to explain.

It is not possible for two people who still have feelings for each other to still be friends, and that's because those feelings will always inevitably surface each time these two people get together. Be that because one party still fancies the other, but is no longer able to act on that or because, when things ended, they didn't end well and thus there are still unresolved issues.

Whatever the permutation, where feelings are involved, it's somewhat impossible for two individuals to go on to enjoy a platonic relationship.

It is, however, perfectly easy where both parties have moved on—be that because they have both found and are involved with other partners, or the relationship was automatically downgraded from an intimate to platonic status before it even ended.

This is often the case where two people no longer desire each other and they wake up a few years down the line, normally from marriage, and realise that they've become more like brother and sister than hot lovers.

I've personally witnessed this situation multiple times.

You have also witnessed it once in this book.

Justin and her.

And there is a little more to their story that I didn't share with you previously. To do so, I'm going to have to temporarily take you back in time.

May 2003.

Justin was returning home after his tour in the Middle East during which he had done a lot of reflecting on his marriage and his life. He knew exactly what he wanted from the future. This included reenlisting into the Marine Corps to secure a salary and grants that would enable his wife to pursue a legal career.

But when Justin got home, she had altogether different plans.

She confessed to something he had not factored into their future; she was pregnant by another man. She then told him that she did not yet know what she was going to do with the baby, whether or not she was going to keep it and try to make a future with M, or abort it and try to make her marriage work.

The one thing that she did agree to do, whilst she made up her mind, was continue to live and sleep with her husband during the evening, whilst talking on the telephone and sending love emails to M during the day.

For Justin, one of the most difficult things he had to endure was to watch his wife's belly swell with the child of another man. Yet there was nothing he could do about this for he was tied to her, not only by marriage but by financial commitment, for she had made it clear to him that it was in both their interests to keep things amicable.

She explained that if he tried to hurt M, either physically or by reporting him to the Marine Corps Command for committing adultery with a fellow marine's wife, she in turn would tell them that she was no longer living with her husband.

Consequently, at best, he'd lose any marriage subsistence, would be forced out of his accommodation and back into the barracks. At worst, he'd lose everything and be charged for defrauding The Corps.

A somewhat naïve Justin wasn't so naïve as to not understand these ramifications.

So, now things started to make perfect sense to me.

It was obvious that these two had long before fallen out of love. This was evidenced by many factors, not least the fact that Justin was so amenable when it came to allowing his pregnant wife to chat to M while he sat in the next room, as well as the fact that that the two of them kept in regular contact with each other like two good pals without so much as a recrimination, an argument, or a tear.

It also explained why Justin was quite pragmatic about the demise of his marriage just months after his wife did a moonlight flit with another man and removed all of his belongings while he was not at home.

Ask yourself, how would *you* feel if you shared a home with someone and then, one day, while you were at work, without telling you, they came over with someone else and removed much of the furniture and other belongings you shared as part of your relationship?

Would you feel ambivalent or angry? As a bare minimum, you'd feel somewhat miffed, no?

That's because, as humans, we *feel*.

These two had emotionally disconnected months before and so it made perfect sense to both of them to keep their interactions amicable and the lines of communication open, and, in the absence of any emotional friction, this was perfectly possible.

It's the very reason I was shocked to learn that she called Justin that night we were having dinner to tell him she had just given birth to another man's baby and he happily congratulated her.

That said, the shock I experienced that evening wasn't so much to do with the fact that these two could still communicate so dispassionately on such a delicate matter; it was more to do with the fact that they were still talking at all.

I had seriously miscalculated the nature of the current status of their relationship—or, more specifically, I hadn't calculated it at all. I'd simply assumed that these two people would not be on speaking terms.

But they were.

And this meant that everything I had shared with Justin would most likely go back to her and it would most likely be distilled how he saw fit.

Luckily (or naively) for me, we agreed that Justin's meeting with me that night would remain secret from both M and her. When I asked him why he didn't want her to know, he said there wasn't any specific reason, but that it was probably best she not know.

That was fine by me.

Yet it didn't explain why a few days after I returned to England I received a phone call from M.

"I hope you're happy with yourself."

"Well, hello to you too. What are you talking about?"

"She's stopped me from seeing my son."

"What? Why?"

"She said that she doesn't want any part of this freak show and now won't talk to me."

"Right, so what's that got to do with me?"

"You just had to go down there to see him. You just couldn't leave it alone."

"She obviously doesn't care about you as much as you think, M."

"Of course *you'd* know that, being the expert and all."

"So you think she'd be able to ditch you so easily if she really loved you, just because I spoke to her husband?"

Silence.

"M?"

"I'm not having this conversation with you."

"Hey, you're the one who called me, remember?"

I hesitated, for, at this time, I was finding it incredibly difficult to be in any way vulnerable around him. "Look, I'm sorry, M. I didn't mean to stir trouble for you. I genuinely wanted to meet him to try and understand the full story."

I could hear him sneer down the phone.

"Believe what you want," I threw back.

"Do you really mean that?"

"Of course I do."

"Well, in that case you won't mind talking to her then."

I froze. "What?"

"She wants to talk to you," he said calmly.

"Well, I don't want to talk to her!" I said quickly.

"I thought you said you were sorry."

"I am."

"Then do this for me, Tony. Tell her the truth."

I scoffed. "The truth? You don't want me to tell her the truth; you want me to lie. Isn't that what this is all about? You trying to completely erase any trace of our whole relationship? I mean, Christ, you must be desperate if you're willing to risk me talking to her."

"Well, it can't get any worse than her not letting me see my son."

So I paused. Could I realistically and rationally hold a conversation with this girl? And what the hell would I actually say?

"What do you want me to say to her?"

"What do you think?"

There was a long pause.

I knew exactly what he wanted me to do. He wanted me to revert to our old cover story: that our relationship never existed, but that he instead was having a relationship with my friend, Cathy.

"Have you absolutely lost your mind? You want me to pretend I never existed? The very thing that I've been struggling with for the best part of a year?"

"If you really cared about me, as you say you do, then you would."

"Fuck you!" I said angrily, and slammed down the phone. (Okay, so it was a cordless phone and I disconnected it by pressing the button, but I did throw the phone on my bed.)

I was incensed.

Not only did M behave as if we'd never existed—on top of the fact that we couldn't exist to the public even when we were together—but now he also wanted me to talk to her and lie about us.

So what do you think I did?

I took her call of course.

Once I had calmed down, I realised just how much it must be hurting M to not be able to see his son.

I felt sad for him, and I felt responsible. I didn't want anything to do with that.

I took her call, most reluctantly, and I hated every second of it.

(I'd love to share her name with you, but I can't, for obvious reasons, so I'm going to refer to her as Tonia, as in Tonia Harding because, at last look, there was a remarkable resemblance.)

"Why is it any of your business? This is between M and Cathy," she whined (and I mean whined), angrily.

"Look, Tonia, if you're going to carry on shouting, I'm going to hang up on you."

"Why is that? Don't you want to hear what I've got to say?"

"Quite frankly, no. But you're the one who wanted this phone call so the least you can do is not give me earache in the meantime."

"Then tell me, why? Why do you believe this is any of your business?"

"I've already told you; because Cathy is my best friend, and if you have friends you'll know that when some asshole decides to cheat on them and hurt them, it becomes your business."

"Well, M obviously didn't want to be with her otherwise he wouldn't have cheated, as you put it."

"As I put it? How else would you define having sex with someone when you're supposed to be committed to someone else, Tonia?"

"Still, none of your business. This is between Cathy and M, and has nothing to do with you. It certainly doesn't give you licence to go sticking your nose in my business and go bothering the one person I care about with your crap."

"He invited me to go meet with him—and surely, if you cared about your husband so much, you wouldn't have had a child with some other bloke, no?"

"As I say, none of your business."

"And as I say, get off your moral high ground, because there's a huge difference between just talking to someone and having sex with them."

"Yeah, well, we all make mistakes, right?"

562

"Oh so it was a mistake then?"

"The mistake was him ever hooking up with your friend and knowing you, and if I'd known he was going to be all of this hassle, I'd never have got with him in the first place."

"Hassle? You mean had you known that he knew someone who'd actually go direct to your husband and get the truth from his mouth rather than the distilled rubbish you keep spouting?"

"Once again, THIS IS NONE OF YOUR BUSINESS!" she shouted down the phone.

"Once again, if you don't stop shouting, Tonia, I'm going to hang up on you."

"Then back off! This has nothing to do with you; it's between M and Cathy. It certainly has nothing to do with you or my husband, so I'd appreciate it if you just stayed away from him."

"Your husband is an adult, isn't he? I'll let him make the decision as to whether or not he wants to talk to me. You've apparently already made your decision to move on to another man..."

"I haven't moved on to anybody! It's M who kept hassling me. If you must know, I discussed all of this with him at the time and it was he who decided he wanted to keep the baby, not me. I didn't care either way. I told him all I wanted from him was the money to get rid of it as I didn't have any."

I went silent after that last comment. I wasn't sure how to process that. I remember feeling selfishly elated. Almost as if I had got her to confess to something, something that could be used in court against her in the trial of whether or not M should even be with her.

But that was ridiculous.

"Hello?" she said.

Then I went from elation to bitter sadness. Was that something she really felt or was she just saying it in the heat of the moment to get back at me? After all, this is the girl who had always wanted children."

"Hello?"

"I'm here."

"I told M that I wasn't interested in moving in with him anyway. Not least because, if it wasn't for him, you wouldn't even have been able to contact my husband. That's why I don't plan to have anything else to do with him. I don't want anything to do with this freak show y'all seem to have going on."

"You're ditching M because he gave me your husband's contact details? You must have cared for him a lot when you decided to have his baby."

"I cared enough to be there when he needed someone, unlike your friend who was never there when he needed her."

"Do you know what, Tonia? I don't have to listen to this crap from you. I agreed to take this phone call because you needed some kind of validation, but I think we've said all there is to say. Goodbye."

I pressed disconnect on the phone.

Yes, I know; probably not the most civilised thing to do, but we were going round in circles. Besides, I'd done my duty for M. I sucked up my pride and gave her the time of day, my precious time to perpetuate the lie and perhaps even dispel any myth that M's relationship was with anyone other than Cathy.

But it wasn't over.

The next attack came via email—and this time my stomach turned over as waves of hot and cold sweats washed over me.

It seemed that she'd obviously shared the result of my conversation with her husband and he, not willing to appear bitter and/or incredible in his recount, added what he had obviously surmised from our conversation.

The following is the transcript of her email in its entirety:

"Hello Tony. I realize that this email may be a bit of a surprise to you as the last and only time I actually spoke to you, you chose to hang up on me.

Mature. Anyway, I talked to my husband last night and he gave me some very disturbing news about our friend M. He basically told me that M and Cathy were never a couple, that in all actuality, YOU and M were the couple?? Forgive me if I sound completely confused... but that is exactly what I am. I was told that you were homosexual ... but M? Just a bit hard to believe. As you may know from talking to my husband, I rarely speak to M. This situation has deviated from anything that resembles normal to me so I've chosen to detach myself from it. The only reason I am writing you is that I was hoping that, since you've taken it upon yourself to use the person I care most about, that maybe you could do me a favor.... Custody, child support, etc. may be an issue with M. If he is what you say he is... he is certainly unfit and has no chance of seeing his child, at least not without supervision. If there is anything you could do to give me some tangible proof that he is this way, it would be much appreciated. Please advise."

My blood ran cold.

The truth was out.

Or at least it seemed that way.

Did I have proof?

Hell, yes: a whole collection of photos and hours of video tape footage, of the kind I described earlier in this book, and more.

I had unequivocal proof.

As well as the burden of putting this thing to bed once and for all.

"Not without supervision..."

Did she seriously believe that if it was proven that M was gay, he would only be able to see his son via supervised visits?

That was absurd.

But what if it was true?

Did I really want that on my conscience?

On the other hand, this story had already rumbled on for long enough.

I was exhausted.

I wanted it all to end and I was under no illusion that whatever civility was left between M and I, there was no turning back from this; I represented a clear and present threat to his future, and there was no doubt in my mind that he'd want to completely sever all ties with me.

So, finally, I had nothing to lose.

This was my chance to get the recognition that I deserved. The validation that, beyond the confines of closed doors, we existed.

64 THE CANVAS OF LIFE

The march of time is relentless.

It mercilessly tramples over our youth, has us question our mortality and contemplate the things we have or have not done, things we should or should not have said, things we still want or must do before our very short time on this earth is at an end.

These things, on the scale of exhilaration, can be as simple as enjoying a portion of humble fish and chips whilst watching the sun disappear under the horizon, or as extreme as bungee-jumping off a bridge in some far-flung corner of the world.

How far we turn that dial of exhilaration tends to be subject to our age; the young will crank it up, the 'mature' will dial it down, whilst the middle-aged just want to smash it.

Some of us ride the roller coaster of life as if it were a bucking bronco, whilst others are content to live theirs with the traits of a goldfish.

An adventurous existence certainly appears glamorous and it's often coveted by many, but it's seldom realised.

Ben Stiller's first outing as actor and director was the reimagining of *The Secret Life of Walter Mitty*.

In the film, Stiller plays the role of a timid and sad photo editor at *LIFE* magazine who often retreats into elaborate fantasies to become an assertive and somewhat heroic figure who jumps onto helicopters, climbs mountains, combats enemies, and travels the globe faster than it would take Phileas Fogg to tie his shoelaces.

The Secret Life of Walter Mitty was first published in 1939 as a short novel by James Thurber; it was then turned into a film in the forties, then a musical, and was subsequently remade by Stiller.

And there's one simple reason this notable story has transcended time, and that's because, not unlike the very book you're reading now, it's the story of most of us: each and every person who leads what most would class as an 'average' existence, often stuck in a job that they don't particularly like, imprisoned there by life's necessities without much hope of escape or parole.

The latest Deloitte Shift Index survey says that a staggering eighty per cent of us hate our jobs. That is eighty per cent of the workforce choose (I used the term loosely) a salary over passion.

It's a pretty sorry state of affairs, but nonetheless a reality that many of us grin and bear on a daily basis.

Yet there are some, the few, who believe they are destined for greater things. They believe their life to be more than the dog's dinner served to them by a tired and unimaginative destiny. These, the few, make a decision to change their life from a monochromatic formulaic syndrome to a Technicolor dream of risk and reward. These intrepid life explorers have no time for the shadows (also known as haters) who spend their lives resenting the fun of others and dragging their sorry souls through a quagmire of self-pity whilst camping out around a raging bonfire of disgruntlement fed by the kindling of their discontent.

The canvas of life is hung out before us from the moment we draw our first breath. The virginal white landscape of peaks and valleys is but ours for the painting, and whilst we may not be able to control each and every brushstroke, we do control the colours these strokes leave on our soul, on our personality, on our perspective and our life outlook. Be it the colour of red love, the grey of sadness, the black of sorrow, the green of envy, the blue of creativity, the orange of happiness, and a myriad of other colours, including the one you'd care to attribute to fear.

Last week I spoke to a young man who had just launched a brand-new company. I asked him if he was excited, "More like terrified!" was his reply.

Quite right.

There's a conglomeration of statistics out there that tell us just how many start-up businesses will fail in their first year. This young man, still in his twenties, had read them all. (Probably not the most inspiring move.)

Yet, he dares to dream.

In our new world of economic uncertainty, even the bravest risk-takers are stepping back from the abyss of the unknown and investing more in certainty.

Hollywood movie studios demonstrate this well by their incessant scraping of the comic-book barrel as well as their investing in scripts based on tried and tested books, whilst their television counterparts make stars out of inexpensive, talentless reality TV caricatures.

It takes guts to put life as you know it on the line and take a risk. Some of the greatest business pioneers have endured some of their biggest failures before making it big.

Marilyn Monroe was famously told that she 'was not pretty or talented enough to be an actress'. Sōichirō Honda was passed over for an engineering job at Toyota and was penniless before he started designing motorcycles and became a billionaire. Vera Wang first failed as an Olympic skater; she then became an editor, was passed over for an editor-in-chief position and started designing wedding gowns. She now heads a multibillion-dollar industry. Walt Disney was fired by a newspaper because he apparently "lacked imagination and had no good ideas". Sir James Dyson went through 5,126 failed prototypes and fifteen years of savings. His name is now one of the bestselling vacuum brands in the world. Stephen King was so frustrated with *Carrie*, his first novel, that he threw it in the garbage. His wife found the manuscript. To date, he has written over thirty novels and sold over 350 million books.

And who can forget the story of novelist J.K. Rowling who was penniless and raising a daughter on social security before *Harry Potter* was unleashed on the world. She's now the first person to become a billionaire through writing.

The canvas of life is as colourful, or as dull, as we paint it. Bad things happen to all of us, indiscriminately, although sometimes it feels as if we're always getting a raw deal.

But, we don't really know everything that goes on in the lives of others, nor should it be that important to us.

Your job may not be the best in the world, but stop for a second to consider, *why exactly do you allow yourself to be imprisoned by it? What exactly does it do for you?*

Well, let's take a look.

Does it pay the bills?

Yes.

Does it put a roof over your head?

Yes.

Does it feed you and your family?

Yes.

Does it clothe your children?

Yes.

Does it fund vacations and other excursions?

Yes.

Well, in that case, the hideous role you perform on a daily basis is actually a wondrous and colourful oasis of security. A sparkling pot of gold at the end of the rainbow of life. Granted, you may not feel that you are accomplishing much and you may not be getting a great sense of job satisfaction—this is when your job doesn't become you, but is more the means to an end, a tool, the fuel that enables you to travel on the road of things that make you happy, the things that add colour to the canvas of your life, that beautiful canvas that you're going to gaze back on in so many years and think, "I did that."

At least until you are brave enough to venture into the unknown, take a risk, like the aforementioned life adventurers, to abandon the status quo, the complacent, the comfortable, and pursue whichever lofty dream your mind has created for you, a dream free from responsibility, risk or hurt.

We can't always control the things that happen to us, any more than we can control the things that happen to the ones we love—the latter often being the most trying of the two because our instinct is to protect our loved ones, to shield them from the greys and the blacks of life, but the reality is *we cannot*. This decision is often taken out of our hands and we have no option but to stand by and watch them make their own choices, forge their own relationships, paint their own canvas, even if we believe we know better.

All we can do is be there when we're needed and do whatever we can to help them restart the journey the best way experience has taught us how.

I know this because many people in my orbit will often ask me for advice, but they don't always take it. In fact, it's this very subject that is almost a weekly conversation.

I've lost count of the times where I've been standing on the metaphorical pavement yelling at friends or family members not to drive down that metaphorical road because they'll crash. I know this because I've either been there or seen it happen to others, countless times. But still they persist on taking the journey.

That's because hope springs eternal.

Just because it happened to you, it doesn't necessarily mean it will happen to me.

Trust me; there's more than often a good chance that it *will* and, equally, that you won't take my word for it because you feel that you want to find out for yourself or that you can change that which history, experience and wisdom have already taught others.

And so the story repeats.

I did not send any of the so-called 'proof' to her. There was absolutely nothing for me to gain from doing so other than to cause M more pain, and we'd inflicted enough of that on each other already.

Rather than exhuming those demons, it was in my own interest to leave them where I had buried them, deep in the heart of North Carolina.

As for M, he is now a sergeant in law enforcement (well, he always did excel in his career choices).

From what I can tell, he is now married to her.

I'm assuming that, in the absence of any hard evidence, she dismissed her husband's allegations as hearsay, spiteful rumours initiated by me in retribution for his cheating on my friend. And, if you met M, you'd appreciate that there is absolutely nothing about him to suggest otherwise.

I'm fine with that now, but it took me some time and lot of hurt to reach that conclusion.

Black things will happen.

They are part of living and are the things that add contrast to life's ultimate masterpiece, provided they are put into perspective with colour.

I can only hope that, if anything, this book has brought you some perspective about your past, your present and perhaps your future.

Painters will often paint their subject (the foreground) in vibrant, bright colours, and their background in darker shades.

Why do you think that is?

Also by Tony Marturano:

"Fear the living, fear the dead,
fear the Unspeakable."

HALLOWEEN 2015

Also by Tony Marturano:

"There's something in the rain, and it wants the darkest
you to come out."

NEW and revised 'Hell on Earth' edition

UNLEASHED 2016

Discover more at
www.tonymarturano.com

Acknowledgements

The Roman philosopher, Cicero, once said, *"Gratitude is not only the greatest of virtues, but the mother of all others"*.

I'm so very grateful to the following individuals who have supported me throughout this book's journey from manuscript to print, as well as those who have actively contributed to its realisation.

THE PROTAGONISTS
Special heartfelt thanks goes to each and every one of the real life protagonists featured in *Coming Up for Air*. You gave generously not only of your time but also of your privacy. I can only hope that I have done each and every one of your stories justice.

CUFA FOCUS/READER'S GROUP
Special thanks goes to my agent, my cat, my dog. Oh, okay, special thanks goes to my team for their time, orientation and tough love! You know who you are, but just in case you've forgotten (in no particular order):
Francesca Marturano-Pratt, Anna Pratt, Tamanda Flynn, Selina Sarah Daley, Calvin Everdell, Kim Everdell, Matthew Ainslie, Slavka Salajova, Karen Harber, and Renee Owens (for trying).

MY EDITORS
Debbie Brunettin and Campbell Hore (for keeping me on the straight and narrow).

Thanks to Anna Pratt, for soothing my neurosis!

UNITED STATES AIR FORCE AND MARINE CORPS
Some of the key stories in this book were made possible and better, thanks to the generous and very patient cooperation of the United States Air Force bases of Lakenheath and Mildenhall in Suffolk, England.
And
The United States Marine Corps base of Camp Lejeune, North Carolina, United States.

THANKS TO MY BEAUTIFUL SISTERS
Special and heartfelt thanks goes to my two beautiful sisters;
Francesca and Rosa.

Francesca, for her unfaltering support throughout the process of
bringing this book to print, and everything else that I turn my hand
to.

Rosa, for putting up with me during my emotional recovery. As
you will have read, it was Rosa's saintly patience that nudged me
back into the land of the living. I can only hope each and every
other emotionally damaged being is lucky enough to have someone
as pure of heart.

BELLA
Although we may no longer share the same path, when it comes
to my writing, you are and always be in my thoughts.

M
It's highly unlikely that any part of this book is in any way
agreeable to you (for obvious reasons). I remain nonetheless
grateful for the times we had and the journey that you (albeit
inadvertently) initiated.

YOU, THE READER
If you're reading this book, there's a good chance you bought it. I'm
obviously very grateful for that. Thank you!
On the other hand, you may have borrowed this book from
somebody else. If so, I'm just as grateful because it would mean that
person believed in this Coming Up for Air so much, they thought
you'd enjoy it also!

Special thanks to Rebecca Souster, for all your help bringing this
book to print, literally!

Oh, and last but not least, Mr *White Cowboy*. You reminded me that
there was still hope for me!